Lecture Notes in Business Information Processing 545

Series Editors

Wil van der Aalst, *RWTH Aachen University, Aachen, Germany*
Sudha Ram, *University of Arizona, Tucson, USA*
Michael Rosemann, *Queensland University of Technology, Brisbane, Australia*
Clemens Szyperski, *Microsoft Research, Redmond, USA*
Giancarlo Guizzardi, *University of Twente, Enschede, The Netherlands*

LNBIP reports state-of-the-art results in areas related to business information systems and industrial application software development – timely, at a high level, and in both printed and electronic form.

The type of material published includes

- Proceedings (published in time for the respective event)
- Postproceedings (consisting of thoroughly revised and/or extended final papers)
- Other edited monographs (such as, for example, project reports or invited volumes)
- Tutorials (coherently integrated collections of lectures given at advanced courses, seminars, schools, etc.)
- Award-winning or exceptional theses

LNBIP is abstracted/indexed in DBLP, EI and Scopus. LNBIP volumes are also submitted for the inclusion in ISI Proceedings.

Sibylle Peter · Martin Kropp · Ademar Aguiar ·
Craig Anslow · Maria Ilaria Lunesu ·
Andrea Pinna
Editors

Agile Processes in Software Engineering and Extreme Programming

26th International Conference
on Agile Software Development, XP 2025
Brugg-Windisch, Switzerland, June 2–5, 2025
Proceedings

Editors
Sibylle Peter
University of Applied Sciences and Arts Northwestern Switzerland
Windisch, Switzerland

Ademar Aguiar
University of Porto
Porto, Portugal

Maria Ilaria Lunesu
University of Cagliari
Cagliari, Italy

Martin Kropp
University of Applied Sciences and Arts Northwestern Switzerland
Windisch, Switzerland

Craig Anslow
Victoria University of Wellington
Wellington, New Zealand

Andrea Pinna
University of Cagliari
Cagliari, Italy

ISSN 1865-1348　　　　　　　　　ISSN 1865-1356　(electronic)
Lecture Notes in Business Information Processing
ISBN 978-3-031-94543-4　　　　　ISBN 978-3-031-94544-1　(eBook)
https://doi.org/10.1007/978-3-031-94544-1

© The Editor(s) (if applicable) and The Author(s) 2025. This book is an open access publication.

Open Access This book is licensed under the terms of the Creative Commons Attribution 4.0 International License (http://creativecommons.org/licenses/by/4.0/), which permits use, sharing, adaptation, distribution and reproduction in any medium or format, as long as you give appropriate credit to the original author(s) and the source, provide a link to the Creative Commons license and indicate if changes were made.

The images or other third party material in this book are included in the book's Creative Commons license, unless indicated otherwise in a credit line to the material. If material is not included in the book's Creative Commons license and your intended use is not permitted by statutory regulation or exceeds the permitted use, you will need to obtain permission directly from the copyright holder.

The use of general descriptive names, registered names, trademarks, service marks, etc. in this publication does not imply, even in the absence of a specific statement, that such names are exempt from the relevant protective laws and regulations and therefore free for general use.

The publisher, the authors and the editors are safe to assume that the advice and information in this book are believed to be true and accurate at the date of publication. Neither the publisher nor the authors or the editors give a warranty, expressed or implied, with respect to the material contained herein or for any errors or omissions that may have been made. The publisher remains neutral with regard to jurisdictional claims in published maps and institutional affiliations.

This Springer imprint is published by the registered company Springer Nature Switzerland AG
The registered company address is: Gewerbestrasse 11, 6330 Cham, Switzerland

If disposing of this product, please recycle the paper.

Preface

With a great pleasure we introduce this volume of research proceedings of XP 2025, the 26th International Conference on Agile Software Development, held during June 2–5, 2025, at the University of Applied Sciences and Arts Northwestern Switzerland in Brugg-Windisch, Switzerland.

Over the years, XP conferences have played a pivotal role in fostering the successful evolution and widespread adoption of Agile practices by teams and organizations—not only within the software industry and academic settings, but also across a broader range of domains.

The theme for XP 2025 was "Adapt - Uncovering better ways to deliver valuable software products", emphasizing the importance of flexibility, learning, and innovation in delivering sustainable value through Agile methodologies.

This volume of the XP 2025 conference proceedings showcases a wide range of research contributions in the field of Agile software development. The papers included explore a broad spectrum of topics such as leadership and culture, coaching for Agile and practices, AI and process, Global and Hybrid development, Continuous Integration and DevOps, as well as team dynamics, product development, and testing. This year the Research Papers track received 46 submissions. Each submission underwent a thorough single-blind review process, with three reviews per paper. Based on this process, 17 papers —— 13 full papers and 4 short papers —— were accepted to be presented at the conference.

We sincerely thank the authors whose work is featured in this volume for advancing the discourse in Agile software development. Our gratitude also goes to the reviewers for their dedication and thoughtful feedback, which ensured the high quality of these papers. We further acknowledge the invaluable contributions of all speakers, sponsors, shepherds, chairs, and volunteers who helped bring this conference to life. A special thanks is extended to the XP Conference Steering Committee and the sponsor, the School of Computer Science of the University of Applied Sciences and Arts Northwestern Switzerland.

April 2025

Sibylle Peter
Martin Kropp
Ademar Aguiar
Craig Anslow
Maria Ilaria Lunesu
Andrea Pinna

Organization

Conference Co-chairs

Sibylle Peter　　　　　　　　　University of Applied Sciences and Arts
　　　　　　　　　　　　　　　　Northwestern Switzerland, Switzerland
Martin Kropp　　　　　　　　　University of Applied Sciences and Arts
　　　　　　　　　　　　　　　　Northwestern Switzerland, Switzerland

Program Co-chairs

Ademar Aguiar　　　　　　　　INESC TEC, Universidade do Porto, Portugal
Craig Anslow　　　　　　　　　Victoria University of Wellington, New Zealand

Publication Co-chairs

Andrea Pinna　　　　　　　　　University of Cagliari, Italy
Maria Ilaria Lunesu　　　　　　University of Cagliari, Italy

Program Committee

Scott Ambler　　　　　　　　　SA+A, Canada
Hubert Baumeister　　　　　　Technical University of Denmark, Denmark
Jan Bosch　　　　　　　　　　　Chalmers University of Technology, Sweden
Nils Brede Moe　　　　　　　　SINTEF, Norway
Frank Buschmann　　　　　　　Siemens AG, Germany
Steven D. Fraser　　　　　　　Innoxec, USA
Torgeir Dingsøyr　　　　　　　Norwegian University of Science and Technology
　　　　　　　　　　　　　　　　and SimulaMet, Norway

Henry Edison　　　　　　　　　Blekinge Institute of Technology, Sweden
Filipe Figueiredo Correia　　　University of Porto, Portugal
Juan Garbajosa　　　　　　　　Technical University of Madrid, Spain
Fabian Gilson　　　　　　　　　University of Canterbury, New Zealand
Alfredo Goldman　　　　　　　University of São Paulo, Brazil
Peggy Gregory　　　　　　　　University of Glasgow, UK
Eduardo Martins Guerra　　　Free University of Bozen-Bolzano, Italy

Neil Harrison	University of Utah, USA
Orit Hazzan	Technion—Israel Institute of Technology, Israel
Kiyoshi Honda	Osaka Institute of Technology, Japan
Victoria Jackson	University of California, Irvine, USA
Christoph Johann Stettina	Leiden University / Centre for Innovation, Netherlands
Fabio Kon	University of São Paulo, Brazil
Martin Kropp	University of Applied Sciences and Arts Northwestern Switzerland, Switzerland
Marco Kuhrmann	Reutlingen University, Germany
Casper Lassenius	Aalto University, Finland and Simula Metropolitan Center for Digital Engineering, Norway
Ville Leppänen	University of Turku, Finland
Lech Madeyski	Wrocław University of Science and Technology, Poland
Antonio Martini	University of Oslo, Norway
Frank Maurer	University of Calgary, Canada
Jorge Melegati	Free University of Bozen-Bolzano, Italy
Tommi Mikkonen	University of Helsinki, Finland
Alok Mishra	Atılım University, Turkey
Jürgen Münch	Reutlingen University, Germany
Anh Nguyen-Duc	University of South Eastern Norway, Norway
Maria Paasivaara	LUT University and Aalto University, Finland
Sibylle Peter	University of Applied Sciences and Arts Northwestern Switzerland, Switzerland
Adam Przybylek	Gdańsk University of Technology, Poland
Eduardo Ribeiro	University of Porto, Portugal
Pilar Rodriguez	Universidad Politécnica de Madrid, Spain
Daniela S. Cruzes	SINTEF, Norway
Tiago Silva da Silva	Federal University of São Paulo, Brazil
Darja Šmite	Blekinge Institute of Technology, Sweden
Viktoria Stray	University of Oslo / SINTEF, Norway
Diane Strode	Open University, UK
Rini Van Solingen	TU Delft, Netherlands
Joost Visser	Leiden University, Netherlands
Stefan Wagner	Technical University of Munich, Germany
Xiaofeng Wang	Free University of Bozen-Bolzano, Italy
Hironori Washizaki	Waseda University, Japan
Agustín Yagüe	Universidad Politécnica de Madrid, Spain
Luciana Zaina	Federal University of São Carlos, Brazil
Franz Zieris	Blekinge Institute of Technology, Sweden

Steering Committee

Peggy Gregory (chair)	University of Glasgow, UK
Hubert Baumeister	Technical University of Denmark, Denmark
François Coallier	École de Technologie Supérieure, Canada
Jutta Eckstein	Independent, Germany
Hendrik Esser	Ericsson, Germany
Juan Garbajosa	Universidad Politécnica de Madrid, Spain
Martin Kropp	University of Applied Sciences and Arts Northwestern Switzerland, Switzerland
Wouter Lagerweij	Lagerweij Consultancy, Netherlands
Maria Paasivaara	LUT University & Aalto University, Finland
Viktoria Stray	University of Oslo, Norway
Xiaofeng Wang	Free University of Bozen-Bolzano, Italy

Sponsoring Organization

School of Computer Science of University of Applied Sciences and Arts Northwestern Switzerland.

Contents

Leadership and Culture

Core Theories in Agile Software Development 3
   Nan Yang, Xiaofeng Wang, Zheying Zhang, Dominik Siemon, and Sami Hyrynsalmi

Agile Coaching Research: A Systematic Mapping Study 19
   Ehikioya Obode, Peggy Gregory, Derek Somerville, and Advait Deshpande

Fostering a Sense of Belonging in Hybrid Work Within Agile Software Development 37
   Sonja M. Hyrynsalmi, Fateme Broomandi, Iflaah Salman, and Maria Paasivaara

Exploring the Role of Agile Mindset in Information Systems: A Systematic Literature Review 52
   Karen Eilers, Tabea Augner, Necmettin Özkan, Christoph Peters, and Ulrich Bretschneider

A Mosaic of Perspectives: Understanding Ownership in Software Engineering 69
   Tomi Suomi, Petri Ihantola, Tommi Mikkonen, and Niko Mäkitalo

Business Agility

Knowledge Sharing and Coordination in Large-Scale Agile Software Development – A Systematic Literature Review and an Interview Study 81
   Franziska Tobisch and Florian Matthes

Investigating User-Side Representatives in Large-Scale Agile Software Development 100
   Morteza Moalagh, Vegard Svesengen, and Babak A. Farshchian

Fostering New Work Practices Through a Community of Practice A Case Study in a Large-Scale Software Development Organization 116
   Franziska Tobisch and Florian Matthes

Engineering

Architecture Refactoring Towards Service Reusability in the Context
of Microservices 129
    João Daniel, Gabriel Mota, Xiaofeng Wang, and Eduardo Guerra

Exploratory Test-Driven Development Study with ChatGPT in Different
Scenarios 145
    Juliano Cesar Pancher, Jorge Melegati, and Eduardo Martins Guerra

Exploratory Software Testing in Scrum: A Qualitative Study 160
    Giulia Neri, Rob Marchand, and Neil Walkinshaw

Mutation Testing in Test Code Refactoring: Leveraging Mutants to Ensure
Behavioral Consistency 176
    *Tiago Samuel Rodrigues Teixeira, Fábio Fagundes Silveira,
and Eduardo Martins Guerra*

Visualization Usage in Technical Debt Management 186
    Marius Irgens and Antonio Martini

Agile Effort Estimation Usage in the Sri Lankan Software Industry 195
    Sean Jonathon Lee and Mali Senapathi

Metrics for Experimentation Programs: Categories, Benefits
and Challenges 210
    Nils Stotz and Paul Drews

Product and Design

Exploring Documentation Strategies for NFR in Agile Software
Development 229
    *Igor Moreira, Luciane Adolfo, Jorge Melegati, Joelma Choma,
Eduardo Guerra, and Luciana Zaina*

Adapt and Overcome - How Agile Practitioners Adapt to Issues
that Impede the Delivery of Value: An Interview Study 245
    Jan-Niklas Meckenstock and Victoria Wallmichrath

Author Index 265

Leadership and Culture

Core Theories in Agile Software Development

Nan Yang[1(✉)], Xiaofeng Wang[2], Zheying Zhang[3], Dominik Siemon[1], and Sami Hyrynsalmi[1]

[1] LUT University, Mukkulankatu 19, 15210 Lahti, Finland
{nan.yang,dominik.siemon,sami.hyrynsalmi}@lut.fi
[2] Free University of Bozen-Bolzano, Bozen-Bolzano, Italy
xiaofeng.wang@unibz.it
[3] Tampere University, Tampere, Finland
zheying.zhang@tuni.fi

Abstract. The lack of core theories is a challenge for the whole software engineering (SE) discipline, particularly crucial for the agile software development (ASD) field, which is largely practice-driven. Without solid and continuous theoretical development glued by core theories, ASD risks repeating wrong practices and oversimplifying real-world phenomena. To address this issue and foster a strong link between empirical evidence and theoretical development, we conduct this critical review using the Complex Network Analysis (CNA) approach, in response to the editors' call on the XP2020 conference. Based on 83 selected articles and 88 identified theories, our analysis traced the originating disciplines of these theories and synthesized 3 key theory communities. We position ASD core theories between empirical generalization and middle-range theories in the SE theory spectrum and offer practical guidelines for researchers to use, borrow, and generate ASD theories. It is further recommended that new theory development be aligned with the theory of coordination and control theory while employing Complex Adaptive Systems (CAS) theory as a theoretical lens when borrowing theories to ASD.

Keywords: agile software development · core theory · complex network analysis · theory of agile · complex adaptive systems

"Nothing is as practical as a good theory."
—From Ivar Jacobson's[1] keynote speech at the General Theory of Software Engineering (GTSE) Workshop 2014.

---

[1] Jacobson is one co-founder of SEMAT (Software Engineering Method and Theory) initiative, which aims to build a rigorous theoretical basis for software engineering practice. This statement was originally by Kurt Lewin, a pioneer in social psychology, and referenced by Jacobson in his speech.

1 Introduction

The discipline of software engineering (SE), shaped by more than 50 years of practice, is still slowly developing on a theoretical basis [12] and has not achieved a consensus on SE core theories yet [3,15,16,26,33,37]. The briefest definition of a theory is that it is a belief that there is a pattern in phenomena [7,38]. Around the year 2010, there was a lot of discussion of core theory and theoretical foundations in the SE field, aiming to make SE as a mature discipline as biology and psychology for example; biology has the theories of the cell and evolution and psychology has the cognitive theory as a core [26]. The trend of developing core theories of SE has decreased in the past ten years marked by the General Theory of Software Engineering (GTSE) workshop ending in 2015.

One key reason for fewer discussions can be attributed to the difficulty and impracticality of encompassing the theoretical foundations of all subfields in SE by a single theory [29]. But without a collection of core theories, a discipline will struggle to generate, accumulate, and preserve knowledge [22,30,32]. Given the above, this study limits the research scope in the agile software development (ASD) field, reviewing and developing core theories under this context and contributing to whole SE general theories development, increasing the rigor of ASD research through developing a theoretical core [3]. We see ASD as a valuable context for core theory development in SE research. Focusing on this more practically narrow scope (contrary to large-scale studies) allows us to study it deeply.

General theories [27], core theories [26], and kernel theories [24], all refer to the foundational theories that underpin this discipline even though they are not explicitly referenced in each paper; they are integral parts of most other theories' conceptualizations [24] in this discipline. We use the term 'core theories' in this study to make our work easy to understand for the whole SE community, including those without any theoretical background. Kernel theories are commonly used as a term in IS as the design science research (DSR) develops. Engstrom et al. [9] aligned SE with DSR to illustrate the relationship between theory and practice, further encouraging researchers to reflect on how to add new knowledge to general theories as research output. We will not go into details of kernel theories in design science research but we want to emphasize the same desire from both SE and IS communities to establish core theories in the fields. Although there has been less discussion of core theories in the SE discipline in the last 10 years (since 2015), more ASD articles have appeared in IS publications. Especially since the year 2020, ASD core theory and related theoretical foundation topics have been gradually brought back to the agenda not in SE but in IS; in Information Systems Journal (2021), Baham and Hirschheim [3] proposed the components of ASD theoretical core to spark a scholarly discussion.

In the 2009 special issue on ASD in the European Journal of Information Systems, Abrahamsson et al. [1] emphasized the backwardness in agile research, which has lagged behind practice, because of a lack of a "theoretical glue" [36] to bind all agile research together. With this glue, a more unified theoretical understanding of ASD [3] will help research keep up with practice. Otherwise, without rigors and solid theoretical foundations, our field risks repeating wrong practices and oversimplifying the phenomenon [3,16]. Especially due to the rapid pace of software technology advancements today—such as in generative artificial intelligence, quantum computing, and the upcoming 6G [2],—the tempo of software development practices has accelerated significantly. Agile practices in the industry have adapted quickly to these shifts [20]. In our research work, adaptation of new software technologies requires ASD core theories serving as a basis to analyze, explain, predict, prescribe, and inspire [11] practices under the exogenous shocks [23] brought by emerging technologies.

Distilling core theories of ASD from both academics and industry and building consensus on them, presents significant challenges that require strategic approaches. Three non-exclusive strategies have been proposed during GTSE workshops [28]:

(i) *Blank Slate.* Use a grounded theory approach to develop core theories from empirical observations.
(ii) *Integration.* Synthesize a core theory using existing theories from SE and reference disciplines.
(iii) *Extension.* Extend and generalize a promising middle-range theory.

Our study primarily adopts the second strategy, integration, by conducting a critical review of ASD literature. We aim to distil and synthesize a few core theories of ASD from existing literature, providing a foundation for building consensus for both researchers and practitioners. Our work responds to Stray et al.'s [34] call on a deeper exploration of theoretical foundations of ASD, which serves as editors' introduction for extended papers on the XP2020 conference (the flagship conference for ASD community).

The paper is structured as follows. Section 2 presents the nature of theory and reviews the trends of theory development in ASD, building on the work of the XP2020 conference. Section 3 details the methodology, including critical review and a network analysis approach. Section 4 analyzes articles, theories, and communities. Subsequently, Sect. 5 positions ASD core theories in the theory spectrum and provides guidelines for ASD theoretical research. Finally, we conclude our work with limitations and contributions in Sect. 6.

2 Trends of Theories Development in ASD

Before we dive into ASD theories, it is necessary to discuss the nature and boundaries of theories within ASD. Theories generated or developed from SE research are often presented as technological rules [9] through reflection in practices [31]. These technological rules are commonly expressed in the form of: To achieve <Effect> in <Situation > apply <Intervention> [9], which demonstrates the causal relationships among components of a theory. This causality formulation focuses on explanation. However, theories are not limited to explanation; they may also aim at other purposes, such as prediction, saying what will be and guiding future action [11]. Thus, the concept of theory should not be narrowly interpreted as technological rules when synthesizing core theories from existing theories. Core theories must serve as a basis to support multiple goals. In the discipline of IS, Gregor [11] provided a broad taxonomy of theories, categorized into five types: (i) Analysis; (ii) Explanation; (iii) Prediction; (iv) Explanation and prediction; and (v) Design and action. Each theory used or developed in ASD may focus on one or several of these goals, at the expense of others; but the core theories must accommodate all these purposes, at the very least, leaving space for further inclusion of all these elements. This broad understanding of the nature of theories provides foundations for adding new knowledge to the core theories of ASD, allowing theory developments based on these core.

In the special section of the XP2020 conference, Stray et al. [34] analyzed publications on ASD in the Scopus database from 2012 to 2021 (10 years). By exploring the publications that mentioned "theory" "theories," or "grounded theory" in the abstract, title, or keywords, they found only 7% of them used or developed theories. We followed the same protocol[2], searching the articles of the recent three years (2022–2024), yielding 1,683 ASD publications with 5% of them used or developed theories. From 7% to 5%, to further understand the declining trend of ASD publications involving theories, we generated the ratio of each year from 2012 to 2024, as shown in Fig. 1. We found that the percentage of publications related to theories has kept falling over the 13 years; the ratio was approximately 10.8% in 2012 whereas it had fallen to around 5.2% by 2024.

When we go deep into the details of these filtered ASD articles to examine their contributions to ASD theory development, we find it difficult due to the noise within the paper. Some articles contain the word "theory" but do not actually conduct their research aligning with the mentioned theory, for example: (i) they borrow theories from other disciplines without fully understanding the origins or contextual relevance; (ii) they claim theoretical contributions but merely replicating or reiterating existing theoretical work; (iii) they adopt theories as analytical lenses rather than directly contribute to development of such theories; and (iv) their research method is grounded theory but fail to produce a rigorous and validated theoretical framework. To avoid criticizing specific studies, we intentionally refrain from citing particular example papers, as our goal is not to blame certain research but to foster consensus on ASD core theories, not division.

3 Methodology

We performed a critical review to understand the status of ASD theories development and investigate the possible core theories. Critical review in SE often investigates theoretical or methodological topics [22]. It is similar in execution

---

[2] We conducted the search in the Scopus database on Dec 19, 2024, using the following query: TITLE-ABS-KEY ("agile development" OR "ASD" OR "agile methodologies" OR "agile methods" OR "agile project management") and limited to the subject area Computer Science and document types to Articles, Conference Papers, Reviews and Book Chapters.

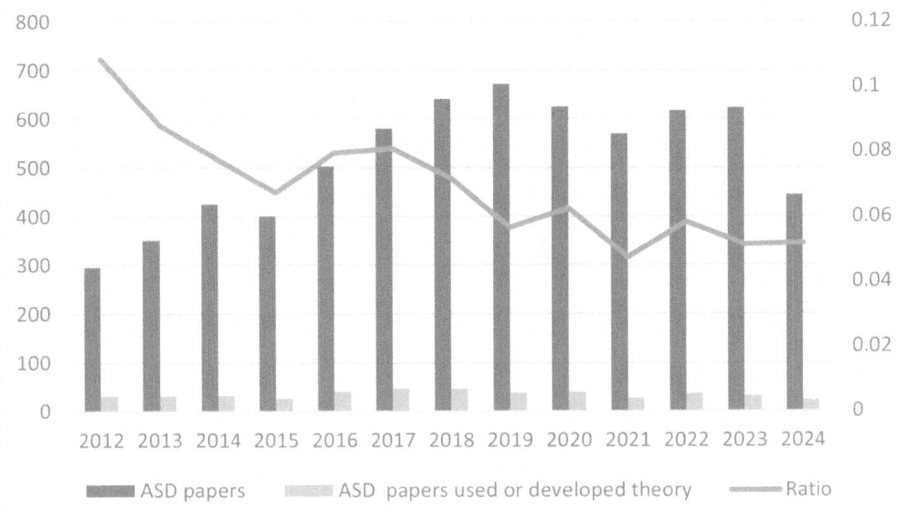

Fig. 1. ASD Publications and the Ratio of Those Using or Developing Theories (2012–2024)

to systematic reviews, except that critical reviews analyze a selected sample of papers with specific characteristics, whereas systematic reviews aggregate all relevant evidence [4]. We aim to answer the following research question (RQ) through this critical review study:

RQ: What are the possible core theories in ASD?

The review process is divided into three phases: literature searching, literature selection, and literature analysis, following Kitchenham and Charters' [18,19] guidelines. Each phase is explained in detail below.

3.1 Literature Searching

We investigate the above RQ by reviewing ASD literature on AIS elibrary, which is the central repository for research papers and journal articles in IS. Instead of choosing XP proceedings or a general database like Scopus, we focus on the scope of IS database and literature because of the following three primary considerations:

(i) The integration strategy [28] we selected for distilling core theories requires synthesizing SE theories with other reference disciplines. IS has become one reference discipline that exchanges ideas in intellectual discourse with other disciplines [5], integrating SE, computer science, psychology, economics, etc.
(ii) Under recent advanced technologies, agile transformation is more than software development transformation; it also largely impacts corporate organizational culture [17,20]. Given this, the core theories of ASD should support

both perspectives of agile-as-a-tool and agile-as-a-culture [23], similar to IS integrating technology and organizations.

(iii) Recently, most key and foundational papers related to ASD core theories have been published in IS venues, while SE and computer science tend to focus more on empirical practices. For instance, the paper "Issues, Challenges, and a Proposed Theoretical Core of ASD Research" was published in *Information Systems Journal* in 2021, sparking a scholarly discussion [3].

We did not limit the time range when searching for articles and included all those published before the end of 2024. Using the search string *subject: "agile software development" OR abstract: "agile software development"*, 199 articles were retrieved.

3.2 Literature Selection

We scanned the remaining articles for theory use and development according to the process shown in Fig. 2. We initially intended to include literature published within the IS 11 Baskets Avenue; however, as only a few studies met this criterion, we decided not to apply filters based on publication name or type, ensuring a broader scope of relevant literature. We excluded 53 articles that do not contain *theor** in all fields through an electronic search and 7 duplicate and inaccessible ones. Through full-text reading of the 139 selected articles, we found that 56 do not explicitly utilize specific theories. For instance, some papers refer to theories in the way of "theoretical lens", "theoretical contribution", or "theoretical exploration" without naming a particular theory. Considering that not all theories include the word "theory" in their title, such as frameworks or models, we further cross-checked whether these articles use theories or not against the list of widely adopted theories in IS provided by Lim et al. [21]. Then 83 articles consist of the final dataset for analysis.

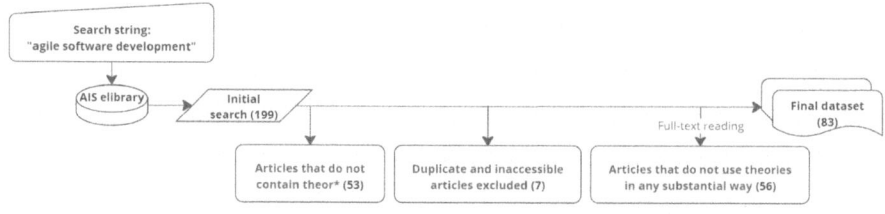

Fig. 2. Literature review process

3.3 Identification of Originating Discipline of Theories

To distil ASD core theories from existing theories used in SE and reference disciplines, we identified the originating disciplines of each theory used in 83 selected articles through the following approach. First, we search for the theories' names in the mapping table of theories and their originating disciplines provided by Lim et al. [21]. This table was constructed by cross-checking several scholarly databases, the Theories Used in IS Research Wiki[3], and validated by multiple researchers. Second, for theories not included in the table, we examined whether they could be classified as subsets of other listed theories. For example, although the Complex Adaptive System (CAS) theory is not explicitly presented in the mapping table, it can be identified as an instance of complexity theory [39], which originates from computer science. CAS is also argued to have originated from the systems science discipline. Still, we will try to trace it to computer science because systems science is interdisciplinary and has drawn heavily from concepts developed within computer science. Lastly, for the remaining theories with undefined disciplinary origins, we applied the same process outlined by Lim et al. [21], building upon their table and contributing to an expanded version.

3.4 Literature-Theory Complex Network Analysis

Using the atlas.ti data analysis tool, we systematically coded all 83 articles, identifying theories and mapping them to their originating disciplines. Based on the coding results, we adopted the Complex Network Analysis (CNA) approach [25] to construct theory networks. The initial step involved building articled-theory networks, as illustrated in Fig. 3, where different node colors of theories indicate different originating disciplines. Subsequently, these article-theory networks were converted into theory networks. To the best of our knowledge, CNA has not previously been applied to analyze theories in the SE discipline and we contribute to this.

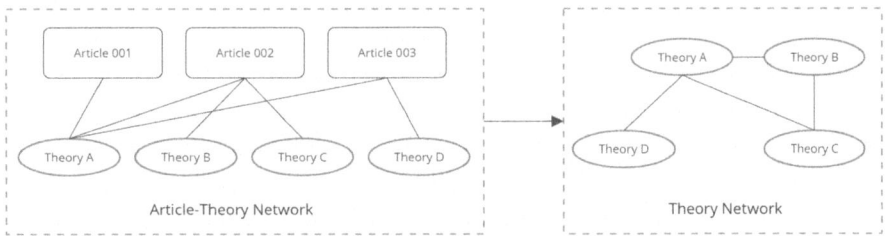

Fig. 3. Construction of Theory Networks

4 Results

From the initial yield of 199 articles on ASD to 83 in the final dataset, approximately 41.7% (83/199) articles used one or several theories in some substantial

---
[3] https://is.theorizeit.org/wiki/Main_Page.

way, which is six times higher than the 7% in the Fig. 1. These 83 articles also include the ones adopting grounded theory as a research method. This high ratio of theoretical work in the searched ASD articles provides a foundation for synthesizing a core theory from existing theories. Among these 83 articles, a total of 88 distinct theories[4] were cited 130 times, with the CAS theory being the most referenced, appearing in 10 articles. The other most used theories are presented in Fig. 4, which shows the long-tail phenomenon. We further examine the theory networks with the CNA method, key communities in the networks, and some noticeable scattered nodes.

Fig. 4. Number of articles using each theory

4.1 Theory Networks and Communities

The theory networks in Fig. 5 contain 88 nodes (theories) and 108 edges which means two theories are used in the same article. Approximately half of the nodes (43 out of 88) are connected to at least one other node, while the remaining nodes are scattered throughout the Figure. The size of each node indicates the number of articles (in Fig. 4) using this node theory. The width of each edge shows the number of articles using both node theories. Most green and red nodes have edges but most blue ones do not.

We categorized the 88 nodes into 3 groups, each colored green, red, and blue. This categorization is based on the findings from Lim et al.'s insights from reviewing two premier IS journals (MIS Quarterly and Information Systems

---

[4] Repository of 83 articles and 88 theories: https://shorturl.at/4sX8v.

Research) theory usage from 1998 to 2006. Their study suggests that theories originating from Psychology and Sociology (blue nodes) tend to be used together, while those from Economics, Strategy, and Organization Science (green nodes) are always together [21]. The remaining disciplines largely related to nature sciences and engineering are in the red group. Our network analysis of ASD articles shows that most green nodes and red nodes are connected closely while most blue ones are not.

Three main communities (densely connected sub-networks), which contain more than 5 nodes, are circled in Fig. 5. The largest community is dominated by 5 theories, ordered from largest to smallest nodes: CAS, theory of coordination, control theory, contingency theory, and leadership theories. These theories skeleton the largest community, with each node in this community being directly connected to at least one of them. (Two nodes are second-degree connected to CAS through complexity theory, which we consider synonymous with CAS as CAS is an instance of complexity theory.) The center theories in the second largest community are agency theory, principle-agent theory, and transaction cost theory; while there is no center node in the third largest one.

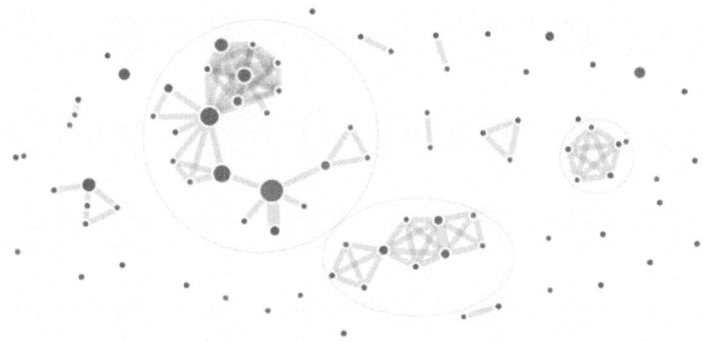

Originating Discipline
- Psychology, Sociology
- Organizational science, Economics, Communication, Strategy, Management
- Computer Science, Statistics, Information systems, Physics, Biology, Software engineering

Fig. 5. Theory networks (Color figure online)

4.2 Theory of ASD - An Isolated Node in Theory Networks

Among all the scattered nodes in Fig. 5, there is one red node without any connection with others, attracting our attention. It is the theory of ASD, proposed by Kakar [16] in 2000. Their study articulates a theory of ASD based on a synthesis of the key concepts underlying Agile principles. The theory of ASD is expressed as a model of relationships and we consider it as another form of agile principles.

Similar to the theory of ASD, another selected article [35] mentioned a theory of agility by citing Conboy's [6] work in 2009. We looked into Conboy's paper and tried to compare the theory of ASD with the theory of agility but failed; because his paper [6] introduces the theory of agility without definition and validation. Due to a lack of rigorous explanation of the theory of agility, we did not include it as a node when analyzing the selected articles.

5 Discussion

The results of CNA indicate that five theories, CAS, theory of coordination, control theory, contingency theory, and leadership theories, act as theoretical glue [6] in existing ASD research; the native theories of agile, agility, and ASD lack of definition or development and hard to gain recognition from our community.

We compare our results with existing studies on ASD theories. Hummel [14] conducted a systematic literature review of 482 ASD papers (38 from IS and 444 from SE included) in the year 2013, identifying the three most frequently applied theories, CAS, control theory, and theory of coordination. CAS and the theory of coordination are also listed in Dingsøyr et al.'s [8] editors' review of the Journal of Systems and Software special issue on ASD. They identified 19 theoretical perspectives used in agile research, analyzed from 452 articles published between 2001 and 2010. These related works and our results show a consistent stream of CAS, theory of coordination, and control theory as the theoretical core of ASD research in the past three decades. These three theories are widely known and used by ASD researchers and can be synthesized to build ASD core theories.

The native theories of ASD are highly grounded in agile principles [6,16,35]. Extracting key concepts from the agile manifesto and principles, Kakar [16] proposes the theory of ASD as: the effectiveness of ASDM arises from a collaborative organizational culture and customer focus that fosters internal and external cooperation, rapid iterative development practices, simplicity, and waste avoidance to provide competitive advantage to the customer, higher team morale, productivity, and customer (user) satisfaction.

To examine whether ASD core theories can be directly synthesized from agile principles, we move toward understanding the relationship between design principles and core theories. These two terms are key concepts in DSR. As a result of examining 47 papers proposing design principles by making use of core theories, Möller et al. [24] claims that core theories can be transformed into specific design principles through meta-requirements. However, design principles cannot be recognized as or simply converted to theories [10]; the systematic mechanism of agile principles to ASD core theories needs further study. We keep the possibility of distilling a native ASD core theory from agile principles but it cannot happen just by synthesizing concepts. Baham and Hirschheim [3] also mentioned there is no core theory inherently derived from agile principles themselves. To promote the development of native core theories in ASD, they propose theoretical core and core theoretical concepts, merging practice with research and contributing to native ASD theories.

5.1 Positioning ASD Core Theories in Theory Spectrum

ASD core theories require consensus from both researchers and practitioners. With CAS, the theory of coordination, and control theory distilled from existing researchers' work, we further consider how these theories are practical and useful for practitioners by positioning them in the theory spectrum. Ralph et al. [28] proposed this theory spectrum according to generality, from practice to theory of everything. In this review, the findings from those searched ASD articles that do not use theories fall into the category of empirical generalizations in this spectrum. Three dominant theories from CNA are classified as either middle-range or grand theories. Grand theories are constituted from mostly axioms, with a low falsifiability scale, and their generation is based on the paradox of induction rather than data; middle-range theories are formed by propositions containing observables, with a high falsifiability scale, and require data to generalize [13]. According to these differences elaborated by Hassan and Lowry [13], CAS is a grand theory whereas the theory of coordination and control theory belongs to the middle range in the context of ASD.

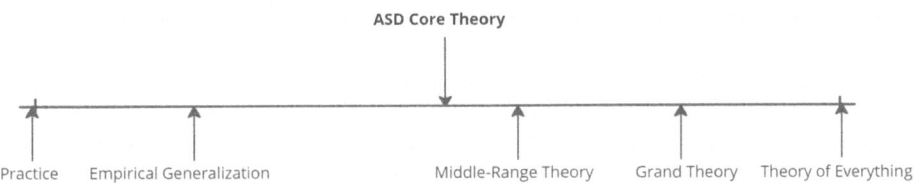

Fig. 6. Theory Spectrum According to Generality [28]

Different from Ralph et al. placing core theories between middle-range theory and grand theory, we position ASD core theories between empirical generalization and middle-range theory and move them closer to middle-range one (shown in Fig. 6) due to the following considerations.

(i) Empirical Grounding for Core Theories

More than half of the ASD articles in AIS elibrary do not use any theories, even more proportion in SE publications [34], but they contribute meaningfully to empirical generalization. To facilitate future research that can align core theories with empirical evidence, the ASD core theories should be grounded in empirical generalizations, to make researchers integrate easily. If core theories are too abstract or distant from practice, researchers may face significant challenges in aligning their work, hindering the development of ASD core theories.

(ii) Practical Usability of Middle-Range Theories

Given the ongoing lack of consensus regarding core theories in SE, Wieringa [38] advocates for a more practical approach: focusing on middle-range theories tailored to specific contexts rather than insisting on developing a single core theory for SE. Middle-range theories, as Wieringa [37] further highlights, are more usable by practitioners. As stepping stones toward core theories, middle-range theories offer the practical and theoretical balance [32,33].

(iii) Evolution of Core Theories

The development and consensus on ASD core theories is an iterative and evolutionary process. While we remain open to the possibility of ASD core theories being more abstract and moving toward grand theories in this theory spectrum [28], as they are adopted by more research. But we need to have something on hand as the starting point of ASD core theories' evolution. Here, we refer to the two identified middle-range theories the theory of coordination and control theory. Their empirical validation in ASD practices supports ASD core theories being abstract enough for generalizations as well as close enough to observation [13].

5.2 Guidelines for Theoretical Work in ASD Research

To accelerate the development of a theoretical basis in ASD and related SE fields and achieve consensus on ASD core theories, we recommend as following for ASD researchers.

When generating new theories from ASD practices, consider their connection with the theory of coordination and control theory. Besides aligning with these two core theories, positioning the proposed theories in the theory spectrum is also needed for more practical validation later. To facilitate other researchers to cite your work and theoretically contribute based on it, it is crucial to give your proposed theories a unique and distinctive name. Otherwise, it may result in being informally labeled after the author's name, diminishing the theory's visibility.

When extracting native theories from ASD principles, clarify the mechanisms used for converting principles toward native theories. These mechanisms could differ for each concept of ASD principles and clear clarification of the scope of each mechanism is necessary. Following a rigorous approach to generating native theories and validation from both academia and industry community are required.

When borrowing existing theories from other disciplines for understanding or predicting ASD phenomenons, consider taking CAS as a theoretical lens. As a grand theory, CAS can be a theoretical view of most ASD practices, assisting newly borrowed theories to better match the ASD context. Remember to cite the originating publication containing these borrowed ones before explaining how they can be used in the ASD context. It is important to distinguish theories with the same name but different meanings in different disciplines, as well as similar theories' names for the same theory content. Also, you should make sure to use the correct name. For example, check when a theory originated, its name is "organizational" or "organization", "theory of ***" or "*** theory".

6 Conclusion

Research left behind practice in the ASD field and we are unable to achieve a common agreement on ASD core theories. This issue is common in SE discipline, and it is particularly relevant with ASD, the field that originated fully from practice. Many researchers have attempted to propose ASD core theories based on empirical generalizations or agile principles. However, without exception, no consensus had been reached until we conducted this research. From these research experiences, we understand that achieving a widely accepted consensus cannot be accomplished through one workshop or a single study. Instead, continuous efforts are needed to examine potential core theories in the ASD field and this research is part of them.

In this critical review, we adopt integration as the main strategy to identify possible core theories in ASD. Through systematic literature selection and CNA processes, we identified theory networks, communities, and key isolated nodes based on 83 filtered articles. Our research does not draw a definitive conclusion about which theories are the core of ASD. Instead, we provide practical guidelines for ASD researchers - connecting applied theories with the theory of coordination and control theory, using CAS as a theoretical lens to borrow new theories, and developing native ASD theories with rigorous methodology.

This research contributes in the following aspects. First, we introduce the CNA approach to SE for analyzing the relationships and development of theories, promoting the theorization of practice in the ASD and broader SE fields. Second, we provide guidelines for researchers on proposing and using ASD theories, addressing the call for theories application and development raised at the XP 2020 conference. Furthermore, building on the work from the GTSE 2014 workshop, we optimize the existing theory spectrum by focusing on the ASD field.

These contributions should be considered in light of several limitations. We may have missed some ASD theories in the selected articles if they were not explicitly labeled as a theory or did not have a clearly identified theory name. Also, this study focuses primarily on the integration strategy for developing ASD core theories, although all strategies are not inclusive. Last, some of the guidelines suggested in this paper, being meta-science, are not directly supported by empirical evidence. In future work, we aim to employ other empirical research methods to validate the proposed guidelines and refine the list of possible core theories proposed in this study.

Acknowledgments. This research was funded by the Business Finland project 6G Bridge - 6G software for extremely distributed and heterogeneous massive networks of connected devices (8516/31/2022); and supported by FAST, the Finnish Software Engineering Doctoral Research Network, funded by the Ministry of Education and Culture, Finland.

References

1. Abrahamsson, P., Conboy, K., Wang, X.: 'Lots done, more to do': the current state of agile systems development research. Eur. J. Inf. Syst. **18**(4), 281–284 (2009)
2. Akbar, M.A., et al.: 6GSoft: software for edge-to-cloud continuum. In: 2024 50th Euromicro Conference on Software Engineering and Advanced Applications (SEAA), pp. 499–506 (2024)
3. Baham, C., Hirschheim, R.: Issues, challenges, and a proposed theoretical core of agile software development research. Inf. Syst. J. **32**(1), 103–129 (2021)
4. Baltes, S., Ralph, P.: Sampling in software engineering research: a critical review and guidelines. Empir. Softw. Eng. **27**(4), 94 (2022)
5. Baskerville, R.L., Myers, M.D.: Information systems as a reference discipline. MIS Q. **26**(1), 1–14 (2002)
6. Conboy, K.: Agility from first principles: reconstructing the concept of agility in information systems development. Inf. Syst. Res. **20**(3), 329–354 (2009)
7. Craver, C.F.: Structure of scientific theories. In: Machamer, P., Silberstein, M. (eds.) The Blackwell Guide to the Philosophy of Science, pp. 55–79. Wiley (2002)
8. Dingsøyr, T., Nerur, S., Balijepally, V., Moe, N.B.: A decade of agile methodologies: towards explaining agile software development. J. Syst. Softw. **85**(6), 1213–1221 (2012)
9. Engström, E., Storey, M.A., Runeson, P., Höst, M., Baldassarre, M.T.: How software engineering research aligns with design science: a review. Empir. Softw. Eng. **25**(4), 2630–2660 (2020)
10. Gregor, S., Jones, D.: The anatomy of a design theory. J. Assoc. Inf. Syst. **8**(5), 312–335 (2007)
11. Gregor, S.: The nature of theory in information systems. MIS Q. **30**(3), 611–642 (2006)
12. Hall, J.G., Rapanotti, L.: A design theory for software engineering. Inf. Softw. Technol. **87**, 46–61 (2017)
13. Hassan, N.R., Lowry, P.B.: Seeking middle-range theories in information systems research. In: International Conference on Information Systems (ICIS 2015), Fort Worth, TX, December, pp. 13–18 (2015)
14. Hummel, M.: State-of-the-art: a systematic literature review on agile information systems development. In: 2014 47th Hawaii International Conference on System Sciences, pp. 4712–4721 (2014)
15. Johnson, P., Ekstedt, M., Jacobson, I.: Where's the theory for software engineering? IEEE Softw. **29**(5), 96 (2012)
16. Kakar, A.K.: A theory of agile software development. In: SAIS 2020 Proceedings, vol. 32 (2020)
17. Kautz, K.: Cultures of agility - agile software development in practice. In: ACIS 2009 Proceedings, vol. 87 (2009)
18. Kitchenham, B., Charters, S.: Guidelines for performing Systematic Literature Reviews in Software Engineering. Technical report, ver. 2.3 EBSE Technical report. EBSE (2007)
19. Kitchenham, B., Madeyski, L., Budgen, D.: SEGRESS: software engineering guidelines for reporting secondary studies. IEEE Trans. Software Eng. **49**(3), 1273–1298 (2023)
20. Lee, J.Y.: A study on agile transformation in the new digital age. Int. J. Adv. Cult. Technol. **8**(1), 82–88 (2020)

21. Lim, S., Saldanha, T.J.V., Malladi, S., Melville, N.P.: Theories used in information systems research: insights from complex network analysis. J. Inf. Technol. Theory Appl. **14**(2) (2013)
22. Lorey, T., Ralph, P., Felderer, M.: Social Science Theories in Software Engineering Research - Replication Package (2022)
23. Magistretti, S., Trabucchi, D.: Agile-as-a-tool and agile-as-a-culture: a comprehensive review of agile approaches adopting contingency and configuration theories. Rev. Manag. Sci. (2024)
24. Möller, F., Strobel, G., Schoormann, T., Hansen, M.R.P.: Unveiling the Cloak: Kernel Theory Use in Design Science Research (2022)
25. Polites, G., Watson, R.: Using social network analysis to analyze relationships among IS journals. J. Assoc. Inf. Syst. **10**(8), 595–636 (2009)
26. Ralph, P.: Possible core theories for software engineering. In: 2013 2nd SEMAT Workshop on a General Theory of Software Engineering (GTSE), pp. 35–38 (2013)
27. Ralph, P., Engels, G., Jacobson, I., Goedicke, M.: 4th SEMAT workshop on general theory of software engineering (GTSE 2015). In: 2015 IEEE/ACM 37th IEEE International Conference on Software Engineering, vol. 2, pp. 983–984 (2015)
28. Ralph, P., et al.: How to develop a general theory of software engineering: report on the GTSE 2014 workshop. SIGSOFT Softw. Eng. Notes **39**(6), 23–25 (2014)
29. Ralph, P., Johnson, P., Jordan, H.: Report on the first SEMAT workshop on general theory of software engineering (GTSE 2012). SIGSOFT Softw. Eng. Notes **38**(2), 26–28 (2013)
30. Sjoberg, D.I.K., Dyba, T., Jorgensen, M.: The future of empirical methods in software engineering research. In: Future of Software Engineering (FOSE 2007), pp. 358–378 (2007)
31. Smolander, K., Päivärinta, T.: Forming theories of practices for software engineering. In: 2013 2nd SEMAT Workshop on a General Theory of Software Engineering (GTSE), pp. 27–34 (2013)
32. Stol, K.J., Fitzgerald, B.: Uncovering theories in software engineering. In: 2013 2nd SEMAT Workshop on a General Theory of Software Engineering (GTSE), pp. 5–14 (2013)
33. Stol, K.J., Fitzgerald, B.: Theory-oriented software engineering. Sci. Comput. Program. **101**, 79–98 (2015)
34. Stray, V., Hoda, R., Paasivaara, M., Lenarduzzi, V., Mendez, D.: Theories in agile software development: past, present, and future introduction to the XP 2020 special section. Inf. Softw. Technol. **152**, 107058 (2022)
35. Strode, D.E.: Coordination effectiveness in an agile software development context. In: PACIS 2011 Proceedings, vol. 183 (2011)
36. Whetten, D.A.: What constitutes a theoretical contribution? Acad. Manag. Rev. **14**(4), 490–495 (1989)
37. Wieringa, R.J.: Design Science Methodology for Information Systems and Software Engineering. Springer (2014)
38. Wieringa, R.J.: Towards middle-range usable design theories for software engineering. In: Proceedings of the 3rd SEMAT Workshop on General Theories of Software Engineering, pp. 1–4 (2014)
39. Xiaofeng, W., Kieran, C.: Understanding agility in software development through a complex adaptive systems perspective. In: 17th European Conference on Information Systems (2009)

Open Access This chapter is licensed under the terms of the Creative Commons Attribution 4.0 International License (http://creativecommons.org/licenses/by/4.0/), which permits use, sharing, adaptation, distribution and reproduction in any medium or format, as long as you give appropriate credit to the original author(s) and the source, provide a link to the Creative Commons license and indicate if changes were made.

The images or other third party material in this chapter are included in the chapter's Creative Commons license, unless indicated otherwise in a credit line to the material. If material is not included in the chapter's Creative Commons license and your intended use is not permitted by statutory regulation or exceeds the permitted use, you will need to obtain permission directly from the copyright holder.

Agile Coaching Research: A Systematic Mapping Study

Ehikioya Obode[1](✉)[iD], Peggy Gregory[1][iD], Derek Somerville[1][iD], and Advait Deshpande[2][iD]

[1] University of Glasgow, Glasgow, Scotland
e.obode.1@research.gla.ac.uk,
{Peggy.Gregory,Derek.Somerville}@glasgow.ac.uk
[2] The Open University, Milton Keynes, UK
advait.deshpande@open.ac.uk

Abstract. Agile coaching has emerged as a key enabler of agile adoption and organisational transformation. Despite its growing prevalence, there has not been much research into agile coaching, and there is a need for a better understanding of the current state of research and where the gaps lie. To fill this gap, we present a systematic mapping study (SMS) of agile coaching to identify and categorise existing research. An initial search identified 497 studies, of which 22 primary studies were selected based on inclusion and exclusion criteria. We provide a thematic analysis of the included papers and a summary of challenges and benefits associated with agile coaching. Key findings indicate a steady rate of research studies since 2013, predominantly from Europe. The most extensively researched areas are coaches' skills, roles, and responsibilities. However, there is a noticeable lack of research depth in other areas and an absence of theory in all papers. Finally, we propose a roadmap for further research, highlighting unexplored aspects of agile coaching, including its impact across diverse organisational contexts. These findings provide a foundation for future research and offer practical insights for practitioners and researchers in the agile domain.

Keywords: Agile coaching · Coaching Challenges · Coaching Benefits · Systematic Mapping Study

1 Introduction

Agile coaching plays a pivotal role in the successful adoption and sustainability of agile practices within organisations and has become more prominent as agile expands beyond software and into large-scale application [1]. As a discipline, agile coaching involves guiding individuals, teams, and organisations through the cultural and practical shifts required to embrace agility, fostering collaboration, adaptability, and continuous improvement [2]. Agile coaches act as facilitators, mentors, and change agents. Their importance lies in bridging the gap between theoretical frameworks and practical application, ensuring that agile principles are not merely implemented but deeply embedded in an organisation's culture. The overall aim being to drive both short-term outcomes and long-term resilience in a rapidly evolving business landscape.

The practice of agile coaching as a discipline distinct from other forms of professional coaching emerged alongside the rise of agile methodologies, particularly following the publication of the Agile Manifesto in 2001 [3]. Initially, agile coaching was embedded in the roles of Scrum Master and Team Lead, but over time, it evolved into a distinct discipline blending coaching, mentoring, facilitation, and teaching [4]. As organisations sought to implement frameworks like Scrum and Kanban, and later to scale agile across larger organisations and even the whole enterprise, the need for skilled practitioners who could guide teams and organisations through the complexities of agile transformation became evident [5]. One of the most interesting elements of agile coaching is its emphasis on fostering psychological safety and team dynamics, recognising that cultural and behavioural shifts are as critical as technical processes and structural change in achieving agility [6]. Another unique aspect is the coach's role as both an observer and a catalyst, balancing non-directive questioning to promote self-discovery with strategic interventions to address organisational impediments. As the field has matured, agile coaches have adopted tools from other domains, such as professional coaching, organisational development, and systems thinking, creating a multifaceted approach that adapts to diverse contexts and challenges.

The aim of this study was to provide a comprehensive overview of empirical academic research into agile coaching. We undertook a systematic mapping study (SMS), which maps the breadth of research literature in a field by identifying themes, trends, gaps, and patterns, rather than a systematic literature review (SLR), which answers a specific research question by synthesising results from published empirical studies. A preliminary search found only one SLR, summarising results related to the tasks, responsibilities, and skills of agile coaches [7], but no SMS overviewing the broad landscape of research into agile coaching, indicating that this research field is rather immature.

2 Research Method

Our SMS procedure is based on Petersen et al. [8] and Kitchenham et al. [9] guidelines on mapping studies. As our aim is to provide an overview of current research and provide a roadmap for future research, we also investigate the benefits and challenges of agile coaching. This paper seeks to achieve our aim by answering the following research questions.

RQ1: What are the publication trends of research on agile coaching?
RQ2: What are the main themes explored in research on agile coaching?
RQ3: What are the benefits associated with agile coaching?
RQ4: What are the key challenges faced in agile coaching?

2.1 Search Strategy

To address the research questions, we carried out a search in the literature using the same broad search query used by Stray et al. for their SLR [7], highlighted below:

"agile coach" OR "agility coach" OR "Scrum coach" OR "Lean coach" OR "Kanban coach" OR "XP coach". OR "DevOps coach" OR "agile coaching" OR "Scrum coaching" OR "Lean coaching" OR "Kanban coaching" OR "XP coaching" OR "DevOps coaching" OR ("internal coach" AND (agile OR scrum OR Lean OR Kanban OR XP OR DevOps)) OR ("team coaching" AND (agile OR Scrum OR Lean OR Kanban OR XP OR DevOps))

We then carried out trial searches across the Web of Science, Google Scholar, and Scopus, and similar to Stray et al. [7], discovered that Scopus provided the most comprehensive results for relevant empirical peer-reviewed papers. It also contained results already found in Google Scholar and Web of Science. Scopus was adopted for this reason and also for its intuitiveness.

We applied our search to Scopus in October 2024 and returned 497 articles related to agile coaching. The articles were screened against the set of inclusion and exclusion criteria we developed for the SMS, shown in Table 1.

Table 1. Inclusion and Exclusion Criteria

ID	Criterion
IC1	Relevant empirical papers published in conference proceedings
IC2	Relevant empirical book chapters to the research topic
IC3	Relevant empirical publications in journals
EC1	Publications where abstract and keywords show paper not related to agile coaching
EC2	Duplicate studies
EC3	Workshop proposals, panels, and tutorials
EC4	Systematic reviews or mapping studies
EC5	Study where full text was not available
EC6	Study where agile coaching is not the main topic of research
EC7	Study of student learning of the agile methods in university courses
EC8	Articles not in English
EC9	Books were excluded

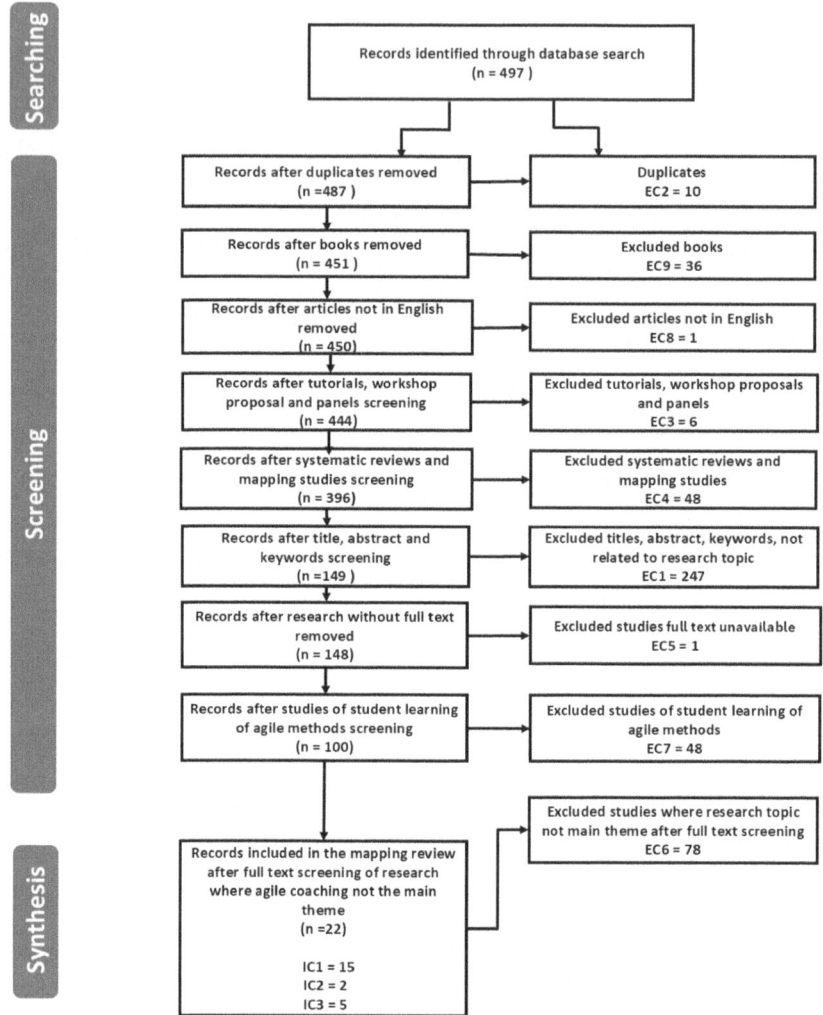

Fig. 1. Flow diagram of systematic mapping study selection process

2.2 Publication Selection

The 497 papers were exported to a CSV file for subsequent analysis. The initial screening of the papers was conducted by the first author, followed by a secondary review performed by the second author. Data analysis was carried out with the assistance of all authors. The study selection process involved screening the titles, abstracts, author keywords and full text using our predefined inclusion (IC) and exclusion (EC) criteria, with each assigned a unique identifier, for easy categorisation during our review. The flow and results of each stage are shown in Fig. 1. Common reasons for our exclusions included studies focusing on software engineering education in undergraduate courses, studies on agile methods where agile coaching was not the main theme of the research, systematic mapping and review studies, books and workshop proposals. Fifteen studies satisfied our inclusion criterion IC1, two satisfied IC2, and five met IC3, making a total of 22 studies used for systematic mapping and narrative synthesis.

2.3 Data Analysis

We conducted a full text screening of our final selection of papers and extracted data related to our research questions. Summary statistics were used to generate figures for year of publication, research methodologies, methods, and theories used. We used Braun & Clarke's thematic analysis approach [10] to generate thematic summaries of three aspects of the included papers: the research topics, the benefits of agile coaching and the challenges of agile coaching. For the thematic analysis of research topics (Table 2), we read the whole paper but particularly the research questions, results, and conclusions to generate a list of codes for each paper. We then reviewed the codes and merged these where appropriate to generate 28 sub-themes and finally grouped them into eight themes. We followed the same overall process for the analysis of the benefits of agile coaching (Table 3) and the challenges of agile coaching (Table 4), in both these cases pulling out relevant data from the papers.

3 Results

In answer to RQ1, we first provide a summary of publication trends, including year of publication, where the research was undertaken, and what data collection methods (surveys, experiments, interviews), methodologies (qualitative, quantitative, or mixed), and theories were used.

Figure 2 shows the number of papers published on agile coaching and agile coaches between 2013 and 2024. From our analysis, regular publications only started in 2013, before which there were no publications on agile coaching that met our inclusion criteria. All pre-2013 publications either had other agile-related studies as their main theme or were not empirical papers, for example, practitioner reports. We also observed an average of two publications per year. However, the trend shows a slight peak in 2023, which may have been because of increased research undertaken during the pandemic. This does not appear to have continued in 2024, with only one publication by October 2024 when we captured our data.

Furthermore, we analysed data on where researchers publish their results. We found that 15 papers were published in conferences, 5 papers were published in journals, and book chapter publications accounted for only 2 papers.

We also examined the geographical distribution of agile coaching research to determine where data contributing to the field was collected. Our objective was to identify the locations in which empirical studies on agile coaching were conducted. Several studies included participants from multiple countries, some

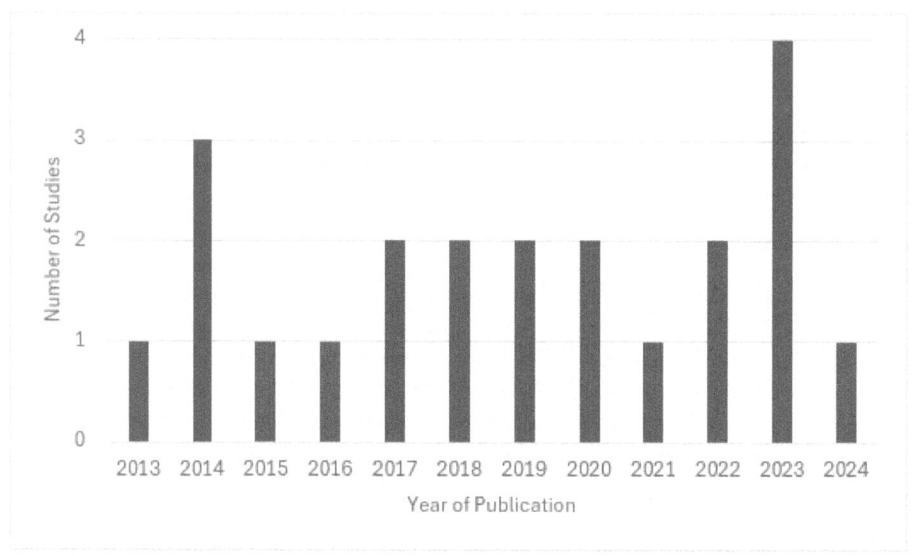

Fig. 2. Publication Trends: Publications by year

within a continent and others across continents. For instance, Klunder et al. [21] interviewed agile coaches in both Spain and Germany in their investigation into fostering an agile mindset within development teams, while Stray et al. [2] interviewed agile coaches across Norway and the USA in their research on the agile coach role.

The geographical distribution indicates a strong representation from Europe. Of the 22 papers analysed, 17 papers collected their data from a single continent, 3 papers collected data across more than one continent. Of the 17 papers that collected data from a single continent, 14 papers collected data solely from Europe. Of the 3 papers that collected data across more than one continent, one collected data from Europe and North America, one from North America and Oceania, and one from Europe, South America, and Asia. Two papers did not specify where data was collected. We have not included those in the analysis. Figure 3 illustrates the distribution of research across different continents. To collate this we looked at the 20 papers that reported research locations, and counted the countries in which research studies had taken place (n = 32). These were then reported by continent for clarity.

We also observed that agile coaching research was carried out across multiple industries, including financial services, education, consulting, music, telecommunications, and healthcare. This indicates a growing interest in agile coaching outside the traditional software industries. Further analysis of the data revealed that 75% of the papers focused on agile coaches or agile coaching within software development teams, while only 10% examined agile coaches working outside the software development domain. 5% of the papers focused on agile coaches working

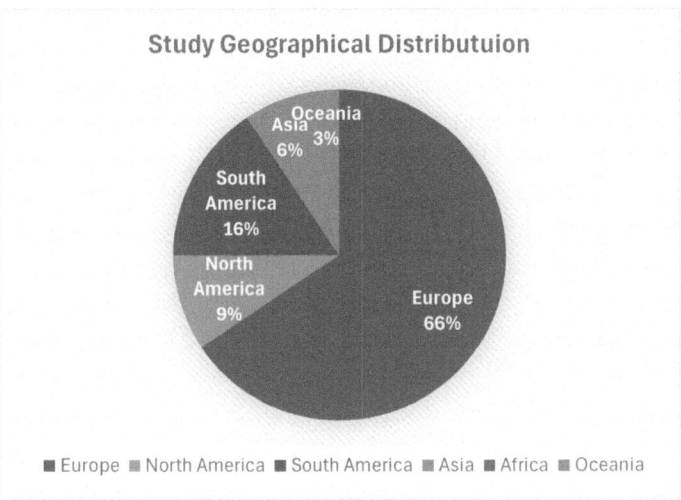

Fig. 3. Agile coaching studies by continent

with software and non-software teams, while 10% of the papers did not specify the type of teams the agile coaches were involved with.

Fourteen of the articles used qualitative methods, seven used quantitative methods, and one used a mixed-method approach. Data collection methods included interviews (12 papers), experiments (5 papers), and surveys (5 papers). We looked for theory use but found that none of the studies used pre-existing theory to shape their studies or interpret their findings. However, two studies used a grounded theory research approach and hence developed theories from their investigations.

3.1 Agile Coaching Research Themes

The twenty-two papers included in this study are highlighted in the Studies column in Table 2. The analysis of topics covered by research identified eight themes and 28 sub-themes (see Table 2), which we discuss below.

Agile Coach Roles and Responsibilities: This explores the roles and responsibilities performed by an agile coach within teams, organisations, and at the leadership level. It was the most researched theme and covered topics relating to the roles, responsibilities, and skills required to fulfill the role, personal characteristics of an agile coach, competencies needed to successfully perform the role, leadership, and the different types of agile coach. Nine papers primarily researched the role and responsibilities aspect, suggesting an active debate around this topic related to agile transformation and its sustainability.

Agile Coaching Practices and Training: This focuses on the methodologies, techniques, tools, and formal training required to develop agile coaching

Table 2. Analysis of research topics: Themes, sub-themes, frequency (#) and studies

Themes	Sub-themes	#	Studies
AGILE COACH ROLES & RESPONSIBILITIES	Roles and responsibilities	9	[2,4,11–17]
	Agile coach types	1	[18]
	Leadership	2	[15,19]
	Coach competencies	1	[2]
	Coach skills	2	[2,4]
	Personal characteristics	1	[21]
AGILE COACHING PRACTICES & TRAINING	Agile coaching tools	4	[2,22–24]
	Agile coaching practices	4	[2,6,11,28]
	Agile coaching metrics	1	[22]
	Agile coach network	1	[1]
	Agile coach certification	2	[20,25]
	Agile coach training	1	[25]
COACHING FOR AGILE ADOPTION & TRANSFORMATION	Coaching for agile adoption	2	[12,14]
	Coaching for agile transformation	2	[13,17]
COACHING FOR TEAM DYNAMICS & PERFORMANCE	Coaching distributed teams	2	[1,19]
	Coaching virtual agile teams	1	[19]
	Team performance	1	[27]
	Team metrics	1	[22]
	Challenges	1	[4]
VALUE & IMPACT OF AGILE COACHING	Agile coach's value	2	[4,26]
	Agile coach's impact	1	[27]
COACHING FOR AGILE CULTURE	Culture change	1	[19]
	Agile mindset	2	[21,25]
	Psychological safety	1	[6]
COACHING THE LEARNING ORGANISATION	Knowledge & management support	1	[14]
	Knowledge sharing	1	[28]
	Importance of context	1	[25]
NEW TRENDS	The AI agile coach	1	[11]

expertise. We identified six sub-themes. Research studies covered a broad range of areas, with agile coaching tools and agile coaching practices being the two most researched sub-themes, followed by research on the agile coach's certification with two studies. The other sub-themes each had one study reporting them, suggesting a spread of research undertaken by researchers on agile coaching practices and training.

Coaching for Agile Adoption and Transformation: This theme emphasises the role of agile coaching in driving successful agile adoption and organisational transformation. We identified two sub-themes with two studies focused on how agile coaches drive agile adoption at both team and organisational levels. Researchers also explored the agile coach's role in the transformation and transitioning of teams and organisations into becoming more agile.

Coaching for Team Dynamics and Performance: This theme explores how agile coaching impacts team collaboration, communication, and overall performance. Two papers related to distributed teams, exploring successful agile coaching in distributed teams and best practices. Coaching for team performance, team metrics, virtual teams and coaching challenges were also researched.

Value and Impact of Agile Coaching: This theme focuses on the tangible and intangible benefits of agile coaching for teams, organisations, and individuals. Researchers explored the value of introducing an agile coach into an organisation and their impact when adopting agile methods. In exploring impact, the researchers compared companies that used an agile Coach for agile adoption with those that did not, with the results showing that using agile coaches provided a better return on investment in agile adoption programmes.

Coaching for Agile Culture: The theme focuses on how agile coaching fosters an organisational culture rooted in agile principles and its challenges. We identified a study that explored the challenges agile coaches encountered when working across different cultures, such as language barriers, different values and norms, and difficulty maintaining trust, especially when working in global software organisations. Researchers also investigated the effectiveness of introducing an agile coach as an intervention to enhance psychological safety. The results showed a substantial improvement in psychological safety perception when compared to a control group without an agile coach.

Coaching the Learning Organisation: This explores how agile coaching contributes to developing a learning organisation that continuously evolves and adapts. Knowledge management, knowledge sharing, and the importance of context were identified as sub-themes within the agile coaching literature. Researchers investigated the role of an agile coach in knowledge management within agile software development teams, highlighting the knowledge offered by agile coaches. Findings indicate that different types of organisational settings will require different types of agile coaches with different qualifications depending on the organisation's specific needs.

New Trends: This theme identifies an emerging trend in agile coaching practice in response to technological advancement. Researchers have experimented using large language models, like ChatGPT, taking on the role of an agile coach within a software development team with positive results.

3.2 Agile Coaching Benefits

We identified 32 benefits of agile coaching from our analysis, which we categorised into eight themes. Each highlighting the pivotal role agile coaches play in organisational transformation. The themes outlined in Table 3 highlight the key benefits of agile coaching in guiding the individual, team, and organisation towards adopting and sustaining agile principles. On the individual level, agile coaching helps individuals improve their understanding of agile, develop new skills, and adopt a growth mindset. Another important benefit of agile coaching is that it enhances team dynamics through tailored agile ceremonies like retrospectives, daily stand-ups, and sprint planning, which improves team processes and team morale while ensuring that team members are aligned on goals and priorities. From a broader organisational perspective, agile coaching helps organisational transformation by facilitating the scaling of agile methodologies across departments, facilitating decision-making, and improving trust with clients while promoting cross-functional collaboration.

3.3 Agile Coaching Challenges

Our analysis identified 11 challenges associated with agile coaching, which have been organised into five sub-themes, as presented in Table 4.

Misunderstanding and Resistance to Agile Principles: These challenges arise due to a lack of understanding of agile principles and the difficulty in aligning team and individual mindsets with agile values. Resistance to change at the organisational, team, or individual level often creates friction in agile coaching efforts.

Stakeholder Alignment and Collaboration: These challenges relate to the complex nature of stakeholder management in agile transformation projects, with each stakeholder pursuing unique priorities and ensuring that coaching efforts are aligned to maximise value. This includes managing competing demands from multiple teams or projects.

Team Dynamics and Change Management: Agile coaches often face challenges in managing dynamic team compositions and ensuring continuity and focus. Challenges also occur in identifying key problems in the midst of evolving team structures, which adds an extra layer of difficulty.

Measuring Effectiveness and Resource Allocation: This focuses on the challenges of determining the right balance in coaching effort and establishing a sustainable business model for agile coaching within organisations. Quantifying the value of coaching and the effective allocation of resources are key challenges.

Table 3. Benefits of agile coaching: Themes and sub-themes

Benefit themes	Benefit sub-themes	Studies
Organisational transformation & agile culture	Facilitate agile transformation	[2, 13, 17]
	Develop agile mindset in organisation	
	Shift organisational culture towards agile	[25]
	Engage management with transformation	
	Aids long-term strategy for organisation	
	Minimises risk of transformation failing	
Team development & morale	Encourages positive team morale	[2, 13, 15]
	Helps motivate teams	
	Helps develop the team	[17, 25]
	Helps teams improve ways of working	
Process improvement & efficiency	Process improvement of agile practices	[1, 6]
	Improves team performance	
	Improves project performance	
	Improves overall efficiency and innovation	
Coaching skills & implementation	Internal coaches help agile adoption	[1, 2, 4]
	Internal coaches can adapt agile to organisational context	
	Coaches bring unique coaching skills	[25]
	Practical experience improves processes	
	Provide technical guidance to team	
Decision making & guidance	Help facilitate decision-making	[1, 2, 13]
	Provide objective guidance to organisation	
	Anticipate challenges in change programs	
Stakeholder engagement & trust	Support stakeholders to apply agile	[1, 2, 16]
	Help to build trust with customers	
	Increases management and business understanding of agile	[17]
Psychological & cost benefits	Enhance psychological safety	[6, 11]
	Potential cost savings	
Learning & continuous improvement	Help individuals/teams/organisations to improve	[2, 19]
	Improve understanding of agile practices	

Remote and Distributed Agile Practices: Coaching teams that are distributed across various locations presents unique challenges, particularly in maintaining collaboration, engagement, and the effectiveness of agile ceremonies.

Table 4. Challenges of agile coaching: Themes and sub-themes

Challenge themes	Challenge sub-themes	Studies
Misunderstandings & resistance to change	Misconception of what it means to be agile	[4, 21]
	Resistance to change for teams/individuals	
	Changing mindset of team and managers	
	Hard for coaches to preserve authority	
Stakeholder alignment & collaboration	Aligning and confirming with stakeholders	[1, 4]
	Selecting which teams to coach to optimise benefits	
Team dynamics & change management	Identifying the real problem to be solved	[4]
	Dealing with team changes	
Measuring effectiveness & resource allocation	Quantifying how much coaching is enough	[1]
	Deciding if individual projects should pay for coaching	
Remote & distributed teams	Running successful agile ceremonies for remote & distributed teams	[19]

4 Discussion

In answer to RQ1, investigating the publication trends of research on agile coaching, we identified 22 papers that met our criteria. Of these, there have been publications every year since 2013, but the average frequency is only two per year. The vast majority of the studies were carried out in Europe, and two-thirds were qualitative. This suggests that agile coaching is an area of interest for researchers, but one that is not yet mature. The widespread use of qualitative research methods and the lack of theory suggest that much of the research is exploratory, and there is not yet a theoretical underpinning. In answer to RQ2, about the main themes explored in the research, we identified eight themes and 28 sub-themes. These cover coaches' roles and practices, the impact of coaching on agile transformation, team performance, culture, and organisational learning, the value of coaching, and the new trend of AI coaching. The variety in the themes shows there are many facets of coaching to explore. However, while the spread of papers is wide, the depth is thin with rarely more than two papers in each sub-theme. To answer RQ3 and RQ4, about the benefits and challenges of agile coaching, we generated eight themes and 29 sub-themes related to benefits and five themes and 11 sub-themes related to challenges. We speculate that the higher number of benefits compared to challenges indicates that the focus of much of the research is on understanding what coaching brings to organisations rather than understanding the problems.

We propose a roadmap for future research into agile coaching, summarised in Table 5. To develop this, we used a framework to aid the identification of research gaps, as missing elements are difficult to spot. Davis et al.'s [29] sociotechnical systems theory was chosen as it provides a holistic view of organisations, emphasising the interconnectedness between human factors and technical systems. First, we mapped sub-themes from this study (sometimes merged for the sake of brevity) to the six framework elements - people, processes and procedures, culture, goals and metrics, technology, and infrastructure, as they represent areas in which some empirical research has been undertaken (see column 2 of Table 5). After this exercise, it was notable that each framework element contained some research areas indicating a certain breadth. Of this research, the majority has focused on coaches as individuals and specific aspects of their practice, especially in supporting team development. This work fits into the 'People' element of the roadmap. However, as we noted in our findings, there is insufficient research depth in any area, so even in the areas covered by current research, more studies are needed. We then identified potential new research topics through discussion between ourselves (see column 3 of Table 5). This list inevitably has limitations because of the speculative nature of the exercise. Unresearched areas include comparing practices in different contexts, exploring the influence of national and organisational culture on agile coaching practices, investigating how coaching can influence deep-seated change in organisations, further work into how AI may support or change coaching practice and comparing coaching models from different industries. Finally, there is a lack of theory in the field, so we encourage future researchers to consider either applying existing theory or developing new theory to aid a better understanding of this practice.

4.1 Threats and Validity

Systematic mapping studies are subject to limitations and potential threats to validity. In carrying out our final search query, we relied on a single database, Scopus, which could potentially produce some bias. We performed trial searches

Table 5. A roadmap for future research in agile coaching

Socio-technical elements	Sub-themes from this study	Research gaps
PEOPLE	Coach roles & responsibilities;	Non-coaches who coach;
	Different types of coaches;	Influence on team dynamics;
	Coaching teams;	Dealing with resistance;
	Coaches' skills, competencies & characteristics	Different teams, online vs f2f, global teams
PROCESSES & PROCEDURES	Coach training & certification;	Novel processes;
	Coaching practices & networks;	Comparing practices;
	Coaching for agile adoption & transformation;	Contextual practices, i.e. different industries, parts of company
CULTURE	Changing culture & leadership;	Techniques for culture change;
	Agile mindset;	National & org culture;
	Psychological safety	Sustaining culture change
GOALS & METRICS	Coaches' value & impact;	Impact on culture change;
	Team performance & metrics	Impact on organisation
TECHNOLOGY	Coaching tools;	Coaching support tools;
	The AI coach	AI coaching and automation
INFRA-STRUCTURE	Knowledge-sharing;	Different coaching models
	Coaching for context	Organisation-wide coaching

in Google Scholar and Web of Science, compared the results of our searches, and discovered that the Scopus database contained results from the other two databases, however, there is a possibility that some papers may have been inadvertently missed. Secondly, the authors performed a thematic analysis of the data, and there is a possibility of some subjectivity on how the data were themed; although we employed census-building techniques to mitigate this risk, some bias may persist. Thirdly, our scope for this mapping study was restricted to empirical research articles published in English. This may have led to the exclusion of other valuable studies published in other languages. Despite these limitations, we believe that this systematic mapping study provides insights into the current state of agile coaching research and identifies areas for further study. Addressing these limitations in future studies will help strengthen the evidence base and provide a more comprehensive understanding of this evolving field.

5 Conclusions

The contributions of our study are an SMS of agile coaching, including a thematic analysis of the topics areas researched, and the benefits and challenges of agile coaching. We also contribute a roadmap for future research. Our analysis highlights the evolving role of agile coaching as a crucial component in facilitating agile transformations, improving team performance, and fostering organisational agility. Key trends indicate a growing interest in understanding the roles and competencies of agile coaches, their roles and responsibilities, their influence on team dynamics, and the measurement of their impact on organisational outcomes. Research on the use of Artificial Intelligence in agile coaching is new and is bound to increase in the coming years.

Our findings offer important implications for practitioners involved in agile coaching. First, the range of areas investigated, such as agile mindset development, team dynamics, and coaching roles, highlight the multifaceted nature of agile coaching. Practitioners can benefit from aligning their coaching approaches with evidence-based strategies tailored to specific challenges of agile coaching at team or enterprise level. Second, the scarcity of empirical studies that focus on agile coaching outcomes and impact indicates a gap in actionable evidence. Practitioners are encouraged to support empirical evaluations of their coaching interventions, contributing to a feedback loop that refines and validates coaching practices. Finally, the study reveals a growing trend in exploring soft skills, psychological safety, and leadership in agile coaching. This suggests that effective coaching goes beyond processes and frameworks. It requires emotional intelligence, communication skills, and the ability to foster trust within teams. Agile coaches should therefore invest in developing these interpersonal competencies alongside technical knowledge.

References

1. Paasivaara, M., Lassenius, C.: Agile coaching for global software development. J. Softw. Evol. Process. **26**(4), 404–18 (2014)
2. Stray, V., Tkalich, A., Moe, N.B.: The agile coach role: coaching for agile performance impact. Presented at the Hawaii International Conference on System Sciences. https://doi.org/10.24251/HICSS.2021.817.2021

3. Althoff, S.: Qualitative interview-based research: an exploratory study on the role of the agile coach and how the coach influences the development of agile teams (Bachelor's thesis, University of Twente) (2020)
4. Daljajev, E., Scott, F., Milani, Pfahl, D.: A study of the agile coach's role. In: Product-Focused Software Process Improvement: 21st International Conference, PROFES: Turin, Italy, 25–27 November 2020. Proceedings, pp. 37–52. Springer, Heidelberg (2020). https://doi.org/10.1007/978-3-030-64148-13
5. Turner, L.R.: Becoming Agile: Coaching Behavioural Change for Business Results. McGraw-Hill Education (UK) (2021)
6. Jocic, D.: Psychological safety perception in community pharmacies: a randomized controlled trial of agile interventions. Explor. Res. Clin. Soc. Pharm. **14**, 100452 (2024)
7. Stray, V., Memon, B., Paruch, L.: A systematic literature review on agile coaching and the role of the agile coach. In: Product-Focused Software Process Improvement: 21st International Conference, PROFES 2020, Turin, Italy, 25–27 November 2020, Proceedings 2021, pp. 3–19. Springer (2020)
8. Petersen, K., Vakkalanka, S., Kuzniarz, L.: Guidelines for conducting systematic mapping studies in software engineering: an update. Inf. Softw. Technol. **64**, 1–18 (2015)
9. Kitchenham, B.A., Budgen, D., Brereton, O.P.: Using mapping studies as the basis for further research-a participant-observer case study. Inf. Softw. Technol. **53**(6), 638–651 (2011)
10. Clarke, V., Braun, V.: Thematic analysis: J. Posit. Psychol. **12**(3), 297–298 (2017)
11. Bera, P., Wautelet, Y., Poels, G.: On the use of chatGPT to support agile software development. In: Short Paper Proceedings of the Second International Workshop on Agile Methods for Information Systems Engineering (Agil-ISE 2023) co-located with the 35th International Conference on Advanced Information Systems Engineering (CAiSE 2023), Zaragoza, Spain, 13 June 2023, vol. 3414, pp. 1–9. CEUR Workshop Proceedings
12. Ng, P.: A canvas for capturing context of agile adoption. In: Ghani, I., Jawawi, D., Dorairaj, S., Sidky, A. (eds.) Emerging Innovations in Agile Software Development, pp. 37–50. IGI Global Scientific Publishing. https://doi.org/10.4018/978-1-4666-9858-1.ch003.2016
13. Gandomani, T.J., Nafchi, M.Z.: Agile Coaches and Champions: Two Hidden Facilitators of Agile Transition (2016)
14. Pavlič, L., Heričko, M.: Agile coaching: the knowledge management perspective. In: Uden, L., Hadzima, B., Ting, IH. (eds.) Knowledge Management in Organizations, KMO 2018. Communications in Computer and Information Science, vol. 877. Springer, Cham. https://doi.org/10.1007/978-3-319-95204-8-6.2018
15. Bäcklander, G.: Doing complexity leadership theory: how agile coaches at spotify practise enabling leadership. Creat. Innov. Manag. **28**(1), 42–60 (2019). https://doi.org/10.1111/caim.12303
16. Miller, G.J.: Project management tasks in agile projects: a quantitative study. In: 2019 Federated Conference on Computer Science and Information Systems (FedCSIS), Leipzig, Germany, pp. 717–721 (2019). https://doi.org/10.15439/2019F117
17. Jovanović, M., Mas, A., Mesquida, A.L., Lalić, B.: Transition of organizational roles in Agile transformation process: a grounded theory approach. J. Syst. Softw. **133**, 174–194 (2017)

18. Allan, K.: Patterns of agile coach roles. In: Proceedings of the 27th European Conference on Pattern Languages of Programs (EuroPLop 2022), Article 3, pp. 1–9. Association for Computing Machinery, New York (2023). https://doi.org/10.1145/3551902.3551963.2023
19. Moe, N.B., Cruzes, D.S., Dybå, T., Engebretsen, E.: Coaching a global agile virtual team. In: 2015 IEEE 10th International Conference on Global Software Engineering, pp. 33–37. IEEE (2015)
20. Griffin, L., Hinek, A.: An analysis of agile coaching competency among practitioners. In: McDermott, O., Rosa, A., Sá, J.C., Toner, A. (eds) Lean, Green and Sustainability. ELEC 2022. IFIP Advances in Information and Communication Technology, vol. 668. Springer, Cham (2022). https://doi.org/10.1007/978-3-031-25741-4-4.2023
21. Klünder, J., Trommer, F., Prenner, N.: How agile coaches create an agile mindset in development teams: insights from an interview study. J. Softw. Evol. Proc. **34**(12), e2491 (2022). https://doi.org/10.1002/smr.2491.2022
22. Pacheco, M., Mesquida, A.L., Mas, A.: Being agile while coaching teams using their own data. In: Systems, Software and Services Process Improvement: 25th European Conference, EuroSPI 2018, Bilbao, Spain, 5–7 September 2018, Proceedings 25, pp. 426–436. Springer (2018)
23. Raith, F., Richter, I., Lindermeier, R.: How project management tools are used in agile practice: benefits, drawbacks and potentials. In: Proceedings of the 21st International Database Engineering & Applications Symposium, pp. 30–39 (2017)
24. Pacheco, M., Mesquida, A.L., Mas, A.: Image based diagnosis for agile coaching. In: Systems, Software and Services Process Improvement: 26th European Conference, EuroSPI 2019, Edinburgh, UK, 18–20 September 2019, Proceedings 26, pp. 481–494. Springer (2019)
25. Ziegler, A., Peisl, T., Ates, A.: The future of agile coaches: do large companies need a standardized agile coach certification and what are the alternatives? In: European Conference on Software Process Improvement, pp. 3–15. Springer, Cham (2023)
26. O' Connor, R.V., Duchonova, N.: Assessing the value of an agile coach in agile method adoption. In: Systems, Software and Services Process Improvement: 21st European Conference, EuroSPI 2014, Luxembourg, 25–27 June 2014. Proceedings 21, pp. 135–146. Springer, Heidelberg (2014)
27. Shamshurin, I., Saltz, J.S.: Using a coach to improve team performance when the team uses a Kanban process methodology. Int. J. Inf. Syst. Proj. Manag. **7**(2), 61–77 (2019)
28. Santos, V., Goldman Filho, A.H.R.: The influence of practices adopted by agile coaching and training to foster interaction and knowledge sharing in organizational practices. In: Proceedings of the Annual Hawaii International Conference on System Sciences, pp. 4852–4861 (2013)
29. Davis, M.P., Challenger, R. Jayewardene D.N.W., Clegg, C.W.: Advancing sociotechnical systems thinking: a call for bravery. Appl. Ergon. **45**(2, Part A), 171–180 (2014)

Open Access This chapter is licensed under the terms of the Creative Commons Attribution 4.0 International License (http://creativecommons.org/licenses/by/4.0/), which permits use, sharing, adaptation, distribution and reproduction in any medium or format, as long as you give appropriate credit to the original author(s) and the source, provide a link to the Creative Commons license and indicate if changes were made.

The images or other third party material in this chapter are included in the chapter's Creative Commons license, unless indicated otherwise in a credit line to the material. If material is not included in the chapter's Creative Commons license and your intended use is not permitted by statutory regulation or exceeds the permitted use, you will need to obtain permission directly from the copyright holder.

Fostering a Sense of Belonging in Hybrid Work Within Agile Software Development

Sonja M. Hyrynsalmi[✉], Fateme Broomandi[iD], Iflaah Salman[iD], and Maria Paasivaara[iD]

Department of Software Engineering, LUT University, Lahti, Finland
{sonja.hyrynsalmi,fateme.broomand,iflaah.salman,maria.paasivaara}@lut.fi

Abstract. The Agile Manifesto emphasizes individuals and interactions over processes and tools. However, after the COVID-19 pandemic, interaction in software development changed, and companies are trying to find new practices in the hybrid environment. Hybrid work research points to the benefits for the individual, whereas companies have begun to form new rules and policies to get employees back to the office. To find a balance benefiting all, companies need to find new ways to connect and communicate. This paper explores how hybrid work impacts the sense of belonging in agile software development. We conducted interviews (N = 38) and a workshop (N = 15) with professionals from three case organizations. Our thematic analysis identifies key factors influencing belonging at the individual, team, and organizational levels. Our findings underline that continuous, conscious, and visible actions are needed at all levels to foster a sense of belonging. As hybrid work reduces spontaneous and random encounters, maintaining a sense of belonging requires planned efforts to recreate the informal interactions that once happened naturally.

Keywords: hybrid work · sense of belonging · agile · hybrid agile development · random interactions

1 Introduction

Hybrid work, i.e., working partially from the office and partially remotely, e.g., from home, has changed the communication and connection between software professionals. It has challenged organizations on the management and maintenance of organizational culture, productivity, employee motivation, and commitment [4,5]. Software development is a knowledge-intensive activity that tackles complex situations and scenarios. Therefore, successful software development usually requires teamwork, communication, and connection between different individuals [15,30]. However, when the COVID-19 pandemic forced professionals to work from home, there was a decrease in synchronous communication and an increase in asynchronous communication. Communication, collaboration, and connection became more difficult, static, and siloed [13,30].

After the pandemic, not all software professionals wanted to return to their offices full-time [5]. Right after the pandemic, most companies were flexible in allowing different hybrid work arrangements. However, recently, a rising number of IT companies have imposed practices and rules to get people back to the offices, claiming that, e.g., culture, communication, and innovativeness would suffer from excessive remote work [14,18]. There seems to be a mismatch of hopes and expectations regarding hybrid work between employees and employers. However, what has been missing in the discussion is the aspect of a sense of belonging. In a work environment, understanding the sense of belonging also helps in understanding how people contribute to the workplace and its success [10]. Therefore, investigating its role in hybrid work in agile software development could give a better understanding of how to succeed while working in a hybrid environment.

This study investigates the sense of belonging in hybrid work in agile software development via two research questions:

- **RQ1: How does hybrid work impact the sense of belonging in agile software development?**
- **RQ2: What strategies can support fostering a sense of belonging in hybrid work in agile software development?**

We address these research questions through empirical research, utilizing interviews of software professionals from two companies, as well as insights gathered from a half-day workshop on hybrid work that we organized for software professionals from three companies.

In the next section, we introduce the background literature on hybrid work in software development and the aspects of a sense of belonging, especially in the context of software development. In Sect. 3, we describe the research design. Section 4 presents the results of our analysis. Section 5 discusses our results and past research. Section 6 concludes the paper.

2 Background

Hybrid work blends remote and office settings, ranging from office-first to remote-first models [23]. Hybrid work offers several benefits to software professionals, such as flexibility, autonomy, reduced commute, improved well-being, and better work-life balance while enhancing team diversity [8]. However, it can weaken team connections, complicate management, and reduce informal interactions vital to collaboration and innovation [8,24]. In addition, challenges such as isolation and a diminished sense of belonging make hybrid setups more complex [5].

In this paper, we define a 'sense of belonging' as a multi-dimensional experience that reflects an individual's feeling of being accepted, seen, and valued within a social group or organizational context. Building on Filstad et al. [10], we conceptualize belonging as a dynamic process shaped by social interactions, organizational culture, and shared practices. It involves continuously negotiating inclusion, experiencing boundaries, and actively engaging in workplace participation. Belonging is both a personal experience and a collective perception of being valued and equal within an organization. According to Scheide Miller and Giblin [22], a sense of belonging is a fundamental need that fosters commitment, motivation, and job satisfaction. They state that feeling valued improves self-worth, performance, and emotional well-being, shaping how employees find meaning in their work. They also claim that flexible schedules and supportive supervisors enhanced both job satisfaction and belonging.

Contrary to common concerns, Gajendran and Harrison [11] claim that hybrid work does not significantly harm workplace relationships or career prospects. However, according to them, extensive remote work may negatively impact coworker relationships. They suggest that these challenges can be managed through well-informed policies [11]. Furthermore, Belle et al. [2] state that remote workers value organizational belonging, experiencing it through work, shared values, or as a means to an end. According to them, belonging differs by individual, influenced by identity and personal freedom. Belonging seems to be multifaceted but central to the organization-employee relationship. Deep belonging blends personal and organizational identity, but for it to be impactful, it must be a shared experience [2].

In software engineering research, the concept of a sense of belonging has been investigated, for example by Trinkenreich et al. [26] via a theoretical framework where two organizational factors, work appreciation, and psychological safety, along with three diversity aspects, gender, tenure, and country culture, affect the sense of belonging within software delivery teams. Trinkenreich et al. [26] found that a lack of sense of belonging is linked to higher burnout levels among software developers. Belonging is also crucial for resilience, job satisfaction, and well-being. Guidelines are provided to foster a sense of belonging in software development teams, ultimately improving developers' well-being [27].

Although the sense of belonging in hybrid work within agile software development has not yet been studied widely, some studies have addressed aspects of it. For example, De Sousa Santos et al. [9] stated in a recent study that workplace relationships enhance belonging, mutual support, job satisfaction, motivation, and teamwork in software engineering. Tkalich et al. [25] found that a sense of belonging in a software development team enhances feelings of being valued and psychological safety, reinforced by frequent spontaneous office interactions and positive feedback exchanges. Moreover, according to De Sousa Santos et al. [9] the ability of software teams to work effectively in hybrid environments, under adverse conditions relies on a strong sense of belonging. Furthermore, De Sousa Santos et al. identified three key factors for a sense of belonging: consistent interaction to build team cohesion, internal feedback to foster inclusion and value, and mutual support from teammates, including non-work-related assistance.

According to Belle et al. [2], a sense of connectedness and belonging at work is strongly linked to employee engagement, which in turn drives productivity and performance. Osborne and Hammoud [19] state that a strong sense of belonging enhances employee engagement, which directly influences an organization's longevity and financial performance. They note that when employees feel connected and valued, their productivity improves, leading to better overall organizational outcomes. The COVID-19 pandemic accelerated the transition to hybrid work, driven also by software professionals' demand for greater flexibility and work-life balance [7]. This shift has fundamentally reshaped how organizations manage teamwork, culture, and collaboration [4]. As hybrid work can weaken employees' sense of belonging, fostering that is essential for maintaining engagement, productivity, and long-term success. Despite its importance, research on the sense of belonging in hybrid work in agile software development remains limited, highlighting the need for further studies in this area.

3 Research Design

We conducted a case study [31] to examine the impact of hybrid work in agile software development on the sense of belonging and to explore strategies that foster it. Case study research is commonly used in software engineering to examine a contemporary software engineering phenomenon by exploring multiple sources of evidence within a real-life setting [21]. Following the guidelines by Brereton et al. [3], we developed a case study protocol and refined it continuously during the research process. Given the importance of triangulation in empirical studies [20], balancing data richness with inherent low precision, we applied data source triangulation (three distinct case organizations) and methodological triangulation (semi-structured interviews and a workshop).

3.1 Case Selection

We examined three case organizations, that were purposefully selected: they were using agile software development in hybrid work environments. To ensure diverse perspectives, we selected companies differing in industry, size, and organizational culture, allowing for a broader understanding of these factors.

Case 1: Telecommunications and Networking Solutions. This global company, founded in 1918, operates in the telecommunications and networking solutions sector. 700 employees are based in Finland, working in one main location. It is known for its strong tradition, with an emphasis on reliability, stability, and long-term growth. While the company collaborates with other global sites, our study focuses on two R&D units employing 65 and 70 persons located on the Finnish site. The organization adopted a customized large-scale agile software development approach based on the Large-scale Scrum (LeSS) framework in 2009 and has continuously developed it further. Before the pandemic, everybody typically worked at the office. During our interviews, their hybrid working mode had just changed from the recommended two days at the office to three office days.

Case 2: Clean Energy Industrial Solutions. Founded in 2017, this company focuses on clean energy industrial solutions and employs 700 people across multiple offices in Finland. It operates in a fast-paced, entrepreneurial environment, constantly innovating to meet market demands. Agile practices based on the Disciplined Agile Delivery (DAD) framework are utilized in the software development unit of around 50 people. The unit operates in three main offices located in different Finnish cities. All agile teams include members from at least two different locations. The hybrid working model is fully flexible, allowing individuals to decide their daily location. Unit days, organized every 1,5 months, collect the whole software development unit for a one-day planning and socializing meeting, while teams organize "team days" a few times per year.

Case 3: Digital Transformation and Technology Consulting. Established in 1996, the company specializes in digital transformation and technology consulting, with 2,100 employees spread across several countries in Europe, while our study focuses on the Finnish offices. It embraces an agile approach to software development and offers a hybrid working environment. This case participated only in the workshop. We will run the interviews later on.

In the results section we use descriptions such as Case 1, Case 2 and Case 3 and interviews ID's are running for Case 1 AI1-AI28 and for Case 2 BI1-BI10.

3.2 Data Collection

We collected data through semi-structured interviews and a half-day workshop. Interviews were the key data collection method, offering insights into human actions, contexts, and historical information [31]. They are ideal for exploratory research, enabling detailed responses and clarifications [12]. A total of 38 interviews were conducted between October and December 2024, including 28 interviews from Case 1 and 10 from Case 2, with voluntary participation and informed consent. Interviewees were selected with the help of case organization representatives according to the wishes of the researchers to ensure diverse roles, experience levels, hybrid work preferences, and representation of different agile teams. The group included developers, coaches, managers, specialists, and Product Owners. 35 interviews were organized remotely via Microsoft Teams, with sessions recorded and transcribed. Three interviews were conducted face-to-face during a visit to the Case 2 organization and were voice-recorded and transcribed. The interview length ranged from 45 min to one hour. The interview guide included questions that were organized into topical groups: hybrid work practices, meeting practices and preferences, sense of belonging and community, well-being, productivity, and improvement suggestions on hybrid work. In this paper, we concentrate only on the topic group *sense of belonging and community*, including six questions. Participants were asked to describe what community and a sense of belonging meant to them, to identify the communities they feel connected to within their company, and to explain their role in those communities. They were also prompted to reflect on how occasional office interactions influence their work and sense of belonging. Additionally, we asked interviewees how they personally contribute to their company's community and whether they belong to other work-related communities.

After the interview round, a half-day workshop was conducted, on the premises of the Case organization 1, in December 2024. Over twenty participants joined the presentations given by the three case organizations on their hybrid work practices, while 15 participants continued for the 1,5 h interactive part: seven from Case 1, six from Case 2, and two from Case 3. The workshop participants were mainly managers, Product Owners, and coaches, most of whom we had interviewed during the interview round. The workshop used the World Café method [16], where participants were divided into four mixed groups of 3–4 participants from 2–3 companies. The groups rotated between rooms with different discussion topics around hybrid work: meetings, well-being, productivity, and the sense of belonging. Each topic had a facilitator from our research team who introduced the topic and posed questions on that specific topic. The questions about the sense of belonging (the topic we concentrate on in this paper) included potential threats to a sense of belonging, existing practices to mitigate these threats, and suggestions for new practices. Participants first wrote their answers on Post-it notes and then presented them to others. The facilitator grouped the answers and engaged participants in a discussion. The Post-its were collected for analysis. The discussions were not recorded for confidentiality reasons.

3.3 Data Analysis

To analyze the interview transcripts and the Post-it notes from the workshop, we used thematic analysis, a popular method for identifying patterns and categorizing data [6]. This method is commonly applied in software engineering research and was particularly useful for exploring the emerging theme of "sense of belonging." We applied an iterative thematic analysis approach using ATLAS.ti. First, responses to questions related to the sense of belonging were coded line-by-line using open coding. Emerging categories were then grouped into higher-level themes through axial coding. For the workshop data, participants and facilitators grouped the Post-it notes during the session. One researcher then reviewed these groups and integrated them with the interview themes. The analysis process followed recommended practices for qualitative thematic analysis in software engineering research [6].

The analysis combined both the interview and workshop data, refining themes to build a comprehensive understanding of the sense of belonging in a hybrid work environment in agile software development.

4 Results

Our analysis revealed that hybrid work in agile software development impacts the sense of belonging in *individual, team, and organizational levels*. As a summary of our analysis, we provide a framework for fostering a sense of belonging in agile software development. Next, the results are presented according to the three levels.

4.1 Individual Level

At the individual level, *belonging* meant our participants being accepted, seen, valued, and being part of the team—but not necessarily being part of the company. The individuals, people who professionals work with and meet daily, were the key players in creating a sense of belonging at the individual level. These people were not necessarily from the respondents' own teams, but they had met them during unit days, in coffee rooms, or in the company's guilds, clubs, or events. In some of the cases, and especially with case 1, people had known their colleagues for decades and had built personal bonds between them beyond team or unit silos:

"Yes, but then it's not belonging at the company level because in that sense it doesn't have anything to do with the company. We are meeting in the company building. We are meeting there because we are working in the same company, but we are not stopping to talk because we belong to the same company, but because we have a good relationship personally."/Case 1, AI1

The challenges at the individual level regarding the sense of belonging were around feeling isolation and disconnection from colleagues, missing informal information ('gossips') which could help either apply for a position inside the company or get an overall understanding on the direction which company is going, lack of recovery time or overall that is not seen or known. As all of the companies had faced challenges due to the economic situation affecting also to the IT industry, some of the respondents highlighted that especially the need to be known and seen was also connected to the fear of potential layoffs. One interviewee described the impact of layoffs on the sense of belonging:

"Someone or yourself feels that you are respected and what you do has some value. That impacts a lot. And we might have some challenges on that nowadays because of some negotiations and changes that we had, so it didn't boost the feeling. Let's say that way."/Case 1, AI11

The feeling of psychological safety, the possibility to be yourself, trust others, and feel that you are treated equally and valued in the company was also strong among the respondents. One of the workshop participants stated:

"It's difficult to show your personality or bond with teammates remotely."/Workshop participant

When asked how interviewees personally contribute to the company's community, how they see their role in their community, or the solutions for the sense of belonging challenges identified in the workshop, participants highlighted the importance of emphasizing the feeling that everyone is valued and seen, the importance of kindness in the working environment and overall just being a good colleague. One interviewee summarized the role of the individuals:

"Trying to be kind of a good team player and keeping up the good spirit when meeting colleagues, I think that's the key point. Taking others into consideration and always trying to do your best, whatever you are doing."/Case 1, AI7

Being able to share something personal and know colleagues on a personal level was highly important, especially in the interviews. Both in the interviews and workshop it was highlighted that at the individual level, the most important thing was that people contributed, to make an effort to know others and, for example, to make new colleagues feel welcome, like in this example:

"When I joined the team, some of my colleagues said that they are going to the gym almost every afternoon and asked me to join, and then my husband made it possible for me to join once a week, and it was kind of a 'nice' 'excuse'. They kind of made me feel that they want me to be there too."/Case 1, AI24

4.2 Team Level

When specifically asked about the community to which interviewees feel they belong, the most common answer was the team they worked for. A few also mentioned the unit they were working for.

The challenges around the sense of belonging at the team level were around a lack of team identity, unstable teams, effects of layoffs, and overall lack of emotional ties and alignment among team members because of not seeing them so often and sharing interactions with them. Sharing the workload equally in the team, trust in the team members, and feeling that team members value respondents' opinions were important, as stated by one of the interviewees:

"That someone or you feel that you are respected and what you are doing has some value. That impacts a lot."/Case 1, AI11

The difficulties in resolving conflicts among team members, especially in the virtual environment, were raised both in the workshop and in interviews. Direct harassment or inappropriate behavior was not mentioned, but in the virtual setup, participants raised challenges in recognizing other feelings or the 'tone' in their messages. There were also clear communication challenges in the virtual settings, both in the availability of colleagues if someone needed help or in the way they were communicating with others, for example, they felt that there was no empathy or caring in the communication. The importance of body language and the feeling that others were reacting and listening was stated as highly important for the sense of being seen and valued. One of the workshop participants summarized guidelines for how he hoped people would pay attention to the communication and connection:

"Be conscious how your behaviour impacts others. Can you be the light (or energy) for the other?"/Workshop participant

Investing in team building and bonding was considered extremely important for fostering a sense of belonging when working in a hybrid mode. The most frequent solutions offered for almost every challenge were around team building, team events, unit level events, afterworks, clubs, or just overall somehow interacting with others, sharing those personal aspects, and learning to know others. But, also learned something useful from the people from other teams, as one of the interviewees told:

"As I am in 'silo' of software development. We don't usually talk to those people (meaning: sales team), but they can bring problems that we have never heard about that come from people who are potentially buying our solutions."/Case 2, BI9

Some practical ways to improve the sense of belonging at the team level include one-to-one discussions with line managers or similar people, mentoring possibilities, and a master-apprentice setup. Overall, participants highlighted that learning together was important for them and gave a possibility to bond with the team members, but also members from other teams:

"Besides the people I already know, there are also colleagues from my team and other teams working in the same area. We got to know them, and plan to organize a learning session since they are working on something closely related to our team."/Case 2, BI1

4.3 Organizational Level

On the organizational level, meaningfulness, shared mission and vision, and the company's impact on the world were some of the key things for a sense of belonging. This was regardless of the way of working-whether remotely, hybrid, or live. Furthermore, the practices for mandatory office days, fixed seating setups, or other hybrid work practices were mentioned really briefly.

The main challenges at the organizational level in hybrid software development were more around the feeling that the organization had siloed, and more 'us versus them' mentalities were reported, or worries about that kind of mentality. Especially in the workshop, there were also raised case examples of people stating that they work better alone, they only focus on their own tasks, and they stay in remote mode although there are a lot of possibilities for live interactions. One of the workshop participants stated his concern:

"One can focus only on his/her tech tasks and therefore lose the connection to the others."/Workshop participant.

Interviewees and workshop participants were especially worried that the element of random interactions would vanish if people worked more only remotely, and solutions for that were seen to happen at the organizational level. Random interactions were a possibility to share something personal on the individual level, but also as they were a source of happiness and fun moments during the workdays, crystallization of the great atmosphere in the company, way to get a piece of informal information from the company and overall that you would be seen and noted in the coffee room were extremely important for people and their sense of belonging:

"In those face-to-face workshops or in some ad hoc coffee meetings at the office, when we go to the sofas in our team room after lunch, we start discussing something. So suddenly, we are, you know, surprisingly solving problems there. So I think this kind of relaxed, safe environment."/Case 1, AI17

Participants noted that people were not attending as regularly and in the same numbers as before COVID-19, in different social or sports clubs, or just some common activities together. However, there were signs that people were gradually coming back to these social activities, and several respondents said that just recently, they had started once again attending these events.

Furthermore, these clubs had been important places to get to know people from different teams and, in that way, feel that you would be part of a larger community than your own team. One of the participants also stated the concern that if social events inside the company were not attracting people anymore and people were encouraged to focus more on sport and other outsourced activities in their free time (with for example, sports benefits), companies would lose their most important tool for fostering the sense of belonging:

"It's going to model that you have this sports and culture benefit that you use how you want. Then people use it for the gym, you go wherever you go in the city center gym, but then it's a completely different thing, you are not doing it with your colleagues in a company gym or a sports club, but you are just exercising. When a company has a Sports Club, its employees play together, spend time together, and create a community."/Case 1, AI2

In addition to doing something social together, respondents highlighted clear and transparent practices as one impactful solution for challenges in the organizational-level sense of belonging. These practices included frequent polls and surveys, collecting feedback, giving it directly to the people, and solving challenges or pain points together after collecting them via survey. Overall, having company-wide practices and routines was felt important:

"Practices are important. Having the routines like dailies, tech meetings, cameras on, and preferably common in-the-office events, talks about seeking discussion, ad-hoc encounters etc."/Workshop participant

4.4 Recommendations for Fostering a Sense of Belonging in Hybrid Agile Software Development

From our findings, we formed a framework for fostering a sense of belonging in hybrid agile software development (Fig. 1). In our framework, we have three impacting levels: *individual, team, and organizational level*. Our analysis shows that actions from all of these three levels are needed and required to foster a sense of belonging.

Fig. 1. Framework for fostering a sense of belonging in hybrid agile software development

In the organizational level, there are tools for regular, transparent practices such as surveys and polls, clubs and events, hybrid work practices (such as a number of office days in a week), creating cooperation between teams to avoid 'us vs. them' silos and overall have a clear, shared goal in the organizational level. What used to happen spontaneously through in-person encounters now requires intentional planning and structured organizational support.

At the team level, the importance of team days, mentoring and other aspects to help professionals grow, recognition of achievement, underlining empathy, tone and conflict resolution in communication, and making sure that workload is shared equally are highlighted. All the actions around team bonding are important.

Individuals also have many possibilities to foster a sense of belonging in companies. Showing kindness and empathy, paying attention to others, practicing good communication skills, supporting the feeling of being seen and valued and receiving that same feeling, supporting and acknowledging psychological safety, feeling open to getting to know colleagues, and welcoming new colleagues were important.

5 Discussion

Our research offers some key takeaways on what to take into account when fostering a sense of belonging in hybrid work in agile software development: *Firstly*, the sense of belonging is built on multiple levels. *Secondly*, continuous and conscious actions are needed from all of the actors, especially managers, and that must also be made more visible when communicating about the sense of belonging in the companies. *Thirdly*, although it can feel that people are not joining social events like before the pandemic, it can be a good idea to give them more time to come back.

Our framework helps stakeholders identify their roles and current actions and prioritize the next efforts to foster a sense of belonging in hybrid work within agile software development.

5.1 RQ1: How Does Hybrid Work Impact the Sense of Belonging in Agile Software Development?

Hybrid work in an agile software development environment influences the sense of belonging at the individual, team, and organizational levels. This supports the findings of Belle et al. [2] that belongingness is most impactful when it is a shared and interrelated experience among organizational members rather than just at an individual level. Our findings in the *individual level* show that belonging is primarily built through daily social interactions. Still, hybrid work limits spontaneous conversations and informal exchanges, making employees feel unseen or disconnected. This relates to the findings of De Sousa Santos et al. [9] that hybrid work creates physical barriers between team members, reducing interactions among professionals.

At the *team level*, we found that hybrid work complicates team identity and emotional ties, as limited in-person interactions reduce shared experiences and trust among members. Conflict resolution also becomes more difficult in virtual settings, where body language and tone are harder to interpret. On the *organizational level*, our study shows that hybrid work can create an "us vs. them" mentality and silos in organizations. This supports previous findings of Moe, Nils Brede, et al. in [17] that firm-wide remote work made the collaboration network more static and siloed. However, our findings show that people are slowly returning to social events and clubs, and that companies should give more opportunities and time for social activities.

5.2 RQ2: What Strategies Can Support Fostering a Sense of Belonging in Hybrid Work in Agile Software Development?

At the *individual level*, our results show that employees in hybrid settings should actively engage in social interactions, practice kindness, and contribute to creating a welcoming team culture. Encouraging personal connections, such as inviting colleagues to activities outside of work, helps strengthen interpersonal bonds. At the *team level*, our findings include fostering psychological safety, ensuring equal workload distribution, and enhancing communication by emphasizing empathy and tone in virtual interactions. Team-building activities, mentoring programs, and cross-team learning opportunities can also improve belonging and collaboration. Regular in-person team events and structured check-ins with managers help maintain emotional connections and trust among team members. These findings support the findings of Scheide Miller and Giblin [22] that supportive supervisors enhanced belonging and also enlarge the research around psychological safety and belonging in software engineering [27,28]. Our results give strategies, especially about the importance of tone and emphasizing empathy in virtual settings. Furthermore, while some of the findings may appear intuitive, such as the value of social connection or informal communication, our results show that these elements require conscious effort and structural support in hybrid contexts. What was once spontaneous now demands strategic design.

On an *organizational level*, our results highlight strategies fostering a sense of belonging. It requires clear hybrid work practices and policies, transparent communication, and opportunities for cross-team interactions. Creating social spaces, such as coffee areas designed for informal interactions, and organizing company-wide events can enhance connections across different departments. Investing in social clubs, sports teams, and shared activities should be continued, although people would come back to them later than to the offices. Social interactions were also the place where professionals may hear about open positions inside the company, so in future research, it would be interesting to test whether the findings by Gajendran and Harrison [11], saying that remote and hybrid working does not significantly harm workplace relationships or career prospects, are still valid. Furthermore, although onboarding was not our focus, early experiences shape belonging, making structured onboarding crucial in hybrid settings. Future work could explore its role in newcomer integration in hybrid settings.

Overall, a strong sense of belonging in hybrid agile software development depends on balancing flexibility with structured engagement, ensuring that employees feel seen, valued, and connected at multiple levels.

5.3 Threats to Validity and Future Work

Next, we discuss the threats of validity according to Wohlin et al. [29]:

Construct Validity: Sense of belonging is a complex term without a shared agreement on how it should be measured, and its literature is broad and theoretically diverse [1]. Therefore, in this research, we approached the sense of belonging via understanding, frameworks, and practices used in software engineering research. In the future, we will expand our findings with an online survey and aim to identify differences between hybrid work practices and software business company models.

Internal validity: There can be a danger of self-selection bias, as participation in the study was voluntary. This may have influenced the fact that those with stronger opinions about the impact of hybrid work were more likely to agree to participate. In future research, we aim to mitigate this by collecting a more diverse and larger sample and incorporating also quantitative data.

External Validity: The findings are based on three large companies and their software development professionals. This can limit the generalizability of the findings for companies in different sectors, sizes or working fully remotely.

6 Conclusions

As hybrid work is becoming the new norm in agile software development, understanding the connection, communication, and commitment of employees is becoming more important. For this research, we conducted interviews (n = 38) and a workshop on hybrid work in agile software development. Our findings show that fostering a sense of belonging happens at the individual, team, and organizational levels and requires constant and conscious work. Our framework helps identify what is already done and where to pay attention when companies desire to focus on fostering a sense of belonging in a hybrid environment.

References

1. Allen, K.-A., Kern, M.L., Rozek, C.S., McInerney, D.M., Slavich, G.M.: Belonging: a review of conceptual issues, an integrative framework, and directions for future research. Aust. J. Psychol. **73**(1), 87–102 (2021)
2. Belle, S.M., Burley, D., Long, S.: Where do i belong? High-intensity teleworkers' experience of organizational belonging. Hum. Resour. Dev. Int. **18**(1), 76–96 (2015)
3. Brereton, P., Kitchenham, B., Budgen, D., Li, Z.: Using a protocol template for case study planning. In: 12th International Conference on Evaluation and Assessment in Software Engineering (EASE), BCS Learning & Development (2008)
4. Byrd, M.Y.: Creating a culture of inclusion and belongingness in remote work environments that sustains meaningful work. Hum. Resour. Dev. Int. **25**(2), 145–162 (2022)

5. Conboy, K., Moe, N.B., Stray, V., Gundelsby, J.H.: The future of hybrid software development: challenging current assumptions. IEEE Softw. **40**(02), 26–33 (2023)
6. Cruzes, D.S., Dyba, T.: Recommended steps for thematic synthesis in software engineering. In: 2011 International Symposium on Empirical Software Engineering and Measurement, pp. 275–284. IEEE (2011)
7. de Souza Santos, R., Adisaputri, G., Ralph, P.: Post-pandemic resilience of hybrid software teams. In: 2023 IEEE/ACM 16th International Conference on Cooperative and Human Aspects of Software Engineering (CHASE), pp. 1–12. IEEE (2023)
8. de Souza Santos, R., Grillo, W.D.N., Cabral, D., De Castro, C., Albuquerque, N., França, C.: Post-pandemic hybrid work in software companies: Findings from an industrial case study. In: Proceedings of the 2024 IEEE/ACM 17th International Conference on Cooperative and Human Aspects of Software Engineering, pp. 68–78 (2024)
9. de Souza Santos, R., Magalhaes, C., Franca, C.: Hybrid work well-being: software professionals finding equilibrium. IEEE Softw. (2024)
10. Filstad, C., Traavik, L.E., Gorli, M.: Belonging at work: the experiences, representations and meanings of belonging. J. Work. Learn. **31**(2), 116–142 (2019)
11. Gajendran, R.S., Harrison, D.A.: The good, the bad, and the unknown about telecommuting: meta-analysis of psychological mediators and individual consequences. J. Appl. Psychol. **92**(6), 1524 (2007)
12. Gray, D.E.: Doing research in the real world
13. Jaspan, C., Green, C.: Developer productivity for humans, part 2: hybrid productivity. IEEE Softw. **40**(02), 13–18 (2023)
14. Jassy, A.: Message from CEO Andy Jassy: strengthening our culture and teams (2024). Accessed 16 Sept 2024
15. Li, H., Xing, Z., Peng, X., Zhao, W.: What help do developers seek, when and how? In: 2013 20th Working Conference on Reverse Engineering (WCRE), pp. 142–151. IEEE (2013)
16. Löhr, K., Weinhardt, M., Sieber, S.: The, "world café" as a participatory method for collecting qualitative data. Int J Qual Methods **19**, 1609406920916976 (2020)
17. Moe, N.B., Stray, V., Šmite, D., Mikalsen, M.: Attractive workplaces: what are engineers looking for? IEEE Softw. **40**(5), 85–93 (2023)
18. Nicholas, K., Hull, D.: Elon musk tells tesla workers to return to the office or lose their jobs (2022). Published in Los Angeles Times, June 1, 2022
19. Osborne, S., Hammoud, M.S.: Effective employee engagement in the workplace. Int. J. Appl. Manage. Technol. **16**(1), 4 (2017)
20. Petersen, K., Gencel, C.: Worldviews, research methods, and their relationship to validity in empirical software engineering research. In: 2013 Joint Conference of the 23rd International Workshop on Software Measurement and the 8th International Conference on Software Process and Product Measurement, pp. 81–89. IEEE (2013)
21. Runeson, P., Höst, M.: Guidelines for conducting and reporting case study research in software engineering. Empir. Softw. Eng. **14**, 131–164 (2009)
22. Scheide Miller, C., Giblin, J.: Improving job satisfaction and belonging through flexible work and leadership cohorts. Adv. Dev. Hum. Resour. **26**(1), 20–47 (2024)
23. Smite, D., Christensen, E.L., Tell, P., Russo, D.: The future workplace: characterizing the spectrum of hybrid work arrangements for software teams. IEEE Softw. **40**(2), 34–41 (2022)
24. Smite, D., et al.: Half-empty offices in flexible work arrangements: why are employees not returning? In: International Conference on Product-Focused Software Process Improvement, pp. 252–261. Springer (2022)

25. Tkalich, A., Šmite, D., Andersen, N.H., Moe, N.B.: What happens to psychological safety when going remote? IEEE Softw. **41**(1), 113–122 (2022)
26. Trinkenreich, B., Gerosa, M.A., Steinmacher, I.: Unraveling the drivers of sense of belonging in software delivery teams: insights from a large-scale survey. In: Proceedings of the IEEE/ACM 46th International Conference on Software Engineering, pp. 1–12 (2024)
27. Trinkenreich, B., Gerosa, M.A., Steinmacher, I., Sarma, A.: Guidelines for cultivating a sense of belonging to reduce developer burnout. IEEE Softw. (2024)
28. Trinkenreich, B., Stol, K.-J., Sarma, A., German, D.M., Gerosa, M.A., Steinmacher, I.: Do i belong? Modeling sense of virtual community among linux kernel contributors. In: 2023 IEEE/ACM 45th International Conference on Software Engineering (ICSE), pp. 319–331. IEEE (2023)
29. Wohlin, C., et al.: Experimentation in Software Engineering, vol. 236. Springer (2012)
30. Yang, L., Hecht, B., et al.: The effects of remote work on collaboration among information workers. Nat. Hum. Behav. **6**(1), 43–54 (2022)
31. Yin, R.K.: Case study research and applications (2018)

Open Access This chapter is licensed under the terms of the Creative Commons Attribution 4.0 International License (http://creativecommons.org/licenses/by/4.0/), which permits use, sharing, adaptation, distribution and reproduction in any medium or format, as long as you give appropriate credit to the original author(s) and the source, provide a link to the Creative Commons license and indicate if changes were made.

The images or other third party material in this chapter are included in the chapter's Creative Commons license, unless indicated otherwise in a credit line to the material. If material is not included in the chapter's Creative Commons license and your intended use is not permitted by statutory regulation or exceeds the permitted use, you will need to obtain permission directly from the copyright holder.

Exploring the Role of Agile Mindset in Information Systems: A Systematic Literature Review

Karen Eilers[1]([✉]) , Tabea Augner[2] , Necmettin Özkan[3] , Christoph Peters[4] , and Ulrich Bretschneider[5]

[1] Institute for Transformation, Max-Brauer-Allee 28, 22765 Hamburg, Germany
karen.eilers@in-transformation.com
[2] SRH University, Sonnenallee 221, 12059 Berlin, Germany
tabea.augner.extern@srh-hochschulen.de
[3] Department of Business, Gebze Technical University, Cumhuriyet 2254. Sk No: 2, 41400 Gebze, Kocaeli, Turkey
n.ozkan2020@gtu.edu.tr
[4] University of the Bundeswehr Munich, Werner-Heisenberg-Weg 39, 85579 Neubiberg, Germany
christoph.peters@unibw.de
[5] Research Center for Information System Design (ITeG), University of Kassel, Pfannkuchstraße 1, 34121 Kassel, Germany
bretschneider@uni-kassel.de

Abstract. The success of agile work heavily depends on people and their approach to challenges, with the agile mindset emerging as a pivotal driver. Despite its importance, Information Systems (IS) research lacks a systematic overview of the contexts where the agile mindset is relevant and the research gaps that remain. This study addresses this gap by systematically examining the factors influencing and resulting from the agile mindset in IS contexts and, for the first time, demonstrating its broad relevance across diverse IS domains.

We conducted a systematic literature review, analyzing 62 relevant papers from IS research. Our findings show that the agile mindset plays a central role in four key areas: (1) implementing agile methods or scaled agile frameworks during agile transformations, (2) applying digital tools and driving digital transformation, (3) supporting coaching, training, and education, and (4) leadership and management. This study's originality lies in highlighting the agile mindset's wide-ranging applicability, offering practitioners actionable insights for designing processes and mechanisms to enhance the success of agile work in IS. Additionally, researchers are provided with a roadmap of open questions and future research opportunities to deepen our understanding of this critical concept in IS contexts.

Keywords: Agile Mindset · Agile Transformation · Digital Transformation · Leadership · Agile Methods · Organizational Agility · Agile Software Development · Education · SLR

Supplementary Information The online version contains supplementary material available at https://doi.org/10.1007/978-3-031-94544-1_4.

© The Author(s) 2025
S. Peter et al. (Eds.): XP 2025, LNBIP 545, pp. 52–68, 2025.
https://doi.org/10.1007/978-3-031-94544-1_4

1 Introduction

Agility has been demonstrated as a positive influencing factor for various outcomes in Information Systems (IS) and beyond. Studies show that agility improves organizational performance [15] and increases job satisfaction [47, 48, 62]. Despite these promising results, agile transformation does not occur without obstacles, and many organizations struggle with its implementation [12, 59]. Challenges arise both in implementing new external structures (often referred to as "doing agile") and, more often, in enabling employees and leaders to develop their internal structures, such as an agile mindset, to truly "be agile" [17, 61]. The individuals affected by agile transformation are a key success factor in bringing agility to life. Moreover, challenges related to the agile mindset can hinder transformation efforts and lead to the failure of agile projects [13, 15, 35].

The agile mindset has primarily been the subject of qualitative research (e.g. [35]), with a number of different conceptualizations exceeding the simplification to living the agile values and principles. Senapathi and Srinivasan [55], for example, stated that an agile mindset requires "requires a continuous change in behavior based on possibility thinking, learning, and growth" [55]. Van Manen and van Vliet [67] identified the three aspects of trust, continuous improvement and collaboration as components of an agile mindset. Based on the existing definitions, Eilers et al. [15] recently developed a comprehensive conceptualization that characterizes the agile mindset as the attitude of an individual in a complex environment that manifests itself through positive evaluations in terms of (1) learning spirit, (2) collaborative exchange, (3) empowered self-guidance and (4) customer co-creation [15].

Agility encompasses both the aspects of "doing" and "being" agile. "Doing agile" refers to the external structural aspects of agility, such as using agile methods, leveraging digital tools for faster decision-making, or promoting technical excellence practices in software development. In contrast, "being agile" focuses on the internal structures of individuals, such as fostering an agile mindset [15, 16]. While aspects of "doing agile" are expected to lead to better outcomes, they do not always achieve all intended results. Previous research has predominantly focused on the "doing agile" aspects, whereas "being agile"—particularly the agile mindset—has emerged as a major challenge in agile transformations [15, 47]. As a result, various researchers call for a deeper understanding of agility and its mechanisms [1, 70]. It is crucial for both practitioners and researchers to gain a comprehensive understanding of what drives successful agile projects and transformations—and what causes them to struggle or fail. The high failure rate was highlighted in a study by Digital.ai [12]-an international survey of the state of agile-where only 48% of respondents reported that all or most of their agile projects were successful. Furthermore, even well-established companies fail to scale new practices and structures effectively to achieve greater flexibility and speed [23, 33, 43].

This issue has also been recognized by other researchers. Barroca et al. [7], cited in Mordi and Schoop [44], noted the growing interest in the human factors of agile transformation: "Investigating human factors in agile transformations has been placed at the top of research agendas, including further research on the agile mindset." While studies indicate that the agile mindset plays a crucial role in successfully implementing agile methods and structures [13, 50], in leadership programs and management [3], and even in enabling the sustainable use of chatbots [39] or low-code development platforms

[49], a synthesized overview of the agile mindset's relevance across different IS contexts is still lacking. More specifically, there is a need for a comprehensive review of how aspects of "doing agile" in IS interrelate with the agile mindset and what outcomes result from this interaction. Such insights are necessary to determine the relevance of the agile mindset and to demonstrate its significance across various IS contexts. Establishing this foundation would provide a solid basis for further theory development and future research [72].

To address this gap, this study conducts a systematic literature review to synthesize existing research on the agile mindset within IS contexts. The objective is to provide a structured overview of how the agile mindset interacts with different aspects of agility, particularly in relation to "doing agile," and how this interaction influences key outcomes. While studies suggest that the agile mindset plays a crucial role in successfully implementing agile methods, leadership programs, and digital transformation initiatives, how the agile mindset influences relevant outcomes or is influenced by different IS settings remains largely unknown. By identifying and describing these IS settings and it's interaction to the agile mindset, this review aims to establish a deeper understanding of the agile mindset's role in IS, highlight its practical implications, and lay the groundwork for future research.

We conducted a systematic literature review in September 2022 to answer the following research questions: 1) *"Which aspects of doing agile affecting the agile mindset in IS are already discussed in literature?"* and 2) *"What outcomes are related to these aspects?"* The remainder of this paper is organized as follows. In Sect. 2, we describe the overview of the research design and the paper selection process. Section 3 delivers the results of the literature review. In Sect. 4, we deliver contributions of the study. Limitations and future research are conveyed in Sect. 5.

2 Research Method

While agility has its roots in software development, people in IS are often confronted with agile projects and transformations. In IS, several structural aspects (aspects of "doing agile"), like digital tools, or meetings / events, offer the possibility to sense and respond more quickly to surrounding issues, and to thereby be more agile. To answer our presented research questions, we followed the approach of Webster and Watson [72] and vom Brocke et al. [69].

To identify a suitable set of scientific literature, we selected two databases known for their comprehensive coverage of IS research: the AIS Library and Elsevier, with a focus on Computer Science. Additionally, a forward and backward search using KARLA [65] and Google Scholar provided further relevant results. This approach ensures that the selected publications are related to IS, either through their publication outlet or topic focus. We searched for the term "agile mindset" in various forms (e.g., agility mindset, agile mind-set) and excluded publications such as books, book chapters, calls for papers, and workshop proceedings. Since research on the agile mindset is not yet extensively available, we thoroughly examined the entire content of each paper for relevant insights, rather than limiting our review to titles and abstracts. No restrictions were applied regarding the publication period, ensuring a comprehensive overview of the existing body of literature. In the initial search, we identified 81 papers. After applying the inclusion (peer-reviewed publication, IS-context, English language, insights to the relevance of the agile mindset in the main text) and exclusion criteria (formats like books, book chapters, calls for papers, and workshop proceedings, doublets) during the screening process, 55 papers were deemed relevant. The forward and backward search yielded an additional 7 relevant papers, further enriching our dataset of finally 62 papers.

3 Findings

An analysis of the publication years reveals that the first relevant publication appeared in 2008. However, by the end of 2022, the number of publications has increased significantly, from two or 4 every year from 2015–2019, reaching up to 16 publications in 2022 till September 2022. This trend highlights the growing research interest in the agile mindset.

We carefully analyzed the publications to assess their insights into the relevance of the agile mindset for IS. It is noticeable that a large number of studies lack a valid conceptualization or definition of the agile mindset. Most studies do not focus explicitly on the agile mindset; however, they still provide valuable insights into how it relates to their respective research contexts. So far, quantitative correlations between the agile mindset and other outcome variables remain an exception—such as in the study by Eilers et al. [15]. The relevance of the agile mindset is primarily inferred from case studies based on qualitative interviews, document analysis, or observational data. Thematically, the studies cover a range of IS research settings and present diverse aspects of "doing agile." A significant portion focuses on the implementation of agile methods, scaling agility in agile transformations, and the challenges associated with these initiatives. Additionally, researchers emphasize the importance of the agile mindset in areas such as the application of digital tools and digital transformation, coaching, training, education, leadership, and management. Furthermore, the studies report various outcomes related to these "doing agile" efforts in IS. In the following, the thematic areas—including aspects of "doing agile," their connection to the agile mindset, and related outcomes—are explored in greater detail.

3.1 The Agile Mindset in Implementing Agile Methods and Large-Scaled Agile

Most of the identified papers addressing the relevance of the agile mindset focus on the implementation of agile methods. In this context, the agile mindset is often highlighted as a major challenge. Qumer and Henderson-Sellers [51] developed a framework (Agile Software Solution Framework, ASSF) and an improvement model (Agile Adoption and Improvement Model, AAIM) for implementing agility, assessing the degree of agility, and improving and adapting agile practices. Their multiple case study revealed that "the most important challenge was the development and encouragement of an agile culture and mindset within the organization" [51]. This finding aligns with Senapathi and Drury-Grogan [56], who concluded that the agile mindset "was recognized as key to sustainable agile transformation" [56]. Ozkan and Gök [46] further argue that "the right way to agility should start with a proper agile mindset instead of applying Agile methods directly" [46]. Similar conclusions were drawn by Zielske and Held [74], Limaj and Bernroider [40], Alami, Krancher, and Paasivaara [3], and Trippensee and Remané [63]. Lindskog [41] identified the agile mindset as a crucial component of agility within an agile project at a government agency. However, she also noted that developing an agile mindset can create learning tensions, which can be addressed through retrospectives as part of agile project management [41].

The literature review further demonstrates that the agile mindset is a significant factor influencing various outcomes. Senapathi, Drury, and Srinivasan [55], along with Senapathi and Drury-Grogan [56], showed through qualitative studies—based on focus group and interview data—that the agile mindset impacts agile adoption and, consequently, productivity, quality, and customer satisfaction. Lalmi, Fernandes, and Souad [38] stated that "adopting an agile mindset increases productivity and maximizes results." However, Könnölä et al. [36] did not observe productivity increases during their measurement period. They investigated three cases of tailored agile methods for embedded system development and noted that for two cases, the agile mindset was unfamiliar, with no prior agile experience. The researchers suggested that transitioning to agility and adopting new ways of working take time and may initially hinder productivity [36]. Alami, Krancher, and Paasivaara [3] examined technical excellence in agile software development and found that the agile mindset—encompassing continuous attention to sustainable code, learning, teamwork, and influencing practices—is essential for achieving technical excellence. Lal and Clear [37] explored planning at different levels within a software vendor and concluded that "the agile mindset for short development cycles, cross-functional effort, adaptation, empowerment, and self-organization must be adopted by vendors, as 'basic agile methods' (Scrum, XP, etc.) provide planning practices limited to the engineering level" [37]. Hummel, Rosenkranz, and Holten [29] investigated specific agile practices and found that some team members struggled with the agile mindset, particularly in terms of frequent face-to-face communication during daily stand-up meetings [29]. Wang et al. [71] explored the combination of agile and lean practices and reported that "Kanban helped the agile mindset to stick in the company" [71]. Researchers in other areas, such as user experience methods, also emphasize the importance of an agile mindset [9], though they often fail to provide a detailed conceptualization.

The agile mindset is also considered crucial in scaling agile methods and facilitating organization-wide agile transformations. Denning [11] conducted a consortium workshop with organizations such as Barclays, Ericsson, Microsoft, and Vistaprint to define agile management. The results emphasized that "the whole organization needs to embrace the Agile mindset and function as an interactive network, not a top-down bureaucracy with just a few teams implementing Agile tools and processes" [11]. Similarly, Mordi and Schoop [44] assert that "there is no agility without an Agile mindset," a statement further supported in their scaling framework [44]. Fuchs [20] conducted a multiple case study and found that across all cases, interviewees reported their firms aimed to introduce cultural values aligned with agile methods and an agile mindset. Heikkilä et al. [27] discovered in their longitudinal case study that many challenges in their project resulted from the immature adoption of large-scale agile models and the agile mindset. This finding is corroborated by Kasauli et al. [32], who explored requirements engineering challenges in large-scale agile system development and identified the agile mindset as a key challenge. The challenges associated with the agile mindset extend beyond the IT sector to industries such as banking [61], energy [54], and government agencies [41]. Fabri et al. [18] developed an agile scaling maturity model with eight capability dimensions (e.g., organization & management, technology, customer collaboration, people-centric & team culture). They emphasize that "spreading and internalizing the agile mindset in the organization and beyond is a success factor" [18].

Several systematic literature reviews, including those by Dikert et al. [13], Putta et al. [50], and Kischelewski and Richter [34], identify success and challenge factors for large-scale agile transformation. They argue that "reasons for agile implementations to fail were deviations from the process, because of which the agile mindset did not take root" [13]. Kischelewski and Richter [34] further state that fostering an agile mindset is the biggest human resource management challenge in large-scale agile initiatives. Regarding the implementation of the Scaled Agile Framework (SAFe), Putta et al. [50] found that "the most commonly mentioned challenges of SAFe adoption are organizational politics, difficulties in establishing an agile mindset, change resistance, and team formation challenges," with 68% of study participants highlighting the agile mindset as a challenge. Agile transformation also involves developing new roles. Lueg and Drews [42] proposed a concept for role development in agile transformations and argue that these roles are distinguished by an embedded agile mindset. In their role development step "role testing and application," they suggest providing additional guidance for those unfamiliar with agile ways of working [42]. An overview of the key findings related to the agile mindset in implementing agile methods and large-scale agility is presented in Fig. 1.

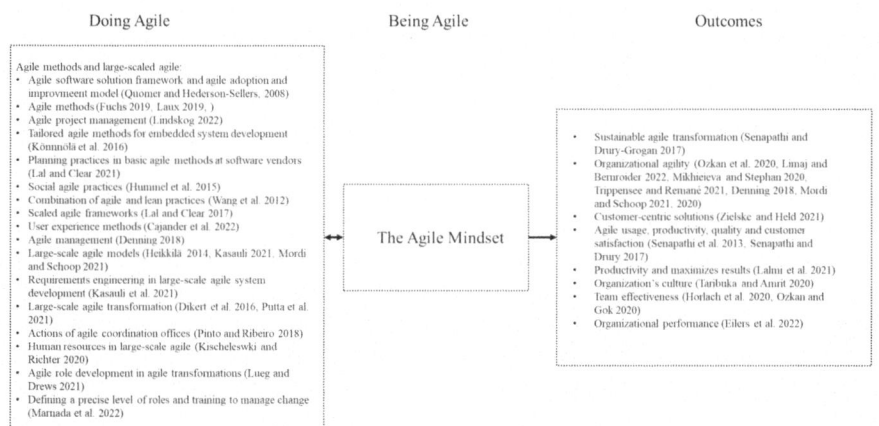

Fig. 1. Overall Results to the Agile Mindset in Implementing Agile Methods and Large-scaled Agile.

3.2 The Agile Mindset in Digital Transformations

Previous research demonstrates that the agile mindset also plays a critical role in digital transformation. Fuchs and Hess [21] describe agile transformation within organizations as part of digital transformation. Organizations aim to address the challenges of the digital world in an agile way. Based on a literature review of challenges and success factors and the socio-technical system theory, Fuchs and Hess [21] conducted two case studies and identified the agile mindset as a motivational challenge for being agile during a digital transformation. Salmela et al. [53] go even further and conceptualize digital agility in their paper published in the *Journal of the Association for Information Systems*. They conclude that the new logic for collaborating with partners requires a co-creation mindset, as demonstrated in the case studies of Volvo and LeadTech. They further describe the case of Spotify, which owes its business advantages not to a specific method but to the establishment of an agile mindset [53]. Salvetti and Bertagni [54] incorporated a development program for the agile mindset to promote digital transformation: "If people lack the right mindset to change, and current organizational practices are flawed, digital transformation will simply magnify those flaws" [54]. This is further confirmed by an interview study by Bitzer et al. [8]. As part of the cultural transformation for the digital transformation of incumbents, they report that "Without a suitable mindset, our IPs [interview partners] expect that neither the best strategy, governance, processes, technologies, nor tools may be enough to leverage the potential of the transformation efforts of DT [digital transformation] and AT [agile transformation]." [8].

In the context of legal services, Janeček et al. [30] investigate the personal characteristics of lawyers who avoid using artificial intelligence and digital technologies at work. They argue that, to fully capture the potential of AI and digital technologies, "The answer is partly in adopting the agile mindset" [30]. Shahalei and Kazan [58] gathered a comprehensive set of data in their longitudinal study on digital product platforms. By building multi-component teams and thereby expanding competencies, the participants reported that this led to an increase in the agile mindset [58]. The agile mindset was also related to low-code development platforms, as found in an exploratory study by Prinz et al. [49]. The researchers identified the agile mindset as a challenge when implementing low-code development platforms. Employees from business departments, who are reluctant to share knowledge and applications, hinder the potential recovery of those platforms [49]. The agile mindset also plays a role in digital servitization in manufacturing. Tronvoll et al. [64] interviewed 33 participants from a global market leader and concluded: "Our findings suggest that an agile mindset was key for coping with the fast-paced development lifecycle of software and digital infrastructure" [64]. Initial insights into the agile mindset have also emerged in research on digital business ecosystems. In a design science research approach, Guerrero Barboza et al. [26] developed design principles for personal services and included the agile mindset in both a theoretical principle ("An agile mindset is required to manage the dynamics and mechanisms of a service ecosystem" [26] and in their final design principle: "For PS [Personal Services] designers and developers to build a DBE [digital business ecosystem], they must [...] foster an agile mindset, whereby agile and innovation practices such as DT [Design Thinking] and Scrum are executed to work closely with their employees, customers, and other partners, leading to co-creating innovative services or products" [26]. Furthermore, the agile mindset of employees is shown to be required for the long-term adoption of conversational agents [39]. Mordi and Schoop [44] conducted a comprehensive mapping, based on case study data, to determine how software tools like task boards, chat, and workflows are related to characteristics of the agile mindset. They found that a task board used by developers and project managers during sprints is related to a feeling of responsibility and ownership, key characteristics of the agile mindset.

A design science study by Fabri et al. [18] developed an agile scaling maturity model with eight capability dimensions (e.g., organization & management, technology, customer collaboration, people-centric & team culture). To develop the people-centric dimension and team culture, the researchers stated that "spreading and internalizing the agile mindset in the organization and beyond is a success factor" [18]. Practices that foster the development of an agile mindset are the main drivers in another design science study by Jung and Rueckel [31]. In their resulting software development lifecycle model for IT sourcing and disruptive development, they describe challenges for each segment and how to overcome them by having a clear distributed rationale, organizing work in small independent units, cultural mediation, and temporary co-location [31]. An overview of the interactions of the agile mindset in digital transformation can be seen in Fig. 2.

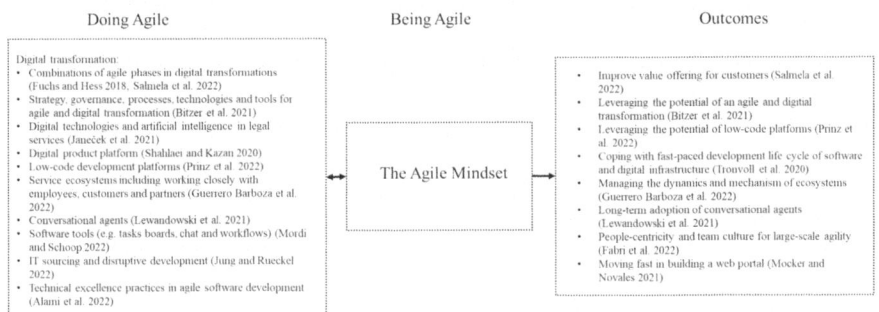

Fig. 2. Overall Results on the Agile Mindset in Digital Transformation.

3.3 The Agile Mindset in Training, Coaching and Education

Gandomani et al. [22] investigate the impact of training on the agile transformation process in their grounded theory study. They found that adequate and functional training can influence the agile mindset of individuals involved in the agile transformation and transition process. Dikert et al. [13] further describe that participation in training sessions alone is not enough; rather, team coaching in the actual working environment is necessary to change the agile mindset. Klünder et al. [35] analyzed how agile coaches can promote an agile mindset in development teams. They elaborate on various activities of agile coaches for fostering the agile mindset, such as "conveying theoretical knowledge," "creating realistic expectations," "working with the team on solutions," and "integrating agile simulations" [35].

Some approaches already exist in education regarding the agile mindset. Raduescu et al. [52] developed course design principles for learning complex information infrastructures. As the researchers concluded that the agile mindset is critical for students' employability, they aimed to support its development by building a complex adaptive system and defined nine characteristics, including agent autonomy, connectivity, interdependence, context awareness, and self-organization. Furthermore, they described four design principles: 1. "Formulate significant learning objectives," 2. "Use valid development learning assessments," 3. "Select learning activities that foster active, engaged learning," and 4. "Supporting element: educational ecosystems" [52]. Salvetti and Bertagni [54] designed a three-day development program for the agile mindset development of young leaders. It includes three content pillars: "teamwork, start-up culture, and matrix management" (p. 1) and various methods like business games, scenario analysis, immersive simulation, as well as keynotes to develop the agile mindset. Another study focusing on the development of students' agile mindset was conducted by Babik [5]. In his Scrum boot camp, students work in two sprints, practicing the Scrum values and practices, while managing their own team staffing, projects, and workload [5]. Furthermore, Van Slyke et al. [68] call for the agile mindset in the context of the COVID-19 pandemic as a future issue for IS education. Gregory et al. [25] suggest that onboarding processes for agile software projects are distinct from other organizational onboarding processes, as they require an understanding of agile practices to contribute to self-organizing teamwork and to develop an agile mindset. Figure 3 summarizes the results regarding the agile mindset in training, coaching, and education.

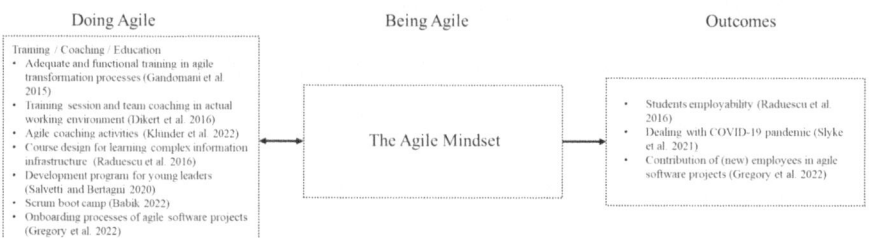

Fig. 3. Overall Results to the Agile Mindset in Training, Coaching, and Education.

3.4 The Agile Mindset in Leadership and Management

Williams et al. [73] investigate how decision makers deal with digital visualization tools. While the tools already promote a strongly agile, prototypical approach, managers still have to cognitively adapt to this new type of visual decision making and develop an agile mindset. Traditional mindset tendencies of analysts as well as decision makers inhibit the potential of visual analytics [73]. Goncalves et al. [24] also investigate incumbents and identify that leaders need an agile mindset to promote agile transformation. The scholars describe that management supports the transformation but was not actively involved and did not directly participate in it. As a result, others felt "a lack of support, transparency, engagement, and courage in communication and decisions" [24]. This inhibits innovation and organizational agility [24]. In an exploratory single case study, Hennel and Dobmeier [28] underline these results. They investigate critical success factors for management affected by using agile methods in a large-scale environment. The agile mindset was one of the obstacles for agile management identified by the scholars [28]. As one participant stated, "If management does not have the agile mindset [...], there is no point in seriously thinking about setting up an agile project" [28]. This parallels with Adie et al. [2], who conducted a literature review on digital leadership and found evidence for the relevance of an agile mindset for digital leaders. Alami et al. [3], who investigate technical excellence in agile software teams, found that leadership support creates an enabling condition for agile mindset development. In addition, Mueller et al. [45] suggest in their study that IT project managers need both a traditional mindset for top management communication and an agile mindset towards their agile IS development teams. Given the relevance of the agile mindset for leaders, Salvetti and Bertagni [54] focused on the agile mindset in their Leadership 5.0 program for leaders in the energy sector. Furthermore, Durbin and Niederman [14] developed managerial approaches to tackle agile challenges and emphasize the importance of implementing them with an agile mindset. The results regarding the agile mindset in leadership and management are summarized in Fig. 4.

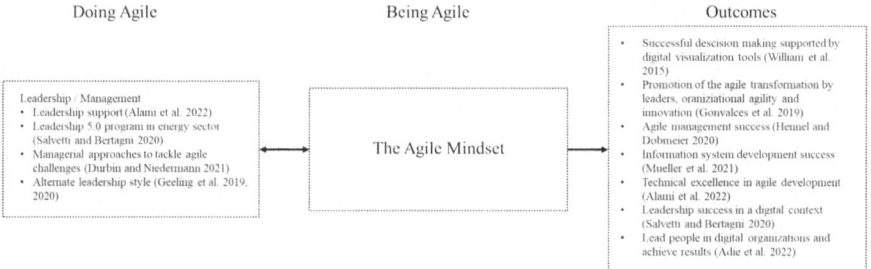

Fig. 4. Overall Results to the Agile Mindset in Leadership and Management.

4 Contributions

4.1 Theoretical Contribution

This systematic literature review provides, for the first time, a comprehensive overview of previous research regarding the agile mindset in IS. While various literature reviews regarding agility exist (e.g. [60]), to the best of our knowledge, none focus specifically on the agile mindset or "being agile," a concept that has increasingly become part of organizational agendas and found its way into research. Given that research on the agile mindset is still in its infancy, this literature review helps to align future research approaches and identify and address relevant research gaps. It provides the following valuable theoretical contributions:

First, it demonstrates the relevance of an emerging construct that is already widely used in practice and gaining increasing attention in IS research. The literature review indicates the wide range of outcomes affected by the agile mindset, such as productivity [38, 55, 56], the long-term adoption of conversational agents [39], students' employability [52], successful decision-making [73], information system development success [3], and leadership success [54]. Moreover, it quantifies the increasing research interest through the rapidly growing number of papers published to date.

Secondly, the literature review provides a comprehensive and structured overview of agile mindset contexts (aspects of doing agile), clustered into four key areas: 1. The implementation of agile methods and large-scale agility, 2. In digital transformations and the application of digital tools (e.g., conversational agents, low-code platforms), 3. In the area of training, coaching, and education, and 4. In leadership and management. It thus benefits several theories that can be extended by the findings.

Agile methods and large-scale agile frameworks have been under consideration for a long time. Regarding the agile mindset, the diversity of different methods is particularly striking, including: user experience methods [9]; tailored agile methods for embedded software development [36]; large-scale frameworks [13]; and even individual practices (e.g., planning practices [37]); social agile practices [29]). The large number of recent papers relating digital transformations (e.g., [30, 53]), the application of digital tools (e.g., low-code platforms [49]), and conversational agents [39]) to the agile mindset underscores its increasing relevance in the IS context. These findings contribute to and extend socio-technical theory [74]. However, it turns out that the agile mindset has thus far only been incorporated into socio-technical theory to a limited extent (e.g., [15, 20]. The literature review also addresses insights regarding IS education, training, and coaching, thus connecting with learning theories. While there are differing opinions on the combination of measures (e.g., training [22]) or coaching and training [13]), there seems to be a consensus on the developability of the agile mindset. It can therefore also be integrated into attitude models, such as learning through models [6] or cognitive dissonance theory [19]. Finally, systematic review expands leadership theories. While various leadership styles have already been discussed in the agile context (e.g., transformational leadership [4]), servant leadership [66]), ambidextrous leadership [16]), the integrated papers present the agile mindset as an overarching attitude that can be manifested in different leadership styles. As far as we know, the agile mindset has never before been considered to this extent in IS. Thus, we broaden the theoretical knowledge of agility in a holistic way by providing a comprehensive overview of previous insights.

4.2 Practical Contribution

In addition to its theoretical contributions, the literature review provides several implications for practice. It shows that the agile mindset is a relevant component in IS that affects several outcomes and mutually influences the use of digital tools, transformation efforts, training programs, and leadership. Beyond the implementation of agile methods, organizations are undergoing extensive agile and digital transformations. For this, the agile mindset has been shown in several case studies to be a critical success factor for productivity [56], quality [57], and performance [15]. At the same time, developing the agile mindset is a major challenge. In this regard, this literature review provides insight into where the agile mindset has already been identified as relevant, and thus awareness needs to be created within organizations. Practitioners should consider the agile mindset when implementing agile methods, agile transformations, and digital transformations. The agile mindset should also be taken into account when introducing new practices and digital tools to exploit their potential.

In this context, designing supportive conditions can help those affected. The agile mindset should already be considered during onboarding processes [25], and employees and managers should be supported in their development through training and coaching [22, 35]. Agile coaches can help to "convey theoretical knowledge," "create realistic expectations," "work with the team on solutions," and "integrate agile simulations" [35]). To increase the employability of students in the IS context, the agile mindset should also be promoted through appropriate teaching concepts, including agent autonomy, connectivity and interdependence, context awareness, and self-organization, as applied in the concepts of Raduescu et al. [52], Babik [5], or Salvetti and Bertagni [54]. Efforts regarding agility that do not include the agile mindset seem to fail. Addressing the agile mindset is therefore essential for practice.

5 Limitations and Future Research

Like all studies, this literature review is affected by limitations. The selection of search terms and databases inherently restricts the scope of retrieved studies, meaning that some relevant research may have been missed, particularly those published in non-peer-reviewed sources. To mitigate this, we relied on two well-established academic databases in IS and carefully included different ways of writing the focus concept to enhance coverage. Moreover, data extraction was performed by a single researcher, introducing the potential for subjective interpretation. While quality assessment criteria were grounded in field expertise, their application remains inherently subjective. Additionally, the contextual nature of primary study results limits their broader applicability. To strengthen the reliability of our findings, ambiguous cases were discussed and resolved through consensus with a all co-authors.

In-depth studies regarding the agile mindset are still limited. The analysis shows that many studies do not focus directly on the agile mindset; instead, the agile mindset is considered a highly relevant influencing factor for several outcomes (e.g., productivity, quality, digital leadership success) but has often played a secondary role in studies to date. Most studies also do not rely on a clear definition or conceptualization of the agile mindset. This points to a need for future research. Future studies should therefore build on a clear definitional basis to avoid confusion and ambiguities regarding the understanding of the agile mindset. Since previous findings are often still undifferentiated or generalized, there is a need for comprehensive specifications and descriptions that respect the role of the agile mindset and how it can be promoted in everyday work through suitable supporting conditions. This aligns with Mordi and Schoop [44], who call for more research regarding the agile mindset and software tools and contexts: "Select specific tools and contexts to extend and enrich our understanding based on individual levels of underlying mindset properties" [44].

In many of the publications the directions of relationships between the agile mindset and other constructs are only vaguely hinted at. For the presentation of the results, we proposed a schematic process, which places the agile mindset as a mediator between the aspects of doing agile and outcomes. This relationship is derived from theory and could be confirmed in research by Eilers et al. [15] and Eilers et al. [16]. Nevertheless, it is conceivable that the agile mindset might also appear as a moderator in certain research contexts. This needs to be considered in more detail in future research. Previous research has also used only limited quantitative approaches to explore the agile mindset. Many correlations have therefore not yet been researched quantitatively and require confirmatory research approaches.

Moreover, the agile mindset can assume different roles (e.g., scrum master, product owner, developer, leader), levels (individual, team, organization) [15], environments, and different IT applications [44]. While this literature review suggests that the agile mindset plays a key role in a wide range of IS research, significant gaps in knowledge remain. Several contexts could therefore be interesting to examine in relation to the agile mindset: For example, the agile mindset could be relevant in IS consortia research to promote fast and iterative cooperation between interdisciplinary research and practice partners. Furthermore, the agile mindset and its scaling within organizations may play a role in corporate venturing or digital hubs, where cultures clash between innovative and traditional business entities. To reach the goals of agile projects, some authors recommend recruiting employees who already possess a high degree of an agile mindset [10, 40]. However, it is still unclear how staffing can be implemented based on the agile mindset and what role the human resources business unit plays in this. Furthermore, design science research should explore possibilities for IT applications to self-monitor the agile mindset of teams and support them in achieving positive outcomes in agile transformations. The literature review results provide an impetus for intensifying the theoretical expansion of socio-technical theory. Due to its relevance for IS, the agile mindset should be investigated further to close the research gaps mentioned above.

Acknowledgments. The authors have no competing interests to declare that are relevant to the content of this article.

References

1. Abrahamsson, P., Conboy, K., Wang, X.: 'Lots done, more to do': the current state of agile systems development research. Eur. J. Inf. Syst. **18**(4), 281–284 (2009)
2. Adie, B., Tate, M., Cho, W., Valentine, E.: Digital leaders and digital leadership: a literature review and research agenda. In: Pacific Asia Conference on Information Systems (2022)
3. Alami, A., Krancher, O., Paasivaara, M.: The journey to technical excellence in agile software development. Inf. Softw. Technol. **150**, 1–14 (2022)
4. Avolio, B.J., Zhu, W., Koh, W., Bhatia, P.: Transformational leadership and organizational commitment: mediating role of psychological empowerment and moderating role of structural distance. J. Organ. Behav. **25**(8), 951–968 (2004)
5. Babik, D.: Teaching Tip: Scrum Boot Camp: introducing students to agile system development. J. Inf. Syst. Educ. **33**(3), 195–208 (2022)
6. Bandura, A.: Self-efficacy: toward a unifying theory of behavioral change. Psychol. Rev. **84**(2), 191–215 (1977)
7. Barroca, L., Carroll, N., Gregory, P., Strode, D.: Agile transformation (ATRANS) workshop: a summary and research agenda. In: Paasivaara, M., Kruchten, P. (eds.) Agile Processes

in Software Engineering and Extreme Programming: XP 2020 Workshops, pp. 148–154. Springer, Cham (2020)
8. Bitzer, M., Hinsen, S., Jöhnk, J., Urbach, N.: Everything is IT, but IT Is not everything: what incumbents do to manage their digital transformation towards continuous change. In: International Conference on Information Systems, n.v., pp. 1–17 (2021)
9. Cajander, Å., Larusdottir, M., Geiser, J.L.: UX professionals' learning and usage of UX methods in agile. Inf. Softw. Technol. **151**, 1–9 (2022)
10. Conboy, K., Coyle, S., Wang, X., Pikkarainen, M.: People over process: key challenges in agile development. IEEE Softw. **28**(4), 48–57 (2010)
11. Denning, S.: How major corporations are making sense of agile. Strategy Leadersh. **46**(1), 3–9 (2018)
12. Digital.ai. 13th annual state of agile report (2019). Accessed 19 Nov 2022. https://www.stateofagile.com/#ufh-i-521251909-13th-annual-state-of-agile-report/473508
13. Dikert, K., Paasivaara, M., Lassenius, C.: Challenges and success factors for large-scale agile transformations: a systematic literature review. J. Syst. Softw. **119**, 87–108 (2016)
14. Durbin, M., Niederman, F.: Bringing templates to life: overcoming obstacles to the organizational implementation of agile methods. Int. J. Inf. Syst. Proj. Manag. **9**(3), 1–18 (2021)
15. Eilers, K., Peters, C., Leimeister, J.M.: Why the agile mindset matters. Technol. Forecast. Soc. Change **179**, 1–14 (2022)
16. Eilers, K., Simmert, B., Peters, C.: Doing agile vs. being agile: understanding their effects to improve agile work. In: International Conference on Information Systems, pp. 1–17 (2020)
17. Eilers, K; Simmert, B; Peters, C; and Leimeister, J.M.: Why the agile mindset matters. In: Academy of Management Proceedings, online (2021) n.p.
18. Fabri, L., Häckel, B., Stahl, B., Beck, S., Gabele, M.: How agile is your IT department?: development and application of an framework-independent agile scaling maturity model. In: European Conference on Information Systems, n.v., pp. 1–18 (2022)
19. Festinger, L.: A Theory of Cognitive Dissonance. Stanford University Press, Standfort (1957)
20. Fuchs, C.: Adapting (to) agile methods: exploring the interplay of agile methods and organizational features. In: Hawaii International Conference on System Sciences, n.v., pp. 7027–7036 (2019)
21. Fuchs, C., Hess, T.: Becoming agile in the digital transformation: the process of a large-scale agile transformation. In: International Conference of Information Systems, n.v., pp. 1–17 (2018)
22. Gandomani, T.J., Zulzalil, H., Abdul Ghani, A.A., Md. Sultan, A.B., Meimandi Parizi, R.: The impact of inadequate and dysfunctional training on Agile transformation process: a grounded theory study. Inf. Softw. Technol. **57**, 295–309 (2015)
23. Gerster, D., Dremel, C., Brenner, W., Kelker, P.: How enterprises adopt agile forms of organizational design. ACM SIGMIS Database DATABASE Adv. Inf. Syst. **51**(1), 84–103 (2020)
24. Goncalves, D., Bergquist, M., Bunk, R., Alänge, S.: The influence of cultural values on organizational agility. In: Americas Conference on Information Systems, n.v., pp. 1–10 (2019)
25. Gregory, P., Strode, D.E., Sharp, H., Barroca, L.: An onboarding model for integrating newcomers into agile project teams. Inf. Softw. Technol. **143** (2022). n.p.
26. Guerrero Barboza, R., Lattemann, C., Gebbing, P., Siemon, D., Robra-Bissantz, S.: Digital business ecosystems: towards design principles for personal services. In: Pacific Asia Conference on Information Systems, n.v., pp. 1–16 (2022)
27. Heikkilä, V.T., Paasivaara, M., Rautiainen, K., Lassenius, C., Toivola, T., Järvinen, J.: Operational release planning in large-scale Scrum with multiple stakeholders – a longitudinal case study at F-Secure Corporation. Inf. Softw. Technol. **57**, 116–140 (2015)

28. Hennel, P., Dobmeier, M.: Critical success factors in agile management: insights for large-scale interdisciplinary projects from an exploratory single case study. In: Americas Conference on Information Systems, n.v., pp. 1–10 (2020)
29. Hummel, M., Rosenkranz, C., Holten, R.: The role of social agile practices for direct and indirect communication in information systems development teams. Commun. Assoc. Inf. Syst. **36**, 273–300 (2015)
30. Janeček, V., Williams, R., Keep, E.: Education for the provision of technologically enhanced legal services. Comput. Law Secur. Rev. **40**, 1–13 (2021)
31. Jung, M., Rueckel, D.: Effective collaboration of distributed development teams through IS sourcing in times of digital transformation. In: Pacific Asia Conference on Information Systems, n.v., pp. 1–17 (2022)
32. Kasauli, R., Knauss, E., Horkoff, J., Liebel, G., de Oliveira Neto, F.G.: Requirements engineering challenges and practices in large-scale agile system development. J. Syst. Softw. **172**, 1–26 (2021)
33. Kiely, G., Kiely, J., Nolan, C.: Scaling agile methods to process improvement projects: A global virtual team case study. In: Americas Conference on Information Systems, n.v., pp. 1–9 (2017)
34. Kischelewski, B., Richter, J.: Implementing large-scale agile: an analysis of challenges and success factors. In: European Conference on Information Systems, n.v., pp. 1–17 (2020)
35. Klünder, J., Trommer, F., Prenner, N.: How agile coaches create an agile mindset in development teams: insights from an interview study. J. Softw. Evol. Process **34**, 12 (2022). n.p.
36. Könnölä, K., Suomi, S., Mäkilä, T., Jokela, T., Rantala, V., Lehtonen, T.: Agile methods in embedded system development: multiple-case study of three industrial cases. J. Syst. Softw. **118**, 134–150 (2016)
37. Lal, R., Clear, T.: Scaling agile at the program level in an Australian software vendor environment: a case study. In: Americas Conference on Information Systems, n.v., pp. 1–12 (2017)
38. Lalmi, A., Fernandes, G., Souad, S.B.: A conceptual hybrid project management model for construction projects. Procedia Comput. Sci. **181**, 921–930 (2021)
39. Lewandowski, T., Delling, J., Grotherr, C., Böhmann, T.: State-of-the-Art analysis of adopting AI-based conversational agents in organizations: a systematic literature review. In: Pacific Asia Conference on Information Systems, n.v., pp. 1–14 (2021)
40. Limaj, E., Bernroider, E.W.: A taxonomy of scaling agility. J. Strateg. Inf. Syst. **31**(3), 1–19 (2022)
41. Lindskog, C.: Tensions and ambidexterity: a case study of an agile project at a government agency. Int. J. Inf. Syst. Proj. Manag. **10**(2), 5–23 (2022)
42. Lueg, R., Drews, P.: Conceptualizing role development in agile transformations: deriving design goals and principles for agile roles. WIRTSCHAFTSINFORMATIK, n.v., 1–17 (2021)
43. Maruping, L.M., Venkatesh, V., Agarwal, R.: A control theory perspective on agile methodology use and changing user requirements. Inf. Syst. Res. **20**(3), 377–399 (2009)
44. Mordi, A., Schoop, M.: Enabling agile environments: software tools revisited with an agile mindset. In: European Conference on Information Systems, n.v., pp. 1–17 (2022)
45. Mueller, L., Albrecht, G., Toutaoui, J., Benlian, A.: Role identity tensions of IT project managers in agile ISD team settings. In: International Conference of Information Systems, n.v., pp. 1–17 (2021)
46. Ozkan, N., Gök, M.Ş., Köse, B.Ö.: Towards a better understanding of agile mindset by using principles of agile methods. In: Proceedings of the Federated Conference on Computer Science and Information Systems (FedCSIS), pp. 721–730 (2020)

47. Peters, C., Simmert, B., Eilers, K., Leimeister, J.M.: Future Organization Report 2019. St.Gallen, Switzerland and Frankfurt, Germany: Institute of Information Systems, University of St.Gallen; Campana & Schott Business Services GmbH (2019)
48. Peters, C., Simmert, B., Eilers, K., Leimeister, J.M.: Future Organization Report 2020. St.Gallen, Switzerland and Frankfurt, Germany: Institute of Information Systems, University of St.Gallen; Campana & Schott Business Services GmbH (2020)
49. Prinz, N., Huber, M., Riedinger, C., Rentrop, C.: Two perspectives of low-code development platform challenges: an exploratory study. In: Pacific Asia Conference on Information Systems, n.v., pp. 1–16 (2022)
50. Putta, A., Uludağ, Ö., Paasivaara, M., Hong, S.-L.: Benefits and challenges of adopting SAFe: an empirical survey. In: International Conference on Agile Software Development, n.v., pp. 172–187 (2021)
51. Qumer, A., Henderson-Sellers, B.: A framework to support the evaluation, adoption and improvement of agile methods in practice. J. Syst. Softw. **81**(11), 1899–1919 (2008)
52. Raduescu, C., Leonard, J., Hardy, C.: Course design principles to support the learning of complex information infrastructures. Assoc. Inf. Syst., n.v., 1–11 (2016)
53. Salmela, H., Baiyere, A., Tapanainen, T., Galliers, R.D.: Digital agility: conceptualizing agility for the digital era. J. Assoc. Inf. Syst. **23**(5), 1–24 (2022)
54. Salvetti, F., Bertagni, B.: Leadership 5.0: an agile mindset for a digital future. Int. J. Adv. Corp. Learn. **13**(2), 1–5 (2020)
55. Senapathi, M., Drury, M., Srinivasan, A.: Agile usage: refining a theoretical model. In: Pacific Asia Conference on Information Systems (2013)
56. Senapathi, M., Drury-Grogan, M.L.: Refining a model for sustained usage of agile methodologies. J. Syst. Softw. **132**, 298–316 (2017)
57. Senapathi, M., Srinivasan, A.: Sustained agile usage: a systematic literature review. In: International Conference on Evaluation and Assessment in Software Engineering, n.v., pp. 119–124 (2013)
58. Shahalei, C.A., Kazan, E.: Digitizing products towards platforms: the case of vehicle motion system. In: International Conference on Information Systems, n.v., pp. 1–17 (2020)
59. Sutherland, J.: Why do 47% of agile transformations fail? (2023). https://www.scruminc.com/why-47-of-agile-transformations-fail/
60. Tallon, P.P., Queiroz, M., Coltman, T., Sharma, R.: Information technology and the search for organizational agility: a systematic review with future research possibilities. J. Strateg. Inf. Syst. **28**(2), 218–237 (2019)
61. Taribuka, D., Amrit, C.: Agile in the banking industry: exploring multiple levels of agile transformation process facilitators and challenges from a people perspective. In: European Conference on Information Systems, n.v., pp. 1–16 (2020)
62. Tripp, J.F., Riemenschneider, C., Thatcher, J.B.: Job satisfaction in agile development teams: agile development as work redesign. J. Assoc. Inf. Syst. **17**(4), 267–307 (2016)
63. Trippensee, L., Remané, G.: Practices for large-scale agile transformations: a systematic literature review. In: Americas Conference on Information Systems, n.v., pp. 1–19 (2021)
64. Tronvoll, B., Sklyar, A., Sörhammar, D., Kowalkowski, C.: Transformational shifts through digital servitization. Ind. Mark. Manage. **89**, 293–305 (2020)
65. UB Kassel: KARLA - Katalogportal der UB Kassel (2023). https://hds.hebis.de/ubks/index.php
66. van Dierendonck, D.: Servant leadership: a review and synthesis. J. Manag. **37**(4), 1228–1261 (2011)
67. van Manen, H., van Vliet, H.: Organization-wide agile expansion requires an organization-wide agile mindset. In: Product-Focused Software Process Improvement, PROFES 2014. LNCS, pp. 48–62 (2014)

68. Van Slyke, C., Topi, H., Granger, M.J.: COVID-19, learning, pedagogy, and educational systems. Commun. Assoc. Inf. Syst. **48**(1), 476–486 (2021)
69. Walter, A.-T.: Organizational agility: ill-defined and somewhat confusing? A systematic literature review and conceptualization. Manage. Rev. Q. **71**, 343–391 (2020)
70. Wang, X., Conboy, K., Cawley, O.: "Leagile" software development: an experience report analysis of the application of lean approaches in agile software development. J. Syst. Softw. **85**(6), 1287–1299 (2012)
71. Webster, J., Watson, R.T.: Analyzing the past to prepare for the future: writing a literature review. Manage. Inf. Syst. Q. **26**(2), xiii–xxiii (2002)
72. Williams, B., Boland, R., Lyytinen, K.: Shaping problems, not decisions: when decision makers leverage visual analytics. In: American Conference on Information Systems, n.v., pp. 1–14 (2015)
73. Winter, S., Berente, N., Howison, J., Butler, B.: Beyond the organizational 'container': conceptualizing 21st century sociotechnical work. Inf. Organ. **24**(4), 250–269 (2014)
74. Zielske, M., Held, T.: Application of agile methods in traditional logistics companies and logistics startups. J. Syst. Softw. **177**, 110950 (2021)

Open Access This chapter is licensed under the terms of the Creative Commons Attribution 4.0 International License (http://creativecommons.org/licenses/by/4.0/), which permits use, sharing, adaptation, distribution and reproduction in any medium or format, as long as you give appropriate credit to the original author(s) and the source, provide a link to the Creative Commons license and indicate if changes were made.

The images or other third party material in this chapter are included in the chapter's Creative Commons license, unless indicated otherwise in a credit line to the material. If material is not included in the chapter's Creative Commons license and your intended use is not permitted by statutory regulation or exceeds the permitted use, you will need to obtain permission directly from the copyright holder.

A Mosaic of Perspectives: Understanding Ownership in Software Engineering

Tomi Suomi[✉], Petri Ihantola, Tommi Mikkonen, and Niko Mäkitalo

Faculty of Information Technology, University of Jyväskylä, Jyväskylä, Finland
{tomi.p.suomi,petri.j.ihantola,tommi.j.mikkonen,niko.k.makitalo}@jyu.fi

Abstract. Agile software development relies on self-organized teams, underlining the importance of individual responsibility. How developers take responsibility and build ownership are influenced by external factors such as architecture and development methods. This position paper examines the existing literature on ownership in software engineering and in psychology, and argues that a more comprehensive view of ownership in software engineering has a great potential in improving software team's work. Initial positions on the issue are offered for discussion and to lay foundations for further research.

Keywords: ownership · software · collaboration

1 Introduction

Independent and self-organized teams are the cornerstone of agile development. In addition to personal properties, the way developers take responsibility depends on external factors such as architecture or development methods. As an example, microservices have become standard practice, leading to more independently scalable and flexible software architecture at the cost of overall system complexity, where large systems have hundreds or even more microservices, often scattering and obfuscating the lines of ownership [5].

Although software ownership has been studied [7], the overall understanding of the topic is scarce. The previous research focuses on individual ownership targets, creating various definitions and ways of measuring ownership. The interplay between working practices, organizational structure, architecture, ownership, and various quality attributes is complex. For example, ownership affects various technical quality metrics as well as intangible factors like teamwork [12] and developer retention [3]. In modern, complex systems, we should better understand the overarching nature of ownership and how to manage it.

This paper introduces initial positions on what ownership studies are lacking and how to fill this gap. Section 2 provides background on ownership research, both in the software engineering context and briefly in psychology. Next, Sect. 3 introduces the research gap and provides six positions based on the analysis of previous research. Finally, Sect. 4 derives concrete research questions, discusses potential strategies to answer them, and concludes our work.

2 Background

2.1 Ownership in Software Engineering

A recent systematic literature review by Koana et al. [7] found 28 definitions for ownership, ranging from code ownership to all the way to organizational ownership. The study focused heavily on *corporeal ownership* side, that refers to development history of an artifact. Moreover, the review divides ownership into three dimensions: What (e.g., code, task, issue, bug, and requirement), Who (e.g., developer, organization, and manager), and How (i.e., dedicated or shared). By using this classification, code was by far the most studied artifact.

Code Ownership. Bird et al. [2] interpreted code ownership as the ratio of commits made by a developer against all commits in that particular component. The study categorized developers into major and minor contributors, based on whether their total number of commits was more or less than 5% of total commits, respectively. The study found the number of minor contributors correlated with pre- and post-release failures in Windows Vista and Windows 7 projects. Correspondingly, top contributor's higher level of ownership negatively correlated with failures, but the effect size was less than that of minor contributors.

Rahman and Devanbu [17] studied ownership of code at code line level, so that ownership refers to the developer who has authored most of the code. The study also considered developer's specialized (experience in particular file) and general experience. The results suggested that specialized experience is more important in writing bug-free code than general experience. Additionally, faulty code was found to be more likely authored by single developer, contradicting the study by Bird et al. [2], where higher number of minor contributors led to more failures. One reason can be the different granularity of metrics, where one study used line level metrics to determine ownership versus commit level, underlining the need for more standard approach on measuring ownership.

Zabarast et al. [23] used Ownership and Contribution Alignment Model (OCAM) to understand the alignment of ownership with relation to the actual contributions. Compared to the two previous studies presented above, ticket data was used in addition to Git data to understand ownership and contributions. The authors found that misalignment of ownership (i.e. owning team is not the main contributor to the component) led to faster accumulation of technical debt. The misalignment can happen for example due to module dependencies, where other team needs to do changes in dependent module. Similar pattern was also found by Bird et al. [2], where it was observed that minor contributor was often major contributor in dependency package.

While the studies of code ownership against faults in code are many, the correlation between the two metrics is still unclear. Where Bird et al. [2] found correlation between number of minor contributors and faults, the replication study by Koana et al. [7] didn't see similar effect. And while Koana et al. [7] saw increase in bugs with higher number of major contributors, Rahman and

Devanbu [17] noticed that buggy code was more likely authored by single developer. In addition there are studies that found no strong correlation between number of developers and defects, such as the one by Weyuker et al. [20]. The reasons for these inconsistencies can be many, such as different product types, or the context of development such as the methodology used. Deeper understanding of ownership and all of its dimensions should help in eliminating the differences in results, which is why further research is required.

Psychological Ownership. Psychological ownership in software engineering context was defined as a feeling of ownership toward an owned entity in a project by Koana et al. [7]. In study by Sedano et al. [19], psychological ownership is related to team code ownership (meaning development approach where anyone within team can modify any part of team's code). The authors state that team code ownership is not simply a decree, but rather a feeling. The feeling of team code ownership was found to be supported by understanding the system context, having contributed to the code, perceiving the code quality as high, feeling that the product satisfies user's needs and finally high perceived team cohesion. The study also found multiple risks towards feeling of ownership, such as knowledge silos, increasing code base and team size, and pressure to deliver.

Psychological ownership has also been studied in context of open-source software participant retention by Chung et al. [3]. The authors investigated value and demands-value fit of developers towards open source projects and found that both negatively impact developer turnover in open-source projects. However, higher feelings of psychological ownership were found to moderate the effect on value fit, meaning even if value fit towards the project was low, high feeling of psychological ownership improved developer retention.

Collaboration can also benefit from psychological ownership in agile development. The study by Nazir et al. [12] investigated both individual and collective (psychological) ownership and suggests that individual ownership can both promote and hinder (e.g. by developer siloing themselves or insisting on solving the issue at hand alone) collective ownership. This aligns well with the discussion on the negative and positive effects of psychological ownership, which are presented in greater detail in Subsect. 2.2. The authors found that collective ownership was "turbocharger" in collaboration, meaning collective ownership improved collaboration, which in turn improved collective ownership. The same study states that collective ownership can develop by high perceived level of control over tasks, shared understanding of the tasks and involvement in collaboration. These are well in line with the routes of psychological ownership presented in Fig. 1. The authors do note however that collective psychological ownership is not universal concept, and for example organizational culture might affect the feeling of collective psychological ownership.

Impact of Organization. Looking at the issue of ownership with even wider lens, organizational structure, and therefore the ownership, has also been shown

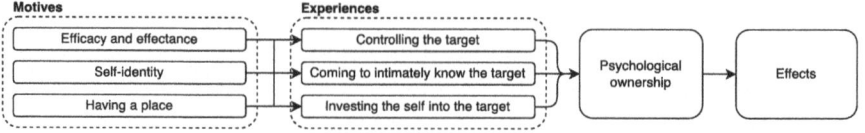

Fig. 1. Motives, experiences and effects of psychological ownership [13].

to affect both software failure-proneness as well as test effectiveness and reliability [6,11]. Herzig and Nagappan [6] studied test effectiveness and reliability, finding that larger organizational subgroups with short communication paths (i.e. test owners are closer to each other in organizational chart) positively correlates with test effectiveness. The study therefore supports the idea that test suites should be owned by individual organizational subgroups. The authors also noted that test suites owned by engineers that have already left the company are less effective.

2.2 Ownership in Psychology

Ownership has been studied vastly in other fields as well, which might provide interesting insights on how to understand ownership in software engineering. Especially interesting are the ownership studies in psychology, where *psychological ownership* is presented in better detail. Psychological ownership is a feeling of ownership towards a target, or "a cognitive-affective state that characterizes the human condition", held primarily by the individual of this feeling [14].

Figure 1 represents the motives and experiences that cause psychological ownership as well as consequences resulting from psychological ownership. On the first column of Fig. 1 we have motives, or roots, of psychological ownership that fulfill basic human motives [14]. The first motive efficacy and effectance, meaning as we interact with target, some change happens, leading to feeling of efficacy [22]. The second motive is self-identity, referring how objects for example can form and express both private and public identity of a person [21]. Finally, the third motive is having a place, for example home, which can provide stable refuge, providing security, simulation and identity for the person [15]. Having a place has also been described as "belongingness" [1].

On the second column of Fig. 1 the major experiences, or routes, from which psychological ownership is born [13] are presented. First there is controlling the target. One way to promote the feeling of control in organizations can be self-managing teams and employee's participation in decision making [8]. Secondly, we have intimately knowing the target. Supporting this, Sedano et al. [19] found that developers in the study felt more ownership towards code when system context was well known to them. Final experience to psychological ownership is investing self into the target. One example is the IKEA effect where consumers value products more when they have assembled it successfully themselves [18].

In addition to motives and experiences, other factors affect psychological ownership as well. One critical element is cultural context, as some cultures are more individualistic and others more collectivistic, which might affect whether ownership is felt either at individual or collective level [14]. This might limit the generalization of any results.

The last column of Fig. 1 simply represents any potential consequences due to psychological ownership. These can be positive or negative. For example, psychological ownership can lead to higher job satisfaction, commitment and intention to stay within the job [1]. On the negative side, person might refuse to share information or resist change [13].

3 Gap in Research

Based on the related work above, there is little doubt about the importance and industrial impact of ownership. From code quality to test efficiency to technical debt accumulation, understanding ownership can allow companies to exploit this phenomenon. From the psychological ownership side, the increased feeling of responsibility, developer retention, and improved collaboration were just few of the many potential effects. The various known and yet to be discovered benefits of understanding ownership combined with the knowledge of how to foster ownership in practice show promise of significant industry impact. Once completed, the results provide practitioners both the theoretical understanding of ownership as well as how it can be embedded into the existing development processes.

Position 1: Ownership Research in Software Engineering has been Scattered, Lacking Full Understanding. In his paper introducing the chaos model methodology, Raccoon stated that, *"It seems to me that we have studied each aspect of software development in isolation, not how all aspects fit together."* [16]. The same appears to be true also for ownership in software engineering: while individual aspects of ownership have been studied, there is no complete model for ownership available that explains how the various pieces work together.

Position 2: Psychological Ownership can Help Understand Ownership in Software Engineering more Comprehensively. For example, we can consider corporeal ownership and psychological ownership. Corporeal ownership was based on the history of an artifact. But looking at the routes of psychological ownership in Fig. 1, it seems unlikely that corporeal ownership exists without psychological ownership. In fact, one paper argued that team code ownership is a feeling [19], meaning it's related to psychological ownership. Similarly, it could be argued that corporeal ownership is, in fact, psychological ownership. Scenario where developer has created large part of a system but doesn't feel psychological ownership towards it seems hard to imagine.

Position 3: Architectural and Methodology Choices Affect the Development and Distribution of Ownership. Continuing on the psychological ownership path, the current assembly line way of software development might have made it more difficult to develop a feeling of psychological ownership towards the entire project. Just like in Ford manufacturing, workers no longer worked on every part of the car, instead they would focus on one or two tasks on an assembly line, which made the work more boring [4] and could arguably have led to loss of feeling of psychological ownership beyond their immediate tasks. It could be argued that software engineering has seen a similar shift towards "assembly line" as well in terms of agile development, where work is iterative and focuses on smaller steps.

Position 4: Time Dimension Must also be Considered in Ownership Studies and Ownership Must be Transferable. While the systematic literature review on ownership in software teams did divide the ownership into components of what, who and how [7], the time component must also be considered. Software engineering teams are dynamic, with people coming and going. Therefore, the ownership model should also be dynamic enough that it doesn't rely on any individual, and even someone with high level of ownership leaving should be manageable without causing unnecessary strain on the development, meaning the ownership must be transferable.

Position 5: To Study Ownership, We Must Understand what Belongs to Software Engineers' Responsibilities to Identify All Possible Routes to Ownership. When talking of overarching ownership strategy, it's also important to consider all responsibilities software engineers have. Ayas et al. [10] studied the roles, responsibilities, and skills of engineers in microservice era based on job-ads. The authors identified 5 families of responsibilities: software development support & infrastructure, software product delivery, software process & team development, professional services delivery and software engineering governance. The implication for ownership study is that there is more to a software engineer's job than simply coding, and ownership studies should not ignore these other responsibilities and how they might affect or be affected by a feeling of psychological ownership. In fact, up to 52% of developer's workday is used in non-development-heavy activities [9].

Position 6: Ownership Must be Integrated as Part of the Software Development Process. Once understood more comprehensively, ownership can be used in practice.

4 A Research Agenda

Inspired by the importance of commitment and self-organization of teams in agile software development, this paper presented the current work done on ownership in software engineering and mirrored research in psychology to software engineering. While in agile methodologies smaller teams can be self-organized, cross-team communication can be challenging in large-scale projects. Although large-scale agile methodologies try to tackle this challenge, we believe ownership can provide interesting pathway to improve agile software development methods at a large scale. It was argued that the ownership research so far has been scattered with no overall understanding of the issue. To guide research further, below are presented research questions to bridge the research gaps discussed.

Based on the position statements, we set the following overarching research challenge: *How can we embed ownership into software engineering process?* This can be operationalized via the following Reserarch Questions (RQ):

RQ1: What is ownership and what does it contain? To understand the *targets and dimensions* of ownership, existing literature must be studied in combination with interviews and surveys with software engineering professionals.

RQ2: How can we measure and influence ownership to understand its benefits? To measure and influence ownership, various *instruments* are needed to create standard ways to measure and affect ownership. The existing literature on ownership on software engineering can be compared against known methods of psychological ownership.

RQ3: How software development context affects ownership in software teams? As software is developed in various contexts (e.g. different methodologies and architectures), their effect on ownership must be understood. The learnings from RQ1 and RQ2 should be studied in practice to understand the fostering of a sense of ownership. Trialing the methods with different contexts allows for the nuances of team context to be studied.

There are different approaches to operationalizing the proposed RQs. For example, we have started to explore RQ1 by analyzing data from the interviews of software security professionals, with the primary goal of identifying the concrete activities that could support the creation of psychological ownership. For example, security task prioritization is one concrete activity under controlling the target route. Related to RQ2, we have started to mine Git data and plan to interpret the results in the light of psychological ownership.

Acknowledgments. This work has been supported by FAST, the Finnish Software Engineering Doctoral Research Network, funded by the Ministry of Education and Culture, Finland. We thank Doctoral Researcher Maha Sroor and Assistant Professor Rahul Mohanani from University of Jyväskylä for their contributions to the preliminary results on security ownership, which will be further explored in an upcoming paper.

Disclosure of Interests. The authors have no competing interests to declare that are relevant to the content of this article.

References

1. Avey, J.B., Avolio, B.J., Crossley, C.D., Luthans, F.: Psychological ownership: theoretical extensions, measurement and relation to work outcomes. J. Organ. Behav. **30**(2), 173–191 (2009). The International Journal of Industrial, Occupational and Organizational Psychology and Behavior
2. Bird, C., Nagappan, N., Murphy, B., Gall, H., Devanbu, P.: Don't touch my code! examining the effects of ownership on software quality. In: Proceedings of the 19th ACM SIGSOFT Symposium and the 13th European Conference on Foundations of Software Engineering, pp. 4–14 (2011)
3. Chung, T.R., Sharma, P.N., Daniel, S.L.: The impact of person-organization fit and psychological ownership on turnover in open source software projects. In: AMCIS (2015)
4. Ford Motor Company: The Moving Assembly Line. https://corporate.ford.com/articles/history/moving-assembly-line.html (nd). Accessed 14 Nov 2024
5. Gluck, A.: Introducing Domain-Oriented Microservice Architecture. https://www.uber.com/en-IN/blog/microservice-architecture/ (2020). Accessed 4 Sep 2024
6. Herzig, K., Nagappan, N.: The impact of test ownership and team structure on the reliability and effectiveness of quality test runs. In: Proceedings of the 8th ACM/IEEE International Symposium on Empirical Software Engineering and Measurement, pp. 1–10 (2014)
7. Koana, U.A., Le, Q.H., Raman, S., Carlson, C., Chew, F., Nayebi, M.: Examining ownership models in software teams. Empir. Softw. Eng. **29**(6), 1–43 (2024)
8. Liu, J., Wang, H., Hui, C., Lee, C.: Psychological ownership: how having control matters. J. Manag. Stud. **49**(5), 869–895 (2012)
9. Meyer, A.N., Barr, E.T., Bird, C., Zimmermann, T.: Today was a good day: the daily life of software developers. IEEE Trans. Software Eng. **47**(5), 863–880 (2019)
10. Michael Ayas, H., Hebig, R., Leitner, P.: The roles, responsibilities, and skills of engineers in the era of microservices-based architectures. In: Proceedings of the 2024 IEEE/ACM 17th International Conference on Cooperative and Human Aspects of Software Engineering, pp. 13–23 (2024)
11. Nagappan, N., Murphy, B., Basili, V.: The influence of organizational structure on software quality: an empirical case study. In: Proceedings of the 30th International Conference on Software Engineering, pp. 521–530 (2008)
12. Nazir, S., Collignon, S.E., Surendra, N.C.: Understanding collective ownership in agile development: Turbo charging the process. Inf. Manag. **61**(6), 104004 (2024)
13. Pierce, J.L., Kostova, T., Dirks, K.T.: Toward a theory of psychological ownership in organizations. Acad. Manag. Rev. **26**(2), 298–310 (2001)
14. Pierce, J.L., Kostova, T., Dirks, K.T.: The state of psychological ownership: integrating and extending a century of research. Rev. Gen. Psychol. **7**(1), 84–107 (2003)
15. Porteous, J.D.: Home: The territorial core. Geographical review, pp. 383–390 (1976)
16. Raccoon, L.: The chaos model and the chaos cycle. ACM SIGSOFT Softw. Eng. Notes **20**(1), 55–66 (1995)
17. Rahman, F., Devanbu, P.: Ownership, experience and defects: a fine-grained study of authorship. In: Proceedings of the 33rd International Conference on Software Engineering, pp. 491–500 (2011)
18. Sarstedt, M., Neubert, D., Barth, K., et al.: The IKEA effect. A conceptual replication. J. Mark. Behav. **2**(4), 307–312 (2017)

19. Sedano, T., Ralph, P., Péraire, C.: Practice and perception of team code ownership. In: Proceedings of the 20th International Conference on Evaluation and Assessment in Software Engineering, pp. 1–6 (2016)
20. Weyuker, E.J., Ostrand, T.J., Bell, R.M.: Do too many cooks spoil the broth? Using the number of developers to enhance defect prediction models. Empir. Softw. Eng. **13**, 539–559 (2008)
21. Wheeler, S.C., Bechler, C.J.: Objects and self-identity. Curr. Opin. Psychol. **39**, 6–11 (2021)
22. White, R.W.: Motivation reconsidered: the concept of competence. Psychol. Rev. **66**(5), 297 (1959)
23. Zabardast, E., Gonzalez-Huerta, J., Tanveer, B.: Ownership vs contribution: Investigating the alignment between ownership and contribution. In: 2022 IEEE 19th International Conference on Software Architecture Companion (ICSA-C), pp. 30–34. IEEE (2022)

Open Access This chapter is licensed under the terms of the Creative Commons Attribution 4.0 International License (http://creativecommons.org/licenses/by/4.0/), which permits use, sharing, adaptation, distribution and reproduction in any medium or format, as long as you give appropriate credit to the original author(s) and the source, provide a link to the Creative Commons license and indicate if changes were made.

The images or other third party material in this chapter are included in the chapter's Creative Commons license, unless indicated otherwise in a credit line to the material. If material is not included in the chapter's Creative Commons license and your intended use is not permitted by statutory regulation or exceeds the permitted use, you will need to obtain permission directly from the copyright holder.

Business Agility

Knowledge Sharing and Coordination in Large-Scale Agile Software Development – A Systematic Literature Review and an Interview Study

Franziska Tobisch(✉) and Florian Matthes

TUM School of Computation, Information and Technology, Department of Computer Science, Technical University of Munich, Munich, Germany
`franziska.tobisch@tum.de`

Abstract. Due to their benefits regarding resilience to change and adaptability, agile methods are widely adopted in the software development industry. Despite being intended for small co-located teams, organizations have started to scale agile methods, e.g., applying them in multi-team projects. Consequently, effective and efficient knowledge sharing and coordination become more complex, and agile intra-team practices are not sufficient anymore. While several case studies investigate knowledge sharing and coordination in the scaled agile context, an overview across multiple organizations is missing. To fill this gap, we combined the results of a literature review of 69 studies and an interview study to gain an overview of how coordination and knowledge sharing are conducted in scaled agile organizations and what factors hinder or facilitate their effectiveness and efficiency. Our findings show that organizations implement various mechanisms, including roles (e.g., Product Owners), meetings (e.g., ad-hoc exchange), tools and artifacts (e.g., chats), and other structures (e.g., Communities of Practice). Organizations struggle particularly with misalignment among teams and units, insufficient communication, and distribution across different working locations. Key enabling factors are documentation efforts, as well as both formal and informal exchanges. Context is crucial and should be regularly reassessed as needs evolve. Also, strong organizational support is needed to facilitate coordination and knowledge sharing.

Keywords: Large-Scale Agile · Coordination · Knowledge sharing

1 Introduction

Agile methodologies have gained great popularity since the creation of the Agile Manifesto at the beginning of the 2000s [22,25]. Many organizations have adopted agile practices to stay competitive despite constantly changing customer needs, technological requirements, and market conditions [60]. Although originally designed for single-team projects [66], their proven success inspired organizations to scale agile methods beyond individual teams [22]. However, scaling agile practices increases complexity and yields several challenges for organizations, including coordination [22,23]. For example, managing dependencies between teams [16] and maintaining technical consistency can be difficult [23]. Also, the distribution of teams complicates coordination [87]. In addition, there is a risk of redundant work, teams or units not sharing their knowledge, and inefficient use of knowledge resources [22,23]. This risk makes cross-organizational and inter-team knowledge sharing essential to create collective knowledge, enhancing organizational performance and innovation [71]. Moreover, agile software development teams, programs, and organizations must adapt to the impacts of remote and hybrid work in our post-pandemic world [81]. Consequently, investigating how coordination and knowledge sharing in large-scale agile contexts can be performed effectively and efficiently is important.

Several researchers have studied this topic (e.g., [2,10]) but mainly investigated a single case in detail or focused on a particular mechanism, like Scrum-of-Scrums (SoS) [62]. While those studies provide initial insights, only a few findings on knowledge sharing [17,39,72,97] and coordination [15,34] across different scaled agile contexts exist. To address this gap, we systematically analyzed the described research area by examining empirical studies and practical insights from an interview study. Our research aims to understand which knowledge-sharing and coordination mechanisms are implemented in practice and what hinders and fosters their success, addressing the following research questions (RQs): *How do knowledge exchange and coordination take place in scaled agile software development settings? (RQ1) What are the barriers to and enabling factors for effective and efficient knowledge sharing and coordination in this context? (RQ2)*

2 Background and Related Work

Knowledge is a key strategic resource for organizations, making its management crucial for success [40]. In the organizational context, *knowledge sharing* refers to transferring skills, technology, and wisdom [89] and stands for the collective routines related to exchanging knowledge, experiences, and skills [55] between individuals, and within and among teams, organizational units, or organizations [42]. *Coordination* is a primary activity connecting different organizational parts to carry out tasks [92]. *Large-scale agile software development* can be defined as implementing agile methods in large teams, organizations, or multi-team settings or applying agile practices and principles across the organization as a whole [25]. Given the high number of studies investigating contexts that fall under this definition, we limit our study to environments with at least two teams, including distributed, remote, hybrid, and co-located settings.

Knowledge management is crucial for collaboration in software engineering [67,99]. Knowledge is shared, for instance, via repositories (e.g., databases), collaborative tools (e.g., wikis), and practices like code reviews, pair programming, and Communities of Practice (CoPs) [67,99]. However, time constraints, geographical distribution, cultural differences, and lack of incentives hinder knowledge sharing [67]. Leadership, a strong knowledge-sharing culture, and clear communication channels improve knowledge flow [67,99]. Co-location fosters informal interactions, while standardized tools and trust facilitate exchanges [99]. Coordination in software engineering usually relies on formal meetings, communication tools, and shared artifacts [38,45]. Task interdependence, geographic distribution, unclear roles, and poor communication can cause inefficiencies [38,45]. Shared goals, frequent communication, structured workflows, and trust can positively affect coordination [45].

Multiple researchers investigated knowledge sharing and coordination in scaled agile settings. The majority of this research investigates a single [2,10, 11,14,18,26,27,58] or a few cases [15,72]. Only some studies take a broader view through reviewing literature [17,34,39,97]. According to these studies, common knowledge sharing mechanisms include CoPs [2,17,39], open workspaces [2,17,39,72], team rotations [72], and cross-team meetings [17]. Common barriers are excessive meetings [2], time constraints [39,72,97], and lack of structured documentation [72]. On the contrary, an open culture [39], organizational support [39,72], open workspaces [17,72], and communication tools [2] facilitate knowledge sharing. Common coordination mechanisms in large-scale agile settings include cross-team meetings [27], open workspaces [14,27], dedicated coordination roles like Product Owners (POs) [11,14,15,34], communication tools, and shared documentation (e.g., dependency documents) [11,14,15,58]. Challenges arise due to inefficient coordination arenas [58] and the complexity of scaled agile settings [14,27]. Alignment [11,18], physical proximity [18,27], central roles [10,15], and collaboration tools [10,18] aid coordination.

Most papers concentrating on either knowledge sharing or coordination still address the other topic to a certain extent since both topics overlap. Effective coordination depends on the exchange of knowledge [10], and knowledge sharing is facilitated by well-structured coordination [27].

While many of the described studies examine coordination and knowledge sharing in scaled agile settings, they typically focus on single organizations, programs, or projects. Even the few studies with broader viewpoints consider only a limited amount of cases or do not focus on coordination or knowledge sharing but on other related topics. Also, despite presenting barriers and enabling factors, few papers present them in a structured way.

3 Methodology

We combined a systematic literature review [43,96] and an interview study [56] for a systematic data collection to gain insights from literature and practice.

3.1 Literature Review

With our literature review [43,96], we aimed to identify and analyze empirical literature on knowledge sharing and coordination in scaled agile software development to synthesize these findings to gain new insights. After an initial search, to get familiar with the topic and get a feeling for relevant papers and potential search strings, we chose six electronic databases (AIS eLibrary, ACM Digital Library, IEEE Xplore, Science Direct, Scopus, Web of Science). We iteratively refined our keyword search string, considering synonyms and spellings over multiple trial searches. We combined sub-strings using boolean connectors [43], leading to the following search string: *(agile OR scrum) AND (large OR large scale OR large-scale OR scaling OR scaled OR inter-team OR multiteam OR distributed) AND (knowledge sharing OR knowledge exchange OR knowledge management OR coordination) AND NOT (manufacturing)*, adapted to each database's syntax rules. Our search covered titles, keywords, and abstracts. For each study, we extracted meta-data (e.g., title, year), when possible, automatized through export. Then, we screened all 1272 studies, removed duplicates, and selected relevant papers based on (1) metadata, (2) abstract, and (3) full-text. To limit the search results and ensure objectivity, we applied inclusion and exclusion criteria [43] (see Table 1). After the full-text filtering, 66 studies remained. Next, we used forward and backward snowballing on key papers [2,10,11,14,15,17,18,26,27,34,39,58,72,97], finding 36 potentially relevant papers. After filtering those papers, three relevant studies remained. Combining these studies with the 66 initially found ones, we included 69 studies[1] (Fig. 1). We analyzed and synthesized the selected literature using qualitative coding [52,70], based on a two-cycle approach. First, we used descriptive coding. Hereby, we summarized relevant text segments with short phrases. Then, we combined deductive and inductive coding. We started by assigning pre-defined high-level codes based on our RQs (e.g., *"Barrier"*) to our previously created descriptive codes. Then, iteratively, we defined and assigned lower-level codes reflecting patterns to the descriptive codes, like specific barriers recurring across different papers and interviews (e.g., *"Missing alignment"*).

Table 1. Inclusion and exclusion criteria

Inclusion criteria	Description
Context	Describing coordination and/or knowledge sharing mechanisms, barriers, and enabling factors in large-scale agile settings, with focus on inter-team, -unit, -project, -program, or cross-organizational
Information amount	Enough data about knowledge sharing or coordination (either more than one mechanism, barrier, or enabling factors or detailed focus on one)
Exclusion criteria	
Language	Not written in English
Accessibility	Not accessible as full-text online
Quality	Insufficient quality (e.g., regarding grammar and spelling)
Publication date	Published before 2001 (creation of the Agile Manifesto [25])
Research approach	No empirical research (e.g., literature reviews)
Version	Earlier version(s) of extended papers

[1] The numbering of the sources listed in the result section exceeds 69 since we refer to the reference list and not a separate numbering for the included studies.

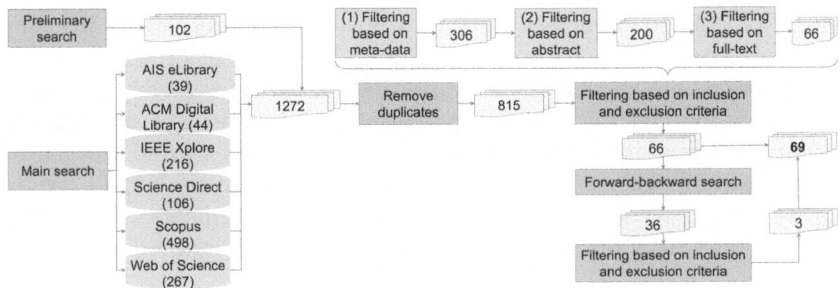

Fig. 1. Literature review process

3.2 Interview Study

To complement and enhance the insights of the literature review with primary data, we additionally conducted semi-structured interviews of experts [29,56,75]. We conducted nine interviews with ten experts between February and April 2024 via videoconferencing tools (see Table 2). Two experts (E7, E8) participated in a joint interview. Using convenience and purposive sampling [44], we contacted potential interviewees directly, e.g., via LinkedIn, and shared a call for participation with existing contacts. Still, we selected only "experts" with working experience in scaled agile settings [25] and, thus, the ability to share relevant experience. To capture diverse perspectives, the interviewees have various roles and work experience in different industries [56]. The interviews had an average duration of 55 min. The questions were mostly open-ended, covering the interviewees' background (e.g., role), knowledge sharing and coordination in current and previous organizations, and experienced barriers and enabling factors. While

Table 2. Interview partner

ID	Role(s)	Organization pseudonym(s)
E1	Software Developer, Project and Development Lead, Solution Train Engineer, Quality Assurance Manager	ConsultCo1
E2	Scrum Master	SoftwareCo1
E3	Software Developer, Project Manager	TeleCo, FoodCo
E4	PO	InsureCo, ConsultCo2
E5	Chapter Lead	InsureCo
E6	Lead Architect, Scrum Master	ConsultCo2
E7	Business Analyst, Requirements Engineer, Rollout Manager	TransportCo
E8	Scrum Master, PO	TransportCo
E9	Change Manager, PO	ConsultCo2, EnergyCo
E10	Scrum Master, PO, Development Lead, Software Architect	SoftwareCo2&3, ConsultCo3

following a predefined guide (see [88]), we adjusted each interview to the conversation's flow. After receiving approval, all interviews were recorded, transcribed, and anonymized. Since we intended to use the interviews to support our literature review findings and identify potential gaps, we reached a certain data saturation after nine interviews [1], as identified insights started to recur. We coded and analyzed the interviews similarly to the literature [52,70]. We used descriptive coding to summarize relevant interview statements, then assigned higher-level codes from our literature analysis and, if required, added new ones.

4 Results

4.1 Mechanisms

We identified various coordination and knowledge-sharing mechanisms in scaled agile settings. Table 3 illustrates the mechanisms sorted in descending order based on their frequency in the literature and interviews. We included only mechanisms reported at least three times across both sources.

Table 3. Knowledge-sharing and coordination mechanisms categorized in line with Berntzen et al. [10]

Mechanisms	Source(s)	#
Tools & artifacts		
Chat tools	E1, E3, E5–8, E10, [2, 10–14, 24, 26–28, 41, 49, 53, 58, 61, 64, 77, 78, 83, 86, 87, 94]	29
Wikis	E5, E6, E8, E10, [2, 3, 6, 10, 13, 14, 20, 24, 27, 61, 64, 72, 87]	17
Videoconferencing tools	E1, E3, E5–8, E10, [2, 6, 13, 20, 26, 32, 61, 62, 80, 87]	17
Project management tools	E1, E5, E6, E8, E10, [2, 10, 11, 13, 14, 26, 27, 58, 64, 72, 87, 95]	17
Task boards	[10–14, 27, 31–33, 53, 63, 64, 84]	13
E-mails	E10, [10, 20, 26, 49, 61, 62, 72, 87]	9
Guidelines* (e.g., for architecture)	[2, 7, 24, 26, 27, 58, 87, 98]	8
Objective & Key Results (OKRs)	[10–12, 14, 59, 86, 94]	7
Dependency documents*	E4, [15, 16, 26, 33, 57, 90]	7
Repositories (e.g., for code)	E1, E6, [26, 64, 72, 82, 87]	7
Shared backlogs*	E5, [6, 11, 14, 24, 87]	6
Road-maps	E8, [10, 14, 26, 91]	5
Whiteboards	E7, E10, [12, 20, 72]	5
Document management systems	E5, E8, E10, [20]	4
Fora**	[61, 64, 72, 78]	4
Organizational structures		
CoPs	E1, E2, E5–8, E10, [2, 10, 11, 14, 31, 37, 54, 59, 61, 78–80, 90, 91]	21
Open workspaces	[2, 11, 14, 18, 24, 27, 28, 58, 71, 72, 78, 84, 85]	13

continued

Table 3. continued

Team member borrowing/rotations	[2, 11, 24, 26, 27, 71, 72, 78, 82]	9
Informative workspaces*	[11, 14, 18, 27, 28, 71, 72]	7
Trainings**	E4, E5, E10, [2, 71, 86, 91]	7
Pair programming	[12, 64, 71, 72]	4
Shared activities like code reviews	[15, 41, 82]	3
Roles		
POs	E5, E6, E8, E10, [7, 8, 11, 13–16, 27, 28, 30, 31, 37, 41, 61, 65, 73, 82, 84, 94]	23
Experts for specific topics, e.g., testers	E5, E7, E10, [3, 10–12, 14, 16, 21, 37, 54, 58, 61, 65, 66, 68, 80, 82, 84, 85, 94]	22
Managers	E3, E5, E10, [3, 6, 10–12, 14, 19, 27, 28, 53, 61, 62, 82, 84, 85, 93, 95, 98]	21
Architects	E8, [3, 10, 11, 14–16, 19, 20, 26–28, 53, 65, 66, 84, 85, 91]	18
Scrum masters	E2, E10, [6, 15, 26–28, 30, 31, 46, 61, 87]	12
Central teams*	[3, 10, 12, 14–16, 37, 51, 98]	9
Task forces	E6, [10, 12, 14, 48, 65, 66, 82]	8
Team leads	[12, 14, 65, 80, 84, 94, 98]	7
Dedicated coordination roles*	[26, 69, 95]	3
Meetings		
Unscheduled, ad-hoc meetings	E1, E2, E4–6, E9, E10, [2, 10–14, 18, 20, 24, 26–28, 49, 53, 58, 64, 65, 72, 77, 78, 80, 82, 84, 86, 94]	32
SoS*	E6, E10, [2, 6, 18, 24, 26–28, 30–33, 35, 36, 53, 61–63, 72, 73, 84–86]	24
Planning meetings	E1, E2, E4, E5, [6, 10, 15, 26, 28, 31–33, 35, 36, 53, 57, 65, 66, 72, 98]	20
Regular meetings of certain roles	E4, E5, E7, E8, [10–15, 24, 26–28, 53, 65, 66, 78, 84, 94]	20
Demonstrations	E4, E8, E9, [10, 11, 14, 18, 24, 26–28, 53, 58, 63, 65, 72, 78]	17
Retrospectives*	E4, E8, [2, 10, 11, 15, 24, 27, 28, 53, 58, 72]	12
Workshops & seminars	[5, 6, 10, 14, 15, 26, 64, 71, 72, 80, 82, 94]	12
Daily/Stand-up meetings	E1, E6, E8, E10, [14–16, 27, 58, 64]	10
Technical presentations	[24, 26–28, 47, 53, 64, 71, 72]	9
Remote site visits	E5, [6, 19, 20, 50, 63, 64, 78, 87]	9
Open spaces	E9, [2, 24, 27, 28, 53, 71, 73]	8
Additional inter-team meetings	E1, E2, E4–6, E9, [6, 12]	8
Lunch talks	E2, [24, 27, 28, 53, 71, 72]	7
Regular meetings of mixed roles	E5, E7, [14–16, 27]	6
Review meetings	E1, [26, 32, 33, 72]	5
Bug related meetings*	[28, 53, 66, 85]	4
Team meetings attended by other teams' members	[18, 26, 41, 58]	4
Expert fora**	E10, [27, 28]	3
Competitions**	E2, [71, 72]	3
Kick-offs*	E2, [20, 63]	3

*only coordination, **only knowledge sharing*

4.2 Barriers and Enabling Factors

We identified 26 barriers to and 33 enabling factors for effective and efficient coordination and knowledge exchange in scaled agile settings. Table 4 and Table 5 illustrate the barriers and enabling factors in descending order based on their fre-

Table 4. Barriers to effective and efficient knowledge sharing and coordination

Barrier	Source(s)	#
Missing alignment, e.g., on goals, processes, or documentation routines between teams	E7, E8, E10, [3–5, 11, 13, 14, 16, 19, 37, 48–51, 57, 59, 61, 62, 68, 69, 77, 78, 87, 90, 93, 95]	28
Lack of exchange and communication, e.g., between teams or roles	E1, E3, E5, E6, E9, E10, [3–5, 14, 26, 48–50, 54, 61, 62, 68, 71, 72, 76–78, 80, 85, 87, 90]	27
Distribution of workplaces, e.g., of teams across time zones, locations, or remote work	E1-3, E5-8, E10, [4, 5, 19, 20, 48–50, 57, 61, 68, 71, 77–79, 83, 86, 87]	25
Hindering organization, project, or program set-up, e.g., hierarchies or high team autonomy	E2, E6, E7, E10, [3, 4, 11, 14, 16, 19, 26, 27, 32, 48, 49, 51, 66, 71, 77, 78, 87, 93, 95]	23
Lack of transparency, e.g., on progress, status, or knowledge between teams	E2–8, E10 [4, 5, 14, 16, 20, 26, 27, 41, 49, 62, 77, 86, 87, 94, 95]	23
Insufficient documentation, e.g. multiple databases, no updates, or missing access	E4, E6–9, [3, 5, 14, 16, 20, 27, 33, 49, 54, 68, 72, 77, 82, 95]	19
Dependencies, e.g., technical or task-related between teams	E3, E4, E7, E10, [4, 14, 16, 19, 26, 28, 50, 51, 57, 71, 76, 78, 93, 95]	18
Lack of involvement, e.g., lack of engagement or attendance in by representatives in exchanges	E2, E3, E5, E6, [10, 13, 14, 54, 61, 62, 69, 72, 76, 79, 80, 86]	16
Hindering organizational culture, e.g., change resistance or fear to share	E1, E3, E5, E7, E10, [2, 3, 26, 32, 59, 61, 62, 71, 72, 76]	15
No focus on big picture, e.g., overall goal	E3, E6, E10, [3–5, 51, 59, 62, 71, 76, 86, 93, 95]	14
Uncertainty & changes, e.g., of staff or priorities	E1, E4–6, [5, 11, 14, 16, 26, 49, 51, 54, 66, 76]	14
Large scale of organizational, project, or program	E2, E4, E6–8, [11, 12, 14, 16, 19, 27, 68, 71, 77]	14
Lack of time to exchange, e.g., due to time pressure or lacking management support	E6, [2, 3, 10, 14, 31, 54, 72, 76, 79, 80, 82, 85]	13
Lack of dependency awareness*, e.g., of teams	E3, E4, [5, 7, 15, 16, 33, 57, 76, 77, 90]	11
Lack of organizational support, e.g., time or resources	[10, 11, 14, 20, 31, 68, 72, 80, 93, 94]	10
Lack of knowledge of "who knows what" within organization, project, or program	E6, E10, [14, 49, 54, 58, 71, 72, 77, 78]	10
Misunderstandings, e.g., between roles or teams	E3, [5, 20, 57, 65, 66, 68, 87, 94, 95]	10
Unclear roles, responsibilities & processes	E1, E7, E10, [3, 14, 49, 59, 69, 77]	9
Low perceived value of mechanisms, e.g., of meetings by teams or roles	E1, E6, [14, 26, 61, 62, 72, 78, 79]	9
Unsuitably organized exchanges, e.g., large size	E1, E5, E7, [14, 36, 58, 62, 71, 76]	9
Insufficient planning activities*, e.g., superficial or top-down planning without teams	E4, E10, [3, 5, 16, 19, 41, 68, 76]	9
Meeting overload, e.g., of roles or teams	E1, E2, E8, [2, 19, 26, 35, 68]	8
Inefficient use of communication tools, e.g., complex chat structure or limited accessibility	E5, E7, E8, [11, 86, 94]	6
Work with external parties, e.g., regulations	E5, E8, [50, 57, 87]	5
Individuals as bottlenecks, e.g., lacking skills	E10, [68, 76, 80]	4
Ad-hoc exchange, e.g., between roles or teams	E10, [49, 94]	3

*only coordination, **only knowledge sharing*

quency in the literature and interviews. We included only barriers and enabling factors reported at least three times across both sources.

5 Discussion

In this section, we discuss the key findings and limitations of our study.

Table 5. Factors enabling effective and efficient knowledge sharing and coordination

Enabling factors	Source(s)	#
Adequate documentation efforts and tools, e.g., single source of truth, regular updates	E1, E4, E6–10, [2,3,6,7,10–14,16,21,24,26,27,33, 47,49,50,53,54,57–59,61,63,64,72,77,79,82,84,86, 87,94,95]	42
Formal exchange, e.g., scheduled meetings between teams or roles	E2–10, [5,10–16,18,24,26–28,30,41,47,53,57,58,63, 65,66,71,72,78,82,84,87,98]	38
Ad-hoc exchange, e.g., un-scheduled meetings or chats between teams or roles	E2, E3, E5–7, E10, [2,10–14,18,24,26–28,49,53,58, 65,71,72,77,78,80,82,84–87,94]	32
Dedicated central entities, e.g., POs, managers, specialists, scrum masters, central teams	E5, E10, [3,7,10–12,14–16,20,21,26,28,30,37,46, 51,54,58,65,66,68,73,78,80,82,87,93–95,98]	32
Alignment, e.g., on goals, used tools, or a shared mental model between teams	E4, E5, E7, E8, E10, [2,10–14,16,18,20,27,30,48, 53,54,58,59,62,66,71,72,78,82,86,87,94,95]	31
Transparency, e.g., on progress, planned tasks, or information between teams	E1, E5, E6, E9, E10, [2,3,6,11,12,14,15,18,21,27, 28,49,53,57,61,66,71,72,82,84,86,87,90,94,95]	30
Chats and digital exchange tools, e.g., chats or videoconferencing tools	E1, E6, E7, E10, [2,10–14,20,26–28,41,49,53,58,61, 64,72,77,78,82,86,87,94]	27
Dependency management*, e.g., through discussions or documentation	E3–6, E9, [10–12,14,15,18,26–28,33,47,50,51,53, 57,63,78,84,85,94,95]	26
Supporting organizational set-up, e.g., flat hierarchies, empowerment, modularity	E2, E4–6, E9, [12,14,15,18,19,24,26,27,37,49,50, 53,54,61,65,66,72,76,78,87]	25
Suitable organization of exchanges, e.g., engaging, with agenda or facilitator	E1, E5, E7–9, [10,11,13,16,18,27,28,36,48,53,61, 62,71,73,78,79,85]	22
Organizational support, e.g., incentives, infrastructure, time, trainings, or by agile coaches	E5, E6, E10, [10,11,14,20,33,48,50,54,59,61,63,71, 72,78–80,84]	20
Co-location, e.g., of collaborating teams	E2, E3, E5, E8, E10, [10,11,14,18,24,26,27,48,53, 57,64,71,72,78,84]	20
In-person meetings, e.g., on-site visits	E3, E5, E7, E8, E10, [6,10,11,13,19,20,28,50,58,63, 64,77,78,87]	19
Exchange structures, e.g., meetings, member rotation, pair programming, or CoPs	E6, E10 [2,12,14,18,54,61,65,66,71,78–80,86,91, 98]	17
Open and informative workspace	E6, [2,10,11,13,14,18,24,27,28,53,58,71,72,78,84, 85]	17
Top-down steering, e.g., clear strategy, Definition-of-Done, or guidelines	E4, E8, [2,7,11,14,20,27,30,48,50,59,64,72,78,98]	16
Supporting organizational culture, e.g., openness	E7, E10, [2,10,15,20,21,47,49,54,59,61,71,72,77, 78]	16
Shared dependency understanding & awareness*, e.g., between teams	E2–4, [12,15,16,26,28,33,47,53,57,78,90]	14
Reflection and adjustment on mechanisms	E2, E8, [2,11,13,18,26,27,41,53,58,72]	12
Good network, e.g., between certain roles	E5, E6, E10, [15,18,20,28,54,64,72,78,80]	12
Focus on big picture, e.g., overall goal	E5, [2,12,13,18,20,50,59,62,72,86,94]	12
Sufficient planning activities, e.g., joint, iterative, considering dependencies	E2–6, [15,16,27,47,57]	10
Context-dependent approach, e.g., based on agile maturity and needs	E2, E8, E10 [13–15,18,27,33,53]	10
Combining different mechanisms, e.g., ad-hoc and scheduled meetings	[11,13,18,26–28,53,59,84]	9
Good interpersonal relations, e.g., between teams or roles	E2, E7, [2,6,10,27,78,87]	8
Value of mechanisms, e.g., interesting topics	E6, E8, E10, [61,72,79,85]	7
Face-to-face communication, e.g., via video	E5, [10,20,58,71,72,78]	7
Time** of teams to exchange	E6, E10 [10,61,72,80]	6
Automation, e.g., status tracking	[10,14,57,65,95]	5
Trust, e.g., between teams and roles	E6, [18,20,47,87]	5
Context knowledge of and experience with framework, technology, domain, or processes	E4, E7, [18,26,80]	5
Involvement, e.g., active discussions	E5, [27,28,79]	4
Motivation, e.g., of roles to share	[53,72,86]	3

*only coordination, **only knowledge sharing

5.1 Key Findings

To answer our RQ1, *"How do knowledge exchange and coordination take place in scaled agile software development settings?,"* we identified more than 51 different mechanisms for knowledge sharing and coordination in agile organizations. Based on our findings, chat tools are the most frequently used tools, ad-hoc meetings are the most implemented format, and CoPs are the dominant structure. Likewise, prior research found informal exchanges as important mechanisms in scaled agile settings [10,11,39]. While POs and managers typically handle coordination and knowledge sharing, we found that in line with Gustavsson [34], not only such typical roles but also experts for specific topics (e.g., testers) contribute, which highlights the need for broad organizational involvement. Some companies even establish dedicated coordination roles, reflecting the task's complexity. Based on the studies' publication dates, the use of most mechanisms remained stable over time, though OKRs seem more common in recent years.

To answer our RQ2, *"What are the barriers to and enabling factors for effective and efficient knowledge sharing and coordination in scaled agile software development settings?,"* we identified 26 barriers to and 33 factors enabling efficient and effective knowledge sharing and coordination in scaled agile contexts. The high number of identified barriers reflects the complexity of successfully realizing both. The impediments reported most frequently in our findings are missing alignment between teams or across the organization (e.g., regarding goals), insufficient communication, and remote work or distribution of teams. While similar barriers were discovered in related studies [11,14,39,72,97], none of them highlights challenges related to workplace distribution. Moreover, problems related to inefficient use of communication tools seem to be more frequent only recently, probably related to their increasing relevance during pandemic times [74]. The most relevant enabling factors are adequate documentation (tools) and formal and ad-hoc exchange. Several other studies also highlight these aspects [2,10,11,14,15,18,39,72]. While ad-hoc exchanges can be an enabling factor due to being fast and easy, they can also be a barrier (e.g., required context switching). Especially organizational support (e.g., resources, time) can help address various barriers (e.g., lack of time) and foster other enabling factors (e.g., alignment). Likewise, other studies found organizational support to be highly relevant [10,11,72]. Our findings also show that context plays an important role. Specific mechanisms like CoPs, wikis, videoconferencing tools, and remote-site visits are predominantly adopted in distributed, hybrid, or remote contexts. In particular, remote, distributed, unsuitable, large, or complex organizational or project settings trigger other barriers (e.g., lack of exchange, dependencies). Also, other authors [11,14,27] highlight scaling agile's complexity as a challenge. Context-dependent approaches to coordination and knowledge sharing and, aligned with the Agile Manifesto [9], adjusting the respective approaches to changes are important. Likewise, as mentioned, and in line with Dingsøyr et al. [26] and Berntzen et al. [11], some mechanisms and barriers have changed their relevance or prevalence over time. In general, respecting agile values and principles [9] is useful. For instance, next to openness to change and reflection to improve, supporting organizational culture, trust, motivation, face-to-face communication, and frequent exchanges are beneficial. However, while the Agile Manifesto puts people and interactions over processes or tools [9], we found documentation and tools as key enabling factors. Likewise, other authors report on the relevance of documentation, especially in distributed, remote, large, and complex settings [2,14,26,27,99].

Most mechanisms we found enable knowledge sharing and coordination, and likewise, most barriers and facilitators impede or foster both. These findings emphasize the tight coupling between knowledge sharing and coordination.

Our findings can serve as inspiration to practitioners on potential mechanisms for coordination and knowledge sharing in scaled agile settings and to help them be aware of barriers and enabling factors. Leadership aiming to enhance coordination and knowledge sharing should ensure sufficient support. Responsible roles should not follow strict guidelines but adapt their approach to their needs. Also, regularly reflecting on and improving these approaches is essential.

5.2 Limitations

To mitigate validity threats in our literature review [100], we followed guidelines [43,96] for systematic database selection, search terms, and study inclusion. We sampled experts with diverse roles and organizational contexts to enhance external validity and generalizability in our interview study. Combining interview findings with literature review results further strengthens external validity, though a larger sample could improve generalizability. For reliability, we adhered to established data collection and analysis guidelines [52,56,70]. Internal validity threats were addressed using consistent interview outlines. Still, the risk of bias in coding and interpretation caused by a single researcher analyzing the data remains.

6 Conclusion and Future Work

Knowledge sharing and coordination are highly relevant to the success of applying agile methods at scale but equally challenging. Existing research provides initial insights into how coordination and knowledge sharing are performed and what factors can facilitate or hinder both. Still, a broad, structured overview of mechanisms, barriers, and enabling factors is missing. To fill this gap, we conducted a systematic literature review and an expert interview study and combined both results. We presented an overview of the various coordination and knowledge-sharing mechanisms (i.e., tools, artifacts, roles, meetings, structures) implemented in practice. The most common mechanisms are chat tools, CoPs, POs, and unscheduled ad-hoc meetings. Moreover, we presented 26 barriers and 33 enabling factors for efficient and effective knowledge sharing and coordination. Both activities are highly related. Misalignment, insufficient communication, and distributed workplaces are key obstacles. Documentation, tools, and both formal and informal exchanges are key enabling factors. Context is critical and should be considered and regularly re-assessed as needs evolve when implementing coordination and knowledge-sharing practices. Future work could extend the interviews to enhance generalizability, study individual mechanisms or enabling factors in-depth, or provide concrete guidance to adopt them. Also, given the scarcity of quantitative empirical research in existing literature, a quantitative study would be valuable.

Acknowledgements. This research has been partly funded by the BMBF through grant 01IS23069. We thank Anil Can Kara for his support.

References

1. Aldiabat, K.M., Le Navenec, C.L.: Data saturation: the mysterious step in grounded theory methodology. Qual. Rep. **23**(1), 245–261 (2018)
2. Almeida, F., Miranda, E., Falcão, J.: Challenges and facilitators practices for knowledge management in large-scale scrum teams. J. Inf. Techn. Case App. Res. **21**(2), 90–102 (2019)
3. Alsaqaf, W., Daneva, M., Wieringa, R.: Quality requirements challenges in the context of large-scale distributed agile: an empirical study. Inf. Softw. Techn. **110**, 39–55 (2019)
4. Amrit, C., Hutten, E.: The effects of modularity on effective communication and collaboration. In: Proceedings of the ACM SIGMIS Conference on Computers and People Research, pp. 33–40 (2017)
5. Badampudi, D., Fricker, S.A., Moreno, A.M.: Perspectives on productivity and delays in large-scale agile projects. In: Baumeister, H., Weber, B. (eds.) Agile Processes in Software Engineering and Extreme Programming, pp. 180–194. Springer, Heidelberg (2013)
6. Bannerman, P.L., Hossain, E., Jeffery, R.: Scrum practice mitigation of global software development coordination challenges: a distinctive advantage? In: Proceedings of the 45th Hawaii International Conference on System Sciences, pp. 5309–5318. IEEE (2012)
7. Bass, J.M.: How product owner teams scale agile methods to large distributed enterprises. Emp. Softw. Eng. **20**, 1525–1557 (2015)
8. Bass, J.M., Haxby, A.: Tailoring product ownership in large-scale agile projects: managing scale, distance, and governance. IEEE Softw. **36**(2), 58–63 (2019)

9. Beck, K., et al.: https://agilemanifesto.org/ (2001). Accessed 04 Apr 2025
10. Berntzen, M., Hoda, R., Moe, N.B., Stray, V.: A taxonomy of inter-team coordination mechanisms in large-scale agile. IEEE Trans. Softw. Eng. **49**(2), 699–718 (2022)
11. Berntzen, M., Stray, V., Moe, N.B., Hoda, R.: Responding to change over time: a longitudinal case study on changes in coordination mechanisms in large-scale agile. Emp. Softw. Eng. **28**(5), 114 (2023)
12. Berntzen, M., Engdal, S.A., Gellein, M., Moe, N.B.: Coordination in agile product areas: a case study from a large fintech organization. In: Šmite, D., Guerra, E., Wang, X., Marchesi, M., Gregory, P. (eds.) Agile Processes in Software Engineering and Extreme Programming XP2024. LNBIP, vol. 512, pp. 36–52. Springer Nature, Cham (2024)
13. Berntzen, M., Moe, N.B., Stray, V.: The product owner in large-scale agile: an empirical study through the lens of relational coordination theory. In: Kruchten, P., Fraser, S., Coallier, F. (eds.) Agile Processes in Software Engineering and Extreme Programming XP2019. LNBIP, vol. 355, pp. 121–136. Springer, Cham (2019)
14. Berntzen, M., Stray, V., Moe, N.B.: Coordination strategies: managing inter-team coordination challenges in large-scale agile. In: Gregory, P., Lassenius, C., Wang, X., Kruchten, P. (eds.) Agile Processes in Software Engineering and Extreme Programming XP2021. LNBIP, vol. 419, pp. 140–156. Springer, Cham (2021)
15. Bick, S., Scheerer, A., Spohrer, K.: Inter-team coordination in large agile software development settings: Five ways of practicing agile at scale. In: Proceedings of the Scientific WKSH XP2016. ACM (2016)
16. Bick, S., Spohrer, K., Hoda, R.: Coordination challenges in large-scale software development: a case study of planning misalignment in hybrid settings. IEEE Trans. Softw. Eng. **44**, 932–950 (2018)
17. Bjørnson, F.O., Vestues, K.: Knowledge sharing and process improvement in large-scale agile development. In: Proceedings of the Scientific WKSH XP2016. ACM (2016)
18. Bjørnson, F.O., Wijnmaalen, J., Stettina, C.J., Dingsøyr, T.: Inter-team coordination in large-scale agile development: a case study of three enabling mechanisms. In: Garbajosa, J., Wang, X., Aguiar, A. (eds.) Agile Processes in Software Engineering and Extreme Programming XP2018. LNBIP, vol. 314, pp. 216–231. Springer, Cham (2018)
19. Bosch, J., Bosch-Sijtsema, P.: Coordination between global agile teams: from process to architecture. In: Agility across Time and Space: Implementing Agile Methods in Global Software Projects, pp. 217–233. Springer (2010)
20. Clerc, V., Lago, P., van Vliet, H.: Architectural knowledge management practices in agile global software development. In: Proceedings of the 6th International Conference on Global Software Engineering Workshop, pp. 1–8. IEEE (2011)
21. Daneva, M., et al.: Agile requirements prioritization in large-scale outsourced system projects: an empirical study. J. Syst. Softw. **86**(5), 1333–1353 (2013)

22. Digital AI: 17th annual state of agile report. https://info.digital.ai/rs/981-LQX-968/images/RE-SA-17th-Annual-State-Of-Agile-Report.pdf?version=0 (2023). Accessed 04 Apr 2025
23. Dikert, K., Paasivaara, M., Lassenius, C.: Challenges and success factors for large-scale agile transformations: a systematic literature review. J. Syst. Softw. **119**, 87–108 (2016)
24. Dingsøyr, T., Moe, N.B., Fægri, T.E., Seim, E.A.: Exploring software development at the very large-scale: a revelatory case study and research agenda for agile method adaptation. Emp. Softw. Eng. **23**, 490–520 (2018)
25. Dingsøyr, T., Moe, N.B.: Towards principles of large-scale agile development. In: Dingsøyr, T., Moe, N.B., Tonelli, R., Counsell, S., Gencel, C., Petersen, K. (eds.) Agile Methods. Large-Scale Development, Refactoring, Testing, and Estimation. XP2014. LNBIP, vol. 199, pp. 1–8. Springer, Cham (2014)
26. Dingsøyr, T., Bjørnson, F.O., Schrof, J., Sporsem, T.: A longitudinal explanatory case study of coordination in a very large development programme: the impact of transitioning from a first- to a second-generation large-scale agile development method. Emp. Softw. Eng. **28**(1) (2023)
27. Dingsøyr, T., Moe, N.B., Seim, E.A.: Coordinating knowledge work in multi-team programs: findings from a large-scale agile development program. Project Mgmt. J. **49**(6), 64–77 (2018)
28. Dingsøyr, T., Rolland, K., Moe, N.B., Seim, E.A.: Coordination in multi-team programmes: An investigation of the group mode in large-scale agile software development. In: Procedia Computer Science. vol. 121, pp. 123–128 (2017)
29. Fontana, A., Frey, J.H.: The interview: from structured questions to negotiated text. In: Denzin, N.K., Lincoln, Y.S. (eds.) Handbook of Qualitative Research, pp. 645–672. SAGE, Thousand Oaks, CA, 2nd edn. (2000)
30. Gupta, R.K., Reddy, P.M.: Adapting agile in a globally distributed software development. In: Proceeding of the 49th Hawaii International Conference on System Sciences, pp. 5360–5367. IEEE (2016)
31. Gustavsson, T.: Practices for vertical and horizontal coordination in the scaled agile framework. In: Andersson, B., Johansson, B., Carlsson, S., Barry, C., M. Lang, H.L., Schneider, C. (eds.) Proceeding of 27th International Conference on Information Systems Development AIS (2018)
32. Gustavsson, T.: Dynamics of inter-team coordination routines in large-scale agile software development. In: Proceedings of the 27th European Conference on Information Systems AIS (2019)
33. Gustavsson, T.: Visualizing inter-team coordination. In: Proceedings of the 24th International Conference on Evaluation and Assessment in Software Engineering, pp. 306–311 (2020)
34. Gustavsson, T.: Assigned roles for inter-team coordination in large-scale agile development: a literature review. In: Proceedings of the XP2017 Scientific WKSHs. ACM (2017)
35. Gustavsson, T.: Changes over time in a planned inter-team coordination routine. In: Hoda, R. (ed.) Agile Processes in Software Engineering and Extreme Programming – WKSHs. XP2019. LNBIP vol. 364, pp. 105–111. Springer, Cham (2019)

36. Heikkilä, V., Rautiainen, K., Jansen, S.: A revelatory case study on scaling agile release planning. In: Proceedings of the 36th EUROMICRO Conference on Software Engineering and Advanced Applications, pp. 289–296 (2010)
37. Heikkilä, V.T., Paasivaara, M., Lassenius, C., Damian, D., Engblom, C.: Managing the requirements flow from strategy to release in large-scale agile development: a case study at Ericsson. Emp. Softw. Eng. **22**, 2892–2936 (2017)
38. Herbsleb, J., Roberts, J.: Collaboration in software engineering projects: a theory of coordination. In: Proceedings of International Conference on Information Systems 2006. AIS (2006)
39. Hustad, E., Nakayama, M., Sutcliffe, N., Beckfield, M.: Knowledge mobilization in agile inf. systems projects: a literature analysis. In: Proceedings of the 23rd European Conference on Knowledge Management, pp. 533–541. Acad. Conf.s & Publishing Int. (2022)
40. Ipe, M.: Knowledge sharing in organizations: a conceptual framework. Hum. Resour. Dev. Rev. **2**(4), 337–359 (2003)
41. Kantola, K., Vanhanen, J., Tolvanen, J.: Mind the product owner: an action research project into agile release planning. Inf. Softw. Techn. **147**, 106900 (2022)
42. King, W.R.: Knowledge sharing. In: Encyclopedia of Knowledge Management, pp. 914–923. IGI Global, 2 edn. (2011)
43. Kitchenham, B., Charters, S.: Guidelines for performing systematic literature reviews in software engineering. Tech. rep., School of Computer Science and Mathematics, Keele University, Keele, Staffs, United Kingdom (2007)
44. Kitchenham, B., Pfleeger, S.L.: Principles of survey research: part 5: populations and samples. ACM SIGSOFT Softw. Eng. Notes **27**(5), 17–20 (2002)
45. Kraut, R.E., Streeter, L.A.: Coordination in software development. Commun. ACM **38**(3), 69–82 (1995)
46. Kristensen, S.H., Paasivaara, M.: What added value does a scrum master bring to the organisation?-A case study at Nordea. In: 47th Euromicro Conference on Software Engineering and Advanced Applications, pp. 270–278. IEEE (2021)
47. Kuusinen, K., Gregory, P., Sharp, H., Barroca, L., Taylor, K., Wood, L.: Knowledge sharing in a large agile organisation: a survey study. In: Baumeister, H., Lichter, H., Riebisch, M. (eds.) Agile Processes in Software Engineering and Extreme Programming XP2017. LNBIP, vol. 283, pp. 135–150. Springer, Cham (2017)
48. Liu, Z., Stray, V., Sporsem, T.: Organizational debt in large scale hybrid agile software development: a case study on coordination mechanisms. In: Kruchten, P., Gregory, P. (eds.) Agile Processes in Software Engineering and Extreme Programming – WKSHs. XP2022/23. LNBIP, vol. 489, pp. 75–84. Springer Nature, Cham (2024)
49. Manteli, C., van den Hooff, B., Tang, A., van Vliet, H.: The impact of multi-site software governance on knowledge management. In: Proceedings of the 6th International Conference on Global Software Engineering, pp. 40–49. IEEE (2011)
50. Martini, A., Pareto, L., Bosch, J.: A multiple case study on the inter-group interaction speed in large, embedded software companies employing agile. J. Softw. Evol. Process. **28**(1), 4–26 (2016)
51. Melo, C., Cruzes, D.S., Kon, F., Conradi, R.: Interpretative case studies on agile team productivity and management. Inf. Softw. Techn. **55**(2), 412–427 (2013)
52. Miles, M.B., Huberman, A.M., Saldaña, J.: Qualitative Data Analysis: A Methods Sourcebook, 4th edn. SAGE, Thousand Oaks, CA (2019)

53. Moe, N.B., Dingsøyr, T., Rolland, K.: To schedule or not to schedule? An investigation of meetings as an inter-team coordination mechanism in large-scale agile software development. Int. J. Inf. Syst. Proj. Mgmt. **6**(3), 45–59 (2018)
54. Moe, N.B., Šmite, D., Börjesson, A.L., Andréasson, P.: Networking in a large-scale distributed agile project. In: Proceedings of the 8th International Symposium on Empirical Software Engineering and Measurement, pp. 1–8 (2014)
55. Moorman, C., Miner, A.S.: Organizational improvisation and organizational memory. Acad. Mgmt. Rev. **23**(4), 698–723 (1998)
56. Myers, M.D., Newman, M.: The qualitative interview in is research: examining the craft. Inf. Organ. **17**(1), 2–26 (2007)
57. Narayanan, N., Joglekar, N., Eppinger, S.: Improving scaled agile with multi-domain matrix. In: Proceedings of the 23rd International DSM Conference, pp. 70–84 (2021)
58. Nyrud, H., Stray, V.: Inter-team coordination mechanisms in large-scale agile. In: Proceedings of the XP2017 Scientific WKSHs. ACM (2017)
59. Olsen, J.O., Stray, V., Moe, N.B.: Business development in large-scale agile software development: barriers and enablers. In: Agile Processes in Software Engineering and Extreme Programming – WKSHs. XP2022/23. LNBIP, vol. 489. Springer Nature (2024)
60. Oosterhout, M.V., Waarts, E., Hillegersberg, J.V.: Change factors requiring agility and implications for it. Europ. J. Inf. Syst. **15**, 132–145 (2006)
61. Paasivaara, M., Lassenius, C.: Communities of practice in a large distributed agile software development organization-case Ericsson. Inf. Softw. Techn. **56**(12), 1556–1577 (2014)
62. Paasivaara, M., Lassenius, C., Heikkilä, V.T.: Inter-team coordination in large-scale globally distributed scrum: do scrum-of-scrums really work? In: Proceedings of the International Symposium on Empirical Software Engineering and Measurement, pp. 235–238 (2012)
63. Pries-Heje, L., Pries-Heje, J.: Why scrum works: a case study from an agile distributed project in Denmark and India. In: Proceedings of the 2011 Agile Conference, pp. 20–28. IEEE (2011)
64. Razzak, M.A.: Knowledge management in globally distributed agile projects–lesson learned. In: IEEE 10th International Conference on Global Software Engineering, pp. 81–89. IEEE (2015)
65. Rolland, K.H.: Scaling across knowledge boundaries: a case study of a large-scale agile software development project. In: Proceedings of the Scientific WKSH XP2016
66. Rolland, K.H., Fitzgerald, B., Dingsøyr, T., Stol, K.J.: Acrobats and safety nets: problematizing large-scale agile software development. ACM Trans. Softw. Eng. Method. **33**(2), 1–45 (2023)
67. Rus, I., Lindvall, M., Sinha, S.: Knowledge management in software engineering. IEEE Softw. **19**(3), 26–38 (2002)
68. Saeeda, H., Ahmad, M.O., Gustavsson, T.: Exploring process debt in large-scale agile software development for secure telecom solutions. In: Proceedings of the 7th ACM/IEEE International Conference on Technical Debt, pp. 11–20 (2024)
69. Saeeda, H., Ovais Ahmad, M., Gustavsson, T.: Navigating social debt and its link with technical debt in large-scale agile software development projects. Softw. Qual. J. 1–33 (2024)
70. Saldaña, J.: The Coding Manual for Qualitative Researchers, 4th edn. SAGE, Thousand Oaks, CA (2021)

71. Santos, V., Goldman, A., Guerra, E., Souza, C.D., Sharp, H.: A pattern language for inter-team knowledge sharing in agile software development. In: Proceedings of the 20th Conference on Pattern Languages of Programs (2013)
72. Santos, V., Goldman, A., Souza, C.: Fostering effective inter-team knowledge sharing in agile software development. Emp. Softw. Eng. **20**, 1006–1051 (2015)
73. Scheerer, A., Hildenbrand, T., Kude, T.: Coordination in large-scale agile software development: a multiteam systems perspective. In: Proceedings of the 47th Hawaii International Conference on System Sciences, pp. 4780–4788. IEEE (2014)
74. Schmidtner, M., Doering, C., Timinger, H.: Agile working during COVID-19 pandemic. IEEE Eng. Mgmt. Rev. **49**(2), 18–32 (2021)
75. Seaman, C.B.: Qualitative methods in empirical studies of software engineering. IEEE Trans. Softw. Eng. **25**(4), 557–572 (1999)
76. Sekitoleko, N., Evbota, F., Knauss, E., Sandberg, A., Chaudron, M., Olsson, H.H.: Technical dependency challenges in large-scale agile software development. In: Cantone, G., Marchesi, M. (eds.) Agile Processes in Software Engineering and Extreme Programming XP2014. LNBIP, vol. 179, pp. 46–61. Springer, Cham (2014)
77. Šmite, D., Dingsøyr, T.: Fostering cross-site coordination through awareness: an investigation of state-of-the-practice through a focus group study. In: Proceedings of the 38th Euromicro Conference on Software Engineering and Advanced Applications, pp. 337–344. IEEE (2012)
78. Šmite, D., Moe, N.B., Floryan, M., Gonzalez-Huerta, J., Dorner, M., Sablis, A.: Decentralized decision-making and scaled autonomy at Spotify. J. Syst. Softw. **200**, 111649 (2023)
79. Šmite, D., Moe, N.B., Levinta, G., Floryan, M.: Spotify guilds: how to succeed with knowledge sharing in large-scale agile organizations. IEEE Softw. **36**(2), 51–57 (2019)
80. Šmite, D., Moe, N.B., Šāblis, A., Wohlin, C.: Software teams and their knowledge networks in large-scale software development. Inf. Softw. Techn. **86**, 71–86 (2017)
81. Šmite, D., Moe, N.B., Hildrum, J., Gonzalez-Huerta, J., Mendez, D.: Work-from-home is here to stay: call for flexibility in post-pandemic work policies. J. Syst. Softw. **195**, 111552 (2023)
82. Spagnoletti, P., Kazemargi, N., Prencipe, A.: Agile practices and organizational agility in software ecosystems. IEEE Trans. Eng. Mgmt. **69**(6), 3604–3617 (2021)
83. Sporsem, T., Moe, N.B.: Coordination strategies when working from anywhere: a case study of two agile teams. In: Stray, V., Stol, K.J., Paasivaara, M., Kruchten, P. (eds.) Agile Processes in Software Engineering and Extreme Programming XP2022. LNBIP, vol. 445, pp. 52–61. Springer, Cham (2022)
84. Stray, V., Moe, N.B., Aasheim, A.: Dependency management in large-scale agile: a case study of devops teams. In: Proceedings of the 52nd Hawaii International Conference on System Sciences, pp. 7007–7016 (2019)
85. Stray, V., Moe, N.B., Strode, D., Mæhlum, E.: Coordination value in agile software development: a multiple case study of coordination mechanisms managing dependencies. In: Proceedings of the 15th International Workshop on Cooperative and Human Aspects of Software Engineering, pp. 11–20 (2022)
86. Stray, V., Moe, N.B., Vedal, H., Berntzen, M.: Using objectives and key results (OKRs) and slack: a case study of coordination in large-scale distributed agile, pp. 7360–7369 (2023)

87. Szabó, D.M., Steghöfer, J.P.: Coping strategies for temporal, geographical, and sociocultural distances in agile GSD: a case study. In: Proceedings of the 41st International Conference on Software Engineering: Software Engineering in Practice, pp. 117–126. IEEE (2019)
88. Tobisch, F., Matthes, F.: Supplementary material. https://doi.org/10.6084/m9.figshare.28705322 (2025). Accessed 04 Apr 2025
89. Tsai, W.: Social structure of "coopetition" within a multiunit organization: coordination, competition, and intraorganizational knowledge sharing. Organ. Sci. **13**(2), 179–190 (2002)
90. Uludağ, Ö., Harders, N.M., Matthes, F.: Documenting recurring concerns and patterns in large-scale agile development. In: Proceedings of the 24th European Conference on Pattern Languages of Programs, pp. 1–17 (2019)
91. Uludağ, Ö., Matthes, F.: Investigating the role of enterprise architects in supporting large-scale agile transformations: a multiple-case study. In: Proceedings of the Americas Conference on Information Systems. 2020. AIS (2020)
92. Van de Ven, A.H., Delbecq, A.L., Jr, R.K.: Determinants of coordination modes within organizations. Am. Soc. Rev. 322–338 (1976)
93. Van Wessel, R.M., Kroon, P., Vries, H.: Scaling agile company-wide: the organizational challenge of combining agile-scaling frameworks and enterprise architecture in service companies. IEEE Trans. on Eng. Mgmt. **69**(6), 3489–3502 (2021)
94. Vedal, H., Stray, V., Berntzen, M., Moe, N.B.: Managing dependencies in large-scale agile. In: Gregory, P., Kruchten, P. (eds.) Agile Processes in Software Engineering and Extreme Programming – WKSHs. XP2021. LNBIP, vol. 426, pp. 52–61. Springer, Cham (2021)
95. Vlietland, J., van Vliet, H.: Towards a governance framework for chains of scrum teams. Inf. Softw. Techn. **57**, 52–65 (2015)
96. Webster, J., Watson, R.T.: Analyzing the past to prepare for the future: writing a literature review. MIS Quarterly, pp. xiii–xxiii (2002)
97. Wihayanti, T., Lubis, M., Fakrurroja, H.: Optimizing knowledge sharing in agile organization: a systematic literature review of strategies, challenges, and opportunities. In: Selected Papers of the 10th International Conference on E-Business and Applications, pp. 108–119. Springer (2024)
98. Xu, P.: Coordination in large agile projects. Rev. Bus. Inf. Syst. **13**(4) (2009)
99. Zahedi, M., Shahin, M., Babar, M.A.: A systematic review of knowledge sharing challenges and practices in global software development. Int. J. Inf. Mgmt. **36**(6), 995–1019 (2016)
100. Zhou, X., Jin, Y., Zhang, H., Li, S., Huang, X.: A map of threats to validity of systematic literature reviews in software engineering. In: Proceedings of the 23rd Asia-Pacific Software Engineering Conference, pp. 153–160. IEEE (2016)

Open Access This chapter is licensed under the terms of the Creative Commons Attribution 4.0 International License (http://creativecommons.org/licenses/by/4.0/), which permits use, sharing, adaptation, distribution and reproduction in any medium or format, as long as you give appropriate credit to the original author(s) and the source, provide a link to the Creative Commons license and indicate if changes were made.

The images or other third party material in this chapter are included in the chapter's Creative Commons license, unless indicated otherwise in a credit line to the material. If material is not included in the chapter's Creative Commons license and your intended use is not permitted by statutory regulation or exceeds the permitted use, you will need to obtain permission directly from the copyright holder.

Investigating User-Side Representatives in Large-Scale Agile Software Development

Morteza Moalagh[✉] [iD], Vegard Svesengen [iD], and Babak A. Farshchian [iD]

Department of Computer Science, Norwegian University of Science and Technology (NTNU), Trondheim, Norway
{morteza.moalagh,babak.farshchian}@ntnu.no

Abstract. User involvement is critical in large-scale agile software development. User representatives bridge access gaps and align development teams with user expectations. However, research primarily focuses on development-side user representatives like product owners or user experience designers, overlooking user-side representatives who bring practical expertise and bridge communication between users and development teams. This highlights a gap in understanding user-side representatives' roles in large-scale agile software development for fostering effective collaboration. In this paper, we ask the following research question: What are the roles, responsibilities, and challenges of user-side representatives in large-scale agile software development? We conducted an exploratory case study within a large public organization using interviews, focus groups, and document analysis to answer this. We investigated two established user-side representative roles: implementation coordinators and change agents. In our distributed case organization, implementation coordinators serve as county-level contact points, overseeing planning, coordination, training, and follow-up of software release implementation. Based in local offices, change agents facilitate requirements elicitation, test software quality, train users, share knowledge, and handle user requests. These roles enhance communication of user needs, support alignment between development and user requirements, and complement development-side user representatives. These findings contribute to a deeper understanding of user involvement in large-scale, distributed agile software development.

Keywords: User Involvement · User Representatives · User-Side Representatives · Large-Scale Agile Software Development · Implementation Coordinator · Change Agent

1 Introduction

Agile software development (ASD) is fundamentally about tight collaboration with the customer and user to deliver usable software. Therefore, user involvement is a cornerstone of ASD to ensure that the developed software aligns with user needs [1]. Schon et al. [2] demonstrate that prioritizing user involvement leads to precise requirements gathering, ultimately improving system success. User involvement is enabled by techniques such as user stories and participatory design workshops in ASD [3]. User involvement is equally or even more important in large-scale ASD. Lage-scale ASD frameworks like SAFe and LeSS advocate iterative feedback to adapt to evolving user needs [4]. However, user involvement with multiple development teams is complex and costly as the number and diversity of users increase [5]. For instance, our case organization has more than 100 agile teams located in Oslo. In contrast, their user organization includes 22,000 employees –internal users –distributed across more than 450 offices throughout Norway. Practicing ASD in such large, distributed organizations means the developed software will target varied users with differing requirements.

Despite its importance, research on user involvement in large-scale ASD is scarce as researchers have focused on developer practices. While scalability challenges have led to the inception of several coordination frameworks for large-scale ASD [6, 7], some of these frameworks isolate users from critical design and implementation phases, limiting involvement in key decisions and diminishing their visibility [8].

In this paper, we unpack the concept of user involvement in large-scale ASD by analytically distinguishing between what we call development-side user representatives (DRs) and user-side representatives (URs). DRs are often members of the development team. Product owners (POs), domain experts, and user experience (UX) designers are typical DRs in an agile team. Large-scale ASD has led to an explosion of DR responsibilities. Maruping and Matook [9], investigated the DR role in a large-scale organization, describing their key responsibilities as managing requirements, ensuring quality, liaising with organizational stakeholders, and fostering trust between development teams and the user organization. As a consequence of these multiple and often contradicting expectations, DRs are criticized for favoring development team needs over users, potentially reducing user involvement in large-scale ASD [10].

On the other hand, URs are not members of the development team but are practitioners on the user side. Some examples are super users, expert users, and champions [11]. Their involvement can significantly enhance the relevance and usability of the software by ensuring that context-specific requirements are handled during development [12]. However, UR involvement in large-scale ASD faces challenges such as limited availability, lack of technical expertise, and organizational constraints [13]. Unlike DRs, which have been studied extensively, URs have received less attention from software engineering researchers [11].

In this paper, we investigate the UR role by posing the following research question: ***What are the roles, responsibilities, and challenges of user-side representatives in large-scale agile software development?*** We address this question through an explorative case study conducted in the Norwegian Labour and Welfare Administration (NAV). NAV is a large public service organization that implemented large-scale ASD in its in-house software development. This organization has internal and external users of its services. In this article, when talking about the users, we mean internal users like counselors and case workers using NAV systems for case management.

NAV has a semi-formal and evolving infrastructure for using URs in user involvement. This infrastructure is what we have investigated in our study. Based on 16 interviews, one focus group, and document reviews, the study highlights how established UR roles in NAV, like implementation coordinators (ICs) and change agents (CAs), collaborate with each other and product development teams. URs have different responsibilities ranging from planning and coordination to participation in development, user training, and leading organizational change. This study contributes to a better understanding of URs and their role in large-scale ASD by providing empirical evidence from an advanced form of UR organization in the real world.

2 Background

2.1 User Involvement in Large-Scale Agile Software Development

Large-scale ASD has gained prominence as organizations adapt to evolving market dynamics and address the complexities of modern systems. Since ASD was first developed for small, co-located teams, the term "Large-Scale" is now often used to refer to projects that have several cooperating teams, complex dependencies, lengthy project durations, and team members that are spread out geographically [14]. Large-scale ASD faces challenges in maintaining direct user involvement due to organizational layers, distributed teams, and conflicting stakeholder priorities. These barriers challenge Agile principles like continuous feedback and collaboration [8]. Therefore, it might be difficult to ensure that software satisfies user needs [4, 13].

Despite several studies demonstrating the benefits of user involvement in large ASD, numerous organizations fail to properly apply it [15]. Tam et al. [16] show that one significant hurdle is a lack of user availability, which limits their ability to participate in iterative design and feedback processes. Furthermore, users frequently lack the competence or communication skills required to participate effectively in ASD processes like user story prioritization and backlog refinement [2]. Organizations also have trouble balancing the expectations of development teams and users, which might lead to decreased effectiveness of user involvement [17]. Furthermore, in their systematic literature review, Dikert et al. [18], demonstrate that the fast-paced nature of large-scale ASD projects frequently favors delivery speed over robust user involvement, resulting in gaps in user feedback throughout important stages of development. Finally, cultural resistance and challenges of collaboration between the development side and the user side of organizations might inhibit teams from involving users, even when research suggests they are effective [19].

2.2 User Representatives in Large-Scale Agile Software Development

User involvement in large-scale ASD is challenging; therefore, various mechanisms, such as implementing user involvement practices and assigning roles as user representatives, have been introduced to address this issue [7, 20]. Practices such as user stories, participatory design workshops, scaled-scrum, and iterative feedback sessions and cycles enable teams to refine designs and improve usability [13]. User stories are widely used in large-scale ASD to capture requirements and enable iterative adjustments. However, they are often criticized for being utilized more as tools to measure team performance rather than genuinely fostering effective user involvement [21]. Moreover, large-scale ASD frameworks incorporate techniques and methods to enhance user involvement, such as Nexus's scrum of scrums and SAFe's program increment planning. As Edison et al. [4] stated, these frameworks employ iterative review cycles and collaborative prioritization mechanisms to facilitate meaningful user involvement. However, some of these approaches can be challenging, as they may distance development teams from users, potentially reducing the emphasis on user experience.

User representatives sometimes referred to as customer representatives in the literature, are a key mechanism for involving users in large-scale ASD [9]. These representatives can take on consultative and participative roles, empowering users by ensuring their requirements are met during the development process [22]. One primary category of user representatives originates from the development side of the organization, referred to in this paper as Development-side User Representatives (DRs). Key roles within this category include product owners (POs), domain experts, designers, and user experience (UX) experts, who are identified as critical contributors to bridging the gap between users and development teams in large-scale ASD [23].

Maruping and Matook's theoretical model describes DRs as dynamic, multi-oriented individuals who balance stakeholder expectations and project constraints through responsibilities such as managing requirements, ensuring quality, liaising with stakeholders, and fostering trust within the development team and organization [9]. Martin et al. further introduced the concept of customer-focused coaches as DR roles, emphasizing their responsibility to collaborate with customers, address challenges, and ensure that users feel valued and supported [24]. Similarly, POs are highlighted as pivotal figures in maintaining feedback loops, prioritizing backlogs, and aligning stakeholder expectations with project goals [10, 25]. Despite their importance, DR roles are criticized for prioritizing development team needs over user expectations, potentially weakening user-centricity in large-scale ASD [10].

The second category of user representatives in large-scale ASD comprises individuals directly sourced from the user side, referred to as URs in this paper. Roles such as super users, expert users, and champion users in the literature are among the roles in this category [11]. Unlike DRs, URs contribute practical expertise and contextual knowledge from their daily interactions with the system. Their involvement can significantly enhance the relevance and usability of the software by ensuring that user requirements are addressed effectively during development [12]. In the software engineering literature, URs have been used in some methods, such as end-user development, but in large-scale ASD, less attention has been paid to the role [11]. Therefore, this study examines this role, its responsibilities, and challenges in large-scale ASD.

3 Research Method

Given the exploratory nature of our research and our aim to understand ongoing phenomena while generating new ideas, we adopted an exploratory case study research strategy [26, 27]. This strategy investigates the context deeply, uncovering patterns and generating insights [28]. This section outlines components of the exploratory case study strategy in this research: the case organization, data collection techniques, and data analysis approach.

3.1 Case Description

The Norwegian Labour and Welfare Administration (Abbreviated as "NAV" in Norwegian language) serves as Norway's central hub for labor and welfare services. With

22,000 employees, NAV provides social and financial services to citizens. With its headquarters (NAV Directorate) in Oslo, NAV oversees 12 county offices ("Fylke" in Norwegian), which coordinate and support 456 NAV local offices in the whole country. These offices, delivering integrated welfare services, range from 20 to over 200 employees in size [29]. NAV Initially relied on external vendors for digitalization between 2006 and 2016 [30]. In 2016, under new leadership, NAV shifted its strategy from outsourcing to insourcing and adopting ASD practices [31]. In 2019, NAV's IT department adopted a product development structure, expanding to approximately 800 employees across eight distinct product areas. This approach increased the frequency of weekly releases and resulted in the creation of over 2,600 code repositories [32]. NAV's success in implementing ASD gained notable recognition, earning the digitalization prize in Norway's public sector [33].

3.2 Data Collection and Analysis

Data Collection. Case studies use qualitative data for a nuanced understanding of complex phenomena and triangulation methods to enhance credibility and minimize bias [34]. In this study, we used semi-structured interviews with internal users from two different NAV counties. We also interviewed participants from three product development teams of two product areas. We aimed to explore two main themes: (1) the collaboration of user-side representatives, such as implementation coordinators (ICs) or change agents (CAs), with other stakeholders, and (2) their roles in the ASD process. 16 interviews were conducted for this study, each lasting between 60 and 120 min. The interview questions were adapted to align with the specific activities of each participant group. Additionally, we conducted a focus group interview (90 min, 22 participants) with all ICs nationwide to discuss collaboration with product development teams and users in local offices. Finally, we analyzed documents, including NAV public reports, strategic documents, and the NAV website, revealing NAV's strategic priorities and the context of organizational change. Table 1 details the data sources. To ensure confidentiality, participants were assigned unique codes (e.g., P1, P2), and specific details about product development teams, ICs, and CAs (like age, years of experience, ...), and local office locations were excluded from the table to prevent identification or inference.

Data Analysis. We used an abductive thematic analysis approach to analyze the data. This method combines inductive and deductive reasoning by establishing connections between empirical data and existing theoretical concepts [35]. By iteratively comparing observations with established frameworks, abductive analysis promotes deeper understanding while maintaining theoretical rigor. This study adhered to Jamie Thompson's eight-step guideline for abductive thematic analysis [36]. Interview recordings, including those conducted in Norwegian, were transcribed, translated into English, and imported into NVivo software along with relevant documents. Using the UR as a unit of analysis, Open coding was employed to identify concepts and patterns, focusing more on responsibilities and stakeholder interactions. A codebook was developed, and themes were created by grouping related codes. For instance, codes like "testing and evaluating software during development" and "acceptance testing of software" formed the theme "Empowering User Voices in Design and Testing." This iterative process involved multiple revisions to ensure the themes accurately represented the codes and supported the study's phenomena. The thematic analysis also linked findings to theories while addressing theoretical gaps.

Table 1. Data Sources

Data Source	Details	#
Semi-Structured Interview	Implementation Coordinators (P1-P3)	16
	Change Agents (P4-P10)	
	Product Leaders (P11-P13)	
	Technical Lead (P14-P15)	
	Domain Expert (P16)	
Focus Group Interview	Network of all implementation coordinators in the NAV with 22 participants (G1)	1
Documents	NAV public reports, Strategic documents, and the NAV website	5

4 Findings

This section presents findings addressing the roles and responsibilities of URs within the studied organization (NAV), describes their responsibilities, and highlights challenges. Pertinent quotations from interviews serve as supporting evidence.

4.1 User Representatives Roles and Network in NAV

Within NAV, product development teams are responsible for the complete ASD process. These teams include several specialized roles, such as product leaders, developers, designers, domain experts, and agile leads. Their main tasks are gathering user requirements, developing and testing functionalities, supporting users, and solving technical issues. Although user involvement is essential to ASD, NAV's large size and geographic distribution create challenges for consistent user involvement. While product leaders and designers primarily manage user involvement, this work is further supported by two semi-formally established roles on the user side: Implementation Coordinators (ICs) and Change Agents (CAs).

The role of an IC is a full-time position at the county level within NAV. The IC coordinates a community of CAs comprising members from the local NAV offices within the respective county. The position is filled through a formal application process, which includes the submission of a resume and participation in an interview. Each county typically has one or two ICs, depending on the population size and the breadth of work within the county. They cooperate closely with the product development teams in the IT department from one side and local offices in different cities in their county from the other side: *"I think our role is to be a connection between what's made and who is doing the task at hand. So we're trying to funnel down the information and be the connection between the offices and the directorate and also to coordinate our region in this"* [P2, Implementation Coordinator].

CAs, the second established UR role in NAV, are typically counselors or caseworkers who assist citizens, follow up on cases, and ensure legal compliance. Appointed by local office leaders, they take on a part-time role to collaborate with users, ICs, and product development teams. Each local NAV office has at least one CA, and the large local offices have one per department: *"The change agent role is about being updated on what is coming and what has recently come of new things. There is an agile development that continuously provides new systems and programs. So, my task is to facilitate and train my co-workers in the office or department on new systems or releases"* [P8, Change Agent].

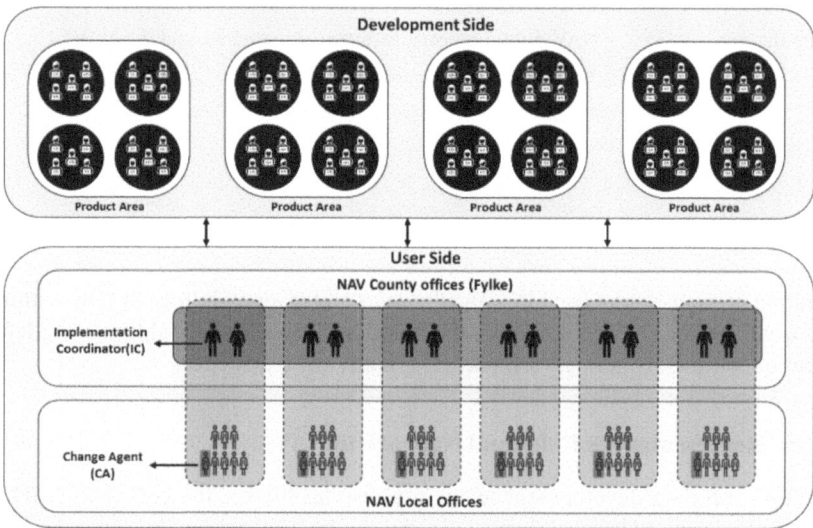

Fig. 1. UR Roles and Networks in NAV

ICs maintain an active network to collaborate and share knowledge via digital tools like Microsoft Teams. This network (See Fig. 1), which is managed centrally by NAV, benefits the company by enabling product development teams to demo products, gather feedback nationwide, and receive county-specific perspectives through ICs as local representatives: *"If you're talking about the network itself or the cause, the big benefit is having different product teams come and present their work and give us their status and sort of update on the direction the organization is taking"* [P1, Implementation Coordinator]. Moreover, CAs and ICs maintain county-level networks via digital tools like Microsoft Teams for coordination, updates, support each other, and knowledge sharing: *"We have created a network, so last week, we had meetings with all the NAV leaders (local office leaders). There are [...] of offices in our region, and we have divided them into seven sorts of regional groups"* [P3, Implementation Coordinator].

4.2 Implementation Coordinators (ICs) Responsibilities

Planning and Leading the Implementation of Large Software Releases. Focusing on continuous releases, product development teams in different product areas release new features each week. If the release is a small one (minor enhancements, bug fixes, or small feature updates), ICs just share the information with CAs, But if the release is large (major features, architectural updates, or system-wide improvements), then it needs to be planned, and users must receive training: *"This network (ICs and CAs in the county) is going to develop a workshop that they are going to bring back to their offices. We are training or learning something new together, and they will take it back to the area and have a workshop there"* [P3, Implementation Coordinator].

Monitoring New Work Processes. As the change leader in their county, ICs are also responsible for establishing new work processes and realizing the value of developed features. They are not only directing the implementation of software systems but also have a critical role in following up and monitoring how new features are used in the local offices: *"It's like, you know, they are just smoothly implemented in their everyday work, and we are monitoring how much they are using and, of course, doing some samples like, was this useful for you? Do you remember this new feature?"* [P2, Implementation Coordinator].

Communicate and Follow up with Different Stakeholders. ICs attend numerous meetings daily and check different communication channels. Meetings range from product demo sessions with product development teams to follow-up meetings on implementation progress or product training and support with various local offices: *"We usually have meetings with the NAV director and someone with the local offices. So mostly meetings, and yeah, I think that's a typical day"* [P3, Implementation Coordinator].

Facilitate Resource Acquisition for Different Product Development Teams. ICs enhance communication between product development teams and local offices and use their understanding of personnel and procedures to assist with user recruitment for different activities in software development: *"For example, they have asked me for three co-workers who have worked under one year. Then, there were another three co-workers who had worked for over three years. To find out how they work differently, how they find information, etc. Then, they interviewed them qualitatively..."* [P1, Implementation Coordinator].

4.3 Change Agents (CAs) Responsibilities

User Advocacy in Requirements Management. In a large and diverse organization like NAV, it is challenging to elicit user requirements. To address this, product development teams leverage CAs as advocates for the broader user community. Through this approach, CAs assist in eliciting requirements on behalf of a diverse group of users: *"And when the developers create a new digital solution, they have perspectives from their backgrounds. At the same time, we users of the systems have different needs and want to make changes that will help the optimal function of a program. So it is important and good for us to be involved"* [P5, Change Agent]. CAs also assist product development teams in setting priorities. Based on their experience with product teams, they attempt to mediate user expectations and development goals: *"I think how we are involved in development is good enough. It is not supposed to be our main job, but we have good opportunities to report wishes and requests. Moreover, we can see in the deployed systems that our requests have been seen and heard."* [P4, Change Agent].

Empowering User Voices in Design and Testing. In the NAV, with thousands of diverse internal users around the country, collecting user feedback during sprints is very difficult before releasing the feature. Therefore, some product development teams use the potential of CAs by having bi-weekly or monthly meetings to show the under-development features and get their feedback: *"So, we invite all (CAs) to see our latest developments. They usually have a lot of viewpoints, which are usually a bit formed by the previous system; we usually get a lot of value from"* [P14, Technical Lead]. Sometimes, product development teams during the sprints contact CAs and request a meeting to review the features being developed: *"We will share a screen, and we will talk with them (CAs) through then. We will ask one of them to take an actual case. A real-life case, and then we toggle on the functionality, and they try it out in a real-life case and see if it works."* [P13, Product Leader]. CAs also collaborate with product development teams in the pilot tests before the organization's widespread implementation of software releases: *"We had five pilot offices testing the solution over almost four months. We started the pilots with informational meetings and talked about our expectations. They had the opportunity to ask questions, and we held a demo"* [P16, Domain Expert].

Train and Implement Large Software Releases in the Local Offices. NAV adopts a "train-the-trainer" approach, where CAs receive instruction from ICs or materials, master new software, and subsequently train colleagues: *"We get courses or training programs, with some documents or maybe power points of how a solution will be when it is finished. Then that is my responsibility to present to my office, and I can decide how to approach it."* [P5, Change Agent]. For training users, some CAs in some local offices employ practices such as "Digi workshop". These practices involve dedicating a week to addressing particular challenges identified by CA: *"We have tried to run what we call" Digi workshop" every other week. This is something we do locally in the office. We try to identify what is new and what our co-workers are struggling with beforehand and then have a workshop."* [P7, Change Agent].

Adopting Users with New Work Processes. In NAV, one of the responsibilities of CAs is to ensure users adapt to new work processes. This task is challenging for product development teams in large, distributed organizations. However, CAs' local presence and user relationships facilitate this process: *"I can see the way people use the different systems. Even though we have the required search functions in Modia (system for unemployment welfare services), we still have people opening Arena (legacy system for unemployment welfare services) to search for the person, copying their national ID number. They paste it into the other system, Modia. So there might not be enough focus on changing the whole work process, rather than just learning the new system."* [P7, Change Agent].

Communicate and Follow up with Product Development Teams. In NAV, CAs communicate with product development teams to stay informed about recent changes or address challenges in implementing new features: *"Every 3rd week, I also meet all of the representatives from all of the offices of the caseworkers, and I want to make sure that then one level office informed about what I'm saying to one level beneath before I do that. So the information flows well, and then the goal is just, I mean, the goal in all of the meetings is just to say what kind of things we are working on"* [P12, Product Leader]. CAs also submit user requests on behalf of their local office for product development teams and follow up with them: *"It is my job to bring user requests from our domain, which we believe will help us work more efficiently. The people who develop the systems have not worked within our subject or domain before. So we are the most experienced in knowing how to work most efficiently"* [P8, Change Agent].

4.4 Challenges of User-Side Representatives in Large-Scale ASD

Motivating Users to Adopt New Work Processes. Although ICs and CAs are responsible for adopting new work processes within NAV, this responsibility presents significant challenges. In particular, ICs often face difficulties in encouraging users to adopt and effectively utilize the newly released features, highlighting the complexities of user involvement in large-scale ASD: *"Some of the users could do their job without using the new features; it has no consequence. But the question is this: how can we make the process work better? Then we need to motivate them"* [G1, One Implementation Coordinator in Focus Group Interview]. Particularly, long-standing employees who have developed established work processes over the years are more challenged to adopt new ones: *"If you have done the same things and handled the same type of cases for 15 years, and then you are suddenly told to do it in a new way, but you are still doing the same thing, that can be frustrating for people…So they usually use a long time to transition to the new ways"* [P5, Change Agent].

Communicate with Different Stakeholders via Multiple Channels. Some ICs are concerned about communicating in multiple channels daily, as their role demands responding to diverse stakeholders across various communication channels: *"We have a job to work in different communication channels. We have many channels, which makes it challenging. Therefore, people become more concerned with where they communicate than what they communicate!"* [G1, One Implementation Coordinator in Focus Group Interview].

Disagreement Between CAs and Product Development Teams in Prioritizing Requirements. While product development teams rely on input from CAs to prioritize requirements, this collaboration can sometimes create conflict. Product development teams balance the organization's strategic goals with users' needs and perspectives. This balancing act might create tensions, making the collaborative dynamic between the two more complex: *"When we are doing software development, we have two main perspectives which are important. One of the perspectives is the strategy and the objectives we have from the state level in our product area. It is very important for NAV (at the state level) that we prioritize getting out of the legacy system we have. Then, it is the other perspective. How does what we create work for the people we create it for, which is the bottom-up approach. Our primary user group is the counsellors at local offices, right?"* [P11, Product Leader].

5 Discussion

In this section, we investigate the research question: **What are the roles, responsibilities, and challenges of user-side representatives in large-scale Agile Software Development?** Our findings highlight the roles, responsibilities, and challenges of established user-side representatives (URs) in the studied organization (NAV), providing theoretical insights and practical implications for large-scale ASD.

5.1 Implications for Theory

Highlight User-side Representative Roles. The findings (summarized in Table 2) contribute to large-scale ASD literature by highlighting implementation coordinators (ICs) and change agents (CAs) as user-side representatives supporting user involvement. These semi-formally established roles in the studied organization support product development teams in large-scale and distributed ASD. ICs act as intermediaries between product development teams and local offices, plan and lead implementations, monitor new work processes, communicate with different stakeholders, and facilitate resource acquisition for different product development teams. This aligns with Zorzetti et al. [15], who highlight the value of structured user involvement in improving software usability in large-scale ASD. CAs complement this by serving as advocates for diverse user groups, empowering user voices in design and testing, training users in local offices, adopting new work processes, and communicating and following up with product development teams, consistent with Tam et al. [16], who emphasize the importance of user involvement in agile success.

ICs and CAs address availability issues by involving users through structured processes, such as training sessions and regular feedback mechanisms, which align with Buchan et al. [17], who stress the need for robust user involvement strategies. These roles also mitigate communication barriers and foster alignment between geographically dispersed users, addressing challenges identified by Dikert et al. [18], regarding inter-team coordination in large-scale Agile contexts. These findings also complement the work of Klemets and Storholmen [11], on using super users as URs in ASD by introducing the roles, responsibilities, and organizational arrangements of URs within large, distributed organizations. By introducing ICs and CAs as distinct roles, this empirical research complements existing literature while providing actionable insights for improving user involvement in large-scale ASD.

Complement Development-Side Representatives (DRs) in Large-Scale ASD. URs, such as ICs and CAs, complement DRs, including POs and UX designers, in large-scale ASD. DRs or customer representatives, as described by Maruping and Matook [9], are primarily responsible for eliciting and prioritizing requirements, managing backlogs, testing software capabilities, and facilitating communication with stakeholders. However, in large and geographically dispersed organizations, direct contact with users is challenging for DRs, which can hinder their ability to address specific user needs. In contrast, URs like ICs and CAs maintain close interactions with users, providing real-time feedback and addressing their challenges. Together, DRs ensure strategic alignment and technical coordination, while URs represent user perspectives, making this dual-role

Table 2 - UR Roles and Responsibilities in NAV

Role	Description	Responsibilities
Implementation Coordinator (IC)	• Full-time role • Selected through a formal recruitment process • County level • Have an active community with other ICs in the country	• Planning and leading the implementation of large software releases • Monitoring new work processes • Communicate and follow up with different stakeholders • Facilitate resource acquisition for different product development teams
Change Agent (CA)	• Part-time role • Appointed by local office leaders • Local office level • Have an active community with ICs and other CAs in their county	• User advocacy in requirements management • Empowering user voices in design and testing • Train and implement large software releases in the local offices • Adopting users with new work processes • Communicate and follow up with product development teams

approach ideal for balancing organizational goals with user involvement in large-scale ASD.

Challenges of URs in Large-Scale ASD. Introducing UR roles may be accompanied by certain challenges. 1) The challenge ICs and CAs face in adopting users, particularly long-standing users, to new work processes—despite their close relationships with users—aligns with the findings of Dikert et al. [18], that resistance in large-scale ASD may driven by the "top-down mandate of changes" by organizational leadership, implemented without sufficient user involvement or justification. This challenge persists despite roles fostering user involvement, highlighting the complexity of overcoming resistance in large-scale ASD. 2) The issue of ICs managing communication across multiple channels relates to the findings of Edison et al. [4], on the challenge of "synchronizing across dynamic and fast-moving teams" during inter-team coordination. This indicates that communication challenges are not limited to the development side but could extend to the user side in large-scale ASD. 3) Conflicts between URs and DRs in prioritizing requirements align with the findings of Kasauli et al. [13], that "frequency of dependencies" complicates the prioritization process. These insights suggest that while introducing URs in large-scale ASD might offer potential benefits, it might also create new conflicts.

5.2 Implications for Practice

Formalizing and Empowering UR Roles. Organizations could formalize the roles of ICs and CAs as essential URs. Table 2 could be beneficial for reviewing a summary of each role and responsibilities. Empowering these representatives with decision-making autonomy could be beneficial for involving users in large-scale ASD. Additionally, establishing structured communication networks connecting URs with agile development teams will enable regular feedback and transparent collaboration between the development side and the user side of organizations.

Providing Comprehensive Training for User-Side Representatives. Comprehensive training programs are vital to equip URs with the necessary skills to navigate large-scale ASD. Training could focus on agile development concepts, communication, and facilitation to strengthen URs' ability to bridge gaps between users and development teams. These programs will also help representatives advocate effectively for user needs, synchronize with agile development teams, and foster collaboration in large and distributed organizations.

Strengthening Communication Strategies and Tools. Efficient communication between URs and Agile or product development teams is essential for overcoming misalignment and inefficiencies. Organizations should adopt communication frameworks and toolkits that support seamless, multi-channel interactions. These tools can facilitate effective collaboration across distributed teams, improve feedback loops, and ensure that user needs are integrated into development processes, enhancing coordination and overall project success.

6 Conclusion and Future Work

This study examines the roles and responsibilities of user-side representatives (URs), specifically Implementation Coordinators (ICs) and Change Agents (CAs), within large-scale agile software development (ASD) in the context of the studied organization. These roles, which are semi-formally institutionalized, play a supportive function by assisting product development teams in the design, development, and implementation of software systems. ICs act as intermediaries between product development teams and local offices, plan and lead implementations, monitor new work processes, communicate with different stakeholders like product development teams and local users, and facilitate resource acquisition for different product development teams. CAs complement this by serving as advocates for diverse user groups in a large and distributed organization, contributing to requirement management, empowering user voices in design and testing, training users in local offices, adopting new work processes, and communicating and following up with product development teams. These roles complement development-side user representative roles, such as PO and UX designers, by providing real-time user insights and addressing contextual challenges. While URs face challenges such as resistance to change and communication inefficiencies, their formalization and empowerment offer significant potential for improving user involvement in large-scale ASD, bridging the gap between users and development teams.

Future research could aim to develop a comprehensive competency framework for User-side Representative (UR) roles, detailing the skills, knowledge, and behavioral attributes required for effective performance. In parallel, it is important to investigate the organizational, cultural, and structural challenges associated with introducing UR roles in large, complex, and geographically distributed ASD environments across both public and private sectors. Further inquiry could also explore the necessary preconditions—such as leadership support, organizational readiness, and stakeholder engagement—that facilitate the successful implementation of a UR structure. Moreover, identifying the specific characteristics that make an organization suitable for adopting a UR infrastructure, such as organizational culture, governance model, and user involvement practices, would provide valuable insights for practitioners and policymakers.

Acknowledgments. This work was supported by the SustainDiT project, funded by the Sustainability Program at the Norwegian University of Science and Technology (NTNU), and research funds from NAV. We would like to express our sincere gratitude to Professor Torgeir Dingsøyr, Associate Professor Marius Mikalsen at NTNU, and Dr. Parastoo Mohagheghi from NAV for their valuable feedback on earlier versions of this paper. We are also thankful to the anonymous reviewers for their thorough reading and constructive suggestions, which have significantly enhanced the clarity and depth of this work. Finally, we extend our appreciation to all NAV employees who generously contributed to the study through interviews.

References

1. Abelein, U., Paech, B.: Understanding the influence of user participation and involvement on system success – a systematic mapping study. Empir. Softw. Eng. **20**(1), 28–81 (2015). https://doi.org/10.1007/s10664-013-9278-4
2. Schon, E.M., Winter, D., Escalona, M.J., Thomaschewski, J. (eds.): Key challenges in agile requirements engineering. Presented at the Agile Processes in Software Engineering and Extreme Programming (XP 2017). Springer, Cologne Germany (2017)
3. Hansson, C., Dittrich, Y., Randall, D.: Agile processes enhancing user participation for small providers of off-the-shelf software. In: Eckstein, J., Baumeister, H., LINK (Online service) (eds.) Extreme Programming and Agile processes in Software Engineering: 5th International Conference, XP 2004. LNCS, vol. 3092. Springer, Garmisch-Partenkirchen (2004)
4. Edison, H., Wang, X., Conboy, K.: Comparing methods for large-scale agile software development: a systematic literature review. IEEE Trans. Softw. Eng., 1 (2021). https://doi.org/10.1109/TSE.2021.3069039
5. Kula, E., Greuter, E., Van Deursen, A., Gousios, G.: Factors affecting on-time delivery in large-scale agile software development. IIEEE Trans. Softw. Eng. **48**(9), 3573–3592 (2022). https://doi.org/10.1109/TSE.2021.3101192
6. Rolland, K.H., Fitzgerald, B., Dingsøyr, T., Stol, K.-J.: Acrobats and safety nets: problematizing large-scale agile software development. ACM Trans. Softw. Eng. Methodol. **33**(2), 1–45 (2024). https://doi.org/10.1145/3617169
7. Berntzen, M., Hoda, R., Moe, N.B., Stray, V.: A taxonomy of inter-team coordination mechanisms in large-scale agile. IEEE Trans. Softw. Eng. **49**(2), 699–718 (2023). https://doi.org/10.1109/TSE.2022.3160873
8. Conboy, K., Carroll, N.: Implementing large-scale agile frameworks: challenges and recommendations. IEEE Softw. **36**(2), 44–50 (2019)

9. Matook, S., Maruping, L.M.: A competency model for customer representatives in agile software development projects. MIS Q. Exec., 77–95 (2014)
10. Berntzen, M., Moe, N.B., Stray, V.: The product owner in large-scale agile: an empirical study through the lens of relational coordination theory. In: Agile Processes in Software Engineering and Extreme Programming: 20th International Conference, XP 2019, Montréal, QC, Canada, 21–25 May 2019, Proceedings, Montreal, Canada. LNBIP, vol. 355. Springer (2019). https://doi.org/10.1007/978-3-030-19034-7
11. Klemets, J., Storholmen, T.C.B.: Towards super user-centred continuous delivery: a case study. In: Bernhaupt, R., Ardito, C., Sauer, S. (eds.) Human-Centered Software Engineering. LNCS, vol. 12481, pp. 152–165. Springer, Cham (2020). https://doi.org/10.1007/978-3-030-64266-2_9
12. Kautz, K.: Participatory design activities and agile software development. In: Pries-Heje, J., Venable, J., Bunker, D., Russo, N.L., DeGross, J.I. (eds.) Human Benefit through the Diffusion of Information Systems Design Science Research, vol. 318, pp. 303–316. Springer, Heidelberg (2010). https://doi.org/10.1007/978-3-642-12113-5_18
13. Kasauli, R., Knauss, E., Horkoff, J., Liebel, G., De Oliveira Neto, F.G.: Requirements engineering challenges and practices in large-scale agile system development. J. Syst. Softw. **172**, 110851 (2021). https://doi.org/10.1016/j.jss.2020.110851
14. Dingsøyr, T., Moe, N.B., Ohlsson, H.H.: Towards an understanding of scaling frameworks and business agility: a summary of the 6th international workshop at XP2018. In: Proceedings of the 19th International Conference on Agile Software Development: Companion, Porto Portugal, pp. 1–4. ACM (2018). https://doi.org/10.1145/3234152.3234176
15. Zorzetti, M., Signoretti, I., Salerno, L., Marczak, S., Bastos, R.: Improving agile software development using user-centered design and lean startup. Inf. Softw. Technol. **141**, 106718 (2022). https://doi.org/10.1016/j.infsof.2021.106718
16. Tam, C., Moura, E.J.D.C., Oliveira, T., Varajão, J.: The factors influencing the success of ongoing agile software development projects. Int. J. Project Manage. **38**(3), 165–176 (2020). https://doi.org/10.1016/j.ijproman.2020.02.001
17. Buchan, J., Bano, M., Zowghi, D., MacDonell, S., Shinde, A.: Alignment of stakeholder expectations about user involvement in agile software development. In: Proceedings of the 21st International Conference on Evaluation and Assessment in Software Engineering, Karlskrona Sweden, pp. 334–343. ACM (2017). https://doi.org/10.1145/3084226.3084251
18. Dikert, K., Paasivaara, M., Lassenius, C.: Challenges and success factors for large-scale agile transformations: a systematic literature review. J. Syst. Softw. **119**, 87–108 (2016). https://doi.org/10.1016/j.jss.2016.06.013
19. Ciriello, R.F., Glud, J.A., Hansen-Schwartz, K.H.: Becoming agile together: customer influence on agile adoption within commissioned software teams. Inf. Manage. **59**(4), 103645 (2022). https://doi.org/10.1016/j.im.2022.103645
20. Berntzen, M., Alette Engdal, S., Gellein, M., Brede Moe, N. (eds.) Coordination in agile product areas: a case study from a large FinTech organization. In: Proceeding of 25th International Conference on Agile Software Development XP 2024. LNBIP, Bolzano, Italy, vol. 512. Springer (2024). https://doi.org/10.1007/978-3-031-61154-4_3
21. Conboy, K.: Enabling promethean leaps: an examination of storytelling techniques in information systems development. CAIS **48**(1), 333–351 (2021). https://doi.org/10.17705/1CAIS.04835
22. Kautz, K.: Customer and user involvement in agile software development. In: Proceeding of 10th International Agile Processes in Software Engineering and Extreme Programming Conference, XP 2009, Sardinia, Italy. Springer (2009)
23. Jones, A., Thoma, V.: Determinants for successful agile collaboration between UX designers and software developers in a complex organization. Int. J. Hum.-Comput. Interact. **35**(20), 1914–1935 (2019). https://doi.org/10.1080/10447318.2019.1587856

24. Martin, A., Biddle, R., Noble, J.: An ideal customer: a grounded theory of requirements elicitation, communication and acceptance on agile projects. In: Dingsøyr, T., Dybå, T., Moe, N.B. (eds.) Agile Software Development: Current Research and Future Directions. Springer, Heidelberg (2010). https://doi.org/10.1007/978-3-642-12575-1
25. Paasivaara, M., Heikkila, V.T., Lassenius, C.: Experiences in scaling the product owner role in large-scale globally distributed scrum. In: 2012 IEEE Seventh International Conference on Global Software Engineering, Porto Alegre, Rio Grande do Sul, Brazil, pp. 174–178. IEEE (2012). https://doi.org/10.1109/ICGSE.2012.41
26. Runeson, P., Höst, M.: Guidelines for conducting and reporting case study research in software engineering. Empir. Softw. Eng. **14**(2), 131–164 (2009). https://doi.org/10.1007/s10664-008-9102-8
27. Yin, R.K.: Designing case studies. Qual. Res. Methods **14**(5) (2003)
28. Oates, B.J., Marie, G., Rachel, M.: Researching Information Systems and Computing. SAGE Publications, London (2022)
29. What is NAV? https://www.nav.no/hva-er-nav/en
30. Mohagheghi, P., Lassenius, C.: Organizational implications of agile adoption: a case study from the public sector. In: Proceedings of the 29th ACM Joint Meeting on European Software Engineering Conference and Symposium on the Foundations of Software Engineering, Athens Greece. ACM (2021). https://doi.org/10.1145/3468264.3473937
31. Bernhardt, H.B.: Digital Transformation in NAV IT 2016–2020: Key Factors for the Journey of Change, pp. 115–134 (2022)
32. NAV IT: NAV IT. https://www.detsombetyrnoe.no/
33. Meland, S.I.: Lots to learn from the Norwegian Public Sector's IT success. Norwegian SciTech News (2023). https://norwegianscitechnews.com/2023/01/lots-to-learn-from-navs-it-success/
34. Noble, H., Heale, R.: Triangulation in research, with examples. Evid. Based Nurs. **22**(3), 67–68 (2019). https://doi.org/10.1136/ebnurs-2019-103145
35. Saldaña, J.: The Coding Manual for Qualitative Researchers, 2nd edn. SAGE, Los Angeles (2013)
36. Thompson, J.: A guide to abductive thematic analysis. TQR (2022). https://doi.org/10.46743/2160-3715/2022.5340

Open Access This chapter is licensed under the terms of the Creative Commons Attribution 4.0 International License (http://creativecommons.org/licenses/by/4.0/), which permits use, sharing, adaptation, distribution and reproduction in any medium or format, as long as you give appropriate credit to the original author(s) and the source, provide a link to the Creative Commons license and indicate if changes were made.

The images or other third party material in this chapter are included in the chapter's Creative Commons license, unless indicated otherwise in a credit line to the material. If material is not included in the chapter's Creative Commons license and your intended use is not permitted by statutory regulation or exceeds the permitted use, you will need to obtain permission directly from the copyright holder.

Fostering New Work Practices Through a Community of Practice A Case Study in a Large-Scale Software Development Organization

Franziska Tobisch(✉) and Florian Matthes

TUM School of Computation, Information and Technology, Department of Computer Science, Technical University of Munich, Munich, Germany
franziska.tobisch@tum.de

Abstract. New Work and agile methodologies share a common foundation in their aim to foster autonomy, collaboration, and adaptability. Their benefits make both concepts highly relevant for organizations as they support agility, innovation, and attractiveness to existing and potential employees. Still, implementing these concepts within large, established companies remains challenging. Therefore, this case study investigates a Community of Practice that promotes New Work principles within a large software organization aiming to be agile and innovative. Our study explores the establishment and functioning of this community and its effectiveness in advancing New Work practices within the case company. The community has been growing and has achieved its first success in promoting New Work, but there remains potential for improvement. In particular, a clearer mandate from the upper management is needed.

Keywords: Large-Scale Agile · New Work · Community of Practice

1 Introduction

New Work has emerged as a response to globalization, digitalization, and employees' changed expectations regarding autonomy, flexibility, and purpose-driven work [1]. The concept aims to empower individuals toward self-determination, fulfillment, creativity, and passion in alternative work models [3]. In recent years, New Work has evolved toward practical applications in organizations [10,16,19]. For organizations, introducing New Work means reorganizing their structures and processes (e.g., reduced hierarchies) [1]. These changes can help organizations to remain attractive to employees, respond fast, and foster innovation [11]. Likewise, agile methodologies have emerged to address the increasing need for speed, flexibility, and innovation, particularly affecting the software development industry [9,23]. As agile methods share similar objectives with New Work (e.g., self-organization, empowerment, collaboration [2]), they are seen as complementary [4,7,12,19]. Still, both concepts face significant implementation challenges [1,6,10], like change resistance, particularly in large, established organizations.

Communities of Practices (CoPs) are groups of people with a shared interest or concern, often from across the organization, that regularly interact to exchange, learn, and support each other [24]. These communities can aid organizations in cultural change [24], such as transformations toward agility at scale [8,15,22]. CoPs allow to share and spread knowledge across the organization, foster empowerment, innovation [8,22], organizational development [15], openness to change, and employees mindset toward collaboration and self-organization [8]. While their alignment with New Work principles makes them a related practice [19], their potential for cultural change also raises the question of whether CoPs can be used as a bottom-up mechanism to foster a New Work culture and roll out related practices in large software organizations aiming to be agile and innovative.

While several studies have investigated New Work and its adoption within organizations (e.g., [1,11,25]), only a few focus on software development companies, in particular large organizations that apply agile approaches [4,7]. Also, empirical studies are scarce [4,7,25]. Moreover, to the best of our knowledge, using CoPs as a bottom-up approach to foster organizational change within such organizations, particularly the adoption of New Work, has not been investigated intensively. Thus, we conducted a case study to answer the following research questions (RQs): *How do employees use a CoP to foster New Work in a large agile software development organization in a bottom-up manner? (RQ1) How successful is such a CoP in fostering New Work in this context? (RQ2)*

2 Background and Related Work

Initially conceptualized by the philosopher Frithjof Bergmann [3], New Work aims to empower individuals by fostering self-determination, creativity, fulfillment, and passion through alternative work models. In recent years, New Work has developed into actionable principles and practices for organizations [10,16,19], which require significant structural changes [1]. For instance, Laloux [10] introduces the concept of "teal organizations," and Robertson [16] "holacracy," which both emphasize decentralized authority and self-management. New Work practices include flexible work models, job rotation, feedback cultures, and retrospectives [19]. Still, hierarchical structures and change resistance complicate a successful adoption [1,10]. Several studies have investigated New Work (e.g., [1,11]) and its implementation (e.g., [4,12,25]). For instance, Wyrzykowska [25] conducted a literature review on teal organizations, highlighting the difficulty of transforming toward this approach, suggesting a gradual implementation, and emphasizing the need for management's openness and developing employees' self-management skills. Sharing goals like self-organization and empowerment [2], agile practices and New Work complement each other, having the potential to promote innovation when combined [4,12] or, concerning

New Work-related concepts like sociocracy, to support autonomy in scaled agile settings [7]. Like introducing New Work [25], transforming organizations toward agility faces many challenges and requires integrating top-down support with bottom-up initiatives [6].

CoPs are groups of individuals who share a common interest or concern and enhance their knowledge and skills through frequent interactions [24]. CoPs can play a key role in driving cultural transformation within organizations [24], like agile transformations [8,15,22]. CoPs can influence organizational culture through their impact on members and teams, paving the way for broader organizational change by allowing the development of a stronger learning culture on a limited scale before expanding to the entire organization [24]. Several researchers have studied CoPs in large software development organizations with the goal of being agile [5,8,15,20–22]. Such CoPs often aim to foster knowledge dissemination, empowerment [5,8,22], innovation [8,21,22], organizational development [15], and a mindset change among employees [8]. However, adopting CoPs is a challenging endeavor. Most studies on CoPs [5,8,15,20,21,24] highlight challenges (e.g., lack of engagement) but also factors contributing to their success (e.g., passionate leads). The alignment of CoPs' characteristics and goals with New Work principles and their potential as a catalyst for cultural change [8,15,22,24] brings into focus whether they can function as a bottom-up mechanism to foster New Work in large software organizations with the goal of agility and innovation. Despite existing studies on New Work and CoPs in scaled agile settings, empirical research on New Work practices [25], for instance in software development settings, especially those using agile approaches [4,7], remains scarce. CoPs' role as a bottom-up driver for New Work adoption in this context is largely unexplored.

3 Methodology

To answer our RQs, we performed a holistic single-case study [26] of a New Work CoP, our single phenomenon of interest, situated within a large international software development organization, constituting our single unit of analysis. We chose the case study format as a research methodology since it allowed us to gain insights into a real-life setting [26], like a CoP for fostering New Work practices in a large agile software organization. We designed our research based on the guidelines of Runeson and Höst [17], with descriptive, exploratory, and explanatory elements. The study took place from July 2024 to January 2025.

The case organization SoftwareCo is a large software development firm with over 100.000 employees in more than 100 countries, offering various solutions and services. SoftwareCo aims to be competitive through innovation, speed, and change responsiveness. Due to its size and product range, the organization does not follow a specific, large-scale agile framework. Some product areas implement custom agile approaches or frameworks like SAFe, while others follow the traditional waterfall model. The New Work CoP has been initiated as an employee-driven initiative to adopt New Work practices at SoftwareCo and, over time, evolved into a more structured format supported by a small Human Resources (HR) team, taking over core responsibilities in CoP leadership and other activities.

We collected our data through interviews and by analyzing meeting notes and documents for data triangulation. We interviewed 13 CoP members with various roles from different company areas and varying activity and responsibility in the CoP (see Table 1). We conducted the interviews between August and November 2024. All interviews followed the same structure: (1) questions regarding the interviewees' background (e.g., role), (2) the CoP (e.g., goals, structure, activities) and the interviewees' role, (3) the CoP's success in fostering New Work and how well the CoP concept aligns with New Work. The latter two sections consisted of open questions to receive in-depth answers and two Likert scale questions [13]. We conducted, recorded, and transcribed all interviews using Microsoft Teams. Interviews not conducted in English were translated afterward. The interviews took 27–49 min. To complement the interview insights, we participated in a retrospective and analyzed the CoP's SharePoint page, Teams channel, handbook, introduction video, and onboarding guide. We analyzed all collected data using qualitative coding [14,18], using high-level codes derived from the interview questions, and iteratively developing lower-level codes during the analysis.

Table 1. Interview partners

No.	Alias	Role	CoP role	Location
1	I1	Manager	Core member	Germany, Site A
2	I2	HR & New Work Practices Expert	Core member	Germany, Site A
3	I3	Design Thinking Coach	Passive member	Germany, Site B
4	I4	Agile Coach/Scrum Master	Passive member	Germany, Site A
5	I5	Product Manager	Active member	France, Site D
6	I6	Consultant	Active member	France, Site D
7	I7	Transformation Lead	Active member	Germany, Site A
8	I8	Manager	Passive member	Germany, Site A
9	I9	HR & New Work Practices Expert	Active member	Germany, Site A
10	I10	Manager	Active member	Germany, Site C
11	I11	Development Manager	Passive member	Germany, Site A
12	I12	Manager	Passive member	Germany, Site A
13	I13	HR & New Work Practices Expert	Core member	France, Site D

4 Results

4.1 Fostering New Work Practices Through a CoP

Purpose and Goals. The CoP's primary goal is to drive cultural change within SoftwareCo by spreading New Work principles and practices to improve the working environment. The community believes *"that by fostering a more people-positive and complexity-conscious way of working, [SoftwareCo] can be more innovative and successful as a company, and an even more inspiring place to work"* (SharePoint). The CoP aims to connect like-minded people and promote empowerment, self-organization, distributed responsibility, and autonomy. The CoP encourages sharing ideas, knowledge, and experiences related to New Work, learning, and collaboration, serving as a safe place for support and experiments.

Establishment. The New Work CoP started in 2017 as a grassroots initiative, with a team that embraced New Work principles in a site of SoftwareCo in Germany. Due to its positive experience, the team launched the monthly knowledge-sharing event "New Work Breakfast," which attracted up to 100 participants, to advocate for the concept in SoftwareCo, and introduced a fellowship program. These fellows then officially started the New Work CoP, relocated the New Work Breakfast to a more central company site, and tried to connect existing New Work grassroots initiatives across SoftwareCo. As the CoP grew, a group of employees within the HR department became responsible for New Work practices at SoftwareCo, taking on leading roles within the community. Since the CoP's growth required a structured yet flexible framework consistent with New Work principles, it adopted a non-hierarchical, self-organized structure based on so-called circles. The community also created a SharePoint page and initiated activities to promote New Work further. Eventually, the HR team responsible for the CoP became part of the Organizational Growth & Health Unit at SoftwareCo.

Governance Aspects. While the CoP is open to everyone in SoftwareCo, some interviewees highlight its limited scope (I3), i.e., to Germany (I9). The CoP has more than 500 members, with up to 100 actively driving the CoP. An inner core, including the HR team and other members (e.g., I1, I2, I13), takes on leadership responsibilities. Some members are facilitators in CoP sessions or coaches and trainers in its offers (e.g., I1, I2, I5–7, I9, I10, I12, I13). The CoP is structured into circles, each taking ownership of a topic (see Table 2), open to all members, and with an elected lead. The CoP also has local sub-communities at specific company sites. The community operates based on New Work principles like distributed leadership, with each circle making decisions on its topic, and working agreements. I5 explains: *"Within the CoP, anyone can come [up] with a proposal. There can be counter-proposals, and if there is no big disagreement, then it's a consent overall."* Despite a missing mandate, many interviewees (I3, I5–13) believe the CoP influences through its members and those participating in its activities, taking their insights with them. The CoP lacks a dedicated budget but can request limited funds. While the HR team works full-time on New Work, other members do it next to their jobs or get time off from their managers. The HR team members report the CoP's activities and achievements to management.

Table 2. Circles of the New Work CoP

Circle	Responsibility
Events	Organization of events like New Work Talks or Breakfasts
Enablement	Creation of trainings and materials to enable New Work
Amplify	Increase of visibility, influence, and impact inside and outside of SoftwareCo
Agreement	Provision of a functional, structured operating system based on agreements
Onboarding	Onboarding of new members with resources, Q&As, and networking events
Coaching/consulting	Improvement of coaching offer

Communication, Documentation, and Offers. The CoP organizes various meetings (see Table 3) and offers SoftwareCo's employees different trainings and a coaching program in which it accompanies teams in their New Work transformation. Also, a SoftwareCo-wide accessible SharePoint page with information about the CoP and resources (e.g., videos) exists. The CoP uses a Teams channel for communication and documentation. Next to a common decision-making channel, each circle and local sub-CoP has a sub-channel. Each channel is accessible to all members. Other used tools are emails, whiteboards, and newsletters.

Table 3. Meetings and Exchanges of the New Work CoP

Meeting	Frequency	Description
Intra-circle sync	Bi-weekly to monthly	Discussion and planning by circle members
Inter-circle sync	Monthly	Synchronization between circle leads
Retrospective	Quarterly	Reflection
New Work Breakfast	Monthly to bi-monthly	Sharing of experiences by SoftwareCo employees
New Work Talk	Monthly to bi-monthly	Sharing of experiences by external guest speakers
Coffee corner	Bi-weekly	Informal onboarding event
Peer consulting	Monthly	Consultation by peers
Ad-hoc exchanges	Ad-hoc	Exchanges between individual members and circles

4.2 Success of the CoP in Fostering New Work Practices

Challenges. A key issue is the limited time of members due to their regular jobs, hindering them from participating in CoP sessions, working on CoP tasks, and contributing to activities. Partly low motivation to take over time-consuming responsibilities, other priorities, and low commitment further negatively impact participation. A key obstacle is limited management support, as some members' managers do not allow much time for the CoP, and, in general, management's support and attention to New Work and the CoP is limited. The CoP has no dedicated budget, official mandate, or "place" in the company's typical set-up. I2 explains: *"This is probably the biggest challenge, is this missing or weak [management] mandate, [...], it's just a predominantly grassroots initiative, and that's* *great, but it's probably not enough on its own."* Also, some interviewees describe a traditional mindset and change resistance as barriers to promoting New Work. Moreover, the CoP faces organizational challenges, such as balancing structure with freedom to align with New Work principles, achieving fair decision-making, broad member representation, and managing diverse members. Finally, the CoP struggles with an often varying understanding of New Work.

Success and Fit. Most interviewees see the CoP as successful in fostering New Work (I1, I4–8, I10, I12, I13) (see Fig. 1), especially with the current limitations in resources and management support (I2, I3, I6). According to many interviewees, the CoP makes gradual progress, changing the way of working at SoftwareCo in small but meaningful steps (I1, I2, I5, I6, I10, I13). Still, there is potential for improvement (I2, I9, I11, I13), and the success in spreading New Work varies across SoftwareCo (I1–3). The CoP members perceive several factors as relevant to increasing success. These factors include increased management support (e.g., interest, budget, resources, time allowance), sufficient time for members, more active participation, and motivation. Management must fully recognize the CoP's and New Work's value, and the culture must become more open. Factors already contributing to success include the CoP's positive atmosphere, motivating engagement, the active inner core, and the diversity of members, bringing different perspectives and increasing reach. Also, management's limited involvement allows for implementing New Work principles. According to I9: *"You as a community can shape a lot because you don't have any pressure. [...] you are self-reliant, you can decide what is important. Nobody demands anything from you."* Additionally, the CoP actively implements measures to foster its success, like a defined governance model, consent-based decision-making, agreements, open and voluntary participation, onboarding activities, suitable communication (e.g., focus on push), and session formats (e.g., room for ad-hoc topics). The CoP also aims to ensure internal and external transparency (e.g., regular syncs), foster engagement, promote the CoP (e.g., inviting non-members to events), regularly adapt (e.g., retrospectives), and guide activities with a clear goal. Most interviewees believe that New Work and CoPs align well (I1-5, I7–13) (Fig. 1), as they are based on similar principles (I1-3, I5, I6, I11).

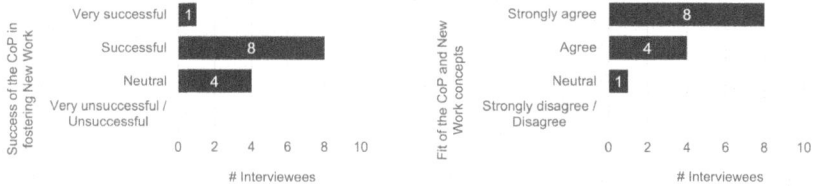

Fig. 1. CoP's success in fostering New Work and fit with New Work

5 Discussion

5.1 Key Findings

To investigate how employees use a CoP to foster a New Work culture within a large agile development organization (RQ1), we investigated a bottom-up initiated New Work CoP within such an organization. Typical for CoPs [24], the community became more integrated and structured as it grew. While open to achieve broad organizational impact [15,24], only few members are active, as typical for CoPs [24]. The community has an inner core responsible for leadership tasks, and its governance model follows sociocracy [7], guided by New Work principles [1,3,10], like distributed leadership (e.g., circle structure). The CoP influences organizational culture indirectly, as employees apply knowledge gained in their work [24]. Typical for bottom-up initiated [22] and non-institutionalized [24] CoPs, the community lacks budget, full- or part-time members, and is barely steered by management. The CoP focuses on adaptability (e.g., retrospectives) and transparency (e.g., open chat channels), aligned with agile and New Work principles [2,3,10,19] and good practices for CoPs [15]. To promote New Work, the CoP offers various initiatives (e.g., trainings) to build employees' skills [25].

To investigate how successful a CoP is in fostering New Work within a large-scale agile organization (RQ2), we examined the CoP's success. The CoP struggles with challenges common for CoPs (in large-scale agile settings) [15,20,24], like limited time of members. Being a bottom-up [22], non-institutionalized initiative [24], the CoP lacks a clear mandate by upper management and integration into official structures. SoftwareCo's hierarchical structure, a common barrier to New Work [1,10], further limits the CoP's impact. CoP members see the potential for greater impact if motivation, engagement, and management appreciation and support are strengthened, factors relevant for CoPs [15,20,24], and New Work introductions [25]. Despite challenges, the CoP has grown, broadened its scope, and become partly integrated into the organizational structure. Members see the impact as incremental yet meaningful, indicating CoPs' potential to support cultural change gradually [24,25]. Key enablers include a positive atmosphere, a committed inner core, and the CoP's independence from top-down steering, supporting CoP success [15,20,24]. Moreover, the CoP implements several measures contributing to its success like alignment with New Work values through governance based on agreements and guiding principles, distributed decision-making, open communication, and continuous feedback and transparency, as also recommended for CoPs [15,20,24]. Our results confirm the alignment of CoPs and New Work principles, indicating that CoPs are suitable for fostering New Work. Our study offers practitioners insights on introducing New Work in large agile organizations through a CoP. Initiators should seek management support while ensuring to preserve the New Work spirit.

5.2 Limitations

Our case study has validity threats [17,26]. As focusing on a single case limits external validity and generalizability, we provided details on the case organization and CoP. Another limitation is the small number of interviews, given the size of the CoP and company, and missing non-member perspectives. Thus, we triangulated data using diverse documents, interviewed members with varied roles and CoP involvement, and followed guidelines for data collection and analysis [14,17,18].

6 Conclusion

Our study explored whether and how CoPs can serve as a bottom-up mechanism to implement New Work in large, established organizations striving for agility and innovation. Through a case study at a large agile development organization, we investigated such a CoP and its success. Emerging from a single-team initiative, the CoP grew in scope and visibility, offering diverse knowledge-sharing formats and living New Work principles through distributed leadership and consent-based decision-making. The CoP has made progress but faces challenges like limited capacity. While the CoP facilitates cultural change gradually by building employees' self-organization skills, a clearer mandate from management is required to strengthen its impact. Future research could expand our study by incorporating non-member perspectives, adopting a longitudinal approach, or exploring alternative methods for introducing New Work.

Acknowledgments. This research is part of a bigger research project between TUM and SAP SE, supported by SAP SE funding. We thank Filip Weidenbach and Markus Meisl for their support.

References

1. Aroles, J., Mitev, N., de Vaujany, F.X.: Mapping themes in the study of new work practices. N. Technol. Work. Employ. **34**(3), 285–299 (2019)
2. Beck, K., et al.: https://agilemanifesto.org/ (2001). Accessed 04 Apr 2025
3. Bergmann, F.: New work new culture: Work we want and a culture that strengthens us, 1st edn. John Hunt Publishing, Hampshire, UK (2019)
4. Bhandari, R., Colomo-Palacios, R.: Holacracy in software development teams: a multivocal literature review. In: Proceed. of the 19th International Conference on Computational Science and Its Applications Applications, pp. 140–145. IEEE (2019)
5. Detofeno, T., Reinehr, S., Andreia, M.: Technical debt guild: when experience and engagement improve technical debt management. In: Proceedings of the XX Brazilian Symposium on Software Quality. No. 25, ACM (2021)
6. Dikert, K., Paasivaara, M., Lassenius, C.: Challenges and success factors for large-scale agile transformations: a systematic literature review. J. Syst. Softw. **119**, 87–108 (2016)
7. Eckstein, J.: Sociocracy: an organization model for large-scale agile development. In: Proceedings of the Scientific Workshop of XP2016. No. 6, ACM (2016)
8. Geffers, K.: Overcoming people-related challenges in large-scale agile transformations: the role of online communities of practice. In: Proceedings of the 32nd European Conference on Information Systems. No. 2178, AIS (2024)

9. Highsmith, J.: Agile Software Development Ecosystems, 1st edn. Pearson Education Inc, Boston, MA (2002)
10. Laloux, F.: Reinventing organizations. Nelson Parker, 1 edn. (2014)
11. Lee, M.Y., Edmondson, A.C.: Self-managing organizations: exploring the limits of less-hierarchical organizing. Res. Organ. Behav. **37**, 35–58 (2017)
12. Liebert, F.: Holacracy as a new approach to new product development in it industry–case study. Sci. Pap. Silesian Univ. Technol. **145** (2020)
13. Likert, R.: A technique for the measurement of attitudes. Arch. Psychol. **22**(140) (1932)
14. Miles, M.B., Huberman, A.M., Saldaña, J.: Qualitative Data Analysis: A Methods Sourcebook, 4th edn. SAGE, Thousand Oaks, CA (2019)
15. Paasivaara, M., Lassenius, C.: Communities of practice in a large distributed agile software development organization-case Ericsson. Inf. and Softw. Technol. **56**(12), 1556–1577 (2014)
16. Robertson, B.J.: Holacracy: The Revolutionary Management System that Abolishes Hierarchy. Penguin Books, London, UK (2016)
17. Runeson, P., Höst, M.: Guidelines for conducting and reporting case study research in software engineering. Empirical Softw. Eng. **14**, 131–164 (2009)
18. Saldaña, J.: The Coding Manual for Qualitative Researchers, 4th edn. SAGE, Thousand Oaks, CA (2021)
19. Schnell, N., Schnell, A.: New Work Hacks. Springer Nature, 1 edn. (2021)
20. Šmite, D., Moe, N.B., Levinta, G., Floryan, M.: Spotify guilds: how to succeed with knowledge sharing in large-scale agile organizations. IEEE Softw. **36**(2), 51–57 (2019)
21. Sporsem, T., Tkalich, A., Moe, N.B., Mikalsen, M., Rygh, N.: Using guilds to foster internal startups in large organizations: a case study. In: Gregory, P., Kruchten, P. (eds.) Agile Processes in Software Engineering and Extreme Programming – Workshops. XP2021. LNBIP, vol. 426. pp. 135–144. Springer, Cham (2021)
22. Tobisch, F., Schmidt, J., Matthes, F.: Investigating communities of practice in large-scale agile software development: an interview study. In: Šmite, D., Guerra, E., Wang, X., Marchesi, M., Gregory, P. (eds.) Agile Processes in Software Engineering and Extreme Programming, XP2024. LNBIP, vol. 512, pp. 3–19. Springer, Cham (2024)
23. Van Oosterhout, M., Waarts, E., Van Hillegersberg, J.: Change factors requiring agility and implications for it. Eur. J. Inf. Syst. **15**(2), 132–145 (2006)
24. Wenger, E., McDermott, R., Snyder, W.M.: Cultivating Communities of Practice: A Guide to Managing Knowledge, vol. 4. Harvard Bus. School, Boston, MA (2002)
25. Wyrzykowska, B.: Teal organizations: literature review and future research directions. Central Europ. Mngmt. Journ. **27**(4), 124–141 (2019)
26. Yin, R.K.: Case Study Research and Applications: Design and Methods, 6th edn. SAGE, Thousand Oaks, CA (2018)

Open Access This chapter is licensed under the terms of the Creative Commons Attribution 4.0 International License (http://creativecommons.org/licenses/by/4.0/), which permits use, sharing, adaptation, distribution and reproduction in any medium or format, as long as you give appropriate credit to the original author(s) and the source, provide a link to the Creative Commons license and indicate if changes were made.

The images or other third party material in this chapter are included in the chapter's Creative Commons license, unless indicated otherwise in a credit line to the material. If material is not included in the chapter's Creative Commons license and your intended use is not permitted by statutory regulation or exceeds the permitted use, you will need to obtain permission directly from the copyright holder.

Engineering

Architecture Refactoring Towards Service Reusability in the Context of Microservices

João Daniel[1(✉)], Gabriel Mota[2], Xiaofeng Wang[1], and Eduardo Guerra[1]

[1] Free University of Bozen-Bolzano, Bolzano, Italy
joao.daniel@student.unibz.it
{xiaofeng.wang,eduardo.guerra}@unibz.it
[2] University of São Paulo, São Paulo, Brazil
gabrielfmota134@usp.br

Abstract. Agility embraces changes in the functional and non-functional requirements. When the latter happens, the architecture needs to evolve, putting architectural refactoring in evidence. Microservices is an architectural style that enables more agility in a system's architecture, as it favors the evolution of the system by adding new operations. But it also has its liabilities: the number of services can explode, with similar ones being created. Ultimately, that harms the system's evolution and maintenance. This work addresses these challenges by proposing a catalog of architecture refactorings to promote reusability in Microservices. These refactorings target patterns that embrace data heterogeneity in the APIs and employ metadata to enhance messages and guide processing. We evaluated the catalog with case studies of three real-world applications and conducted change impact analysis in two scenarios: adding a new data provider, and adding a new processing algorithm. The results showed that embracing heterogeneous data in the API enables a more seamless addition of new data providers, and using metadata can strongly decouple the processing algorithms from the data they use. Furthermore, the results point to other improvements in observability, scalability, and infrastructure.

Keywords: Service Reusability · Architecture Refactoring · Metadata

1 Introduction

In Agile processes, changes in requirements are embraced, requiring updates and refactorings in the code. However, these changes are also common in non-functional requirements [20], which creates a demand for the evolution of the software architecture. While architectural practices were scarce at the beginning of the Agile movement, in the last years, some frameworks and techniques arose, such as Continuous Architecture [6] and ArchHypo [16]. In this context, architectural refactoring is an essential pillar for architectural evolution.

Microservice architectural style (MSA) is frequently pointed out as having a good synergy with agile principles. It is characterized by having its parts collaborating as services to each other, i.e., offering on-demand their capabilities and features. The support for heterogeneous components and the modularization of microservices makes adding new services easy, and consequently, favors the system's growth.

However, this characteristic that helps introduce new services can also lead to an explosion of them. In some cases, the system can be designed in a way that requires the continuous creation of small and specific services. For instance, the architecture might require a dedicated operation to register the activity log for each different domain entity. Consequently, each new entity introduced in the system would require a new operation to be created. This scenario creates obstacles to the system's evolution and its maintenance.

Some patterns propose the usage of metadata in service APIs to create more reusable services [12]. However, little work has been conducted to propose refactorings that can drive the architecture in that direction. Hence, the goal of this work is represented by the following Research Question: *How to refactor the architecture towards more reusable services?* To answer that question, we present a catalog of architecture refactorings to promote the reusability of remote APIs. Our catalog was evaluated with three case studies, following Change Impact Analysis and ALMA [3].

The results showed the embracing heterogeneous data in the API enables a more seamless addition of new data providers, and the usage of metadata can strongly decouple the processing algorithms from the data they use.

2 Related Work

In Daigneau (2012) [5], the book presents patterns for the design of services, i.e., systems work in favor of a functionality to be consumed by a 3rd-party. It contains the "Web Service Evolution" chapter, where the focus is aligned with this work. In this chapter, the patterns address the evolution at the API level, from which we highlight **Single-Message Argument** and **Tolerant Reader**. The former proposes that messages should contain all data in a single package, whereas the latter guides the API Contract to accept variances in the structure of received messages.

In Lercher et al. (2024) [11], the goal is to identify the challenges faced and strategies adopted by practitioners during the evolution of MSA. They report a large usage of REST APIs and a consistent adoption of REST **API Gateway** as an approach to decouple external clients from the internal distributed system. As challenges, they present two major causes of breaking changes: new functionalities and technologies. As workarounds, practitioners often replicate operations to accommodate the required changes and then adopt versioning and deprecation strategies. Another challenge is the maintainability of APIs and the degradation of their usability over time, mainly caused by the overhead in handling outdated versions, and the increase in technical debt by backward compatibility.

Two slices of an API refactoring catalog are presented by Stocker et al. [18, 19]. The goal of the catalog is to propose refactorings to the API Contract that benefit their evolution. It contains 15 refactorings (divided into 8 in the first slice, and 7 in the second one), spanning from high-level policies for the API Contract, down to the operations and their exchanged messages. From the catalog, we highlight the refactorings **Extract Operation**, **Split Operation**, and **Merge Operations**, as well as **Add Wish List**, due to the similarities with the ones presented in the present work. The first three highlighted work on the operation level, increasing or reducing the number of operations, or specializing the existing ones. The fourth highlight proposes specialized metadata as an approach for the best fit between clients' needs and the provided service data.

In previous works [12], we proposed a pattern language for reusability of APIs that leverages metadata. **Flexibilize the Ingestion**: make the API support an operation that accepts heterogeneous data. By doing so, different clients can integrate with it more seamlessly. **Enrich with Metadata** helps making sense of the heterogeneous data. It is also undesirable to face heterogeneous metadata, so it is important to **Agree on Meta Structure**. The integration is not completely seamless because of the enrichment with metadata. There are autonomous but composable strategies to it: **Embed Metadata**, **Configure Meta in Runtime**, and **Configure Meta during Deploy**. When such changes in the API Consumer or API Provider are not possible, **Adapt the Ingestion** so that, by having a mediator, the metadata can be injected. Finally, when the API Provider supports to **Plug the Processors In**, it can handle the processing of the heterogeneous data accompanied by the metadata.

3 Methodology

The goal of this work is to propose refactorings that improve service reusability and evaluate their impact on system evolvability. This study comprises two steps: (i) the formal definition of the refactorings; and (ii) the refactorings' assessment. The former is based on previous experiences and in a pattern language for reusability in service APIs [12]. The refactorings follow the same format and guidelines adopted by [18].

We adopted the multiple case studies research method [15,21,22]. This method is suitable because a real-life context is being considered, and the boundaries between the phenomenon and the context are not evident [22] – in this study, respectively the proposed refactorings and the target system architecture.

The three projects of the case studies were selected using purposive sampling [2], since the projects required a scenario suitable for the target refactorings. The following was considered as inclusion criteria: (a) the project should have a microservices-based architecture; (b) the system should have ingestion and processing of data from multiple sources; (c) it should be desirable to improve the extensibility to add new data sources with the respective processing of this data.

The evaluation of the resulting structure of the refactorings in each case study was based on the ALMA method [3]. In its first step, we defined the specific goal of each evaluation: according to modifiability, to compare the initial architecture with the resulting one from the refactorings. Next, we had to produce a description of the architectures, so for each case, we applied a mix of techniques: (a) meetings with the maintainers to understand the drivers and desirable quality attributes, as well as to acquire an overview of their applications' architecture; (b) inspection of the code and related assets, such as the structure of exchanged messages and databases. Since we already had the selection criteria defining a few quality attributes, the formal third step of ALMA required just the description of the scenarios.

Then, we performed the final step of ALMA: we applied the refactorings as they fit the applications, and performed the assessment through an architecture change impact analysis [23]. The change impact analysis approach adopted can be classified as experimental [10]. We evaluated the extent of a change in two change scenarios: "A" the addition of a new data provider; and "B" the inclusion of a new processing algorithm.

4 Refactoring Catalog

The catalog comprises three architecture refactorings. They are related to each other, but more importantly, it is possible to progressively adopt them. When...

- ... a service replicates a single capability in different feature-specific API Operations, then **Join API Operations with Heterogenenous Data**. After that, when...
- ... different algorithms need to be selected based on data, then **Extract Pluggable Processors**;
- ... dealing with the differences of the heterogeneous data leads to high complexity, then **Introduce Metadata**; finally, when...
- ... the differences are hard to represent just with metadata, then **Extract Pluggable Processors**.

(Refactoring) Join API Operations with Heterogenenous Data

Motivation - A system might offer its capabilities as services to be consumed. The ways to consume such capability might vary from consumer to consumer, due to changes in data, for example. In extreme cases, a single capability is offered in multiple operations, each dedicated to a feature. This replication in the API Contract cascades into the implementation, and in the medium- to long term can harm the service and its evolution.

Stakeholder Concerns

#**DRY**: (*Don't Repeat Yourself*) reducing component replication as a maintainability driver; #**Decoupling**: keeping a low degree of coupling between API Provider and its Consumers, ensuring autonomy in evolving to both parts; #**LowComplexity**: avoiding additional complexity of the implemented solution on top of the business inherit complexity; #**Extensibility**: easing the incorporation of new features to an existing Capability; for example, extending the tax calculation to a new sector or country.

Initial Structure - A given service offers a capability with an arbitrary number of features. Each feature is exposed in a dedicated API Operation, and implemented by a dedicated component. The data structure of each API Operation is defined based on its API Consumers, compromising the coupling between them and the API Provider. Also, since the components implement the logic of the same capability, there might be undesirable replication of responsibilities.

Design Smells

- **Non-parameterized operations**: the API Contract supports many Operations that do not support parameters; an instance for RESTful APIs, the API Contract offers two Operations GET /furnitureproducts and GET /decorproducts instead of a single parameterized one;
- **Unclear choice of operation**: a potential API Consumer faces a hard time choosing which API Operation to call, due to the large number of similar Operations supported for the same Capability in the API Contract; oftentimes, that leads to creating a new dedicated Operation for that specific Consumer;
- **Replication of internal components**: since the API Consumers consume the same capability of the API Provider, but it requires support to different features due to the heterogeneous data structures, the implementation of the service is prone to having component replication;
- **Tight coupling with clients**: it is hard to evolve each API Operation for the Capability; since it is defined based on the data structures provided by the API Consumers, it strongly tights the parts; it is particularly critical when the number of Operations grows;
- **High maintenance cost**: the API Contract is hard to maintain because of the inherent complexity of being extensive; as there are multiple features to the same capability, the API Contract becomes too long supporting multiple Operations.

Steps

1. Add to the API Contract a new Operation that exposes the Capability and accepts heterogeneous data as the content of the incoming message;
2. Implement the joined Operation as a single component for the different messages;
3. Join the calls from the API Consumers into the new Operation; i.e., migrate the API Consumers into using the new Operation;
4. Update the API Contract by deprecating or removing the feature-specific API Operations, as they are no longer being used by any API Consumers.

Target Structure - After this refactoring, the API Contract shall be reduced in the number of supported Operations, joining the features of the same capability into a single Operation that accepts heterogeneous data. The API Consumers consuming that capability do so by referring to the same Operation without changing the provided data structure. Also, the replication of components in the implementation is removed, as there shall be a single component.

This refactoring drives the API Contract definition to follow the "Flexibilize the Ingestion" pattern [12].

(Refactoring) Introduce Metadata

Motivation - The term "heterogeneous" has been carefully selected, avoiding misusing "unstructured". We selected "heterogeneous" because, considering the group of different clients and their data types, there is no particular common structure. Nonetheless, it is most likely that, from each client's perspective, the data has a well-defined structure.

One task of the service is the triage of the messages, and according to their data perform some processing. The heterogeneous data imposes a challenge to the navigation and identification of the containing information – sometimes it is feasible; but other times, it leads to considerably complex implementations.

Stakeholder Concerns

#**DataReadability**: increasing the readability (i.e., understandability) of a record of data, regardless of its context; for instance, a data record found in a tracing tool; #**Integrability**: promoting a more seamless usage of the data by other systems, i.e., reducing the friction of integration; #**LowComplexity**: implementing code for data exploration that does not require in-depth navigation, extensive elaboration, or an intricate combination of criteria.

Initial Behavior - A capability of an API Contract is consumed in various contexts with heterogeneous data structures as input, but the processing in the API Provider is homogeneous for all of them. The received data undergoes a complex conditional that identifies its information, and then the rest of the processing follows.

Design Smells

- **Rigidity or Closure to change**: when it is hard to extend the message processing, harming "The Open-Closed Principle" [13];
- **Sea of IFs**: the triage of incoming messages undergoes a complex conditional structure, that identifies specific fields in the data; e.g., deep nested `if-else` statements.

Steps

1. Identify the different metadata needed for the processing; one approach is to consider metadata that points to specific attributes of the data, e.g., for a unique identifier that might be a composed key;
2. To define where and how to introduce the metadata, classify the different pieces of metadata and potential API Consumers:
   (a) for those that the responsible for setting it should be the API Provider, then mark them as **"internal"**; the rest, mark them as **"external"**;
   (b) for those that the same structure repeats for an arbitrary long sequence of messages, then mark them as **"stable"**; for the rest, mark them as **"volatile"**;
   (c) for the API Consumers that are unable or unwilling to change, mark them as **"fixed"**; for the rest, mark them as **"changeable"**;

3. The introduction of the metadata happens by crossing the classification of metadata pieces and potential API Consumers, as so:
   (a) for the pieces of metadata marked as *"internal"*, introduce them as deploy-time configuration in the API Provider;
   (b) for the *"external"* metadata, when the candidate is *"fixed"*, then introduce the metadata as an external component that acts as an adapter between the candidate and the API Provider; do nothing to the candidate, mark the adapter as *"changeable"*, and proceed to treat it as another candidate;
   (c) for the *"external"* metadata, for the *"changeable"* candidates,
      i. with *"stable"* metadata, extend the API Contract to comprise Operations that allow API Consumers to set their stable metadata once to be reused with its messages;
      ii. else (i.e., *"volatile"* metadata), introduce the metadata as part of the message, to be sent by the candidate along with the data;

4. Implement a component in the API Provider that aggregates the metadata for a message from all the different sources (the pieces embedded in the message, and those pre-defined either using the configuration API or the deploy-time configuration);
5. Implement the metadata-based processing algorithm in a new component in the API Provider and replace the old one with it.

Target Behavior - The capability is defined and consumed as before, and the processing remains homogeneous. The received data no longer undergoes a complex identification; instead, it uses the metadata provided in various ways to guide the identification of the data, and then the rest of the processing follows. This refactoring is towards a set of patterns: "Enrich with Metadata" and "Agree on the Meta Structure"; depending on the combinations "Configure Meta in Runtime", "Configure Meta during Deploy", "Embed Metadata", and "Adapt the Ingestion" [12].

(Refactoring) Extract Pluggable Processors

Motivation - After the triage of the messages, the service has to process them. The algorithms employed for that can vary depending on actual data or the data structure (e.g., when paying with a credit card, there might be interest rates for a person and a company). In other situations, the metadata is not enough to represent the differences between data structures. Then, the metadata tends to get too intricate and hard to use and process. Such obstacles in the way to process data lead to implementations hard to predict due to complexity or harm the abstractions that represent the real world.

Stakeholder Concerns

#**Flexibility**: promoting the design of parts to enable recombination in different contexts; #**CodeReadability**: ensuring the code makes explicit the design decisions made and the solutions adopted; #**Extensibility**: favoring the inclusion of new features and capabilities seamlessly;

Initial Structure or Behavior - The system has data-specific processors, each tight to each capability's feature.

Design Smells

- **Changing input changes output**: when small changes to the input lead to unproportionate changes to the output;
- **Null-heavy abstractions**: the abstractions created to support the processing are forced to contain frequent `null` fields; that indicates a mismatch between the abstraction and the reality;
- **Unnecessarily complex processing**: the processing of data follows intricate paths, often branching to handle corner cases;
- **Complex metadata**: if using metadata, it can get too complex to define the pieces or to process them;

Steps

1. Identify all the different paths the processing can go;
2. Identify the commonalities between different behavior;
3. Define an interface with those commonalities, to have different implementations;
4. (Optional) Allow the combination of implementations, for example, by also adopting Decorators or Composites [9];
5. For each different behavior, implement the common interface and allow its usage to be dynamically configurable, making them plugins;
6. (Optional) Define metadata as a hint of the plugin (or plugin combination) required for that piece of data.

Target Structure or Behavior - This implementation follows the pattern "Plug the Processors In" [12].

5 Case Studies

Case: Startup Digi Dojo

The Startup Digi Dojoplatform was based on MSA. It had a gateway to route and balance the requests and 4 microservices with business logic: "Startups and Users" (SU), "Virtual Spaces" (VS), "Tasks and Calendars" (TC), and "Assistant". The former three interacted with each other to support basic capabilities, such as the creation of startups and hiring of personnel (SU), setup of virtual personal offices and meeting rooms (VS), and scheduling and project management (TC), among other related capabilities. Meanwhile, the Assistant offered an API Operation for each event emitted by the other microservices. For every operation, its behavior was to ingest the data – i.e., receive and store –, then when queried for a research report or an insight for the user, it operated on the raw data by combining different records. Figure 1a illustrates this situation.

In this case, a major challenge to the system's evolution was the tight coupling the Assistant API Contract held about its API Consumers (SU, VS, and TC). By having a dedicated operation to each event of the other microservices, it would require the API Contract to be updated whenever there was a change in

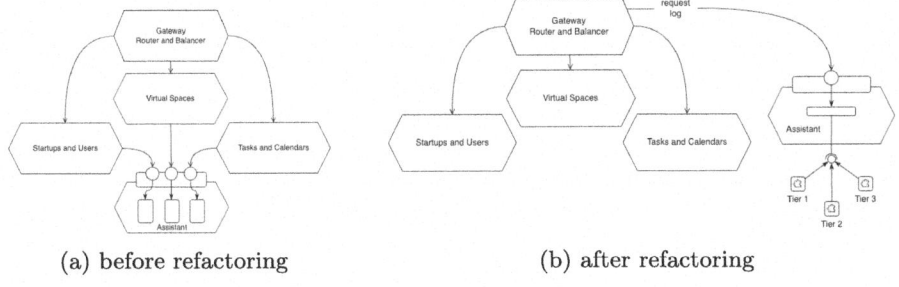

(a) before refactoring   (b) after refactoring

Fig. 1. Initial and refactored architecture of the Startup Digi Dojoplatform

the existing events, or if there would be new events to be included. Consequently, the actual processing of the data to support the reports and insights had to be postponed to the moment of request, instead of pre-calculation.

We applied the three refactorings to this initial architecture. One interesting aspect was that during the INTRODUCE METADATA refactoring, we decided to leverage the "Gateway Router and Balancer" to implement the metadata adapter, by making it log every request to the Assistant. That was beneficial, because it brought the metadata closer to the origin, i.e., the user interaction frontend.

There were three tiers of accuracy for the plugins: tier 1 was the baseline that would be able to operate in all situations, but with less precision; tier 2 would override tier 1 because it adopted a better-informed algorithm, but it might not be possible to operate in all cases; and tier 3 would operate based on metadata, and it would override the others. The result is illustrated in Fig. 1b.

Scenario "A" Before refactoring, the addition of a new data provider means the creation of a new event of interest to the Assistant. It would require including a new API Operation dedicated to that event in its API Contract. In other words, the maintainers of the Assistant would need to get to know the event, and then understand the structure of an external data structure to implement the operation on the Assistant API.

After the refactoring, the new event of interest to the Assistant characterizes the addition of a new data provider. With the API Operation that embraces heterogeneity in data, there is no need to include a new operation, as the existing one is suitable.

Scenario "B" Before refactoring, the structure accepts a new component. But the important aspect of it is the challenge to implement it, rather than the extension of the service. As the data comes to the service as-is, the processing algorithm needs to know the structure and meaning of the data.

After refactoring, no changes to the extensibility, but the implementation can take place seamlessly. As the data comes enriched with metadata, there is no more need for previous knowledge and understanding of the data. Moreover, the structure of the metadata is well-defined in agreement between the involved parts, so it is possible to assume pre understanding of its structure and meaning during development time.

Case: Catch-Solve

Catch-Solve is a software startup that offers monitoring and quality checking services [17]. Its platform had two web servers, a shared database, and two types of data collection agents: one focused on inspecting Web frontends, and another focused on collecting Android app error logs. While the former operates triggered by a scheduler, the latter is an autonomous agent that acquires the logs whenever an error happens in the app and sends it whenever there is a network connection. One highlight of this architecture is that the API Contract for the Ingestion already was shaped as a single operation that joined the API Consumers. One piece of data injected in each request made to the Ingestion API was a pair of identifiers: the customer ID, that made reference to the application it was exploring; and the test ID, that communicated the type of record that request contained. These IDs were used to identify the processing needed. Figure 2a illustrates the starting architecture of this case.

The behavior of the Web frontend agent required more attention, as it implemented a set of detections. For the maintainers of this architecture, the relationship between a single test ID and a set of detections was limiting the extensibility of this agent, as it was planned to incorporate new detections in the future. The test ID was tight coupled with the processing of its results because whenever there would be changes in the set of detections, there would have to be changes in the processing as well. Furthermore, as a single agent doing multiple detections was limiting the implementation of such detections, it would be beneficial to allow the adoption of technologies better suited for each detection.

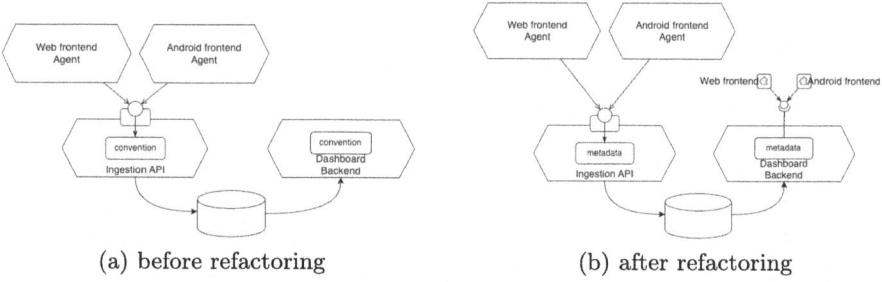

(a) before refactoring   (b) after refactoring

Fig. 2. Initial and refactored architecture of the Catch-Solve platform

Given the API Contract of the Ingestion API, it did not require the first refactoring. We faced challenges related to the technology restrictions for detection and identification of detection results. For that, we followed the INTRODUCE METADATA. We defined the metadata would represent the structure of the results, making the detection independent of the processing. With that, it would be possible to adopt different technologies for the detections without compromising the processing of their results. Lastly, we followed EXTRACT PLUGGABLE PROCESSORS to match the metadata, i.e., the structure of the detection results. We ended up with two groups of plugins, due to the differences in the nature of the data: a group of plugins dedicated to the structures related to Web frontend inspections, and another for the Android error reports. Figure 2b illustrates the resulting architecture.

For this particular case, since the API already followed **Flexibilize the Ingestion** [12], we did not apply the JOIN API OPERATIONS WITH HETEROGENEOUS DATA. That makes the **Scenario "A"** less impacting to the analysis because the compared versions of the architecture have the very similar structures.

The difference worth mentioning regards the usage of metadata: before the refactoring, the processing was based on a test ID, while after that it used metadata. This is relevant for adding a new data provider in the sense that a new data provider might conduct a new test identified by a new ID – which would not trigger any processing. But there would be a problem if we consider a new data provider as a new version of the existing one, that changed which parts it included in its data. This type of change, in the initial version, would require changes to processing algorithms, or risk exceptional states. Alternatively, after refactoring, metadata driving the processing enables partial handles of data, avoiding exceptional states in the application.

Scenario "B" We highlight the positive impact of metadata and its usage as scope for data processing. Before refactoring, a new algorithm would lead the application to either lack data – when the processing is implemented before the tests are providing the new piece of data –, or cause unexpected states by lack of algorithms. The refactored version does not suffer from these limitations.

Case: Open Data Hub

Open Data Hub[1] is an aggregation platform comprising data from a wide range of data providers, such as meteorological data, social and touristic events, and other smart devices for smart-cities infrastructure. This large amount of data is then provided to the innovation community in a standardized shape. Hence, the main task of the platform is to collect large amounts of heterogeneous data, transform it into a structured way, and provide it under a service API. The initial architecture follows a serverless architecture, where for each data provider there is a dedicated data transformer that pulls data from the source, transforms it, and stores it in the aggregated database. Although this solves the functional requirement, it presents challenges to the evolvability and maintenance of the platform, mainly due to code replication. Figure 3a illustrates the architecture.

For this case, the application of the JOIN API OPERATIONS WITH HETEROGENEOUS DATA refactoring was adapted, because each transformer wrote directly into the database. So, we created the "Ingestion Service" with the single API Operation that otherwise would join the other operations. Additionally, to the same service, we created a second API Contract to handle implementation details of the INTRODUCE METADATA refactoring: the runtime configuration of the metadata (step 3, item c-i). We also applied EXTRACT PLUGGABLE PROCESSORS, and used metadata as a description of the structural features of the data,

---

[1] https://opendatahub.com.

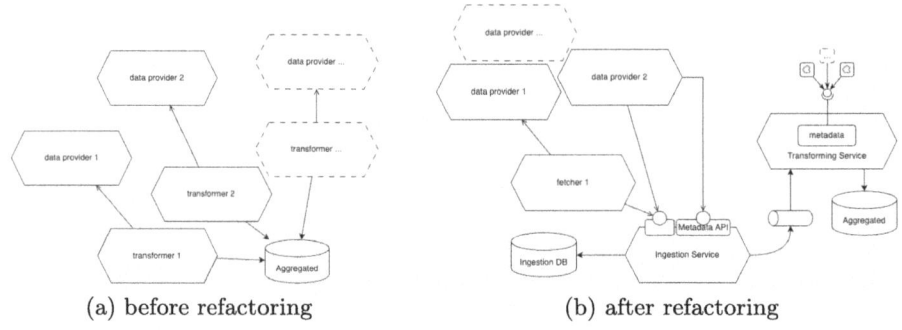

Fig. 3. Initial and refactored architecture of the data aggregation platform

forming a Domain-Specific Language that acted as a key for the composition of plugins to process a piece of data.

In this case, due to the particular scale of the data being collected and transformed, we decided to split ingestion and processing into two separate components that communicate via a message queue. Also, some data providers could not agree to directly send data. For these cases, the adapter option was implemented as a data fetcher. In Fig. 3b, we depicted two examples where "data provider 1" required the adapter, while "data provider 2" did not; but beyond those examples, there were other data providers that required a different combination of the solutions pointed in the INTRODUCE METADATA refactoring.

Scenario "A" Before refactoring, the architecture performed below the desired standards. Adding a new data provider means creating a new component that collects the data, processes it and ultimately stores it in the production database. This process has limited quality by two major factors: it does not allow autonomous data providers, and it heads towards unnecessary code replication.

The refactored version solved both of these issues. The newly created ingestion API enabled data providers to directly integrate with the platform. Moreover, the responsibilities of processing the data and storing it could be shared among different situations, reducing unnecessary code replication.

Scenario "B" Before refactoring, the architecture suffered to create a new dedicated component. From the conversation with the maintainers, this task was a big concern in many aspects, from the poor maintainability due to code replication to a lack of motivation for doing repetitive activities. In practice, even when a similar processing was already implemented, it was hard to benefit from the existing code.

After refactoring, the architecture performed considerably better. Decoupling the processing from the concrete data – via the enrichment with metadata – allowed a simpler implementation, not to mention the possibility of reusing code with the plugin approach.

6 Discussion

Refactoring, as the systematic process of improving software quality by changing its internal implementation without impacting its external functionality [8], offers natural challenges. The immediate one to mention is how to change how a *solution* is implemented without changing the *solution* itself. From our catalog, the JOIN API OPERATIONS WITH HETEROGENENOUS DATA refactoring works directly to simpler cases. But it also can be perceived as a partial solution to more complex scenarios. Embracing heterogeneity will likely introduce challenges. But, as the goal of the proposed refactoring catalog is to promote reusability, there is value to the JOIN API OPERATIONS WITH HETEROGENENOUS DATA refactoring. One can even argue that the Catch-Solve platform supports that: it had already an implementation of **Flexibilize the Ingestion** pattern [12], and it worked fine to support reusability of its API.

The Startup Digi Dojo and Open Data Hub case studies also support the value of the JOIN API OPERATIONS WITH HETEROGENENOUS DATA refactoring. In both cases, the refactoring led to a more reusable API, a structure similar to the **Tolerant Reader** [5], which handles gracefully unforeseen structures. Additionally, it is important to consider that a major part of the efforts in evolving heterogeneous and distributed systems is the technicalities surrounding the implementation, instead of the business rules [1]. The reusability promoted by JOIN API OPERATIONS WITH HETEROGENENOUS DATA reduces reworking and replication.

One important quality of the refactored versions comes from the decoupling between data ingestion and data processing. One important enabler – despite not being necessary – is the usage of metadata, a consequence of the INTRODUCE METADATA refactoring: data processing can rely solely on metadata to perform its task. As a beneficial side effect of this decoupling, in all three cases, the ingestion avoided data loss and, consequently, became less chatty with the original data providers. That reinforces the system's autonomy, a desirable characteristic of MSA that still has room for improvements [1]. That is particularly true when considering its evolution: the raw data ingested was stored internally, so if there are any internal changes, the processing can be redone easily, e.g., in the case of updates in metadata.

Structurally, for all the cases studied, the addition of metadata to the data flow was not a problem; instead, the hard task was to define what information the metadata would bring. As INTRODUCE METADATA attempts to promote abstraction of the structure by describing its information, DDD domain events [7] can play an important role in defining such metadata. Furthermore, a useful tool to elicit the events is the Event Storming workshop [4].

While the EXTRACT PLUGGABLE PROCESSORS refactoring does not directly promote the reusability of the API, it does benefit the adaptability of the processing component in the implementation. By following a plugin architecture (or microkernel [14]), the processing component behind the API becomes extensible and enables the reuse of the plugins in multiple workflows.

Throughout the analysis of the results, we found interesting elements that went beyond the proposed scope. By condensing all the load of one service into a single Operation, it might get easier to measure the service demand. With that, the definition of the scalability parameters in the infrastructure improves.

7 Conclusion

This work addresses the evolution challenges of MSA when there is an exploding number of similar services. We build on top of the "Pattern Language for Leveraging Metadata to Reusability in APIs" [12], and here proposed a catalog of refactorings towards the patterns in that collection. These refactorings instruct to JOIN API OPERATIONS WITH HETEROGENENOUS DATA, INTRODUCE METADATA, and EXTRACT PLUGGABLE PROCESSORS.

We evaluated our refactorings based on three real-world case studies. Following Change Impact Analysis and the model ALMA [3], we considered the addition of new data providers and processing algorithms. The results showed the promotion of seamless addition of providers, and the reduction of coupling between data and the algorithms. We also noticed relevant impacts of the refactorings into other quality attributes, such as scalability, observability, and infrastructure.

References

1. Assunção, W.K., Krüger, J., Mosser, S., Selaoui, S.: How do microservices evolve? An empirical analysis of changes in open-source microservice repositories. J. Syst. Softw. **204** (2023). https://doi.org/10.1016/j.jss.2023.111788
2. Baltes, S., Ralph, P.: Sampling in software engineering research: a critical review and guidelines. Empirical Softw. Eng. **27**(4), 94 (2022). https://doi.org/10.1007/s10664-021-10072-8
3. Bengtsson, P.O., Lassing, N., Bosch, J., Van Vliet, H.: Architecture-level modifiability analysis (ALMA). J. Syst. Softw. **69**(1-2), 129–147 (2004). https://doi.org/10.1016/S0164-1212(03)00080-3
4. Brandolini, A.: Introducing EventStorming An act of Deliberate Collective Learning. Leanpub (2018)
5. Daigneau, R.: Service Design Patterns. Addison-Wesley (2012)
6. Erder, M., Pureur, P.: Continuous Architecture - Sustainable Architecture in an Agile and Cloud-Centric World (2016)
7. Evans, E.: Domain-Driven Design Tackling Complexity in the Heart of Software. Tech. rep. (2003). www.domainlanguage.com
8. Fowler, M.: Refactoring Improving the Design of Existing Code. Addison-Wesley Professional (1999)
9. Gamma, E., Helm, R., Johnson, R., Vlissides, J.: Design Patterns, elements of reusable object-oriented software. Addison-Wesley (1995). https://doi.org/10.1007/978-1-4302-0096-3_10
10. Lehnert, S.: A taxonomy for software change impact analysis. In: Proceedings of the 12th International Workshop on Principles of Software Evolution and the 7th Annual ERCIM Workshop on Software Evolution, pp. 41–50. ACM, New York, NY, USA (2011). https://doi.org/10.1145/2024445.2024454

11. Lercher, A., Glock, J., Macho, C., Pinzger, M.: Microservice API evolution in practice: a study on strategies and challenges. J. Syst. Softw. **215** (2024). https://doi.org/10.1016/j.jss.2024.112110
12. Lino Daniel, J.F., Wang, X., Martins Guerra, E.: Pattern language for leveraging metadata to reusability in APIs. In: Proceeding of the 29th European Conference on Pattern Languages of Programs (2024). https://doi.org/10.1145/3698322.3698344
13. Martin, R.C.: The Clean Architecture (2012). http://blog.8thlight.com/uncle-bob/2012/08/13/the-clean-architecture.html--
14. Richards, M.: Software Architecture Patterns - Understanding Common Architecture Patterns and When to Use them (2015)
15. Runeson, P., Höst, M.: Guidelines for conducting and reporting case study research in software engineering. Empirical Softw. Eng. **14**(2), 131–164 (2009). https://doi.org/10.1007/s10664-008-9102-8
16. Silva, K., Melegati, J., Silveira, F., Wang, X., Ferreira, M., Guerra, E.: ArchHypo: managing software architecture uncertainty using hypotheses engineering. IEEE Trans. Softw. Eng. (2024). https://doi.org/10.1109/TSE.2024.3520477
17. Silva, K., Melegati, J., Wang, X., Ferreira, M., Guerra, E.: Using hypotheses to manage technical uncertainty and architecture evolution in a software start-up. IEEE Softw. **41**(4), 7–13 (2024). https://doi.org/10.1109/MS.2024.3383628
18. Stocker, M., Zimmermann, O.: API refactoring to patterns: catalog, template and tools for remote interface evolution. In: ACM International Conference Proceeding Series Association for Computing Machinery (2023). https://doi.org/10.1145/3628034.3628073
19. Stocker, M., Zimmermann, O., Kapferer, S.: Pattern-oriented API refactoring: addressing design smells and stakeholder concerns. In: Proceedings of the 29th European Conference on Pattern Languages of Programs, People, and Practices, pp. 1–24. ACM, New York, NY, USA (2024). https://doi.org/10.1145/3698322.3698334
20. Viviani, L., Guerra, E., Melegati, J., Wang, X.: An empirical study about the instability and uncertainty of non-functional requirements. In: Lecture Notes in Business Information Processing. vol. 475 LNBIP, pp. 77–93. Springer Science and Business Media Deutschland GmbH (2023). https://doi.org/10.1007/978-3-031-33976-9_6
21. Wohlin, C., Rainer, A.: Is it a case study?—A critical analysis and guidance. J. Syst. Softw. **192**, 111395 (2022). https://doi.org/10.1016/j.jss.2022.111395
22. Yin, R.K.: Case Study Research, design and methods. SAGE, 4th edn. (2009)
23. Zhao, J., Yang, H., Xiang, L., Xu, B.: Change impact analysis to support architectural evolution. J. Softw. Maintenance Evol. Res. Pract. **14**(5), 317–333 (2002). https://doi.org/10.1002/smr.258

Open Access This chapter is licensed under the terms of the Creative Commons Attribution 4.0 International License (http://creativecommons.org/licenses/by/4.0/), which permits use, sharing, adaptation, distribution and reproduction in any medium or format, as long as you give appropriate credit to the original author(s) and the source, provide a link to the Creative Commons license and indicate if changes were made.

The images or other third party material in this chapter are included in the chapter's Creative Commons license, unless indicated otherwise in a credit line to the material. If material is not included in the chapter's Creative Commons license and your intended use is not permitted by statutory regulation or exceeds the permitted use, you will need to obtain permission directly from the copyright holder.

Exploratory Test-Driven Development Study with ChatGPT in Different Scenarios

Juliano Cesar Pancher[1(✉)], Jorge Melegati[2], and Eduardo Martins Guerra[2]

[1] Instituto de Pesquisas Tecnologicas do Estado de São Paulo, Av. Prof. Almeida Prado, 532, São Paulo, SP, Brazil
`juliano.pancher@ensino.ipt.br`

[2] Free University of Bozen-Bolzano, Piazza Università, 1, 39100 Bozen-Bolzano, Italy

Abstract. Generative AI has been rapidly adopted by the software development industry in various ways, offering innovative approaches to transforming requirements into working software. Combining Generative AI with Test-Driven Development (TDD) presents a creative method to accelerate this transformation. However, questions remain about ChatGPT's readiness for this challenge, including the techniques and best practices required for success and the scenarios where this approach can consistently deliver results. To explore these questions, we designed a study where a group of master's students performed programming assignments using TDD, first independently and then with the support of ChatGPT. The three assignments represent distinct scenarios: mathematical calculations (function), text processing (class), and system integration (class with dependencies). We performed a qualitative analysis of the submitted code and reports identifying key strategies that significantly influence success rates, such as providing contextual information, separating instructions in prompts following an iterative process, and assisting AI in fixing errors. Among the scenarios, the integration task achieved the highest performance. This study highlights the potential of leveraging Generative AI in TDD for software development and presents a list of effective strategies to maximize its impact. By applying these positive strategies and avoiding identified pitfalls, this research marks a step toward establishing best practices for integrating Generative AI with TDD in software engineering.

Keywords: Test-Driven Development · TDD · Generative AI · ChatGPT · Strategies

1 Introduction

Since its initial release to the public on November 30, 2022, ChatGPT attracted over one million subscribers within just one week. The Generative Artificial Intelligence (GenAI) tool surprised the world with its capacity to execute remarkably complex tasks from education to public health [6].

Recent research results indicate that the GenAI tools can aid a range of common software development and engineering tasks [1,10,16,31,36]. The use of a Development Bot (DevBot) is a trend that started with simple and repetitive tasks, and now the DevBots do code review, create test scripts, and collaborate with code generation and requirement elicitation [23]. Apart from the context of a DevBot, the ChatGPT tool can simply provide debugging assistance, bug prediction, and bug explanation to help solve programming problems [34]. By generating ideas, offering solutions, and offering feedback on design choices, ChatGPT can be utilized as a collaborative tool to support human software architects in the design process [16,19,22].

Although GenAI applications in Software Engineering show promise, a noticeable gap exists in the literature concerning substantial studies that explore its integration with Test-Driven Development (TDD). Existing research often focuses on predefined methodologies leveraging GenAI's capabilities to address complex software challenges, however, there is a lack of references where the participants are given the freedom to engage with the AI tool, allowing for the identification of emerging strategies that most contribute to positive outcomes across multiple scenarios. To address this gap, we focused on answering the following research questions: **(RQ1)** *Can Generative AI effectively support software development using TDD?*, and **(RQ2)** *What strategies can enhance the effectiveness of Generative AI in software development employing the TDD methodology in different scenarios?*

To answer these questions, we conducted a study involving master's students where, after implementing three code challenges using the traditional TDD, they were prompted to tackle the same challenges using GenAI to guide their TDD process. Besides the production and unit test code, each student also wrote a report detailing their strategies when working with GenAI, along with general comments and impressions about their experience. Additionally, they provided a full log of the prompts used during the exercises.

The focus of the analysis was qualitative, started by collecting some metrics from the source code, like the number of lines and the test coverage, and validated the production code through the reference unit tests. As the students were free to define the way to interact with the AI tool, we followed an inductive coding scheme with the aim of identifying the emerging good and bad strategies. Our findings indicate that Generative AI, particularly ChatGPT, can indeed aid in software development. Furthermore, we identified several strategies that can improve implementation success, such as manually correcting minor errors in the code generated by the GenAI tool and adopting an iterative approach separating the requests in different prompts, and others that can create complications like giving the full list of requirements in a single prompt.

Following the introduction, the article is structured into four additional sections. Section 2 delves into the background and theoretical underpinnings of TDD and GenAI. Section 3 outlines the methodology employed in this study. Section 4 presents the results and Sect. 5 brings the discussion. Finally, Sect. 6 outlines avenues for future research, and concludes the article.

2 Background

Test-Driven Development [14]. TDD is an iterative software development process where developers first write automated tests before writing the implementation code [2,4,17]. TDD has the word driven meaning the tests influence the design [17], and according to software industrial case studies, the quality improved with TDD when compared with non-TDD approach but the time to develop also increased [5]. The TDD approach leads to cleaner code and easier to understand [8], simpler design [18] and low defect rates [5]. Validate the TDD efficacy is difficult and many times inconclusive [13], and also not easy to implement due to lack of knowledge and experience, difficulty to shift to TDD mindset, technical complexity in a few scenarios such as GUI development, lack of detail upfront design [33].

Large Language Models. AI has existed in the human mentality for a long time now, the term was coined by John McCarthy in 1956 when defining the engineering of making intelligent machines [25]. This area of knowledge developed in different subsets, Machine Learning (ML) allows systems to learn from experience without implementing the rules [26], Deep learning (DL) makes use of neural networks to learn from complex datasets [21], Natural Language Processing (NLP) focuses on the interaction between computers and humans through natural language, beyond the literal meaning, in a way that would be possible to apply this technology to translation, chatbots, text summarization and others [10].

Large Language Models (LLM) is a type of DL model trained on huge datasets capable of predicting the next token in a sequence given the preview context [28]. The research of large Pre-Trained Models (PTM) started to gain traction with the creation of some large-scale supervised datasets [30]. It did not take long to integrate the PTM with a Transformer [15], which quickly became the standard neural structure for natural language generation.

The Generative Pre-Trained Transformer (GPT) was the first technology that combined the modern Transformer architecture and the self-supervised pre-training objective [15]. ChatGPT, a chatbot launched in November 2022 by the company OpenAI, had a geometric growth reaching 100 million active users monthly in only 4 months [3]. It's applications in the Software Engineering field are happening in software architecture [1,19,22], enhancing software engineering education [9], helping with software debugging and testing [16], and also to control managing existing AI models to solve complex AI tasks, including task planning, model selection, and result summarization across multiple domains [31].

TDD with LLMs. The study by Piya and Sullivan [29] explores using LLMs for TDD, focusing on ChatGPT generating code for 70 LeetCode problems in Python. Instead of providing the requirements as inputs as we do in our research, test cases are given in the prompt. Key findings include ChatGPT sometimes producing unexpected outcomes due to ambiguous test function names and string-based problems were easier for ChatGPT to solve than integer-based problems. The studies from Matheuw and Magappan [24] and Fakhoury et al. [11] introduced a framework and a workflow to improve the effectiveness of the code generation by GenAI, to resolve MBPP's and HumanEvals' problems. A collaboration between the developer and GenAI to overcome the barrier of not having enough developers experienced in TDD practices to use TDD is proposed by Mock et al. [27]. As one of the results, this study identified that having quality code supervision was important for the success of the implementation.

3 Research Design

The research objective is to identify good and bad strategies for using ChatGPT to support the practice of TDD to create software based on a given set of requirements. Additionally, we want to verify how the different scenarios may affect the results. Finally, we also capture the developer's perspective: how they feel about the approach of working with an AI tool to execute part of the work they were used to doing by themselves. A general view of the methodology is represented in Fig. 1.

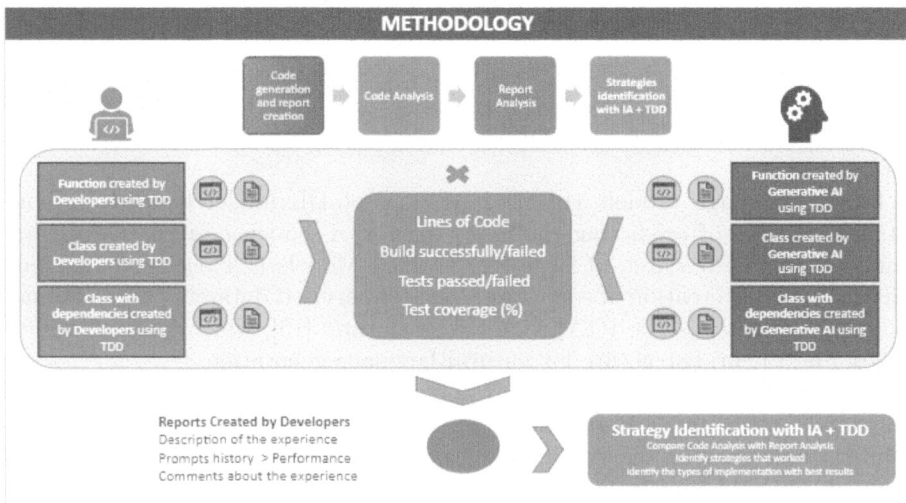

Fig. 1. Study Methodology

The study can be considered an exploratory empirical study, based on the principles of within-subject experiments [20]. In this method, the experimental units are exposed to multiple treatments, and each subject serves as its own control. That aligns with the goals of our study, since after performing TDD in a task, it is possible to compare this experience when ChatGPT is introduced. The study used master's students as subjects but didn't consider them as proxies for professionals [12]. All of them had programming experience and had a basis of TDD in the course. So, they are considered suitable considering the exploratory aspect of the study and its goals.

3.1 Task Description

Three TDD exercises were assigned to a group of master's students from the Free University of Bozen-Bolzano, located in Italy. The participants should first implement the exercises using TDD, and after the same task use ChatGPT support. While the regular assignments were part of the course activities, reimplementing them with ChatGPT was optional and performed voluntarily. The following describes the tasks:

- **Complex Calculation and Business Rule Enforcement Scenario** From a given student's points in practical assignments and exam grades, this function must calculate the final grade based on multiple rules and conditions, emphasizing precision in business logic. This scenario reflects the development of a function, with well-defined parameters and return, and the implementation involved mathematical calculations.
- **Text Processing with Context-Aware Translation Scenario** Building a word and sentence translator with a focus on incremental functionality and flexibility in translation rules. This scenario required handling strings to ensure context sensitivity in translations. As an example of the latter, there is a requirement to avoid translating words with the first letter capitalized in the middle of a sentence, to differentiate proper nouns from regular words. This scenario reflects the development of an independent class, in which the students should define its methods and interface.
- **Mocking and Integration with External Dependencies Scenario** Designing an Automated Teller Machine (ATM) system using mock objects to simulate external dependencies that represent hardware and remote services. The complexity of this scenario was in the orchestration between dependencies that are responsible for different responsibilities. This scenario reflects the development of a class with dependencies, which should be represented by Mock Objects [32] in the tests.

3.2 Data Collection and Analysis

The inputs used in the analysis were: (a) the source code generated by the students when completing the assignments using TDD without the help of ChatGPT; (b) the source code created by the students with ChatGPT support using TDD to produce the same result, and (c) the reports created by the students, including comments about the strategies, results, impressions, and prompt logs. **Code Analysis.** The code Analysis evaluated the source code against the corresponding requirements, analyzed the coverage of the unit tests, and measured the size in lines of code.

To evaluate the requirements a set of reference unit tests were elaborated for each scenario to be used as a reference: (a) for the first scenario 6 unit tests were written to verify if the grade calculation was correct; (b) for the second scenario the basic translation was evaluated by 9 unit tests, and 4 additional tests covered optional requirements; (c) the third scenario, because of the difference in the structure of the solutions, the tests needed to be adapted based on the students test for each case, but in all cases, it was verified that all the requirements were covered. We performed a comparison of the failed tests between the assignment developed by the student using TDD without ChatGPT assistance with the second attempt using TDD assisted by ChatGPT.

The test coverage was verified for all submitted assignments, using IntelliJ, leveraging its report capability to provide a coverage percentage by classes, methods, lines, and branches. Branch coverage shows the rate coverage of all possible executed paths in statements like if-else or switch. Finally, the number of lines of code was calculated using the plugin Statistic for IntelliJ, ignoring the blank and comment lines. The size was measured both for production and test code.

Report Analysis. To analyze the reports, we followed an inductive coding scheme. This approach was chosen to explore participants' perspectives on the results and strategies adopted when using the ChatGPT support [35]. The analysis began with a thorough reading of the reports to become deeply familiar with the data. Specific text segments were then identified, labeled, and converted into initial codes [7]. After that, the identified codes were refined to identify the good and bad strategies the students applied. The report information complemented the code analysis, providing a perspective of the process adopted for the source code generation.

4 Results

This section presents the results of the data analysis performed in the study data. The next subsections cover the code analysis results and the codes identified in the reports. This information is used to build the context and understand the factors and conditions experienced by the students, to identify factors that influenced the outcomes. The replication package with the complete study data is available at https://zenodo.org/records/14691979.

4.1 Code Analysis

For the Complex Calculation and Business Rule Enforcement scenario, as seen in Table 1, 4 of 12 received submissions developed by the student passed all six tests, and 9 of 12 passed at least four tests. When considering the source code generated by ChatGPT through the student prompts, only one of 12 passed the six tests, and 5 of 12 passed at least four tests. Only in two cases did the ChatGPT-generated code present a better performance on tests than the student-generated one, three cases kept the same performance, and all the rest of the 7 instances got a worse result when using GenAI to code. Most of the unit test failures for the students, also failure for the ChatGPT-generated code.

In the Text Processing with Context-Aware Translation scenario, three students delivered a code that passed all mandatory tests, and the AI-generated

Table 1. TDD Performance of Student x ChatGPT

Coder	Complex Calculation and Business Rule Enforcement	Text Processing with Context-Aware Translation	Mocking and Integration with External Dependencie	Total
Student	4/12	3/12	8/11	15/35
ChatGPT	1/12	1/12	10/11	12/35
Totals	5/24	4/24	18/22	27/70

code had one case only with the same performance. Except for one student who improved performance when using AI, 5 of 12 achieved the same results, and the other 6 had fewer unit tests passing for the code generated by the AI.

The Mocking and Integration with External Dependencies scenario presented the best performance for all scenarios, as 8 of 10 deliverables passed all tests without in the student's code, and 10 of 12 in the AI code.

The unit tests created using TDD with ChatGPT assistance for the complex calculation scenario have a higher coverage on average, while the opposite happens for the other two scenarios with fewer business rules and math calculations, as presented in Table 2.

Table 2. Test Coverage

Scenario	Method	GPT Method	Line	GPT Line	Branch	GPT Branch
Complex Calculation and Business Rule Enforcement	98%	95%	99%	92%	93%	83%
Text Processing with Context-Aware Translation	89%	94%	87%	88%	80%	85%
Mocking and Integration with External Dependencies	83%	92%	70%	73%	52%	63%
Totals	90%	94%	86%	85%	76%	78%

The number of lines of code for GPT implementation on average as seen in Table 3, was smaller than the implemented by the students, for all three scenarios, and significantly smaller in the Mocking and Integration with External Dependencies scenario implementation where GPT presented a very optimized code on average, with the better success rate between all scenarios, as shown in Table 1.

4.2 Report Analysis

From the inductive coding analysis performed in the reports, a few strategies were identified that positively or negatively contributed to the outcomes, as seen in Fig. 2.

Separate instructions in prompts following an iterative process was the most frequent strategy identified, mentioned by 18 of 35 assignments, as stated by one student: "*I tried to make requests in a more structured and step-by-step manner,*

Table 3. Lines of Code

Scenario	Implementation	GPT Implementation	Tests	GPT Tests
1.Complex Calculation and Business Rule Enforcement	61	57	89	76
2.Text Processing with Context-Aware Translation	81	61	114	100
3.Mocking and Integration with External Dependencies	118	61	194	120
Total geral	86	60	131	98

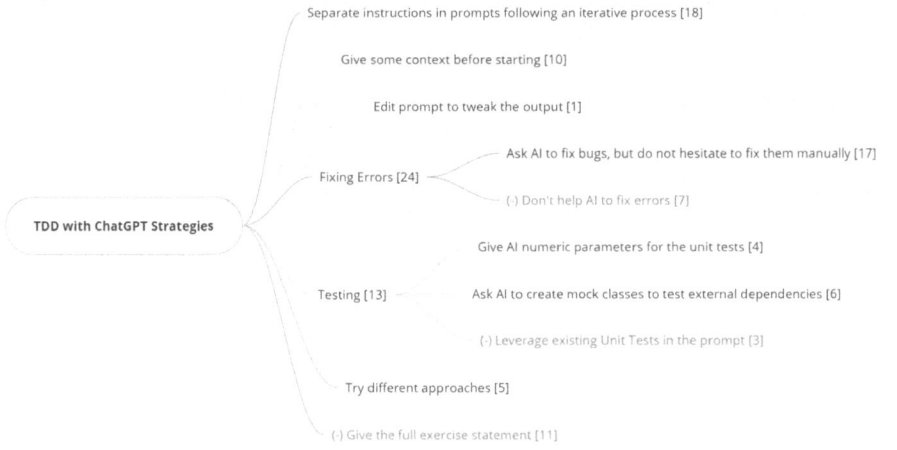

Fig. 2. Strategies identified in the reports

and it worked. It took me little time, and all the tests are successful." (S1), aligned with the iterative approach required for any TDD implementation.

The strategy to fix the errors when using AI to generate the code was defined by each student, and they were grouped into two different categories, based on the outcomes observed in each case. The first one, with hopeful outcomes, is to ask the AI to fix the errors, but not hesitate to fix them manually noted in 17 of 35 assignments. The second is asking AI to fix the errors, and avoid helping it motivated by different reasons *"I would like to preserve the original code generated by ChatGPT"* (S15), as observed in 7 of 35 assignments, most of them, resulting in a failed implementation.

In 11 of 35 assignments, students opted to give the full exercise statement to the AI right at the beginning. This approach diverges from the principles of TDD, as recognized by one student: *"So I gave it the whole requirements file that I had, in order to get a better output.[...] In a way, this was not TDD"* (S3). On the other hand, separating instructions in prompts following an iterative process helped the AI better understand the requests and define boundaries for its responses, often leading to more satisfactory outcomes. This strategy was employed in at least 10 of 35 assignments, with interesting outcomes.

A common highlight across the assignments was ChatGPT's ability to refactor code. While most students appreciated its skills in this area, some encountered challenges, as illustrated by one participant: *"I asked the bot to refactor the whole class so that there is no method with more than 10 lines of code. It did that but that broke quite a few test cases"* (S10).

Nine students reported that ChatGPT was able to implement tasks with relative ease. This was particularly noted in two scenarios: Text Processing with Context-Aware Translation (three instances) and Mocking and Integration with External Dependencies (six instances). In contrast, the math-oriented scenario did not receive any feedback indicating ease of implementation. Some students perceived GPT as having difficulties with more complex tasks, such as adhering to specific calculation rules or combining multiple tasks within a single function, and 5 out of 12 students chose to avoid delivering the optional and more complex requirements for the text processing scenario.

Regarding the quality of the generated code, six students described ChatGPT's output as clean, and two noted that the AI-produced code was simpler than their own. These students highlighted the AI's good naming conventions and the scalability of its code. However, opinions on the AI's ability to handle tests were more negative. While some praised its competence with mock techniques, as one student noted, *"I was surprised when ChatGPT implemented the tasks with Mocks, without having suggested it to him."* (S9), others criticized its inability to provide accurate and comprehensive test cases. A recurring complaint was that the AI struggled to supply relevant test data for the assigned methods.

5 Discussion

Based on our analysis, we identified a set of strategies to maximize the effectiveness of developing software applications using TDD in combination with GenAI. Additionally, we pinpointed strategies that should be avoided in this context to ensure optimal results. Finally, we also explore a comparison between the different scenarios and recognize some of the study limitations.

5.1 Emerging Strategies

Separate Instructions in Prompts following an Iterative Process: This strategy is about following TDD: a) give a piece of the requirement and ask GenAI to create the unit tests; b) ask AI to implement the code to pass the tests; c) ask ChatGPT to refactor the code if needed. In each step of the iteration, be clear to ask exactly what you expect it to do. Some students (S3, S6, S10, S13, and S15) used this strategy in more than one scenario and were satisfied with the result *"I am really pleasantly surprised by how well it went and how easy it is to generate working code using TDD"* (S15). The iterative approach creates a checkpoint on each step: *"After verifying that all tests passed, I moved on to the fifth rule"* (S6) and provides a better level of control during the entire process *"After that I decided to continue but passing the requirements one by one. I kept the production code it generated at the first time, but to understand if it was correct I preferred to focus on generating the test one by one."* (S10).

Ask AI to Fix Bugs, but do not Hesitate to Fix them Manually: different approaches to deal with bugs were observed: *"For any errors, I analyze them myself and told the AI how to fix"* (S13), *"For this I decide to try to fix it manually, since I already attempted to instruct the bot without success"* (S10), and *"I have noticed that it tends to reuse past code it wrote, even if it made my tests fail. So the only solution is to actually ask it to approach the problem differently, such that it sets up a whole new solution."* (S7). All of these approaches contributed somehow to a positive outcome, and using the more convenient for each context seems to be a winning strategy. However, fixing bugs from the AI-generated code might not be easy: *"This left me bug fixing code I have never written and scouting for errors I have not made, which was very tedious and time-consuming"* (S3) and *"fixing the stuff where it failed took longer than the time I needed for programming it from scratch without the help of AI"* (S5).

Give Some Context Before Starting: Start the conversation with ChatGPT with a short and balanced briefing that may include the intention to follow TDD methodology, specify Java as the programming language to use, and JUnit as the library for building unit tests. The total absence of initial context can bring some problems, as observed by one student: *"My first idea was [...] splitting up the task into several subtasks and prompting GPT only parts of the whole application.[...] ChatGPT did not understand me and was just inventing context for application for itself"* (S3).

Give AI Numeric Parameters for the Unit Tests: For the complex calculation scenario, there were complaints about the limitation of the ChatGPT to create appropriate tests to validate the requirements, as observed by this student: *"ChatGPT appeared to be pretty unreliable/inefficient at creating tests. According to my experience, just telling it to test the borders of a value's ranges wouldn't really work, so if I wanted them tested, I had to calculate the values themselves. Also, I had to constantly remind it of the ranges of certain values (lab points and exam points)."* (S13). That's why helping the AI to define the numerical inputs and the expected outcome for each scenario is a very positive strategy.

Edit Prompt to Tweak the Output: Instead of adding more prompts to ask for minor adjustments, you can edit the previous prompt to direct the output to the expected objectives. Using this tool, it is possible to give or change the names used in the output code, add additional information and clarification to avoid misunderstanding or remove items that produce bad elements in the output: *"With the new editing feature, I was able to quickly find issues in my prompts and further tweak the results"* (S3).

Ask AI to Create Mock Classes to Test External Dependencies: For the scenario with external dependencies, a student said: "I requested a complete solution with mock class implementations and tests" (S8). There were comments regarding ChatGPT's expertise with mocks: "*I was surprised when ChatGPT implemented the tasks with Mocks, without having suggested it to him. But this demonstrates that this is the best way to do it*" (S9).

5.2 Strategies with Negative Outcomes

The following strategies haven't contributed to a positive outcome and should be avoided when developing software following TDD using a Generative AI tool.
Give the Full Exercise Statement: By giving the full exercise statement to ChatGPT you are not using TDD. Many assignments started this way, however, none of the students repeated this strategy in all three scenarios. Although TDD was not used, some cases worked "*I tried to dump all the requirements at ChatGPT and it surprisingly responded really well in sieving out the requirements and genera ng clean and working code.*" (S15).
Don't help AI to Fix Errors: Sometimes, AI gets stuck and can't fix a bug. Avoiding touching the code, can be a big blocker, or slow down the development, as observed in that case: "*I spent 80% of the time trying to tell it what to look for, because I saw what the problem was and wanted the AI to figure it out on its own, without its own hints*" (S2).
Leverage Existing Unit Tests in the Prompt: The use of existing unit tests in a prompt is a risk that might lead to incomplete code implementation, depending on the coverage and quality of the tests. The cases observed in this study started with an initial good result and ended up having problems adding more complex requirements: "*Initially [...] the result was surprisingly good, it provided the code that had 5 out of 10 test passing. [...] The two extra tasks about punctuation and capital preservation were a different story. ChatGPT was not able to have the same function that provided that many services, it kept deleting what was done before to add not working code, so after a long struggle I gave up*" (S4).

5.3 Scenario Comparison

For complex calculation and text processing scenarios, the GenAI performance was below expectation, as it struggled to deal with interdependent business rules and context-sensitive logic. In the first case, to overcome the challenges was important to fix bugs manually and help AI define test parameters and scenarios. In the second case, part of the mandatory requirements wasn't well understood by the students, as both deliverables, with and without GenAI, failed the same requirement.

The success rate of the Mocking and Integration with External Dependencies scenario was surprising. As it was the third assignment for all the students, maybe the experience acquired with the other two implementations contributed to this improvement. Furthermore, it was impressive that the GPT's code, on average, has almost half of the lines compared with the students' implementation and a similar success rate.

5.4 Limitations

The results of this study are limited to the specific scenarios analyzed, and alternative scenarios not covered may yield different strategies. Additionally, the level of expertise of the participants, who were still in the process of learning TDD as evidenced by one of them "*I asked for help from friends since I didn't understand the whole mocking and TDD concept from the beginning*" (S17), likely influenced the outcomes.

6 Conclusion

Our goal was to verify if Generative AI can effectively support software development using TDD in different scenarios and also identify the strategies that can maximize the performance using TDD with the ChatGPT tool. We observed a hopeful path using ChatGPT following TDD, with better performance for low complexity applications, and a path to evolve when complex calculations or business rules reinforcement are needed, especially when leveraging the right strategies identified in this study.

The primary strategies contributing to successful outcomes include separate instructions in prompts following an iterative process, asking AI to fix bugs but also helping it to fix them manually, giving some context before starting, and providing AI with accurate test data scenarios. Conversely, giving full exercise in prompt and not helping AI to fix errors should be avoided.

For future development, the same study could be repeated, asking the participants to follow the strategies mapped in this work. Another interesting research aim would be proposing a framework using TDD with GenAI, for a team organized in different roles, to develop a complex piece of software.

References

1. Ahmad, A., et al.: Towards human-bot collaborative software architecting with ChatGPT". en. In: Proceedings of the 27th International Conference on Evaluation and Assessment in Software Engineering, Oulu Finland, pp. 279–285. ACM, June 2023. isbn: 9798400700446. https://doi.org/10.1145/3593434.3593468. https://dl.acm.org/doi/10.1145/3593434.3593468, Accessed 19 May 2024
2. Astels, D.: Test-driven development: a practical guide. eng. 3. print. The Coad series. Upper Saddle River, NJ: Prentice Hall PTR (2003). isbn: 978-0-13-101649-1
3. Bartz, D.: As ChatGPT's popularity explodes, U.S. lawmakers take an interest. In: Reuters, February 2023. https://www.reuters.com/technology/chatgpts-popularity-explodes-us-lawmakers-takean-interest-2023-02-13/
4. Beck, K.: Aim, fire [test-first coding]. IEEE Software **18**(5), 87–89 (2001). issn: 0740-7459, 1937-4194. https://doi.org/10.1109/52.951502, https://ieeexplore.ieee.org/document/951502/ Accessed 11 May 2024
5. Bhat, T., Nagappan, N.: Evaluating the efficacy of test-driven development: industrial case studies

6. Biswas, S.S.: Role of Chat GPT in Public Health. Ann. Biomed. Eng. **51**(5), 868–869 (2023). issn: 0090-6964, 1573-9686. https://doi.org/10.1007/s10439-023-03172-7, https://link.springer.com/10.1007/s10439-023-03172-7, Accessed 25 May 2024
7. Creswell, J.W.: Research Design: Qualitative, Quantitative, and Mixed Methods Approaches. 4th edition. Sage Publications, Chap. 8 (2013)
8. Crispin, L.: Driving software quality: how test-driven development impacts software quality. IEEE Software **23**(6), 70–71 (2006), issn: 0740-7459. https://doi.org/10.1109/MS.2006.157, http://ieeexplore.ieee.org/document/4012627/ Accessed 18 May 2024
9. Daun, M., Brings, J.: How ChatGPT will change software engineering education. en. In: Proceedings of the 2023 Conference on Innovation and Technology in Computer Science Education V. 1. Turku Finland, pp. 110–116. ACM, June 2023, isbn: 9798400701382. https://doi.org/10.1145/3587102.3588815, https://dl.acm.org/doi/10.1145/3587102.3588815 Accessed 19 May 2024
10. Devlin, J., et al.: BERT: pre-training of deep bidirectional transformers for language understanding. arXiv:1810.04805 [cs], May 2019. http://arxiv.org/abs/1810.04805 Accessed 17 May 2024
11. Fakhoury, S., et al.: LLM-based test-driven interactive code generation: user study and empirical evaluation. arXiv:2404.10100, October 2024. arXiv:2404.10100, https://doi.org/10.48550/arXiv.2404.10100, http://arxiv.org/abs/2404.10100
12. Feldt, R., et al.: Four commentaries on the use of students and professionals in empirical software engineering experiments. Empir. Softw. Eng. **23**(6), 3801–3820 (2018). https://doi.org/10.1007/s10664-018-9655-0
13. Ghafari, M., et al.: Why research on test-driven development is inconclusive? en. In: Proceedings of the 14th ACM/IEEE International Symposium on Empirical Software Engineering and Measurement (ESEM), pp. 1–10, October 2020. arXiv:2007.09863 [cs]. https://doi.org/10.1145/3382494.3410687, http://arxiv.org/abs/2007.09863 (visited on 05/18/2024)
14. Guerra, E., Aniche, M.: Achieving quality on software design through test-driven development. In: Software Quality Assurance, pp. 201–220. Elsevier (2016)
15. Han, X., et al.: Pre-trained models: past, present and future. In: AI Open 2, pp. 225–250 (2021). issn: 26666510. https://doi.org/10.1016/j.aiopen.2021.08.002, https://linkinghub.elsevier.com/retrieve/pii/S2666651021000231 Accessed 19 May 2024
16. Jaber, M.A., Beganović, A., Almisreb, A.A.: Methods and applications of ChatGPT in software development: a literature review, vol. 12, no. 1 (2023)
17. Janzen, D., Saiedian, H.: Test-driven development concepts, taxonomy, and future direction. Computer **38**(9), 43–50 (2005), issn: 0018-9162. https://doi.org/10.1109/MC.2005.314, http://ieeexplore.ieee.org/document/1510569/ Accessed 18 May 2024
18. Janzen, D., Saiedian, H.: Does test-driven development really improve software design quality? IEEE Software **25**(2), 77–84 (2008), issn: 0740-7459. https://doi.org/10.1109/MS.2008.34, http://ieeexplore.ieee.org/document/4455636/ Accessed 18 May 2024
19. Maranhão, J.J., Guerra, E.M.: A prompt pattern sequence approach to apply generative AI in assisting software architecture decision-making. In: Proceedings of the 29th European Conference on Pattern Languages of Programs, People, and Practices, pp. 1–12 (2024)
20. Kampenes, V.B., et al.: A systematic review of quasi-experiments in software engineering. Inf. Softw. Technol. **51**(1), 71–82 (2009)

21. LeCun, Y., Bengio, Y., Hinton, G.: Deep learning. Nature **521**(7553), 436–444 (2015). issn: 0028-0836, 1476-4687. https://doi.org/10.1038/nature14539, https://www.nature.com/articles/nature14539 Accessed 25 May 2024
22. Maranhão, J.J., Jr., Correia, F.F., Guerra, E.M.: Can chatgpt suggest patterns? an exploratory study about answers given by AI-assisted tools to design problems. In: International Conference on Agile Software Development, pp. 130–138. Springer, Cham (2024)
23. Marques, V.S.S.: DevBots can co-design APIs. arXiv:2312.05733 [cs]. December 2023. http://arxiv.org/abs/2312.05733 Accessed 17 May 2024
24. Mathews, N.S., Nagappan, M.: Test-driven development for code generation. arXiv:2402.13521 [cs]. February 2024. http://arxiv.org/abs/2402.13521 Accessed 11 May 2024
25. McCarthy, J., et al.: A proposal for the dartmouth summer research project on artificial intelligence, 31 Aug 1955. AI Mag. **27**(4), 12 (2006)
26. Mitchell, T.J., Creasey, D.P.: Evolutionary sound matching: a test methodology and comparative study. In: Sixth International Conference on Machine Learning and Applications (ICMLA 2007). Cincinnati, OH, USA, pp. 229–234. IEEE, December 2007. isbn: 978-0-7695-3069-7. https://doi.org/10.1109/ICMLA.2007.34, http://ieeexplore.ieee.org/document/4457236/ Accessed 25 May 2024
27. Mock, M., Melegati, J., Russo, B.: Generative AI for test driven development: preliminary results. arXiv:2405.10849, May 2024. arXiv:2405.10849, https://doi.org/10.48550/arXiv.2405.10849, http://arxiv.org/abs/2405.10849
28. Ozdemir, S.: quick start guide to large language models: strategies and best practices for using ChatGPT and other LLMs. eng. OCLC: 1432719739. [Place of publication not identified]: Addison Wesley Professional 2023. (2023). isbn: 978-0-13-819933-3
29. Piya, S., Sullivan, A.: LLM4TDD: best practices for test driven development using large language models. arXiv:2312.04687 [cs]. December 2023. http://arxiv.org/abs/2312.04687 Accessed 18 May 2024
30. Russakovsky, O., et al.: ImageNet large scale visual recognition challenge. Int. J. Comput. Vision **115**(3), 211–252 (2015). https://doi.org/10.1007/s11263-015-0816-y
31. Shen, Y., et al.: HuggingGPT: solving AI Tasks with ChatGPT and its Friends in Hugging Face
32. Spadini, D., et al.: To mock or not to mock? an empirical study on mocking practices. In: 2017 IEEE/ACM 14th International Conference on Mining Software Repositories (MSR), pp. 402–412. IEEE. (2017)
33. Staegemann, D., et al.: A literature review on the challenges of applying test-driven development in software engineering. Complex Syst. Inf. Model. Quart. **31**, 18–28 (2022)
34. Shafiq Surameery, N.M., Shakor, M.Y.: Use chat gpt to solve programming bugs. In: International Journal of Information technology and Computer Engineering, vol. 31, pp. 17–22, January 2023, issn: 2455–5290. https://doi.org/10.55529/ijitc.31.17.22, https://journal.hmjournals.com/index.php/IJITC/article/view/1679 Accessed 17 May 2024
35. Thomas, J., Harden, A.: Methods for the thematic synthesis of qualitative research in systematic reviews. BMC Med. Res. Methodol. **8**(1), 1–10 (2008)
36. White, J., et al.: A prompt pattern catalog to enhance prompt engineering with ChatGPT. arXiv:2302.11382 [cs]. February 2023. http://arxiv.org/abs/2302.11382 Accessed 25 May 2024

Open Access This chapter is licensed under the terms of the Creative Commons Attribution 4.0 International License (http://creativecommons.org/licenses/by/4.0/), which permits use, sharing, adaptation, distribution and reproduction in any medium or format, as long as you give appropriate credit to the original author(s) and the source, provide a link to the Creative Commons license and indicate if changes were made.

The images or other third party material in this chapter are included in the chapter's Creative Commons license, unless indicated otherwise in a credit line to the material. If material is not included in the chapter's Creative Commons license and your intended use is not permitted by statutory regulation or exceeds the permitted use, you will need to obtain permission directly from the copyright holder.

Exploratory Software Testing in Scrum: A Qualitative Study

Giulia Neri, Rob Marchand, and Neil Walkinshaw

The University of Sheffield, Sheffield, UK
{grneri1,n.walkinshaw}@sheffield.ac.uk

Abstract. Exploratory Testing (ET) is a dynamic software testing approach that emphasises creativity, real-time learning, and defect discovery. The integration of ET into structured frameworks like Scrum remains insufficiently explored and presents distinct challenges. This qualitative study investigates how ET is implemented in Scrum workflows and identifies key factors enabling its effective application.

Interviews with 20 industry professionals highlight ET's role in enhancing test coverage, uncovering usability issues, and addressing edge cases often missed by automated or scripted tests. The results demonstrated that the critical enablers of effective ET are the tester's eagerness to learn about the system under test and the ability to adopt a user-centric perspective. Other key factors include testers' curiosity, creativity, domain knowledge, and organisational support. Participants noted that ET complements Scrum's iterative cycles, enabling teams to identify defects dynamically and improve software quality.

Despite its advantages, ET faces challenges within Scrum, including time constraints and the need for traceability. Lightweight documentation practices, such as annotated mind maps and screen recordings, emerged as effective strategies to bridge these gaps. This study underscores ET's potential to enhance Scrum workflows, providing actionable insights for optimising testing strategies in Agile environments.

Keywords: Exploratory Testing · Agile Software Development · Scrum

1 Introduction

Exploratory Testing (ET) is a dynamic software testing approach that emphasises creativity, adaptability, and real-time learning. Unlike traditional scripted testing, which relies on predefined test cases, ET integrates test design, execution, and learning into a single iterative process. This enables testers to dynamically explore system behaviours, uncovering defects and issues that other testing methods might overlook. ET's flexibility makes it particularly effective for addressing ambiguities, identifying edge cases, and exploring complex interactions within systems [1,10].

The application of ET within structured methodologies such as Scrum remains underexplored [2]. Scrum is the most widely adopted Agile framework, characterised by defined roles, ceremonies, and iterative workflows [5,20]. While previous research has investigated Agile's emphasis on iterative development, collaboration, and adaptability [12,14], how ET fits within Scrum workflows has received limited attention.

This investigation explores how ET is applied in Scrum environments. Using a qualitative approach that incorporates interviews with 20 industry professionals, it uncovers key success factors and challenges associated with integrating ET into Scrum. Additionally, it examines how ET supports testing needs within Scrum, contributing to enhanced software quality. By analyzing the insights and experiences of practitioners, this inquiry offers actionable recommendations for Agile teams striving to optimise their testing strategies.

The findings reveal that ET can address gaps in test coverage, usability issues, and collaboration, while also identifying key success factors such as tester curiosity, creativity, eagerness to learn, knowledge of the user's perspective, and organisational support. Additionally, the findings highlight the constraints imposed by time limitations and traceability requirements.

The rest of the paper is structured as follows: Sect. 2 provides a detailed background on ET and its relevance to Agile practices, and formulates the research questions. Section 3 outlines the methodology used in this study, including data collection and analysis. Section 4 presents the key findings, while Sect. 5 discusses their implications. Section 6 outlines the study's limitations. Finally, Sect. 7 concludes the paper and offers recommendations for practice and future research directions.

2 Background

ET aligns well with Agile methodologies, which embrace incremental development and fluid requirements [14], as ET does not depend on detailed system requirements. However, certain characteristics of ET - such as its flexibility, reliance on human intuition, and limited automation - may pose challenges to its effective implementation in an Agile setting. In this section, we explore these complementarities and tensions, providing the context and motivation for the qualitative study outlined in Sect. 3.

The tension between ET's exploratory freedom and Scrum's structured nature raises critical questions about how these methodologies can complement each other effectively. Moreover, existing research often provides general insights into ET in Agile contexts [12,14] but lacks a specific focus on Scrum, leaving a gap in understanding the practicalities of its implementation within this framework.

Addressing this gap is essential for practitioners and teams seeking to refine their testing strategies and enhance software quality. By investigating how ET is used within Scrum workflows and identifying the factors that enable or hinder its success, this study aims to bridge the divide between theory and practice.

The research seeks to uncover actionable insights that can inform the systematic integration of ET into Scrum, providing value not only for testing teams but also for the broader Agile community.

Itkonen, Mäntylä, and Lassenius [10] argue that the defining feature of ET lies in the **intent of the tester to explore, rather than check**. Unlike confirmatory or test-case-based techniques, where testers or automated tools adhere to predefined instructions to verify that software behaves as expected, ET involves seeking defects in unforeseen areas and uncovering new insights about the system. The rationale is that these discoveries can then inform the creation of new confirmatory tests, bridging the gap between exploration and validation.

An Adaptive Testing Approach: ET is consistently defined as an adaptive testing approach. Hendrickson [9] described ET as a process of "simultaneous learning, test design, and execution," where insights from one test guide subsequent tests. This iterative process allows testers to address areas not covered by predefined test cases, making it particularly effective in detecting system-wide defects and edge cases [8].

Effectiveness and Complementarity: ET has been shown to outperform traditional test-case-based methods in terms of defect identification and efficiency, particularly in time-constrained or ambiguous scenarios [1]. Additionally, ET complements other testing approaches, such as automated testing, by uncovering nuanced issues and refining testing models [7,11].

Key Enablers for ET: Success factors for ET have been identified by the literature. These are years of experience [2,6–8,10–12,14,18,19], domain knowledge (subject matter and user perspective knowledge) [1,2,6–8,10–14,18,19], system knowledge (technical details and features) [1,2,6–8,10–14,19], software engineering knowledge [1,2,6–8,10–12,14], personality (such as curiosity, creativity, and eagerness to learn), [11–13,18], organisational factors [2,10,12,14,18,19] use of tools [2,10,12,14,18,19] and "right" level of exploration [8,19]. This refers to striking an effective balance between providing sufficient structure-such as clear objectives, charters, or checklists-to guide testing efforts, and allowing the flexibility needed for creative and thorough exploration of the system [8].

Potential in Agile Workflows: The literature identified Agile development, particularly continuous integration workflows, as an environment for ET [12]. Agile's iterative cycles and emphasis on collaboration align conceptually with ET's adaptability. However, this review highlighted a lack of systematic research on ET's integration into specific frameworks like Scrum. Collaboration also plays a significant role in enabling effective ET. Mårtensson [14] emphasised the value of involving team members, including developers and testers, in exploratory sessions. This collaborative approach broadens the scope of testing by integrating various perspectives and improving the overall understanding of the team's behaviour of the system. Such practices align closely with Agile principles of teamwork and shared responsibility for quality.

Scrum is the most widely implemented Agile framework across industries, therefore it represents a significant portion of modern software development. It offers structured workflows, defined roles, and time-boxed deliverables that prioritise incremental improvements [5,20]. While these characteristics may present opportunities for ET to enhance testing practices, they may also impose constraints that challenge ET's flexibility.

This exploration leads to the formulations of the following research questions:

- **RQ1: How is ET used in Scrum environments?** This question investigates how ET is practiced in Scrum, including its roles, processes, and tools, and how these elements fit into Scrum workflows.
- **RQ2: What factors enable efficient and effective ET in Scrum?** This question explores the enablers of successful ET in Scrum teams, such as collaboration, team expertise, organisational culture, and structured exploratory practices, and examines how these factors influence testing outcomes.

3 Methodology

3.1 Overview

This section outlines the research methodology used to investigate the integration of ET within Scrum workflows. The approach included structured interviews, qualitative data analysis, and a follow-up survey. Data collection spanned several months, ensuring a comprehensive and diverse sample of industry professionals with practical ET experience in Scrum environments. Ethical considerations were prioritised throughout, including participant consent, data confidentiality, and voluntary withdrawal. The methodology was carefully designed to ensure reliability, minimise bias, and enhance the validity of findings.

3.2 Data Collection

The data collection process occurred between December 2022 and June 2023, following research ethics approval.[1]

Recruitment Process. Participants were selected through non-discriminative snowball sampling. The researchers emailed invitations to professional contacts, outlining the study's purpose, participant requirements, and ethical assurances, including data confidentiality and the right to withdraw at any time. Initial contacts were encouraged to share the invitation with colleagues, ensuring the inclusion of individuals with relevant, hands-on experience.

Participants. Participants in this study were required to have practical experience with ET within Scrum teams, or to manage/coach individuals engaged in ET. A total of 20 participants were recruited, reflecting practices used in similar research on ET success factors [13,14].

---
[1] The full dataset is available from Figshare.

Interview Script. The script was structured into three parts, each with specific objectives:

- **Part I**: Gather general opinions about ET in Scrum, including views on the use of ET in Scrum and key factors enabling effective ET.
- **Part II**: Collect background information about participants and their practical experiences, including educational and professional background, roles and responsibilities, and frequency, approach, and purposes of ET in their work.
- **Part III**: Gather participants' opinions on the success factors for ET, as identified in the literature (see Sect. 2). Part III also provided an opportunity for participants to offer additional insights, expand on the listed factors, or suggest new factors not covered by the literature.

The order of the sections was carefully maintained to ensure participants shared their unprompted opinions in Parts I and II before being introduced to the success factors identified by the literature. This design aimed to reduce bias and encouraged authentic responses.

3.3 Data Analysis

In Vivo Coding. In this study, in vivo coding was employed as the primary method for analysing qualitative data. This approach involves identifying and using participants' exact words as codes to capture their authentic perspectives and experiences [16]. It is particularly suited for exploratory research where participants' language offers deep insights into the phenomenon under study. In vivo coding provided a systematic yet flexible approach to understanding how ET is integrated into Scrum workflows. By using participants' actual words, the analysis captured the subtleties of their experiences. This method aligns with best practices in qualitative research, as outlined by Saldaña [16], Braun and Clarke [3], and Creswell and Poth [4]. These references highlight the importance of grounding analysis in participants' language to ensure authenticity and rigor in qualitative inquiry.

Ratings. A rating system was applied to specific aspects of participants' responses. The researchers assigned ratings based on transcript content to systematically categorise and quantify elements of the data. For questions related to success factors in ET, a five-point Likert scale was used, ranging from 1 (not important at all) to 5 (extremely important). This evaluation covered factors such as curiosity, creativity, knowledge of the user's perspective, and eagerness to learn. For questions on the use of ET in Scrum, responses were rated on a scale from 1 (very negative) to 5 (very positive) to capture participants' overall attitudes.

Follow-Up Survey. We conducted a follow-up survey to integrate multiple data sources and strengthen the research findings, following McCartan's [15] recommendation to use data triangulation.

A key concern in this study was the potential subjectivity involved in categorising participant statements and assigning ratings during analysis. The primary aim of the survey was therefore to assess the extent to which respondents agreed with the themes and ratings identified by the researchers during the interview analysis, thereby validating these categorisations and enhancing the trustworthiness of the findings.

Participants were recruited via email using snowball sampling. Existing respondents forwarded the link to the 20-question survey to others in their network who met the inclusion criteria (i.e. familiarity with ET and Scrum). All responses were anonymous. Interview excerpts were randomly selected to minimise selection bias and ensure a diverse representation of perspectives.

Respondents completed two main tasks: rating the importance of factors influencing ET in Scrum on a scale from 1 to 5, and matching predefined themes to highlighted statements. Themes included elements such as getting into the user's mindset, curiosity, creativity, subject matter knowledge, and organisational support-all derived directly from the coding and thematic analysis of the interview transcripts.

4 Findings

4.1 Participants' Backgrounds and Experience in SDLC

The 20 participants represented diverse roles and backgrounds across the SDLC, with experience ranging from 1 to 21 years (average 11.3 years, median 12). Their Scrum roles included Principal Test Engineer, Software Tester, Senior Software Engineer, QA Engineer, Product Owner, Test Manager, and others-reflecting a mix of technical and managerial positions.

Educational backgrounds varied: 15 participants held undergraduate degrees in fields such as Liberal Arts, Law, Pharmacy, Psychology, Software Engineering, Physics, and Computer Science. Five had either no higher education or completed professional certifications instead. Among those with degrees, eight held advanced qualifications (MSc or PhD). Half of the participants had formal software testing qualifications (e.g. ISTQB), two were pursuing certification, and eight had no formal testing credentials.

4.2 RQ1: How Is ET Used in Scrum?

ET is highly regarded for its ability to uncover hidden issues, enhance test coverage, and improve user experience in Scrum. Of the 20 participants, 15 described their use of ET in Scrum as either "highly effective" or "effective," reflecting its strong alignment with Agile principles. Participants highlighted its value in adapting to Scrum's iterative cycles, with one noting, "It's mostly to try to make sure that the combination of features we've added as a team makes sense in the overall workflow."

ET was frequently praised for its effectiveness in detecting defects that scripted tests might miss, ensuring that workflows function properly, and providing critical insights for new features. Of the 20 participants, 12 emphasised its value in identifying bugs, while others highlighted its role in exploring complex features, ensuring usability and addressing accessibility issues. One participant noted, "To confirm that your software under test is working in the expected way... and to improve the experience of the user."

ET was seen as highly adaptable to Scrum workflows. Participants noted that it complements Scrum's iterative and feedback-driven nature by addressing gaps left by automated or scripted testing. Six participants reported integrating ET directly into sprint activities, such as reviews, ensuring that exploratory efforts were part of the iterative process rather than an afterthought. Another participant shared that ET allowed their team to test evolving features, even when requirements were incomplete, stating, "If it's a situation where we don't actually know what the answer should be, that's when we will use exploratory work."

Participants employed a range of approaches to ET. Four participants used structured methods, such as mind maps or lists of specified expectations, to ensure thorough exploration and maintain focus. One participant explained, "Our method often begins with a mind map or a list of known specified expectations to ensure thorough exploration of the system." Another group of four participants favoured intuitive approaches, thinking like users to explore system behaviour and identify potential defects through real-world scenarios. ET was also highlighted by three participants for its ability to uncover bugs missed by automated tests and gather feedback on risky or unpredictable areas of the system.

ET also served as an educational tool for two participants, who used it to help team members familiarise themselves with new systems and workflows. Additionally, five participants mentioned integrating ET into sprints to refine user journeys and ensure comprehensive test coverage. Participants described tailoring ET to fit their Scrum workflows, reflecting its adaptability as a testing practice.

Overall, ET was seen as a vital practice that complements more formal testing approaches, addressing gaps left by scripted methods and enhancing software quality. While five participants used ET regularly to refine workflows and expand test coverage, two employed it primarily as a final validation step, depending on the project context and system complexity.

4.3 RQ2: What Factors Enable Efficient and Effective ET in Scrum?

The factors below reflect the participants' unprompted opinions and were identified during Part I of the interview (see Sect. 3.2).

- **Product Knowledge vs. User-Centricity:** Fifteen participants emphasised the importance of balancing product knowledge and user-centricity for effective ET. This balance enables testers to focus on relevant use cases and system flows. One participant noted that "a strong understanding of the use cases for the product ensures that ET is carried out in an informed and efficient way."

- **Curiosity and Passion:** Curiosity and passion were identified as key motivators by 14 participants, who highlighted their role in driving testers to deeply explore and uncover hidden insights. As one participant remarked, "Curiosity is really important. I would say critical."
- **Structure, Organisation, and Clear Goals:** A structured approach to ET was emphasised by 12 participants. Time-boxed sessions, small objectives, and clearly defined goals were seen as essential for maintaining focus and distinguishing ET from ad-hoc testing. One participant explained, "You need to timebox yourself because you could be there for hours. Small objectives and notes keep it efficient."
- **Autonomy and Tester Agency:** Autonomy was valued by 10 participants, who stressed that it empowers testers to explore effectively, provided they have the support and freedom to focus on relevant areas. One participant stated, "It's how much agency and autonomy the tester has that determines their success."
- **Experience and Collaboration:** Nine participants highlighted the importance of experience and collaboration in ET. They described how combining experienced testers' insights with fresh perspectives improves outcomes. Paired programming and team retrospectives were also mentioned as effective collaborative practices. As one participant shared, "Paired programming really helped-having someone to drive ET made it more thorough."

The factors below, derived from the literature (see Sect. 2), were introduced during Part III of the interviews (see Sect. 3.2) for participants to reflect on, critique, and expand upon. They are presented here in order from the most important to the least, based on the participants' opinions.

- **Eagerness to learn about the SUT:** All participants (20 out of 20) viewed eagerness to learn as critical to successful ET. This factor was rated as "very important" by 16 participants and "important" by 4. The participants highlighted that the more testers want to learn about the system, the more effective their ET becomes, as they are better equipped to challenge the system and explore its weaknesses ("It makes testers explore much more" P15).
- **Curiosity:** 18 out of 20 participants viewed curiosity as important (very important for 14 and important for 4) to ensure successful ET because it encourages testers to explore, think critically, and approach testing creatively. However, P2 noted "curiosity without the tools or the knowledge is sadly kind of useless."
- **Creativity:** 19 out of 20 participants emphasised the importance of creativity (very important for 8 and important for 11). This enables testers to think outside the box, simulate unexpected user behaviours, and uncover unusual issues. Creativity complements curiosity to drive exploration and problem-solving.
- **Knowledge of User Perspective:** 16 out of 20 participants emphasised the importance of understanding the user perspective (very important for 9 and important for 7). Understanding the user perspective is essential for

uncovering issues that might not be addressed by formal test cases, with participants stressing the importance of realistic scenarios and diverse user perspectives to guide ET effectively. P4 points out that adhering to realistic user scenarios is crucial: "There's a certain value... but if you fiddle with some of the underlying Windows settings, our software is on, you can cause all sorts of weird software behaviour and bugs, but none of my customers are ever going to do that. Of which point, whilst you'd find bugs, they're not necessarily bugs that are that important for you to fix."

- **"Right" level of exploration:** In the opinion of 18 participants, this factor is "important." The level of exploration should depend on the situation. The approach to freestyle ET and the level of detail in charters/checklists vary widely among participants, with many adjusting the amount of information based on the situation and the needs of the team. Freestyle testing is valued for its ability to uncover unforeseen issues, but some participants prefer to rely on more structured methods to guide their exploration.
- **Organisational factors:** This factor was rated as "very important" by 6 participants and "important" by 10. Most participants emphasised that successful ET requires a supportive workplace that provides sufficient time, resources, autonomy, and a collaborative culture, alongside opportunities for knowledge sharing, retrospectives, and flexible management practices.
- **Use of Tools:** The tools were considered valuable for documenting tests, automating repetitive tasks, and improving efficiency. This factor was rated as "very important" by 5 participants and "important" by 10.
- **Knowledge of the features of the SUT:** Many participants emphasised that understanding the system's features enhances test coverage, efficiency, and the ability to identify critical areas and subtle issues. This factor was rated as "very important" by 4 participants and "important" by 8.
- **Subject Matter Knowledge:** This knowledge is valuable for understanding software use and identifying relevant issues. This factor was rated as "very important" by 3 participants and "important" by 6.
- **General software engineering knowledge:** While many participants agreed that software engineering knowledge is helpful, opinions varied on how essential it is. This factor was rated as "very important" by 1 participant and "important" by 14.
- **Knowledge of the technical details of the SUT (i.e., code):** While participants recognized that technical knowledge could improve ET, many emphasised that curiosity, user-focused perspectives, and collaboration often matter more. This factor was rated as "very important" by 1 participant and "important" by 8.
- **Experience (years in SDLC):** While experience in testing or software development is helpful for identifying common issues and improving with practice, participants emphasised the need to balance experience with fresh perspectives to avoid biases and encourage creativity. This factor was rated as "important" by 6 participants.

4.4 Findings from the Follow-Up Survey

Eight respondents completed the survey (see Sect. 3.3). The findings demonstrated strong overall alignment, with respondents largely validating the researchers' categorisations and evaluations. Unanimity was observed in areas such as curiosity, importance of ET in Scrum, and eagerness to learn, where all participants aligned with the researchers' classification of these traits as critical for ET. Similarly, themes related to structured versus freestyle testing, organizational support, and getting in the user's mindset were supported by seven participants, validating the researchers' ratings in these areas. One question, about experience in software development, showed greater variability. Five respondents rated a statement as highly important, while the researchers had previously rated it as not important.

The survey results mostly aligned with the findings of the interviews, demonstrating strong agreement between participants and the researcher's themes and ratings.

5 Discussion

5.1 ET as a Natural Fit for Scrum

The claim in Mårtensson [14] that "Agile is killing exploratory testing" reflects frustrations with how ET is sometimes de-prioritised or misunderstood within Agile frameworks. However, findings from this study suggest that ET not only aligns with Agile principles but also enhances them when integrated effectively (e.g. *Build projects around motivated individuals.* [17]).

Agile methodologies, including Scrum, prioritise working software, team collaboration, and responsiveness to change over extensive documentation or rigid processes [5,20]. These principles create opportunities for ET to thrive. ET was frequently highlighted as a key tool for exploring ambiguities, uncovering hidden defects, and addressing rapidly changing requirements. It has proven effective in identifying edge cases and usability issues that are often missed by automated or scripted tests, and it also plays a significant role in simulating diverse user interactions, ensuring a more user-centric perspective during development.

ET's adaptability complements Agile's iterative and feedback-driven workflows. It can be used to explore features still in development, taking advantage of the opportunity to test in environments with incomplete or evolving requirements. Additionally, ET serves as a bridge between automated testing and manual processes, allowing teams to explore system behaviours and uncover issues beyond the scope of predefined test scripts.

Mårtensson's MaLET model [13] supports these findings by illustrating how ET progresses through maturity levels, culminating in a collaborative stage that aligns closely with Agile principles. Specifically, the model underscores the importance of cross-team collaboration and clear reporting mechanisms, which this study corroborates. Cross-functional ET sessions, often involving developers, testers, and product owners, foster shared understanding of system functionality and potential risks.

5.2 Challenges in Scrum-Enabling ET

Despite the synergies, challenges in fully leveraging ET within Agile workflows were identified. One recurring theme was the tension between ET's exploratory nature and the need to maintain a shared understanding of outcomes. While Agile is lightweight on documentation, there remains a need for traceability and actionable insights, especially in complex systems or regulated industries. Lightweight approaches, such as screen recordings, annotated mind maps, or rapid reporting tools, were recommended to capture key findings without burdening the team with excessive documentation.

Another challenge was balancing ET with Agile's fast-paced sprint cycles. Time constraints often limit the ability to engage deeply with exploratory activities, especially when automated testing dominates sprint planning. It was suggested that dedicated ET sessions be incorporated into sprint reviews or retrospectives to ensure that exploratory efforts are treated as an integral part of the process rather than an afterthought. In Agile environments with hybrid or legacy components (e.g., Waterfall teams working alongside Scrum teams), the need for traceable, predefined test cases can inadvertently restrict the exploratory freedom that ET requires.

5.3 Key Success Factors for ET in Scrum

ET in Scrum benefits significantly from testers who proactively learn about the system under test, as their knowledge sharpens workflows, identifies risks, and improves product quality. Traits like curiosity and creativity are critical, enabling testers to uncover issues through unconventional workflows and diverse user interactions. A user-centric approach further reveals usability and accessibility flaws often overlooked by scripted workflows, while a strong understanding of the system helps prioritise high-impact areas during time-constrained sprints. Both experienced testers, with their knowledge of common failure points, and less experienced testers, with their fresh perspectives, bring complementary value. Collaboration within teams and organizational support, including dedicated time for ET, are vital to embedding it effectively in Scrum. Balancing structure and freedom through time-boxed sessions with clear objectives ensures ET remains focused and aligned with Scrum s iterative goals while maintaining its creative essence.

The findings highlighted several insights that complemented the literature. The value of fresh perspectives from less experienced testers was emphasised, as they can uncover unique issues and approach testing with creativity. Eagerness to learn during testing was considered crucial for adapting to new scenarios and identifying hidden bugs. While subject matter knowledge was seen as valuable, there was caution against over-reliance, advocating for a balance between expertise and exploratory freedom. Autonomy was recognized as essential, with advocacy for independent or paired exploration, supported by organizational backing.

Collaborative practices, such as pairing testers of varying experience levels and retrospectives, were endorsed to enhance learning and testing outcomes. Practical use of tools like screen recording and mind mapping provided actionable strategies to document and share ET findings effectively. Additionally, freestyle testing was highlighted as valuable for exploring new features and validating systems in dynamic scenarios.

Mårtensson's MaLET model [13] aligns closely with these findings, highlighting curiosity, creativity, and organizational support as critical enablers of ET. Additionally, the model underscores the importance of balancing structured approaches with flexibility, such as using time-boxed sessions or lightweight documentation-strategies that were endorsed in this study.

6 Limitations

6.1 Threats to Internal Validity

Potential for Social Desirability Bias. Participants may have tailored their responses to align with what they perceived as socially desirable or best practices, particularly when discussing their own competencies or organisational processes. However, the interview questions were intentionally designed to maintain neutrality, avoiding any judgment of the participants' performance, skills, or their organisation. Furthermore, the questions were crafted as open-ended to reduce bias and encourage candid and accurate responses (see Sect. 3.2).

Subjectivity in Data Interpretation. The categorisation of interview data may reflect researcher subjectivity. This was mitigated by a follow-up survey, which validated the themes and ratings against broader practitioner perspectives, supporting the credibility of the findings (see Sect. 3.3).

6.2 Threats to External Validity

Sample Size and Representation. The relatively small sample size (20 participants) and the use of professional contacts and snowball sampling may limit the generalisability of the findings. The sample might not fully represent all Scrum teams or ET practitioners across industries. However, the choice of 20 participants is in line with what has been done in [13,14].

Variability in Practices. The diverse ways Scrum is adapted across teams and organisations, coupled with variations in participants' experience and approaches to ET, may affect the applicability of findings to all Scrum environments. There is a risk that findings may be overinterpreted or assumed to apply universally.

Limited Focus on System Types. The lack of inquiry into the types of systems under test (e.g., gaming software, banking apps, or enterprise systems) introduces variability. However, the findings focus on universally applicable aspects of ET, such as curiosity, creativity, and organisational support, which transcend specific system types. Additionally, the diversity of participants' backgrounds and industries partially offsets this limitation by introducing insights from a variety of contexts without overgeneralising.

7 Conclusion and Future Work

This paper aimed to investigate how ET is integrated into Scrum workflows and the factors that enable its effective implementation. Through detailed qualitative research, the findings challenge the claim by a participant in Mårtensson [14] that "Agile is killing exploratory testing." Instead, this study demonstrates that ET complements Scrum's principles of collaboration, adaptability, and continuous feedback when thoughtfully incorporated into its processes.

The participants consistently highlighted the ability of ET to address the gaps left by scripted and automated testing by uncovering usability issues, edge cases, and unexpected defects. Its flexibility aligns naturally with Scrum's iterative nature, where teams adapt to evolving requirements and rapidly changing priorities. Testers reported integrating ET into various stages of the Scrum process, such as sprint reviews, and ongoing development, allowing teams to identify defects dynamically and improve the quality of the software.

Key enablers of successful ET in Scrum include testers' curiosity, creativity, and eagerness to learn about the SUT. Participants emphasised the importance of subject matter knowledge and experience, which enable testers to prioritise high-impact areas. At the same time, fresh perspectives from less experienced testers were found to uncover issues that might otherwise be overlooked. Collaboration across Scrum roles, supported by a culture that values exploratory efforts, emerged as vital for integrating ET effectively. Lightweight documentation practices, such as screen recordings and annotated mind maps, helped bridge the gap between the unstructured nature of ET and the need for actionable outcomes of Scrum.

While ET faces challenges within Scrum, such as time constraints and the need for traceability, these can be addressed through structured approaches like time-boxed exploratory sessions and focused charters. The participants also stressed the importance of organisational support, including dedicated time and resources for ET, to ensure its effectiveness.

In conclusion, this paper shows that ET is not only compatible with Scrum but also a vital practice for achieving its goals. ET's adaptability, user-centred focus, and defect-finding capabilities enhance Scrum workflows, ensuring robust, high-quality software delivery. Far from diminishing ET, Scrum provides a framework where its exploratory nature can thrive, fostering innovation and improving software development outcomes. By embracing ET's strengths and addressing its challenges, Scrum teams can ensure its continued relevance and value in modern Agile development.

Future work could explore the integration of ET into Agile frameworks beyond Scrum, such as Kanban, to assess the generalisability of current findings. Quantitative studies may help validate key success factors-like tester curiosity and domain knowledge-and contribute to the development of metrics for assessing ET's effectiveness and traceability. Investigating the role of enabling tools, including AI-driven assistants and lightweight documentation practices, could further support ET's adaptability across different contexts. Additionally, exploring ET's use in regulated industries and remote work settings may offer valuable insights into how its inherent flexibility can be balanced with compliance and collaboration demands.

Beyond practical considerations, future work should also aim to establish a stronger theoretical foundation for ET within Scrum. While this study offers empirical observations, synthesizing existing literature into a cohesive conceptual model could help define ET's core principles, uncover key interdependencies, and highlight areas in need of deeper inquiry.

Acknowledgments. Giulia extends her heartfelt gratitude to the staff at Phasefocus Ltd., especially the Technical Team, for introducing her to the fascinating world of Exploratory Testing. She also wishes to thank Tom Lee for his invaluable support, inspiration, and extraordinary patience. Finally, she expresses her sincere appreciation to the 20 participants, whose insights and experiences were instrumental in shaping the findings of this research.

Disclosure of Interests. The authors have no competing interests to declare that are relevant to the content of this article.

References

1. Afzal, W., Ghazi, A.N., Itkonen, J., Torkar, R., Andrews, A., Bhatti, K.: An experiment on the effectiveness and efficiency of exploratory testing. Empir. Softw. Eng. **20**(3), 844–878 (2014). https://doi.org/10.1007/s10664-014-9301-4
2. Asplund, F.: Exploratory testing: do contextual factors influence software fault identification? Inf. Softw. Technol. **107**, 101–111 (2019). https://doi.org/10.1016/j.infsof.2018.11.003
3. Braun, V., Clarke, V.: Using thematic analysis in psychology. Qual. Res. Psychol. **3**(2), 77–101 (2006). https://doi.org/10.1191/1478088706qp063oa
4. Creswell, J.W., Poth, C.N.: Qualitative Inquiry and Research Design: Choosing Among Five Approaches, 4th edn. SAGE Publications, Thousand Oaks, CA (2017)
5. Digital.ai: 17th state of agile report. https://stateofagile.com/ (2023), Accessed 19 March 2025
6. Frajtak, K., Bures, M., Jelinek, I.: Exploratory testing supported by automated reengineering of model of the system under test. Cluster Comput. **20**, 855–865 (2017). https://doi.org/10.1007/s10586-017-0773-z
7. Şahin Gebizli, C., Sözer, H.: Automated refinement of models for model-based testing using exploratory testing. Softw. Qual. J. **25**, 979–1005 (2017). https://doi.org/10.1007/s11219-016-9338-2

8. Ghazi, A., Petersen, K., Bjarnason, E., Runeson, P.: Levels of exploration in exploratory testing: from freestyle to fully scripted. IEEE Access **6**, 26416–26423 (2018). https://doi.org/10.1109/ACCESS.2018.2834957
9. Hendrickson, E.: Explore It!: Reduce Risk and Increase Confidence with Exploratory Testing. Pragmatic Bookshelf, Raleigh, NC (2013)
10. Itkonen, J., Mäntylä, M., Lassenius, C.: Test better by exploring: Harnessing human skills and knowledge. IEEE Software **33**(4), 90–96 (2016). https://doi.org/10.1109/MS.2016.66
11. Itkonen, J., Mäntylä, M.V., Lassenius, C.: The role of the tester's knowledge in exploratory software testing. IEEE Trans. Softw. Eng. **39**, 707–724 (2013). https://doi.org/10.1109/TSE.2012.55
12. Mårtensson, T., Ståhl, D., Bosch, J.: Exploratory testing of large-scale systems - testing in the continuous integration and delivery pipeline, vol. 10611 LNCS (2017). https://doi.org/10.1007/978-3-319-69926-4_26
13. Mårtensson, T., Martini, A., Ståhl, D., Bosch, J.: The malet model - maturity levels for exploratory testing. In: Proceedings of the IEEE International Conference, pp. 78–85. IEEE (2021). https://doi.org/10.1109/SEAA53835.2021.00019
14. Mårtensson, T., Ståhl, D., Martini, A., Bosch, J.: Efficient and effective exploratory testing of large-scale software systems. J. Syst. Softw. **174**, 110890 (2021). https://doi.org/10.1016/j.jss.2020.110890
15. Robson, C., McCartan, K.: Real World Research: A Resource for Users of Social Research Methods in Applied Settings. Wiley (2016)
16. Saldaña, J.: The Coding Manual for Qualitative Researchers, 2nd edn. SAGE Publications, Thousand Oaks, CA (2013)
17. Scrum Alliance: Key values & principles of the agile manifesto. https://resources.scrumalliance.org/Article/key-values-principles-agile-manifesto (nd), Accessed 19 March 2025
18. Shah, S., Gencel, C., Alvi, U.S., Petersen, K.: Towards a hybrid testing process unifying exploratory testing and scripted testing. J. Softw. Evol. Process **26**(2), 220–250 (2014)
19. Shah, S., Torchiano, M., Vetro, A., Morisio, M.: Exploratory testing as a source of technical debt. IT Professional **16**(3), 44–51 (2013)
20. Tenório, N., Pinto, D., Silva, M.J., Almeida, I.C., Bortolozzi, F.: Knowledge management in the software industry: how scrum activities support a knowledge management cycle. Navus **10**(1), 1–13 (2020). https://doi.org/10.22279/navus.2020.v10.p01-13.928

Open Access This chapter is licensed under the terms of the Creative Commons Attribution 4.0 International License (http://creativecommons.org/licenses/by/4.0/), which permits use, sharing, adaptation, distribution and reproduction in any medium or format, as long as you give appropriate credit to the original author(s) and the source, provide a link to the Creative Commons license and indicate if changes were made.

The images or other third party material in this chapter are included in the chapter's Creative Commons license, unless indicated otherwise in a credit line to the material. If material is not included in the chapter's Creative Commons license and your intended use is not permitted by statutory regulation or exceeds the permitted use, you will need to obtain permission directly from the copyright holder.

Mutation Testing in Test Code Refactoring: Leveraging Mutants to Ensure Behavioral Consistency

Tiago Samuel Rodrigues Teixeira[1](✉), Fábio Fagundes Silveira[2], and Eduardo Martins Guerra[3]

[1] Institute for Technological Research (IPT), São Paulo 05508-901, Brazil
tiagosamfito@gmail.com
[2] Federal University of São Paulo (UNIFESP),
São José, dos Campos 12247-014, Brazil
[3] Free University of Bozen-Bolzano (UNIBZ), 39100 Bolzano, Italy

Abstract. Previous research has identified mutation testing as a promising technique for detecting unintended changes in test behavior during test code refactorings. Despite its theoretical support, the practical adoption of this approach has been hindered by a lack of corresponding tools. Consequently, these studies have been unable to fully validate the effectiveness of mutation testing as a guardrail to ensure the consistency of the refactored test behavior, leaving an in-depth empirical validation open for future research. To address this gap, this study examines `MeteoR`, a tool developed as a reference implementation to support test refactoring by using mutation testing. We leverage `MeteoR` to validate the practical applicability of the mutation testing approach across diverse test refactoring scenarios. This evaluation uses a catalog of common test refactorings that reflect real-world practices. The results indicate that `MeteoR` effectively detects changes in test behavior in most cases, demonstrating the efficacy of mutation testing to identify problems during test code refactoring. However, the study also identifies limitations, particularly the occurrence of false negatives when refactorings modify the way tests handle dependencies. These findings highlight the potential of the approach and contribute to the state-of-the-art by identifying limitations that can be addressed in future studies.

Keywords: Software Engineering · Test Code Refactoring · Test Smells · Test Behavior · Mutation Testing

1 Introduction

As asserted by Fowler [4], refactoring entails restructuring software by applying a series of code changes without altering its observable behavior. However, in the context of test code refactoring, van Bladel and Demeyer [1] highlight the challenge of providing the effectiveness of refactored tests, noting the absence of a definitive method to guarantee that the behavior of a test suite remains unchanged after refactoring.

To address the challenge of preserving the intended behavior of refactored tests, Teixeira et al. [12], building upon the work of Parsai et al. [8], explored the use of mutation testing and proposed a tool-based approach to automate the validation process. Mutation testing involves deliberately injecting faults into the application code to evaluate the effectiveness of the test suite [7]. Parsai et al. [8] demonstrated that mutation testing can detect behavioral changes in refactored tests by comparing mutation scores before and after refactoring.

Although Parsai et al. [8] introduced the concept of using mutation testing to validate test refactorings, they did not provide a concrete tool to support their proposal. To fill this gap, MeteoR was introduced by Teixeira et al. [11] as a reference implementation of the approach. The present study extends this prior work by offering a more comprehensive evaluation of MeteoR, while also addressing aspects that had not been previously explored. Accordingly, we present four key contributions: (1) the release of a stable version of MeteoR as a reference implementation of the proposed approach; (2) the development of a comprehensive catalog of common test refactorings, as detailed in Table 1; (3) a qualitative evaluation of MeteoR's effectiveness across a variety of refactoring scenarios using this catalog; and (4) the identification of previously unreported limitations, which provide deeper insights into the applicability of the approach and lay the groundwork for future research.

2 Adopting Mutation Testing for Test Behavior Observability in the MeteoR

Given that test refactoring inherently involves verifying behavior, assessing test behavior in this context requires adopting techniques that enable such observability. Studies in the literature [2,5,8–10,13] present various approaches for this purpose, differing in complexity, required effort, and level of abstraction.

Mutation testing [8,13] stands out for dynamically verifying whether the refactored test code preserves its fault detection capability by executing tests against induced faults. Compared to *static analysis* [2,5] and *instrumentation-based* [9,10] techniques, mutation testing demands less preparatory effort and offers greater robustness and practicality. Nevertheless, its application in test refactoring scenarios remained underexplored, mainly due to the absence of dedicated tools that supported comprehensive evaluation.

MeteoR[1] is an Eclipse IDE plugin that implements the mutation testing approach and integrates seamlessly with *PITclipse*[2], a plugin for *PITest* [3] - a mutation testing tool. By simulating potential faults through code mutations, it evaluates the continuity of the test suite robustness by comparing mutation scores and the states of mutants ("killed", "survived", or "not covered") extracted before and after refactoring.

---
[1] https://github.com/meteortool.
[2] Source code for *PITclipse*: https://github.com/pitest/pitclipse.

3 Evaluation of the Mutation Testing Approach

Therefore, through the use of MeteoR, this study conducts a qualitative evaluation of the efficacy of mutation testing in verifying the consistency of the test behavior after refactoring. Using MeteoR as the primary tool, this research aimed to explore its abilities to identify changes in test behavior that may have been compromised during refactoring.

To conduct the experiment, it was first necessary to select the types of refactorings to be applied. For this purpose, we adopted an initial catalog proposed by Guerra and Fernandes [5] as the basis, supplementing it with two additional refactorings from Martins et al. [6]-namely assertThrows and assertAll-to incorporate more recent practices introduced with *JUnit5*.

3.1 Research Method

The evaluation used a controlled, experiment-specific code project rather than conducting a large-scale study across real-world projects. The code[3] was created specifically for this experiment based on the test refactoring descriptions and examples, as it is impractical to find all instances of each type of refactoring in a single real-world project.

To analyze refactorings, a paired approach was used, similar to that adopted in the study by Teixeira et al. [12], for each type of refactoring: one refactoring was performed correctly to ensure proper behavior maintenance, while another was misapplied, introducing errors that change the test behavior. This dual approach allowed for the evaluation of MeteoR's ability to detect the scenario in which the behavior is maintained and the one in which it is not. Thus, each refactoring type was assessed through both positive (**A**) and negative (**B**) scenarios as shown in Table 1.

In positive scenarios, it is expected of MeteoR the corrected identification of unchanged behavior when refactoring was performed appropriately. This involved selecting test classes requiring improvements and conducting mutation tests on the relevant application classes to establish a baseline. After performing a proper test code refactoring, mutation testing was repeated, and the results were recorded. The mutation testing score and each mutant's state before and after refactoring were individually validated as unchanged to confirm that the refactoring was successful.

Negative scenarios assessed MeteoR's ability to detect unintended behavioral changes resulting from improper refactoring. The project was restored to its initial state, and improper refactoring was performed, which affected the test behavior without altering test execution results. Mutation testing was performed again, and the results were compared with the baseline. Any changes in the mutation testing score or individually in the state of mutants indicated improper refactoring. In these scenarios, a detailed analysis of both surviving and killed

---

[3] Refactoring project code: https://github.com/meteortool/final_assessment/tree/main/project-sample.

mutants was conducted to validate whether the observed changes aligned with the expected impact of the incorrect refactoring.

The following mutation operators, which are the default operators[4] in *PITest* were utilized: *Conditionals Boundary Mutator, Increments Mutator, Invert Negatives Mutator, Math Mutator, Negate Conditionals Mutator, Void Method Call Mutator, Empty Returns Mutator, False Returns Mutator, True Returns Mutator, Null Returns Mutator,* and *Primitive Returns Mutator*.

Specifically, the comparative test mutation reports generated by `MeteoR` with mutation data before and after refactoring were scrutinized to identify the reasons behind mutants being killed or surviving post-refactoring, ensuring that changes were indeed expected within the scope of the incorrect refactoring. In the experiment-specific project, 3,820 mutations were generated and evaluated before and after refactoring, resulting in a total of 7,640 mutants analyzed at two different points in time.

The experimental data were systematically compiled, consolidated, and summarized. The results are presented in Table 1 and made available in the `MeteoR` assessment repository[5].

4 Result Analysis and Discussions

Results indicate that `MeteoR` effectively identified issues across the majority of test code refactoring types. Despite the summarized data presented in Table 1, `MeteoR` evaluated each mutant and its respective state before and after refactoring in detail. This in-depth analysis was applied to all refactorings indiscriminately.

Of the 34 tests conducted, including both positive (correct refactoring) and negative (incorrect refactoring) scenarios, only three positive scenarios did not yield the expected results. Specifically, the tool incorrectly indicated that the refactoring was unsuccessful in these cases. This indicates that the tool achieved accuracy in 31 out of the 34 test refactoring types. In negative scenarios where the refactoring was performed improperly, the tool detected unintended changes in the test behavior in all scenarios, which means that misidentifications occurred only in positive scenarios. In Sect. 4.1, we discuss why these particular refactoring types posed challenges for `MeteoR`. It is important to note that these instances highlight limitations of the approach in specific contexts, rather than deficiencies in the tool itself.

In positive scenarios, such as tests where refactoring failures were incorrectly identified, test effectiveness degradation is less likely to occur. In contrast, in negative scenarios, where refactoring errors were intentionally introduced, the tool should be more proficient at preventing the degradation of refactored tests by accurately detecting changes in their behavior. In these cases, the tool was effective in all scenarios.

---

[4] https://pitest.org/quickstart/mutators/.
[5] The dataset is provided in the worksheet 'Consolidated_Mutation_Data.xlsx', accessible at https://doi.org/10.6084/m9.figshare.25954066.

Table 1. Final validation report data for the refactoring types proposed by Guerra and Fernandes [5] (1–15) and Martins et al. [6] (16–17), including positive and negative scenarios.

Scenario	#	Refactoring Type	Scenario Type	Result
1	1A	Add assertion explanation	Positive	OK
1	1B	Add assertion explanation	Negative	OK
2	2A	Create equality method	Positive	NOK
2	2B	Create equality method	Negative	OK
3	3A	Simplify usage scenario	Positive	NOK
3	3B	Simplify usage scenario	Negative	OK
4	4A	Separate action from assertion	Positive	OK
4	4B	Separate action from assertion	Negative	OK
5	5A	Decompose assertion	Positive	OK
5	5B	Decompose assertion	Negative	OK
6	6A	Add fixture	Positive	OK
6	6B	Add fixture	Negative	OK
7	7A	Extract setup method	Positive	OK
7	7B	Extract setup method	Negative	OK
8	8A	Extract teardown method	Positive	OK
8	8B	Extract teardown method	Negative	OK
9	9A	Merge incremental tests	Positive	OK
9	9B	Merge incremental tests	Negative	OK
10	10A	Merge similar tests with different data	Positive	OK
10	10B	Merge similar tests with different data	Negative	OK
11	11A	Mirror hierarchy for tests	Positive	OK
11	11B	Mirror hierarchy for tests	Negative	OK
12	12A	Pull test up in hierarchy	Positive	OK
12	12B	Pull test up in hierarchy	Negative	OK
13	13A	Pull test down in hierarchy	Positive	OK
13	13B	Pull test down in hierarchy	Negative	OK
14	14A	Create template test for abstract functions	Positive	OK
14	14B	Create template test for abstract functions	Negative	OK
15	15A	Separate test from aggregated class	Positive	NOK
15	15B	Separate test from aggregated class	Negative	OK
16	16A	Surround assertions with assertAll method [6]	Positive	OK
16	16B	Surround assertions with assertAll method [6]	Negative	OK
17	17A	Replace try/catch, @Test expected, and @Rule annotations with assertThrows method [6]	Positive	OK
17	17B	Replace try/catch, @Test expected, and @Rule annotations with assertThrows method [6]	Negative	OK

4.1 Considerations About the Failed Cases

The three correct refactorings that the tool failed to confirm in this experiment can be grouped into two main change types: Scenario 2A (*Create equality method*) increased the mutation score, and Scenario 3A (*Simplify usage scenario*) and Scenario 15A (*Separate test from aggregate class*) decreased the mutation score.

Tests that Changed Behavior Due to Increased Mutation Scores. Scenario **2A**, which involves the *creating an equality method* refactoring, assumes that the refactoring applies the use of a method from the class under test to check the equality between objects of that class type. This change leads to an automatic improvement in the mutation score, meaning that the mutation coverage is increased, since the tests now exercise an additional method that was not previously tested. Consequently, the observed increase in the mutation score in this case can be a false indication of refactoring failure.

In this scenario, although the states of some mutants change as a result of the refactoring, the overall effectiveness of the tests actually improves. Therefore, mutation testing may not be the most suitable method for determining the success of this type of refactoring, as it may not accurately distinguish between unintended changes in test behavior and intentional enhancements.

In Code Snippet 1.1 the test method *testEquality* checks the equality of two *Customer* objects by comparing their names and accounts. The refactored version of the test method applies the proposed refactoring by using the *equals* method in the *Customer* class.

Code Snippet 1.1. Test method before and after proper refactoring.

```
 1    // Before Refactoring
 2    @Test
 3    public void testEquality() {
 4        Customer customer1 = new Customer("Customer 1", new LocalAccount()),
 5            customer2 = new Customer("Customer 1", customer1.getAccount());
 6        assertEquals(customer1.getName(), customer2.getName()) ;
 7        assertEquals(customer1.getAccount(), customer2.getAccount()) ;
 8    }
 9
10    // After Refactoring
11    @Test
12    public void testEquality() {
13        Customer customer1 = new Customer("Customer 1", new LocalAccount()),
14            customer2 = new Customer("Customer 1", customer1.getAccount());
15        assertEquals(customer1, customer2) ;
16    }
```

In Table 2, the mutation scores before and after the refactoring of the previously presented code shows the increase in mutation coverage.

Table 2. Mutation score before and after refactoring.

Number of Classes	Before Refactoring (mutation score)	After Refactoring (mutation score)
6	15/48 (0.3125)	20/48 (0.4167)

Tests That Changed Behavior Due to a Decrease in Mutation Score.
Both scenario **3A** and scenario **15A** involved refactorings that used mocks to simplify the test code as the example shown in Code Snippet 1.2. As a result, the mutation score decreased, indicating a reduced mutation coverage since the tests now executed mock code instead of the real code that was previously tested. This change in the mutation score may be a false indication of a refactoring failure.

It is recommended that in the case of a decrease in the mutation score, this may stimulate the creation of tests (if they do not already exist) that cover the indirect code that was being tested previously and is now no longer being tested, thus avoiding a decrease in the mutation score when all tests are run together.

Code Snippet 1.2. Test method before and after proper refactoring.

```
// Before Refactoring
@Test
public void checkIsCustomerIsNotVIP() {
    Customer customer = new Customer("John doe", new LocalAccount());
    customer.getAccount().addDeposit(new Deposit(customer.getAccount(), 900, null));
    customer.getAccount().addDeposit(new Deposit(customer.getAccount(), 950, null));
    customer.getAccount().addDeposit(new Deposit(customer.getAccount(), 800, null));
    assertFalse(customer.isVIP(), "The customer must not be vip") ;
}

//After Refactoring
@Test
public void checkIsCustomerIsNotVIP() {
    Customer customer = new Customer("John doe", new LocalAccount() {
        public double getAmountDepositAvg() {
            return 999;
        }
    });
    assertFalse(customer.isVIP(), "The customer must not be vip") ;
}
```

Table 3 illustrates that the mutation scores display a reduction in mutation coverage following the refactoring of the aforementioned code.

Table 3. Mutation score before and after refactoring.

Number of Classes	Before Refactoring (mutation score)	After Refactoring (mutation score)
6	12/48 (0.2500)	3/48 (0.0625)

4.2 Production and Test Code Refactorings

Another significant challenge identified during this study was the difficulty in managing simultaneous refactorings of both the production and test code. When changes are made to the application code, new mutants can be introduced, or existing ones disappear, complicating the test code's analysis. The refactorings evaluated in scenarios **12A** and **13A** demonstrated that when both the production code and the test code are modified together, `MeteoR` struggle to isolate the impact of the test code refactoring.

Changes in the production code affect the mutation landscape as stated by Parsai et al. [8], making it difficult to isolate the impact of test code refactoring. To mitigate this, we performed the refactoring in two phases: first, adjusting the production code and then refactoring the test code accordingly. Although this approach was effective in the experiment, the separation of refactoring phases may not always be practical in real-world scenarios, especially for structural refactorings that inherently involve both production and test code.

4.3 Study Limitations

The study utilized test code, production code, and test refactorings created based on descriptions from the chosen catalogs. While this controlled setup facilitated detailed mutant's inspections and the exploration of specific refactorings, it may not fully capture the complexity of real-world projects, limiting the generalizability of the results. The study focused exclusively on these types of refactorings, incorporating qualitative mutant analyses to address cases where behavior maintenance was not correctly assessed. Furthermore, it highlighted challenges in mutation testing for complex refactorings that blur the boundaries between test and production code, as such scenarios may obscure the broader implications of changes spanning both domains.

5 Conclusion

This study evaluated the effectiveness of mutation testing in detecting behavioral changes during test code refactoring. The investigation achieved its four main objectives. First, `MeteoR` was released following the model proposed by Teixeira et al. [12] and incorporating improvements since its preliminary version [11]. Second, the test refactoring catalog has proven to be adequate in helping to identify key gaps in the approach. It successfully facilitates the evaluation process by providing a framework for evaluating the effectiveness of mutation testing in measuring the impact of refactorings on behavior and identifying such impacts. Third, the study conducted using the test refactoring catalog applied to the `MeteoR` tool allowed the qualitative analysis of the results, which had not been carried out previously, provided in-depth evidence of the effectiveness of mutation testing in various test refactoring scenarios. Fourth, the study identified the limitations of applying mutation testing to test refactoring. Specifically, the approach proved less effective in scenarios involving mocks, often introduced during refactoring to simplify the test code. Since mocks replace real interactions, they can obscure mutation testing's ability to detect behavioral changes, leading to false positives or negatives in the mutation score. Previous works [1,5,8,11–13] did not raise this limitation, and its identification was only possible through the qualitative analysis performed. The approach also faces challenges when both the production and test codes are refactored simultaneously. In such cases, mutation testing may struggle to accurately assess the impact of the refactoring, as changes in the application code can introduce or eliminate mutants, making it difficult to isolate the effects of test code refactoring alone.

The correct assessment of the change in test behavior achieved in most of the test refactoring scenarios demonstrates the approach's efficacy. However, three types of refactoring were identified in which the `MeteoR` erroneously pointed out an error in the refactoring, showing that it has limitations in these cases.

Thus, these results provide a comprehensive perspective on the mutation testing approach. By leveraging `MeteoR`, the applicability of mutation testing in the context of test code refactoring becomes more evident, thereby increasing confidence in its adoption as a quality assessment strategy. Furthermore, the proposed model opens the door for the development of other tools based on the same principles, potentially supporting a broader range of programming languages. The findings discussed, particularly the limitations highlighted in Sect. 4.1, not only reveal aspects previously unrecognized in earlier studies [1,8,12,13], but also provide valuable input for the evolution of a more complete and robust catalog of refactorings.

Expanding in future work the tool's evaluation scope to include large-scale production scenarios with real-world projects would be highly valuable. Additionally, future efforts could focus on enhancing the tool's integration capabilities, enabling its use within *DevOps* pipelines in batch mode. This would allow for automated and continuous validation of test code refactorings in real development workflows. Moreover, the tool could be adapted to integrate with large language models (LLMs) to assist in identifying and recommending refactorings, further increasing its potential to support intelligent and automated test maintenance at scale.

Acknowledgments. The authors thank the São Paulo Research Foundation (FAPESP) – grant 2023/14646-1 – for partial financial support.

References

1. van Bladel, B., Demeyer, S.: Test refactoring: a research agenda. In: Proceedings SATToSE (2017)
2. Bladel, B.v., Demeyer, S.: Test behaviour detection as a test refactoring safety. In: Proceedings of the 2nd International Workshop on Refactoring, p. 22-25, IWoR 2018, Association for Computing Machinery, New York, NY, USA (2018), ISBN 9781450359740
3. Coles, H., Laurent, T., Henard, C., Papadakis, M., Ventresque, A.: Pit: a practical mutation testing tool for java (demo). In: Proceedings of the 25th International Symposium on Software Testing and Analysis, pp. 449–452, ISSTA 2016, Association for Computing Machinery, New York, NY, USA (2016), ISBN 9781450343909
4. Fowler, M.: Refactoring: Improving the Design of Existing Code. Addison-Wesley signature series, Addison-Wesley, USA (2019), 9780134757599

5. Guerra, E.M., Fernandes, C.T.: Refactoring test code safely. In: International Conference on Software Engineering Advances (ICSEA 2007), pp. 44–44 (2007)
6. Martins, L., Ghaleb, T., Costa, H., Machado, I.: A comprehensive catalog of refactoring strategies to handle test smells in java-based systems. Softw. Qual. J. 1–39 (2024)
7. Offutt, A.J., Untch, R.H.: Mutation 2000: Uniting the Orthogonal. Springer, US, Boston, MA (2001). 978-1-4757-5939-6
8. Parsai, A., Murgia, A., Soetens, Q.D., Demeyer, S.: Mutation testing as a safety net for test code refactoring. In: Scientific Workshop Proceedings of the XP2015, XP 2015 workshops, Association for Computing Machinery, New York, NY, USA (2015), ISBN 9781450334099
9. Pizzini, A.: Behavior-based test smells refactoring : toward an automatic approach to refactoring eager test and lazy test smells. In: 2022 IEEE/ACM 44th International Conference on Software Engineering: Companion Proceedings (ICSE-Companion), pp. 261–263 (2022)
10. Pizzini, A., Reinehr, S., Malucelli, A.: Sentinel: a process for automatic removing of test smells. In: Proceedings of the XXII Brazilian Symposium on Software Quality, pp. 80–89, SBQS 2023, Association for Computing Machinery, New York, NY, USA (2023), ISBN 9798400707865
11. Teixeira, T., Silveira, F., Guerra, E.: Meteor: a tool for monitoring behavior preservation in test code refactorings. In: Anais do XXXVIII Simpósio Brasileiro de Engenharia de Software, pp. 755–761, SBC, Porto Alegre, RS, Brasil (2024)
12. Teixeira, T.S.R., Silveira, F.F., Guerra, E.M.: Moving towards a mutant-based testing tool for verifying behavior maintenance in test code refactorings. Computers **12**(11) (2023)
13. Xuan, J., Cornu, B., Martinez, M., Baudry, B., Seinturier, L., Monperrus, M.: B-refactoring: automatic test code refactoring to improve dynamic analysis. Inf. Softw. Technol. **76**, 65–80 (2016)

Open Access This chapter is licensed under the terms of the Creative Commons Attribution 4.0 International License (http://creativecommons.org/licenses/by/4.0/), which permits use, sharing, adaptation, distribution and reproduction in any medium or format, as long as you give appropriate credit to the original author(s) and the source, provide a link to the Creative Commons license and indicate if changes were made.

The images or other third party material in this chapter are included in the chapter's Creative Commons license, unless indicated otherwise in a credit line to the material. If material is not included in the chapter's Creative Commons license and your intended use is not permitted by statutory regulation or exceeds the permitted use, you will need to obtain permission directly from the copyright holder.

Visualization Usage in Technical Debt Management

Marius Irgens(✉) and Antonio Martini

Department of Informatics, University of Oslo, Oslo, Norway
{mariuir,antonima}@ifi.uio.no

Abstract. Visualization is a promising technique in TD management, but with various tools offering visualization, the question arise: is it being used effectively by practitioners? Through an analysis of survey data from 417 participants across seven international companies, we examine the current use of visualization and its perceived potential to improve TD management. Our findings reveal that while visualization tools are not widely used, there is a clear desire for enhanced visualization capabilities.

Keywords: technical debt · management · visualization · tools · survey

1 Introduction

Technical Debt (TD) refers to the downstream consequences of compromises made during software development. These consequences manifest as deteriorating code quality, reduced maintainability, declining morale, and escalating costs over time. Agile development, with its focus on quick time-to-market and frequent releases, can be especially prone to TD accumulation, as immediate business value is often prioritized over code maintainability. This makes continuous TD management especially important in agile development, enabling teams to sustain the increased throughput over extended periods. Visualization transforms complex data into intuitive, comprehensible formats. By providing insights into the structure, quality and evolution of software systems, visualization can enable agile developers to continuously monitor code maintainability and detect areas where TD accumulates. Code analysis tools like SonarQube, CodeScene and Arcan incorporate visualization techniques specifically designed for these purposes. However, despite the potential benefits, it remains unclear how much visualization is being applied in TD management across the industry. Few studies have explored its real-world usage. This study seeks to address this gap by presenting data from a comprehensive survey on TD management, which includes statements regarding the use of visualization. It will focus on the following questions:

RQ1: Are organizations currently utilizing visualization to manage TD?

RQ2: Do employees believe that more use of visualization would improve the effectiveness of TD management?

2 Related Work

Several studies have examined the practical use and capabilities of tools for managing TD. A study by Avgeriou et al. [1] provides an overview of the popularity of various TD measurement tools. Their findings show that SonarQube is by far the most widely used tool among practitioners and researchers, followed by NDepend, while other tools such as CAST and SonarGraph have a more limited presence. Fontana et al. [2] conducted a comparative study of five TD measurement tools, focusing on how these tools calculate Technical Debt Indexes (TDIs). The study found significant differences in how the tools assess TD. Martini et al. [4] examined TD tracking practices in 15 large organizations through a survey and multiple case studies. Their results show that while TD management is acknowledged as important, it is often informal and unsystematic, with only 26% of respondents using a tool to track TD, and only 7% *methodically* tracking it. Lenarduzzi et al. [3] conducted a survey on code analysis tools used for software maintenance prediction. Their study highlights a lack of readily available and reliable tools in this domain. They emphasized that many tools used in research are often prototypes or discontinued, limiting their practical applicability. While these studies offer valuable insights into the use of tools in TD management, they do not address the use of visualization specifically.

3 Survey Insights on TD Visualization

This study draws on the TD Pulse survey method developed by Martini et al. [5], which provides a comprehensive framework for assessing TD management practices across organizations. The TD Pulse survey focuses on eight key aspects, including tool usage and development processes. Analyzing both technical and non-technical roles, it provides actionable insights into TD management and identifies gaps and areas for improvement. To answer the posed research questions, this study explores survey data collected from 417 participants across seven international companies, including managers and developers, spanning all experience levels and team sizes. Presented visually, the data provides insights into the current state of visualization usage and its perceived potential to enhance TD management. Figure 1 presents the participants' responses to the two survey items related to visualization. To avoid repetition, these items will be referred to in a shortened form throughout the paper. The first item, 'We confidently use the output of a tool to visualize the overall level of TD in our system(s), its costs and risks to plan future development' will be referred to as simply 'We confidently use visualization.' The second item, 'Which areas would you improve in your organization to make your TD management more efficient? Provide more TD visualization' will be referred to as 'Need for improved visualization.' The survey results and some reflective thoughts around them are presented together in this same section.

Examining Fig. 1a, it is evident that visualization is not widely used to manage TD. Only 12% of participants report confident use of visualization. In Fig.

188   M. Irgens and A. Martini

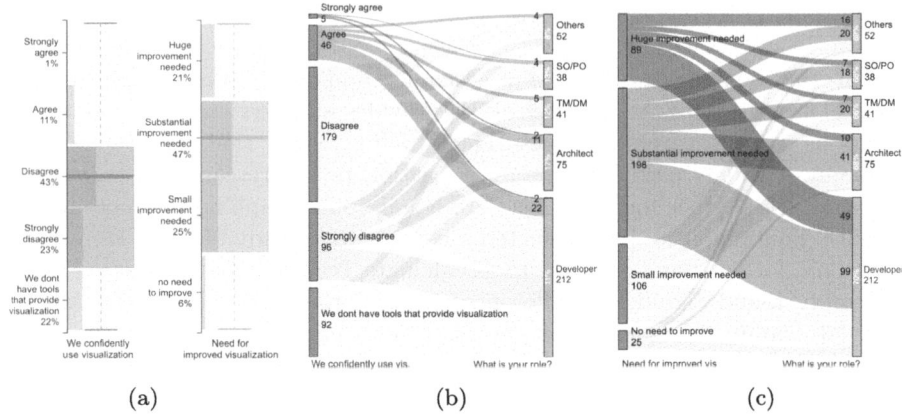

Fig. 1. The distributions of the two main statements and their associations with the participants roles. TM/DM: Team/Development Manager. SO/PO: Service/Product Owner. Others: Includes various roles such as testers, analysts, consultants, and security engineers.

1b, the highest use is seen in the 'Architect' category, where 17% agree they use visualization confidently. In contrast, the category 'Others' reports the lowest usage, with only 8% agreeing. The remaining categories hover around 12%. Figure 1c shows that all roles perceive roughly the same need for improved visualization, with 66% to 70% indicating substantial or huge improvement is needed. This highlights a significant gap between the limited use of visualization and the widespread recognition of its potential to enhance TD management.

To further investigate how TD visualization relates to broader TD management practices, this study examines associations between the two main statements and four selected statements. These were chosen primarily due to notable associations observed in the dataset. By focusing on these associations, the analysis offers insights that may indirectly inform future TD visualization tool research and development.

Figure 2a shows the association between the ease of understanding TD risk and the use of visualization. The data suggests that visualization may aid in risk assessment, as 69% of participants who confidently use visualization agree that it is easy to assess whether the current TD in their system is risky or not. This is slightly higher than the 58% of participants who do not confidently use visualization or lack access to such tools.

In Fig. 2b, the association between peer review of TD removal and visualization usage is more notable. 69% of participants who confidently use visualization report that someone will check if TD was successfully removed. In contrast, only 36% of participants who do not confidently use visualization report the same, and only 26% among those without access to visualization tools. One explanation for this association could be that visualization tools makes it easier for

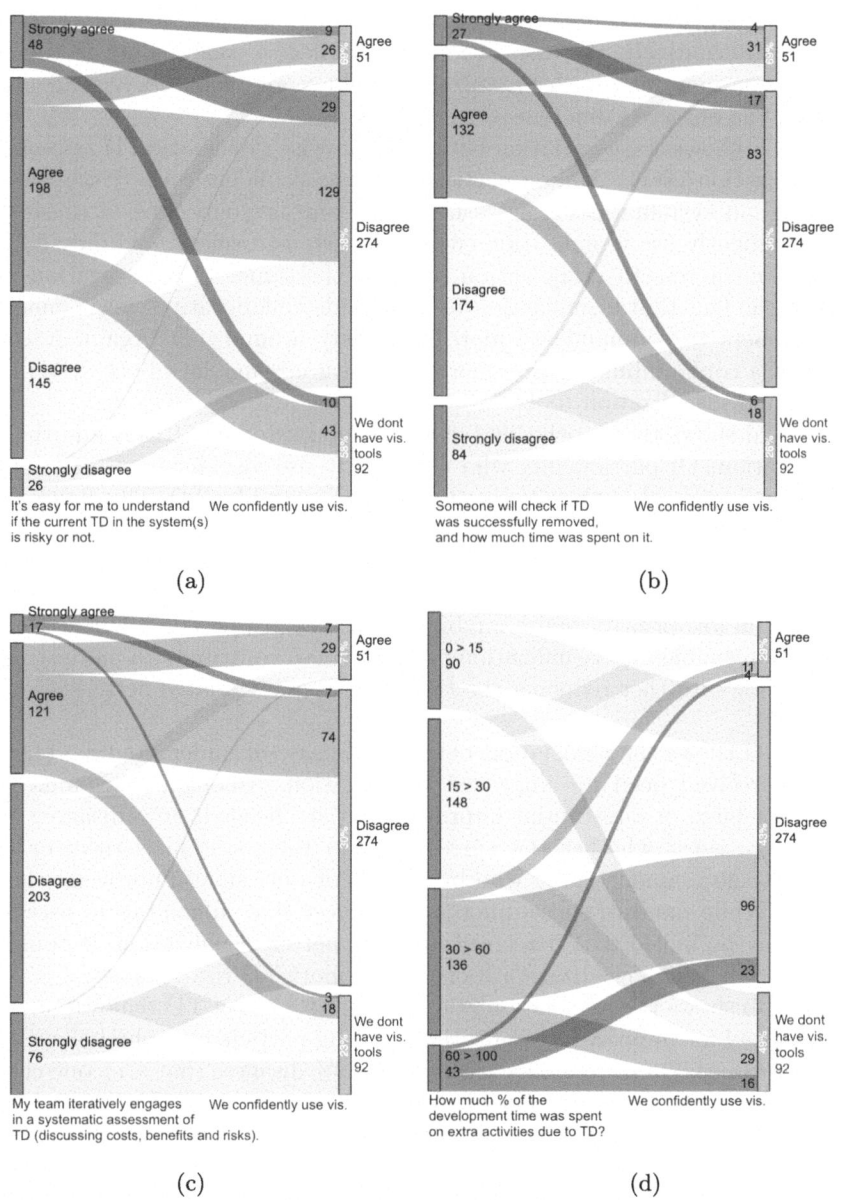

Fig. 2. In each figure, there are different statements on the left axis and 'We confidently use visualization' on the right axis. The exact number of responses for each possible answer is displayed below each node label on the right side of the axes. The number of participants who provided a specific combination of answers to both statements is shown at the end of each focused link on the left side of the right axis. Each node on the right axis highlights the percentage-wise distribution of the focused responses from the left axis in white text. The focused responses are 'Agree' and 'Strongly agree' in the first three figures, and '30 to 60' and '60 to 100' in the last figure.

teams and managers to plan, delegate, and track TD removal and reviewing activities. Alternatively, the association could reflect a confounding factor: less mature teams may lack both organized workflows and tools for visualization, explaining the observed differences.

Figure 2c shows the association between teamwise systematic TD assessment and visualization usage. Among participants who confidently use visualization, 71% engage in systematic TD assessment. In contrast, only 30% of those who do not confidently use visualization engage in such assessment, and only 23% of those without access to visualization tools do the same. This association may be due to the fact that visualization tools provide collaborative views, enabling team members to communicate more effectively around TD. Again, it could also reflect a confounding factor, where less mature teams lack both systematic processes and visualization tools.

Figure 2d shows the association between time wasted due to TD and the use of visualization. Of participants who confidently use visualization, 29% report spending 30% or more of their time on activities caused by TD. This figure rises to 43% for participants who do not confidently use visualization and 49% for those without access to such tools. Visualization tools may help teams prioritize TD more effectively, allowing them to focus on high-impact areas and reduce time spent on low-priority maintainability tasks. Improved communication and collaboration enabled by visualization tools may also contribute to more streamlined workflows, further reducing the time spent on TD-related activities.

Figure 3a shows the association between the ease of understanding TD risk and the perceived need for improved visualization. Among participants who believe that huge or substantial improvements are needed, 46% disagree that it is easy to assess whether the current TD in their system is risky or not, compared to 30% among those who believe no or only small improvements are necessary. While modest, these differences suggest that difficulties in assessing TD risk may be linked to a perceived need for better visualization. It could be because they believe visualization tools can support TD risk analysis.

Figure 3b shows the association between peer review of TD removal and the perceived need for improved visualization. Among participants who believe that huge or substantial improvements are needed, 69% disagree that someone checks whether TD has been successfully removed. In comparison, 47% of participants who believe no or only small improvements are needed disagree with the same statement. These results suggest that participants who do not perform or experience regular review of TD removal are somewhat more likely to see a need for improved visualization, perhaps because they think visualization tools could help facilitate such activities.

Figure 3c shows the association between teamwise engagement in systematic TD assessment and the perceived need for improved visualization. Among participants who believe that huge or substantial improvements are required, 73% disagree that their team iteratively engages in systematic TD assessment. This figure drops to 53% among participants who believe only small or no improve-

Visualization Usage in Technical Debt Management 191

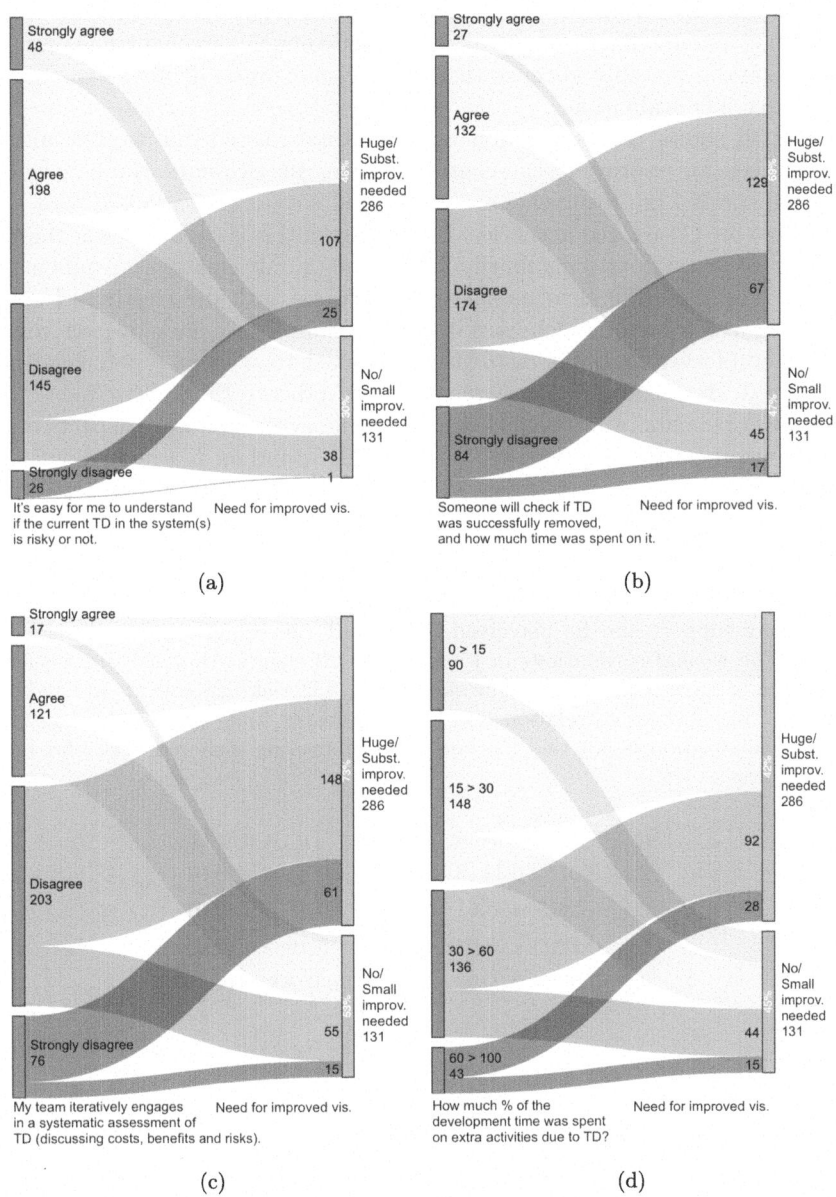

Fig. 3. In each figure, there are different statements on the left axis and 'Need for improved TD visualization' on the right axis. The exact number of responses for each possible answer is displayed below each node label on the right side of the axes. The number of participants who provided a specific combination of answers to both statements is shown at the end of each focused link on the left side of the right axis. Each node on the right axis highlights the percentage-wise distribution of the focused responses from the left axis in white text. The focused responses are 'Strongly disagree' and 'Disagree' in the first three figures, and '30 to 60' and '60 to 100' in the last figure.

ments are needed. This difference suggests that participants whose teams do not engage in systematic TD assessments are more likely to perceive a need for better visualization, possibly because they view visualization as a way to enhance collaborative TD evaluation.

Figure 3d shows the association between time wasted due to TD and the perceived need for improved visualization. Among participants who believe that huge or substantial improvements are needed, 42% report spending 30% or more of their time on TD-related activities. Interestingly, this is slightly lower than the 45% observed among participants who believe no or only small improvements are necessary. This lack of a clear association contrasts with the trends in Figs. 3a, 3b, and 3c, where factors such as not understanding risk, lack of peer review, and absence of systematic assessments are linked to a greater perceived need for improved visualization. These results may indicate that participants view the potential benefits of visualization as valuable across different aspects of TD management, regardless of the time they actually spend on TD-related activities (Table 1).

Table 1. Spearman correlation coefficients and p-values for the statements from Figs. 2 and 3. Mild to moderate correlations in Figs. 2b, 2c, 3a, 3b, and 3c suggest that visualization may support and be perceived to support the respective TD management practices. The weaker correlations in Figs. 2a and 2d suggest that *existing* visualization tools may have a limited role in supporting TD risk assessment and reducing time waste. The lack of correlation in Fig. 3d indicates that the perceived need for improved visualization is not tied to time waste, reflecting a shared desire for better tools regardless.

Figure	ρ	p-value	Figure	ρ	p-value
2a	0.0782	0.1118	3a	−0.1800	< 0.01
2b	0.2567	< 0.01	3b	−0.1826	< 0.01
2c	0.2993	< 0.01	3c	−0.1988	< 0.01
2d	0.0867	0.0768	3d	0.0198	0.6892

4 Final Thoughts

Figures 2 and 3 presents associations between visualization and certain TD management practices. Figure 2 suggests that using visualization is associated with improved TD management, while Fig. 3 indicates that worse TD management is linked to a perceived need for improved visualization. Despite the potential benefits of visualization and the interest in it, the actual use remains limited. Several factors may contribute to this. One possible reason for the limited use of visualization tools is the cost of integrating them into existing development workflows. Agile-driven companies often focus on maintaining throughput, which can make it challenging to adopt new tools, particularly when those tools require significant customization or training. As a result, even though employees recognize the benefits of visualization, the investment required can hinder adoption. This aligns with what Telea and Voinea noted in one of their case studies on Software Visualization [6], stating that 'simplicity is the key to making visualization gain wider acceptance in software engineering at large ... it has to provide clear benefits with limited investment.' Additionally, even when tools are already integrated, insufficient training may lead to low confidence in their usage. Of course, it is also possible that the existing visualization tools do not fully meet the expectations of the employees, and as a result, are discarded from their workflow. Despite this, the desire for improved visualization persists because employees can envision what an ideal tool would look like – something that would provide the insights and functionalities they need, but that current tools does not offer.

The findings from this study suggest some key considerations for future research on TD visualization tools. First, as noted by Telea and Voinea, and further suggested by the low adoption observed in industry, visualization tools need to be easy to integrate into existing workflows. Second, it would be beneficial to support users across all roles and experience levels; as shown in Fig. 1c, every role recognizes the need for improved visualization. Third, features that facilitate TD risk assessment, effective organization of TD removal and systematic team assessment of TD may be of particular value – a notion supported by the observed link between challenges in these areas and an increased perceived need for visualization. Conducting an empirical study on employees' expectations to further identify the features they would find most helpful could provide additional insights. Ultimately, future tools should strive to close the gap between these expectations and the current functionality of the tools that are available.

References

1. Avgeriou, P.C., et al.: An overview and comparison of technical debt measurement tools. IEEE Softw. **38**(3), 61–71 (2020)
2. Fontana, F.A., Roveda, R., Zanoni, M.: Technical debt indexes provided by tools: a preliminary discussion. In: 2016 IEEE 8th International Workshop on Managing Technical Debt (MTD), pp. 28–31. IEEE (2016)
3. Lenarduzzi, V., Sillitti, A., Taibi, D.: A survey on code analysis tools for software maintenance prediction. In: Ciancarini, P., Mazzara, M., Messina, A., Sillitti, A., Succi, G. (eds.) SEDA 2018. AISC, vol. 925, pp. 165–175. Springer, Cham (2020). https://doi.org/10.1007/978-3-030-14687-0_15
4. Martini, A., Besker, T., Bosch, J.: Technical debt tracking: current state of practice: a survey and multiple case study in 15 large organizations. Sci. Comput. Program. **163**, 42–61 (2018)
5. Martini, A., Besker, T., Posch, T., Bosch, J.: Td pulse: assessing the systematic management of technical debt. IEEE Softw. **40**(3), 54–62 (2022)
6. Telea, A., Voinea, L.: Case study: visual analytics in software product assessments. In: 2009 5th IEEE International Workshop on Visualizing Software for Understanding and Analysis, pp. 65–72. IEEE (2009)

Open Access This chapter is licensed under the terms of the Creative Commons Attribution 4.0 International License (http://creativecommons.org/licenses/by/4.0/), which permits use, sharing, adaptation, distribution and reproduction in any medium or format, as long as you give appropriate credit to the original author(s) and the source, provide a link to the Creative Commons license and indicate if changes were made.

The images or other third party material in this chapter are included in the chapter's Creative Commons license, unless indicated otherwise in a credit line to the material. If material is not included in the chapter's Creative Commons license and your intended use is not permitted by statutory regulation or exceeds the permitted use, you will need to obtain permission directly from the copyright holder.

Agile Effort Estimation Usage in the Sri Lankan Software Industry

Sean Jonathon Lee and Mali Senapathi(✉)

Auckland University of Technology, Auckland, New Zealand
`mali.senapathi@aut.ac.nz`

Abstract. Accurate effort estimation in the software development industry remains a significant challenge due to requirements' complexities, technology variability, and insufficient skilled members. To provide up-to-date insights on the state of effort estimation practices in Sri Lanka, we surveyed agile practitioners to identify the effort estimation techniques, types of metrics employed, levels of accuracy, and reasons for inaccuracies in estimates. Our analysis of 93 valid responses reveals that Planning Poker was the most popular estimation technique at 50.5%, while story points were the most widely used metric utilized by 61.3% of participants. Expert estimation was employed by 30% of respondents, and man-hours were used by 23.7%. The combination of Planning Poker and story points was most used, with a prevalence of 70.2%. Regarding the accuracy of estimations, respondents who used a combination of Planning Poker (61.7%) and expert estimation (25.5%) could complete their work within the estimated time without any extra effort. The top three categories of inaccurate estimates were quality-related, project management, and team-related issues.

Keywords: Effort estimation · Agile software development · Software engineering

1 Introduction

Effort estimation accurately predicts the effort, cost, and duration needed to schedule work items [1] effectively. During planning an iteration, such as a sprint, an agile software development (ASD) team selects a set of work items (e.g., task, user story) to include in the sprint, ensuring that the total estimated effort for these items aligns with the sprint's capacity [1]. Sprint capacity refers to the total effort a team can dedicate to work during a sprint, which is determined based on the estimated effort involved in the work items completed in previous sprints [1]. For effective sprint planning, it is crucial that the estimated effort accurately represents the size or development time required for each work item. Timely delivery of high-quality software begins with an accurate estimation process. The estimation includes identifying necessary resources, such as manpower, assessing dependencies, recognizing potential risks, estimating the time needed to deliver a quality product or feature, and the associated costs [2]. Accurate software estimations offer numerous benefits. They enable decision-makers within an organization to make informed choices regarding project feasibility, optimal resource allocation, and effective risk management [3]. Furthermore, reliable estimates can assist in determining initial budget requirements and delivery timelines, facilitating alignment among all stakeholders [4]. However, factors such as customer pressure, varying demands, and outdated estimation methods often lead to overly optimistic estimates, affecting software delivery, quality, and the budget allocated for development [5]. Effort estimation in ASD, presents particular challenges due to the constantly evolving requirements, as the estimates must be progressively adjusted for each sprint to ensure timely delivery [6]. Despite the existence of various estimation techniques within ASD, achieving accuracy continues to be a major hurdle.

While effort estimation has been extensively studied in structured software development such as the waterfall method, there has been a recent rise in interest, particularly within the ASD community, to better [2, 7, 8] understand and improve the effort estimation practices [9]. Most research on Agile effort estimation has focused on conducting a large number of systematic literature reviews (SLRs)) [10–12], and a limited number of case studies [9, 13], and a few surveys such as [14, 15] to explore the state of estimation practices (e.g., techniques, metrics). Most studies have not examined the accuracy of estimations or the reasons behind inaccurate estimations [1]. Recent research indicates that a high accuracy rate in effort estimation significantly increases the likelihood of delivering a successful and high-quality product [16]. On the other hand, inaccurate estimates can negatively affect software project development. This can lead to two outcomes: underestimations may cause project terminations due to exceeded budgets and schedules, while overestimations can result in wasted resources [17]. By identifying the common causes of these inaccuracies, we can address the fundamental issues in effort estimation and ultimately aim to enhance prediction accuracy.

To provide empirical evidence about the state of effort estimation practice, level of accuracy, and the relationship between accuracy and estimation technique, and to contribute to providing more generalizable findings, we conducted an exploratory survey to address the following questions: (a) What agile methodologies are used in the Sri Lankan software industry? (b) What estimation techniques are used? (c) What estimation metrics are used to capture effort estimates? (d) What is the level of accuracy of the estimations? (e) What are the reasons for inaccurate estimation?

The survey study conducted in 2024 collected over ninety-three responses from Sri Lankan software practitioners. The results of the study are particularly noteworthy given the growing popularity of Business process outsourcing (BPO) services in the South Asian region, which includes countries such as India, Sri Lanka, and Bangladesh [18]. BPO services range from low-cost, repetitive tasks to knowledge-intensive value-added service providers utilized by Western nations such as the USA, Canada, Europe and the UK. According to Statista, a global company specializing in business intelligence through data collection and processing, the BPO market in South Asia is projected to reach a revenue of US$8.99 billion in 2024 [18]. With the growth of the BPO industry in this region, the Sri Lankan software sector primarily comprises companies that offer offshore software development services [19]. Accurately predicting project timeframes is not merely a project management activity; it is vital in BPO services where timely delivery is paramount.

The remainder of this paper is structured as follows: Sect. 2 reviews studies related to agile effort estimation. Section 3 outlines the research methodology, including the data collection process and the survey design. Section 4 presents the results. Finally, Sect. 5 concludes the paper, discussing the study's limitations.

2 Related Work

Most related work in agile effort estimation consists of SLRs [10–12, 16, 20], but empirical research providing detailed insights into estimation in ASD settings is limited, with a few exceptions, including case studies [9, 13] and surveys [14, 15].

Usman et al. [10] conducted an SLR on effort estimation in ASD based on analyzing 25 primary studies. They found that subjective estimation methods, such as expert judgment, planning poker, and Use Case Points (UCP), are commonly employed for agile estimation. While UCP and Story Points (SP) were the most frequently used size metrics, Mean Magnitude of Relative Error (MMRE) and Magnitude of Relative Error (MRE) were used as accuracy metrics. Many of the techniques examined did not achieve acceptable prediction accuracy, meaning the estimated values were often far from the actual values. More significantly, the authors concluded that practitioners would find little useful guidance on effort estimation in ASD from the current literature [12]. This is due to the low accuracy of these techniques and the lack of consensus on the appropriate cost drivers in different Agile contexts.

Two updated SLRs were published based on Usman et al.'s [10] original study. The first study used a forward snowballing approach to select 24 new papers published from 2014 to 2017 [11]. The second study analyzed the data extracted from 73 new papers published between 2014 to 2020 [12]. The findings revealed that expert-based estimation methods (e.g., Planning poker) and size metrics (e.g. story points) played an important role in six agile methods: Scrum, eXtreme Programming and four others. While achieving accuracy remains challenging, the updated SLRs observed some improvements. On the one hand, while an increasing number of studies reported acceptable accuracy values, many still demonstrate inadequate results [12]. On the other hand, nearly 29% of the papers that included accuracy metrics also addressed aspects related to model validation, and 18% reported effect sizes when comparing models [12].

Another SLR based on 12 studies published between 2000 and 2015 examined the performance of effort estimation methods, their objectivity, the factors influencing these estimations, and the accuracy of the different methods and approaches [20]. As with previous SLRs, most primary studies employed subjective expert effort estimation techniques, including Planning Poker, Expert Judgment and Story Points. Estimation by analogy was also commonly employed.

A systematic mapping study on effort estimation in ASD analyzed 25 primary studies published between 2018 and 2022 [16]. The findings included commonly used expert-based estimation methods/techniques, such as Story Point Estimation and Planning Poker. MMRE, Prediction Evaluation (PRED), and Mean Absolute Error (MAE) were identified as the most frequently employed performance evaluation measures. The study also identified several challenges and factors that complicate the estimation process, such as feasibility, experience, and the delivery of expert knowledge.

A survey of data collected from 60 agile practitioners from 16 different countries, found that (i) Planning poker (63%), analogy (47%) and expert judgment (38%) were the frequently employed estimation techniques; (ii) Story points, the most frequently (62%) employed size metric; (iii) Team's expertise level and prior experience were the most commonly used cost drivers, and (iv) 52% of the respondents believed that an error under/overestimated their effort estimates on average [10]. Similar findings were reported in a recent survey of 53 valid responses from agile practitioners [6]. Tanveer et al. [21] conducted a case study involving three agile teams in a German multinational company to examine the estimation process and its accuracy in ASD. Their findings highlighted that various factors—such as the developer's knowledge, experience, and the complexity and impact of changes on the underlying systems significantly influence both the magnitude of estimates and estimation accuracy.

In summary, most studies have focused primarily on various estimation techniques and metrics used in ASD without considering the accuracy levels and the reasons behind inadequate estimates. An exception is a recent SLR, which analyzed 82 studies published after 2001 and identified five themes that explain the reasons for inaccurate estimation: information quality, team dynamics, estimation practices, project management, and business influences [1]. To contribute to this area of literature, which has limited empirical evidence, we used an empirical approach to explore and analyze how agile effort estimation is used and experienced by organizations in the real-world software industry. Our aim was to identify the techniques and metrics employed, as well as the accuracy of estimations.

3 Research Methodology

This section provides an overview of the research setting, including details about data collection and survey design.

3.1 Data Collection

After receiving approval from the university's ethics committee, the survey was launched on March 1, 2024, and remained active for the entire month. An open invitation outlining the study's purpose was posted on the first author's LinkedIn profile, inviting software practitioners to participate. A reminder was posted two weeks after the survey opened. Consequently, participant recruitment was based on availability, utilizing a convenience sampling method. Although this approach has drawbacks and potential biases, it is still acceptable. Convenience sampling is reported to be the dominant method used in surveys within the field of software engineering [22]. Of the 109 responses received, 93 were deemed valid after omitting missing and incomplete data values.

3.2 Survey Design

The survey was developed using the Qualtrics survey tool. It consisted of fifteen questions based on relevant literature and empirical studies on agile effort estimation, including a recent study on effort estimation in ASD [6]. It included a participant information sheet and a consent form that thoroughly outlined the project's topic, goal, and privacy policies. A draft questionnaire was developed based on the guidelines proposed by Molléri et al. [23]. The questionnaire was then piloted by a senior academic and a senior software professional from Sri Lanka to check its consistency and legibility. The questions were divided into the following sections:

Background information on the practitioners and their organizations consisted of the following questions: the highest level of education, years of experience in software development, role/position in the organization, and whether they had completed an agile certification program.

Usage of agile effort estimation consisted of the following questions: the agile methodology used, team size, frequency of effort estimation, usage of specific estimation techniques, and usage of specific estimation metrics.

Level of accuracy section had questions related to the ability to complete within the estimated time and reasons for inaccurate estimates.

4 Results

This section presents the results and compares them to earlier studies on agile effort estimation.

4.1 Background Information

The number of valid responses was 93. Regarding the highest qualifications of participants, 62 respondents held a Bachelor's degree, 30 had a Master's degree, and one possessed a Diploma/Certificate level qualification. The respondents were working in various positions in their organizations. The main roles of the respondents were developers/programmers (n = 28) and quality assurance engineers (n = 23). Table 1 presents the respondents' positions, and Fig. 1 shows respondents' experiences in software development. Almost 97% of participants had more than three years of software industry experience: 18.28% had 3 to 5 years, 40.86% had 6 to 8 years, 29% had 9 to 12 years, and 8.6% had more than 13 years. 78.5% of the respondents had more than 5 years of experience, which highlights the involvement of senior practitioners in the ASD estimation process, and increases our confidence in the validity of the responses [14]. Comparatively, a recent study found that only 62.3% of respondents had more than three years of experience, with none reporting over five years of experience in ASD [6]. 72 (77.4%) respondents indicated they had completed an Agile certification program.

4.2 Usage of Agile Effort Estimation

As most participants were highly experienced practitioners, as expected, 88 (94.6%) participants selected that the key Scrum roles of Scrum Master and Product Owner were identified in their teams.

Regarding the type of agile methodology used (see Fig. 2), Scrum was the most commonly used methodology employed by 74 participants (79.57%), hybrid methods (e.g., Agile – Kanban) used by 10 participants (10.75%), followed by Kanban (n = 6,

Table 1. Position of participants

Position	Count (n)	Percent
Developer/Programmer	28	30.1%
Quality Assurance Engineer	23	24.7%
Engineering Manager	9	9.7%
Scrum Master/Project Manager	9	9.7%
Software Architect	7	7.5%
DevOps Engineer	5	5.4%
Business Analyst	4	4.3%
Product Owner	3	3.2%
Other	5	5.4%
Total	93	100

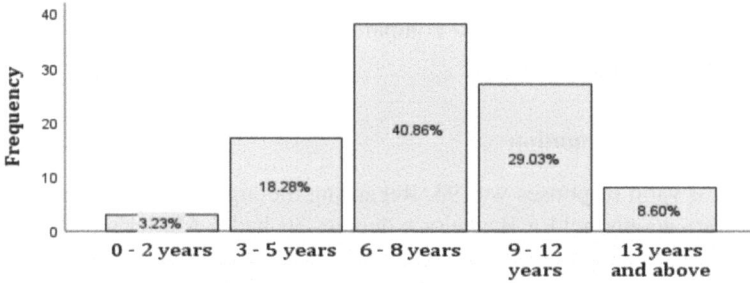

Fig. 1. Experience of participants

6.45%) and Waterfall (n = 3, 3.2%) was the least used. While the wide usage of Scrum and the use of hybrid approaches (e.g., Scrumban) aligns with previous surveys such as HELENA [24] and others [6], it is interesting to note that approaches such as XP (none selected) and Waterfall are rarely used in Sri Lanka.

Most respondents work in teams of up to 12 members (see Table 2); 15 participants (16.1%) reported a team size between 1 and 5, 46 (49.5%) between 5 and 8, and 20 between 8 and 12 (21.5%). Twelve reported a team size greater than 12 (12.9%).

The frequency of performing effort estimation is shown in Table 3. While most respondents (n = 68, 73.1%) reported making the estimates at every sprint, 11 said estimates were made ad-hoc, i.e., when the management or the client requested them.

Effort Estimation Techniques

This study included Planning Poker, Three-point estimation, Top-down estimate, Dot Voting, Expert estimation, Bucket system, and Swimlane sizing as the estimation techniques. Figure 3 details the responses to ASD estimation techniques practiced, along

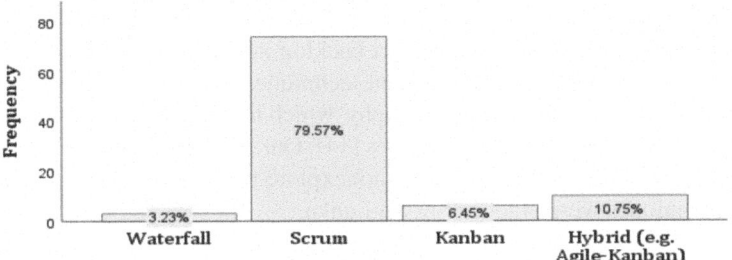

Fig. 2. Agile methods used

Table 2. Team size of participants

Team Size	Count (n)	Percent
1–5	15	16.1%
5–8	46	49.5%
8–12	20	21.5%
more than 12	12	12.9%
Total	93	100

Table 3. Frequency of estimates

Frequency	Count (n)	Percent
Every Sprint	68	73.1%
Before a task/story/requirement	6	6.5%
Monthly/Quarterly	3	3.2%
After reaching a defined project milestone	5	5.4%
Adhoc	11	11.8%
Total	93	100

with the corresponding frequencies and percentages. Planning poker is the most frequently used effort estimation technique, employed by 50.5% of respondents, followed by expert estimation at 30.1%. The estimation techniques used in Sri Lanka align more closely with an older study [14], which reported that 63% of participants practiced planning poker, and 38% used expert judgment. In contrast, in a more recent study [6] story points was the most popular estimation technique, utilized by 26.1% of respondents, followed by planning poker at 20.7% and expert estimation at 17.6%. It is important to note that their study [6] included story points as an estimation technique. However, we chose not to include story points in our survey because they measure the effort required to implement a product backlog item or user story fully. In contrast, story point estimation refers to assigning story points to a product backlog item or user story [25]. Nevertheless, the popularity of subjective assessment techniques like planning poker and expert judgment aligns well with the agile philosophy, which manages much knowledge tacitly and emphasizes people and their interactions [14]. Our survey did not allow participants to select multiple techniques, so we could not explore the combinations in which effort estimation techniques were practiced in Sri Lanka.

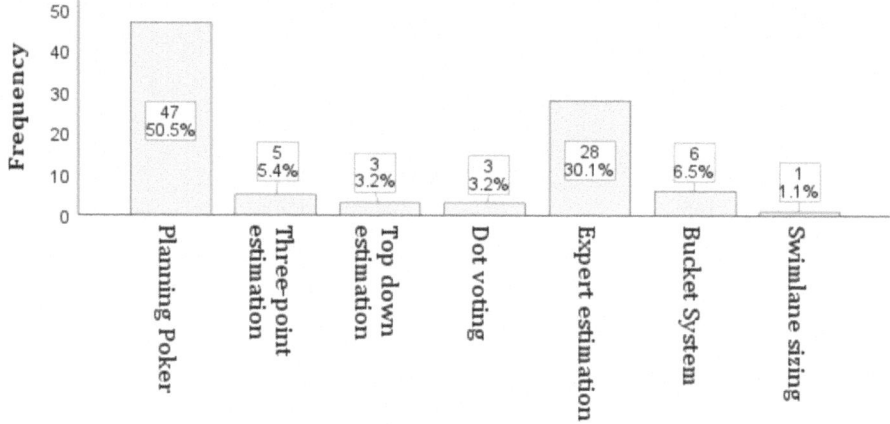

Fig. 3. Effort estimation techniques

Effort Estimation Metrics

To determine the estimation metric used by software practitioners in Sri Lanka for capturing effort estimates, the survey presented four types of metrics: man-hours (estimating the number of hours to complete a task), man-days (estimating the number of days required to finish a task), story points, and t-shirt sizing. Respondents did not report any additional metrics in the *Other* option provided. Figure 4 displays the responses regarding the estimation metrics, including their corresponding frequencies and percentages. 57 respondents, representing 61.3%, chose story points as their preferred sizing metric. This finding is consistent with the study by Usman et al. [12], which reported that 61% of participants also utilized story points. Additionally, this result aligns with the previously discussed estimation techniques, where planning poker emerged as the most commonly used estimation method.

Table 4 illustrates the use of effort estimation metrics in relation to the estimation techniques employed by survey respondents. The use of Planning Poker with story points is the most common method, with a prevalence of 70.2%. Man-hours, man-days, and T-shirt sizing are frequently utilized metrics in expert estimation techniques. Given that most participants were experienced senior practitioners, it is unsurprising that there is a higher usage of man-day and man-hour metrics within expert estimation. T-shirt sizing is also employed in Planning Poker, top-down estimation, and expert estimation

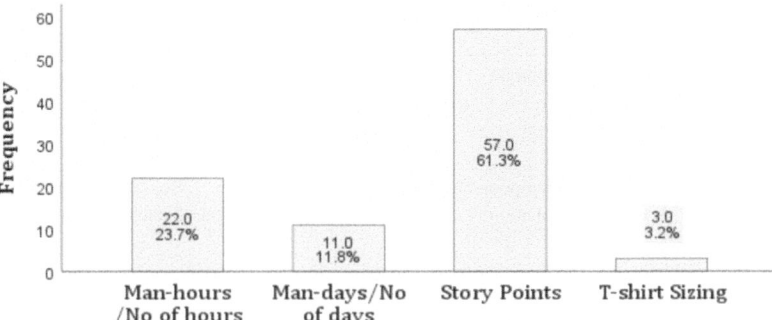

Fig. 4. Estimation metrics

techniques. On the other hand, Swimlane sizing and dot voting are the least commonly used methods.

4.3 Accuracy of Estimations

Level of Accuracy
This section of the questions aimed to determine the accuracy of estimations and the reasons behind inaccurate estimates. Figure 5 displays the results of the first question, which asked respondents to rate the accuracy of their estimations using five options: (i) never able to meet the estimate provided, (ii) a lower chance of meeting the estimate, (iii) able to reach the estimate with extra effort, (iv) able to complete the task within the estimate (with extra effort), and (v) always able to complete the task comfortably within the estimate.

Out of the 93 respondents, 47 (50.5%) indicated that they could complete their tasks within the estimated time without requiring any extra effort, while 33 respondents (33.5%) reported that they could meet the estimate but needed to exert additional effort. The finding that 33.5% of practitioners needed extra effort suggests a trend of underestimating the actual effort required. This aligns with existing literature indicating that the tendency to underestimate effort is more prevalent than the tendency to overestimate it. Usman et al. [14] found that 35% of their respondents reported effort estimates were, on average, underestimated by 25% or more, while 7% indicated underestimation by 50% or more. Underestimation results from various factors, including overoptimism, team members' inexperience in ASD, neglecting non-functional requirements, and disregarding test and code review efforts [1, 14].

Accuracy Level vs Estimation Techniques
The accuracy levels of completing tasks comfortably within estimated timeframes, as well as finishing within estimates without extra effort, can be viewed as a healthy and sustainable approach to estimation without the risk of burnout. The analysis of the accuracy level of various estimation techniques (see Table 5) shows that 61.7% (n = 29) of respondents used Planning Poker along with expert estimation 25.5% (n = 12) to complete their work within the estimated time without any extra effort. All other

Table 4. Estimation metrics used by estimation technique

Estimation Metric %wi = %within Estimate Metric		Estimation technique							Total
		Planning Poker	Three-point estimation	Top down estimation	Dot voting	Expert estimation	Bucket System	Swimlane sizing	
Man-hours/ No of hours	Count	5	4	1	1	9	2	0	22
	%wi	22.7%	18.2%	4.5%	4.5%	40.9%	9.1%	0.0%	100.0%
Man-days/ No of days	Count	1	0	1	0	7	2	0	11
	%wi	9.1%	0.0%	9.1%	0.0%	63.6%	18.2%	0.0%	100.0%
Story Points	Count	40	1	0	2	11	2	1	57
	%wi	70.2%	1.8%	0.0%	3.5%	19.3%	3.5%	1.8%	100.0%
T-shirt Sizing	Count	1	0	1	0	1	0	0	3
	%wi	33.3%	0.0%	33.3%	0.0%	33.3%	0.0%	0.0%	100.0%
Total	Count	47	5	3	3	28	6	1	93
	%wi	50.5%	5.4%	3.2%	3.2%	30.1%	6.5%	1.1%	100.0%

estimation techniques had lower ratings for higher accuracy options. Additionally, the combination of Planning Poker and expert estimation emerged as the most popular combination of multiple estimation techniques utilized by both high and low-accuracy groups. The findings indicate that respondents frequently employed the techniques in conjunction, as they may not be effective when used independently. In the low-accuracy groups, which indicate a lower likelihood of meeting estimates and achieving them with additional effort, nearly 35% to 40% of respondents selected either Planning Poker or expert estimation techniques. While our findings suggest that using either a single estimation method or a combination of techniques may impact estimation accuracy, further investigation is required before any generalizations can be made.

Reasons for Inaccurate Estimates

The second question asked participants to identify the reasons for inaccurate estimates, with the option to select multiple responses. The reasons for these inaccuracies, drawn from relevant literature [1, 6], were categorized into four main groups: *Quality-Related Issues, Team-Related Issues, Project Management-Related Issues*, and *Business Influence Issues*. These reasons are discussed below and summarized in Table 6.

The *Quality-related* issues category received the most contributions, with 117 respondents. Unclear requirements or requirements that are too large to estimate, and overlooking non-functional requirements (NFR) stem from a lack of detail during effort estimation (e.g., user stories, requirements), which can lead to inaccurate estimation [26]. The accuracy of these estimates can be improved when requirements are clearly understood, and when NFRs are considered [14].

Team-related issues (102 respondents) such as lack of experience and insufficient stakeholder participation or absence (e.g., development team, clients, and scrum master)

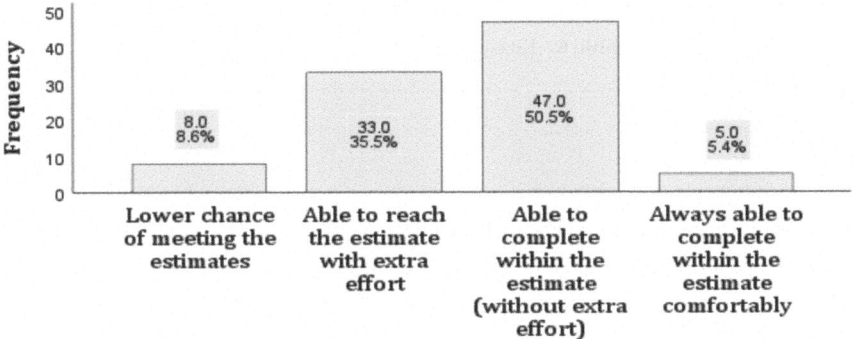

Fig. 5. Level of accuracy of estimations

during the estimation process have been reported to significantly influence over- and under-estimations and the team's ability to deliver [14, 26].

Table 5. Accuracy level vs estimation techniques

			Planning Poker	Three-point estimation	Top-down estimation	Dot voting	Expert estimation	Bucket System	Swimlane sizing	Total
AL	LC	Count	3	0	0	0	3	2	0	8
		%wi	37.5%	0.0%	0.0%	0.0%	37.5%	25.0%	0.0%	100.0%
	EE	Count	11	4	2	1	13	2	0	33
		% wi	33.3%	12.1%	6.1%	3.0%	39.4%	6.1%	0.0%	100.0%
	WEE	Count	29	1	0	2	12	2	1	47
		% wi	61.7%	2.1%	0.0%	4.3%	25.5%	4.3%	2.1%	100.0%
	CC	Count	4	0	1	0	0	0	0	5
		% wi	80.0%	0.0%	20.0%	0.0%	0.0%	0.0%	0.0%	100.0%
Total		Count	47	5	3	3	28	6	1	93
		% wi	50.5%	5.4%	3.2%	3.2%	30.1%	6.5%	1.1%	100.0%

Legend used in Table 5:
AL: Accuracy Level
LC: Lower chance of meeting the estimates
EE: Able to reach the estimate with extra effort
WEE: Able to complete within the estimate (without extra effort)
CC: Always able to complete within the estimate comfortably

The *project management* category (110 respondents) highlighted issues such as scope creep and technical challenges related to development, testing, infrastructure, and deployments following estimation. If these issues are not managed effectively, they can adversely affect development time and project costs, increasing the risk of estimation errors [14, 26].

Table 6. Reasons for inaccurate estimates

	n	Percent
Quality issues		
Unclear requirements or information	65	70%
Too large to estimate (unable to slice the task into sub-tasks)	27	29%
Overlooking non-functional requirements (e.g., performance, security)	25	27%
Total	**117**	
Team-related		
Inexperienced team members/New members	30	32%
Unplanned absence of team members	33	35%
Knowledge gaps related to agile estimations	20	22%
Distributed team (working from home or different locations)	4	4%
Changing team members (no fixed team as team members are allocated and removed periodically)	15	16%
Total	**102**	
Project Management		
Scope creep (change of requirements after estimation)	62	67%
Technical related (facing tech challenges related to development, testing,infrastructure and deployments after estimating)	48	52%
Total	**110**	
Business Influence		
Purposely underestimating to obtain work/retain client	10	11%

The *business influence* issue relates to over-optimism (10 respondents), and purposefully underestimating the effort needed to secure a contract or retain a client is an unfair practice and a clear violation of the ethical code for software engineers [14].

5 Conclusion and Limitations of the Study

By using an exploratory survey of 93 Sri Lankan agile practitioners, this study aimed to analyze the state of agile effort estimation practice. The results indicate that Planning Poker was the most popular estimation technique at 50.5%, while story points were the most widely used metric utilized by 61.3% of participants. The combination of Planning Poker and story points was most used, with a prevalence of 70.2%. Regarding the accuracy of estimations, respondents who used a combination of Planning Poker

(61.7%) and expert estimation (25.5%) could complete their work within the estimated time without any extra effort. The top three categories of inaccurate estimates were quality-related, project management, and team-related issues.

The paper makes the following contributions to research and practice: i) it provides more generalizable and up-to-date results on the state of agile effort estimation practice in Sri Lanka, using first-hand industrial insight on how effort estimation techniques and metrics are being used in the real-world industry. The findings may be advantageously leveraged by other organizations using effort estimation through a better understanding of the methods and practices that their peers are using as well as their benefits and challenges ii) The results identify the accuracy level of estimations and reasons for inaccuracies, which has significant implications for practitioners, underscoring the importance of conducting detailed analyses or confirming information with stakeholders before making effort estimations. Such measures are especially crucial for ensuring the quality of requirements, and iii) The results serve as a foundation for future research by pinpointing the most commonly used agile estimation practices and their accuracy. These findings should inform the research agenda of other initiatives, such as case studies or experiments, that delve deeper into the specific challenges organizations encounter with agile effort estimation and lead to the development of automated approaches for improving the quality of effort estimation.

While our focus on Sri Lanka may limit the generalizability of our results, we believe that our findings offer valuable insights into the software industry as a whole, especially within the South Asian region. We consider the Sri Lankan software industry an appropriate population for this study. To obtain a broad and representative sample of our target population, we took several steps, including advertising our survey on online platforms like LinkedIn. We believe these efforts contributed to achieving a sample that is diverse in terms of experience and job roles.

References

1. Pasuksmit, J., Thongtanunam, P., Karunasekera, S.: A systematic literature review on reasons and approaches for accurate effort estimations in agile. ACM Comput. Surv. **56**(11), 269 (2024). https://doi.org/10.1145/3663365
2. Jorgensen, M., Shepperd, M.: A Systematic Review of Software Development Cost Estimation Studies. IIEEE Trans. Software Eng. **33**(1) (2007). https://doi.org/10.1109/TSE.2007.256943
3. Qi, K., Boehm, B.W.: Process-driven incremental effort estimation, pp. 165–174 (2019). https://doi.org/10.1109/ICSSP.2019.00030
4. Rosa, W., et al.: Empirical effort and schedule estimation models for agile processes in the US DoD. IEEE Trans. Softw. Eng. **48**(8), 3117–3130 (2022). https://doi.org/10.1109/TSE.2021.3080666
5. Pospieszny, P., Czarnacka-Chrobot, B., Kobylinski, A.: An effective approach for software project effort and duration estimation with machine learning algorithms. J. Syst. Softw. **137**, 184–196 (2018). https://doi.org/10.1016/j.jss.2017.11.066
6. Sandeep, R.C., et al.: Effort estimation in agile software development: a exploratory study of practitioners' perspective, pp. 136–149 (2022). https://doi.org/10.1007/978-3-030-94238-0_8
7. Kitchenham, B.A., Mendes, E., Travassos, G.H.: Cross versus within-company cost estimation studies: a systematic review. IEEE Trans. Software Eng. **33**(5), 316–329 (2007). https://doi.org/10.1109/TSE.2007.1001

8. Shepperd, M., MacDonell, S.: Evaluating prediction systems in software project estimation. Inf. Softw. Technol. **54**(8), 820–827 (2012). https://doi.org/10.1016/j.infsof.2011.12.008
9. Tobisch, F., et al.: Investigating effort estimation in a large-scale agile ERP transformation program, pp. 70–86 (2024). https://doi.org/10.1007/978-3-031-61154-4_5
10. Usman, M., et al.: Effort estimation in agile software development: a systematic literature review. In: Proceedings of the 10th International Conference on Predictive Models in Software Engineering, pp. 82–91. Association for Computing Machinery, Turin, Italy (2014)
11. Dantas, E., et al.: Effort estimation in agile software development: an updated review. Int. J. Softw. Eng. Knowl. Eng. **28**(11n12), 1811–1831 (2018). https://doi.org/10.1142/s0218194018400302
12. Fernández-Diego, M., et al.: An update on effort estimation in agile software development: a systematic literature review. IEEE Access **8**, 166768–166800 (2020). https://doi.org/10.1109/ACCESS.2020.3021664
13. Usman, M., et al.: Effort estimation in large-scale software development: an industrial case study. Inf. Softw. Technol. **99**, 21–40 (2018). https://doi.org/10.1016/j.infsof.2018.02.009
14. Usman, M., Mendes, E., Börstler, J.: Effort estimation in agile software development: a survey on the state of the practice. In: Proceedings of the 19th International Conference on Evaluation and Assessment in Software Engineering, p. 12. Association for Computing Machinery: Nanjing, China (2015)
15. Sandeep, R.C., et al.: Effort estimation in agile software development: a exploratory study of practitioners' perspective. In: Lecture Notes in Business Information Processing. (2022).https://doi.org/10.1007/978-3-030-94238-0_8
16. Rodríguez, C.A.P., et al.: Effort estimation in agile software development: a systematic map study. INGE CUC **19**(1), 22–36 (2023). https://doi.org/10.17981/ingecuc.19.1.2023.03
17. Rastogi, H., Dhankhar, S., Kakkar, M.: A survey on software effort estimation techniques. In: 2014 5th International Conference - Confluence the Next Generation Information Technology Summit (Confluence) (2014). https://doi.org/10.1109/CONFLUENCE.2014.6949367
18. Statista: Business process outsourcing - Southern Asia (2024). https://www.statista.com/outlook/tmo/it-services/business-process-outsourcing/southern-asia
19. Ranasinghe, R.K.C., Perera, I.: Effectiveness of scrum for offshore software development in Sri Lanka. In: 2015 Moratuwa Engineering Research Conference (MERCon) (2015). https://doi.org/10.1109/MERCon.2015.7112364
20. Schweighofer, T., et al.: How is effort estimated in agile software development projects? In: SQAMIA, 5th Workshop of Software Quality, Analysis, Monitoring, Improvement, and Applications. Budapest, Hungary (2016)
21. Tanveer, B., Guzmán, L., Engel, U.M.: Effort estimation in agile software development: case study and improvement framework. J. Softw. Evol. Process **29**(11), e1862 (2017). https://doi.org/10.1002/smr.1862
22. Sjoeberg, D.I.K., et al.: A survey of controlled experiments in software engineering. IEEE Trans. Software Eng. **31**(9), 733–753 (2005). https://doi.org/10.1109/TSE.2005.97
23. Molléri, J.S., Petersen, K., Mendes, E.: Survey guidelines in software engineering: an annotated review. IEEE Computer Society (2016). https://doi.org/10.1145/2961111.2962619
24. Kuhrmann, M., et al., Helena stage 2 results (2018)
25. Herranz, R.: What is story point estimation? (2025). https://resources.scrumalliance.org/Article/story-point-estimation
26. Conoscenti, M., et al.: Combining data analytics and developers feedback for identifying reasons of inaccurate estimations in agile software development. J. Syst. Softw. **156**, 126–135 (2019). https://doi.org/10.1016/j.jss.2019.06.075

Open Access This chapter is licensed under the terms of the Creative Commons Attribution 4.0 International License (http://creativecommons.org/licenses/by/4.0/), which permits use, sharing, adaptation, distribution and reproduction in any medium or format, as long as you give appropriate credit to the original author(s) and the source, provide a link to the Creative Commons license and indicate if changes were made.

The images or other third party material in this chapter are included in the chapter's Creative Commons license, unless indicated otherwise in a credit line to the material. If material is not included in the chapter's Creative Commons license and your intended use is not permitted by statutory regulation or exceeds the permitted use, you will need to obtain permission directly from the copyright holder.

Metrics for Experimentation Programs: Categories, Benefits and Challenges

Nils Stotz(✉) and Paul Drews

Institute of Information Systems, Leuphana University Lüneburg,
Lüneburg, Germany
nils.stotz@stud.leuphana.de, paul.drews@leuphana.de

Abstract. Experimentation programs are vital for enabling data-driven decision-making within product development. However, evaluating their overarching success remains a significant challenge. Current metrics, such as conversion rates, primarily focus on individual experiments, leaving a gap in assessing broader program efficiency and impact. This paper addresses this gap by presenting a structured overview and analysis of 18 program-level metrics, categorized into six domains: Volume, Outcome-Based, Quality, Engagement, Process Efficiency and Strategic Alignment. Metrics such as experimentation throughput, time-to-decision and experimentation coverage are examined for their implications on operational efficiency, cultural adoption, and strategic alignment. Based on interviews with 48 experimentation practitioners, this work provides a description of these metrics and discusses their benefits and challenges. The results offer actionable insights for advancing experimentation practices and aligning them with organizational goals.

Keywords: Continuous Experimentation · Experimentation Metrics · Program-Level Evaluation · A/B Testing

1 Introduction

One of the greatest challenges for modern experimentation teams is assessing the success and efficiency of their experimentation programs beyond individual experiments [1]. Controlled experiments, such as A/B tests, have become the cornerstone of data-driven decision-making [33]. But organizations often lack guidance to evaluate and improve the operational, cultural and strategic performance of their experimentation programs [29]. An experimentation program refers to a coordinated approach to managing experiments across teams, products, or initiatives, leveraging shared resources and infrastructure to optimize decision-making and align with organizational goals. These programs vary in scale but consistently focus on measuring aggregate impact and driving scalable, data-driven innovation [1]. Metrics used at the individual experiment level, such as conversion rates or revenue impact, provide valuable insights into specific hypotheses but fail to capture the broader impact, scalability and business value of experimentation efforts [2–7]. Without the ability to measure program-level outcomes, organizations risk underutilizing experimentation as a strategic capability.

Experimentation programs, particularly in larger organizations like Google [10], Microsoft [9], Meta [8] and Amazon [11] are increasingly critical for driving innovation and product development. These companies rely on experimentation not only to validate features but also to foster a culture of evidence-based decision-making [12,13]. However, scaling experimentation introduces new complexities, such as managing throughput, ensuring reliable results and aligning experimentation efforts with strategic goals [14,15]. Recent literature highlights the need to develop robust metrics that evaluate experimentation programs holistically, focusing on dimensions such as efficiency, scalability and cultural adoption [2,14].

While frameworks like the RIGHT model [14] and the Flywheel model [12] offer valuable insights into the processes and infrastructure required for continuous experimentation, they lack detailed guidance on metrics for assessing program-level success. Other existing studies predominantly focus on metrics tied to individual experiments [6,17–21] or specific aspects of these metrics [22,23] as well as the lifecycle of experiment metrics [24] but provide limited insights into actionable program-level metrics that can guide organizations toward higher levels of experimentation maturity. Systematic literature reviews [2,16] underscore this gap, calling for a more nuanced understanding of how metrics can drive the success, scalability and business value of experimentation programs. This paper seeks to address this gap by answering the following research questions:

RQ1: Which metrics are used by experimentation teams to evaluate their experimentation programs and how can they be categorized?

RQ2: What are the benefits and challenges of these metrics in driving organizational success?

Through an empirical study based on interviews with experimentation practitioners, this paper identifies and organizes program-level metrics and investigates their role in operational efficiency, cultural integration and strategic alignment. Unlike prior studies that focus on individual experiment outcomes, this paper emphasizes program-level evaluation, contributing to discussions in both academia and practice on scaling experimentation.

The contributions of this paper are threefold. First, it advances experimentation metrics research by categorizing experimentation metrics into six categories (Volume, Outcome-Based, Quality, Engagement and Adoption, Process Efficiency and Strategic Alignment) while also illustrating their application across organizational contexts. Second, it synthesizes and addresses the gaps in the experimentation literature identified by Quin and Auer by suggesting metrics to measure the success and applicability of the frameworks and model focusing on the process of experimentation [2,16]. Third, it extends the literature by enhancing the experimentation maturity models through metrics to include engagement, cross-functional collaboration and the integration of metrics into strategic decision-making, providing a more flexible foundation for scaling experimentation programs effectively.

2 Background

To evaluate the success and scalability of experimentation programs, it is essential to address what metrics are used to measure outcomes, how experimentation is operationalized through processes and how experimentation programs evolve during different maturity stages. This paper focuses on three key streams of literature: experimentation metrics, experimentation process and experimentation maturity. These streams provide the theoretical grounding necessary to understand how metrics guide experimentation teams toward improved decision-making and scalability as well as better alignment with organizational objectives.

2.1 Experimentation Metrics

Metrics are traditionally classified based on their function such as validating experimental setups, measuring success and diagnosing unexpected outcomes [5,19]. Foundational work by Kohavi et al. [33] already emphasized the importance of Overall Evaluation Criteria (OEC) metrics, which are designed to align experimental outcomes with long-term business objectives. Similarly, guardrail metrics were introduced later and serve as protective measures against adverse effects on critical dimensions, including performance and user satisfaction [6].

Building on these foundations, Mattos et al. [24] introduced a detailed activity and metric framework that integrates metrics into distinct phases of the experimentation lifecycle, such as pre-quality checks, online evaluations and post-analysis validation. This framework categorizes metrics to ensure their relevance and reliability at each stage of experimentation. OEC metrics focus on summarizing overall success and alignment with strategic objectives, while guardrail metrics act as safeguards to prevent harm to critical aspects of the system. The framework also emphasizes diagnostic metrics, which provide granular insights to explain movements in higher-level metrics and feature-specific metrics, while evaluate localized changes in functionality or performance [24].

In addition, recent systematic literature reviews underscore the widespread acknowledgment of metrics as a cornerstone of experimentation practices [2, 16]. These reviews provide insights into how metrics are selected, applied and analyzed within experimentation frameworks, emphasizing the role of metrics in ensuring both validity and meaningfulness in outcomes [2,16]. They further highlight the need for robust methodologies to evaluate the utility of metrics, particularly in the context of scaling experimentation practices across diverse organizational contexts.

Despite their utility, these metrics predominantly address individual experiments and are less focused on program-level evaluation. As highlighted by Fabijan et al. [29], the scalability of experimentation requires broader metrics to assess the maturity and efficiency of the overall program. Metrics such as throughput, decision velocity and experimentation coverage are crucial for understanding how organizations can scale their experimentation practices effectively, yet they remain underexplored in the literature [29].

In summary, there are metric frameworks that are structured and categorised in prior research [24]. However, they focus on the individual experiment and do not help to assess the success of the experimentation program itself. They also do not provide guidance on other important factors such as scalability, efficiency and cross-functional alignment. Due to the lack of standardized frameworks and categories on a program-level it is still challenging to compare different experimentation programs across diverse organisational contexts. Without these standardized and cateogrised metrics, it is equally challenging to surface actionable insights that are based on the performance of various different experimentation programs.

2.2 Experimentation Process

The experimentation process provides the operational framework through which experimentation teams design, implement and scale their activities. It emphasizes systematic workflows, robust infrastructure and scalable methods that allow organizations to transform ideas into measurable outcomes. Key frameworks such as the RIGHT Model [14], HYPEX Model [13] and the HURRIER Process Model [32] are important contributions that help to understand the process of continuous experimentation.

The RIGHT Model [14] emphasizes the iterative nature of experimentation by focusing on rapid, high-frequency testing. It applies the "Build-Measure-Learn" feedback loop as a concept to connect experimentation with strategic business goals. The RIGHT model also identifies critical elements, such as the need for proper instrumentation, experiment design and the seamless integration of results into product roadmaps. A central contribution of the RIGHT model is its holistic perspective, linking technical execution with business objectives to enable continuous value delivery [14].

Complementing this, the HYPEX Model [13] addresses the challenge of closing the feedback loop between product development and customer insights. It outlines a structured process for hypothesis-driven experimentation, which begins with identifying gaps in feature performance and iteratively validating hypotheses. This approach ensures that product decisions are guided by empirical evidence rather than opinions. Notably, the HYPEX Model emphasizes the integration of both qualitative and quantitative feedback with the goal to enable organizations to move toward a data-driven culture [13,25].

The HURRIER Process [32] is tailored for experimentation in B2B mission-critical systems, emphasizing risk mitigation and close collaboration with customers. It structures the experimentation process into stages such as internal validation, single-customer validation and multi-customer validation. Unique features like "passive launch" and "restricted launch" allow safe deployment and data collection in complex environments. By integrating iterative feedback loops from both internal and customer sources, the HURRIER Process ensures the delivery of high-quality solutions while addressing the unique challenges of mission-critical contexts [32].

Despite their distinct contributions, these models share a common emphasis on embedding experimentation into the core operational and strategic processes of organizations. They stress the importance of cultural transformation, technical capabilities and organizational alignment as prerequisites for success. The most noticeable gap of all these models lies in the discussion of the success metrics. They do not differentiate between different business models or different contexts of companies and lack metrics for evaluating process efficiency and long-term scalability. Existing models often focus on isolated experiments rather than holistic program-level evaluations.

2.3 Experimentation Maturity

The concept of experimentation maturity describes the evolution of organizational capabilities from traditional development processes towards adopting and scaling experimentation practices [31]. It captures the progression from ad hoc testing to systematic and strategically aligned experimentation programs. Existing models such as the Stairway to Heaven model [27] the Experimentation Growth Model [3, 29] as well as the Flywheel model [12] provide structured frameworks to understand this journey.

The Stairway to Heaven model outlines five stages, starting with traditional development and culminating in "R&D as an Innovation Experiment System" [28]. In this stage, continuous experimentation drives product development and strategy. This final stage integrates rapid feedback loops across product management, development and customer-facing functions, requiring significant cultural and organizational transformation [27].

Bosch et al. [30] also refined these ideas in the Stairway to Heaven 2.0 framework, emphasizing the role of data-driven decision-making and its integration into strategic processes. At advanced stages, organizations embed evidence-based decision-making into their operational and cultural frameworks, transforming into agile, innovation-driven entities [30]. These models highlight the role of cultural shifts, robust infrastructure and alignment with strategic goals in advancing maturity.

Building on these existing frameworks, the Experimentation Growth Model [3, 29] proposes four stages—Crawl, Walk, Run and Fly—focusing on increasing self-sufficiency, technical capabilities and cultural integration. The model mentions metrics only as individual experimentation metrics that are important for throughput, decision velocity and standardization of experimentation practices [3, 29] but do not explain how to measure this on a program-wide level.

The Flywheel Model [12] provides another dynamic framework for scaling experimentation. It conceptualizes the iterative relationship between value creation and investment, underscoring the importance of showing incremental results to maintain momentum. The Flywheel Model emphasizes investments in infrastructure, cultural change and education to reduce friction in the experimentation process and sustain growth. The model also suggests program level metrics to use for measuring the success of scaling the experimentation program but does not explain the benefits and challenges when using these metrics [12].

While these frameworks provide valuable insights, they often focus on metrics at the experiment level rather than at the program level. Metrics such as the number of experiments conducted, time-to-decision and experimentation coverage remain underexplored but are critical for assessing operational efficiency and cultural integration. They also do not address the challenge of tracking and using these metrics in everyday practices. Additionally, existing models predominantly draw from large-scale online companies, limiting their applicability to other domains such as regulated industries or traditional enterprises.

In summary, the literature on experimentation maturity underscores the importance of systematic growth in experimentation capabilities. This paper contributes to research by addressing gaps in program-level metrics, offering a deeper understanding of how organizations can measure and improve their experimentation programs to achieve strategic alignment and scalability. A systematic way to measure the performance of experimentation programs in different organisations helps to surface more insights based on the differences in metric development within different organizational contexts.

3 Method

To explore how experimentation teams evaluate the success of their experimentation programs through metrics, this study adopts a qualitative-empirical approach, inspired by the inductive methodology of Gioia et al. [26]. This methodology enables a systematic development of theory based on the rigorous analysis of qualitative data, ensuring that the findings are grounded in the experiences and insights of practitioners.

Data Collection. The study involved semi-structured interviews with 48 experts in the field of experimentation. Participants were selected based on their diverse roles within the experimentation ecosystem, ensuring a comprehensive view of how metrics are utilized across different contexts. The expert pool included the following categories: (1) In-Company Experimentation Team Members: Practitioners embedded within organizations that run large-scale experimentation programs. (2) Experimentation Platform Vendors: Representatives from companies providing tools and platforms for conducting and managing experiments. (3) Consultants from Experimentation Agencies: Specialists advising organizations on experimentation strategies and processes. (4) Academic Researchers: Scholars with a focus on experimentation and related methodologies.

To ensure diverse perspectives, participants were selected from organizations of varying sizes, ranging from small startups to multinational enterprises, across different industries, including technology, e-commerce and media as well as from different geographic locations such as the EU, UK and USA. The participants were contacted through LinkedIn by the first author who is participating in various practitioners communities. The interviews were conducted between January and August 2024, remotely via video conferencing tools. Each session lasted approximately 45-60 min and was recorded and transcribed for subsequent analysis. The transcriptions were created with otter.ai and were manually reviewed and refined to ensure accuracy. The interview guide[1] was designed to encourage open-ended responses, enabling participants to share their experiences and insights on the role of metrics in experimentation programs. Key topics included: The types of metrics used to assess experimentation efforts, the benefits and challenges associated with these metrics, the role of metrics in driving organizational adoption of experimentation and recommendations for improving the measurement of experimentation success.

Data Analysis: The analysis of the interview data was conducted in a systematic, multi-step process using MAXQDA, a qualitative data analysis tool. The initial step involved extracting all individual metrics explicitly mentioned by participants during the interviews. This resulted in a dataset containing 158 mentions of metrics. While the overall volume of responses was extensive, only 18 unique metrics were identified, indicating a high degree of homogeneity across the programs. To ensure consistency, similar metrics were grouped under broader terms. For example, statements such as "number of experiments per week" and "number of successful experiments per week" were consolidated under the overarching metric "number of experiments." This grouping allowed us to focus on the underlying themes rather than the specific wording of individual responses, ensuring a comprehensive representation of program-level metrics. In some instances, participants initially misunderstood the concept of program metrics and referred to success metrics for individual experiments. When this occurred, the concept of program metrics was clarified during the interview, prompting participants to adjust their responses accordingly. These clarifications were crucial to maintaining the integrity and relevance of the dataset. Subsequent analysis examined patterns and relationships among the 18 unique metrics, leading to their organization into broader themes or categories. For example, metrics like "Ease of use" and "Time-to-insights" were grouped under process efficiency, while "number of teams engaging with the experimentation platform" and "Active use of tools" were categorized as metrics related to Engagement and Adoption. This phase involved iterative coding to ensure that the grouping reflected the practical and theoretical significance of the metrics. As part of the analysis, we also captured the benefits and challenges associated with each metric. For example, participants noted that throughput metrics are beneficial for demonstrating scalability but cautioned against overemphasizing quantity at the expense of quality. Similarly, metrics like "trust in results" were valued for

---

[1] A supplemental file with the interview questions and additional material can be viewed here: https://zenodo.org/records/15031610.

fostering stakeholder confidence, but achieving statistical rigor was often cited as a key challenge.

This multi-layered approach enabled the development of a structured list of program-level metrics, linking individual metrics to broader themes and contextualizing their practical applications and limitations. By documenting the process of metric aggregation and ensuring clarity in definitions, this analysis offers a robust framework for understanding how experimentation teams measure success and provides actionable insights for both researchers and practitioners in the field.

4 Findings

4.1 Success Metrics

Based on the analysis of interview transcripts, metrics were grouped into six high-level categories: Volume, Outcome-Based, Quality, Engagement and Adoption, Process Efficiency and Meta-Metrics. These metrics are listed and enriched with the respective metrics in Table 1.

Table 1. The 6 identified metric categories as well as the selected metrics

Category	Metric
Volume	Number of experiments conducted
Volume	Breadth and depth of experimentation
Volume	Experiment creation velocity
Outcome-Based	Revenue generated
Outcome-Based	Customer lifetime value (CLV)
Outcome-Based	Avoided losses
Outcome-Based	Uplift in specific KPIs
Outcome-Based	Proportion of successful or conclusive experiments
Quality	Hypotheses quality
Quality	Proper sample sizes
Quality	Adherence to power calculations
Engagement and Adoption	Number of teams engaging with platform
Engagement and Adoption	Number of unique users engaging with platform
Engagement and Adoption	Active use of tools or features
Process Efficiency	Time to insights (duration from setup to results);
Process Efficiency	Ease of use for creating and iterating experiments
Meta-Metrics	Percentage of decisions influenced by experimentation
Meta-Metrics	Ratio of validated changes to total changes

Volume Metrics are among the most frequently mentioned, with three distinct metrics highlighted. The number of experiments conducted per team or organization tracks overall activity levels within experimentation programs and helps assess whether experimentation is being used consistently. The breadth and depth of experimentation measures both the number of teams engaging in experimentation and the average number of experiments per team, serving as an indicator of program adoption across the organization. The experiment creation velocity captures the speed at which new experiments are designed and launched, reflecting the efficiency of workflows and how quickly teams can iterate. Together, these metrics provide insight into the scale and reach of experimentation within an organization, as well as its ability to sustain a high tempo of activity.

Outcome-Based Metrics focus on the results and impact of experimentation, with five unique metrics in this category. Revenue generated is a critical measure of success, as experiments directly influencing revenue are key drivers for decision-making. Customer lifetime value (CLV) assesses the long-term financial impact of experiments by measuring how they affect customer retention and spending over time. Avoided losses captures the ability of experiments to identify and mitigate potential negative impacts, preventing costly missteps. Uplift in specific KPIs, such as conversion rates or average order value, provides a direct measure of how effectively experiments improve key business outcomes. The proportion of successful or conclusive experiments evaluates the reliability and decisiveness of experimentation efforts, ensuring that insights lead to actionable decisions. These metrics tie experimentation efforts to tangible business results, reinforcing their value to stakeholders.

Quality Metrics ensure the rigor and reliability of experimentation, with three key metrics highlighted. Hypotheses quality measures the clarity and validity of experimental hypotheses, ensuring they are well-defined and testable. Proper sample sizes evaluate whether experiments include enough participants to achieve statistical significance, reducing the risk of misleading results. Adherence to power calculations tracks whether experiments are designed to detect meaningful effects, ensuring that conclusions are based on sufficient statistical power. These metrics collectively reinforce the importance of maintaining scientific rigor to produce actionable and reliable results.

Engagement and Adoption Metrics reflect the level of organizational adoption and engagement with experimentation platforms. The number of teams engaging with the experimentation platform indicates how widely experimentation practices are embraced across the organization. The number of unique users engaging with the platform measures the diversity of roles interacting with experimentation tools, highlighting cross-functional involvement. Active use of tools or features, such as feature flagging or dashboards, tracks how frequently teams leverage key functionalities to support experimentation. These metrics provide insights into the reach and influence of the experimentation program across different teams and roles, helping assess overall adoption.

Process Efficiency Metrics focus on reducing the time and effort required to conduct experiments. Time to insights measures the duration from experiment setup to actionable results, reflecting operational efficiency and the ability to make timely decisions. Ease of use for creating and iterating experiments evaluates how intuitive and accessible the tools and processes are, ensuring that teams can experiment with minimal friction. These metrics highlight opportunities to streamline workflows, enabling faster and more frequent decision-making.

Meta-Metrics provide a strategic view of the experimentation program's impact on broader organizational goals. The percentage of business decisions influenced by experimentation evaluates how integral experimentation is in shaping strategic and operational choices, ensuring data-driven decision-making. The ratio of validated changes to total changes assesses the reliability and success rate of experimentation-driven modifications, indicating the program's effectiveness in reducing uncertainty. These metrics emphasize the program's alignment with and contribution to high-level organizational objectives, reinforcing its value.

4.2 Benefits and Challenges

When evaluating the metrics used to measure experimentation success, various advantages and disadvantages were associated with each category. Insights from the interviews provide a nuanced understanding of how these metrics influence program outcomes and highlight both their strengths and limitations.

Volume Metrics are related to the volume of experimentation, such as the number of experiments conducted or breadth and depth of experimentation, were frequently cited as foundational in tracking program activity but tend to become less important once the maturity level of the program increases. "The number of experiments shows us whether the program is being adopted," noted one participant (ID 4). These metrics are particularly valuable for organizations in the early stages of building an experimentation culture, as they provide a straightforward measure of engagement. However, over-reliance on volume metrics can encourage superficial experimentation. "If teams are only focused on hitting numbers, they might run low-impact experiments just to meet quotas," explained another interviewee (ID 7). This potential for gaming the system underscores the need for complementary metrics that emphasize quality and outcomes over quantity.

Outcome-Based Metrics such as revenue generated or customer lifetime value (CLV), provide a clear link between experimentation and business impact. Several participants praised these metrics for their ability to demonstrate value to senior leadership. "Revenue impact is the language the C-suite understands," one interviewee emphasized (ID 10), reflecting the importance of tying experimentation outcomes to organizational goals. Yet, the complexity of isolating experimentation's effects in dynamic business environments presents a challenge that only more mature programs seem to be able to address. "It's hard to attribute revenue changes directly to an experiment when there are so many influencing factors," shared one respondent (ID 12). Additionally, an overemphasis on revenue or CLV can discourage teams from running exploratory or learning-focused experiments, which may have longer-term benefits but lack immediate financial outcomes.

Quality Metrics such as hypotheses quality and proper sample sizes, were widely recognized as critical for maintaining scientific rigor in experimentation. "If we don't ensure proper sample sizes and power calculations, the results are meaningless," asserted one participant (ID 16). These metrics help organizations build trust in experimentation as a reliable decision-making tool. However, some respondents highlighted the resource-intensive nature of implementing quality metrics. "Not every team has the expertise to calculate statistical power or design high-quality hypotheses," noted one interviewee (ID 18), pointing to potential barriers for less mature organizations. Additionally, focusing too heavily on rigorous standards could slow down experimentation velocity, particularly in fast-paced environments.

Engagement and Adoption Metrics measure the platform adoption, such as the number of teams and unique users engaging with experimentation tools, were praised for their ability to track the program's reach. "Seeing more teams adopt the platform is a sign that experimentation is becoming part of our culture," one interviewee explained (ID 20). Engagement metrics also help identify gaps in platform usage, guiding targeted interventions to increase adoption. Nonetheless, some participants raised concerns about the limited scope of these metrics. "Just because people are using the platform doesn't mean they're using it effectively," observed one respondent (ID 23). Metrics focused solely on engagement may overlook deeper issues, such as whether experiments are well-designed or producing actionable insights.

Process Efficiency Metrics like time to insights and experiment creation velocity, were celebrated for their ability to identify bottlenecks and streamline workflows. "Reducing the time it takes to go from idea to actionable result has transformed how we work," shared one participant (ID 27). These metrics are particularly useful for organizations aiming to scale their experimentation efforts without sacrificing agility. However, the focus on speed can sometimes come at the expense of quality. "If we're too focused on being fast, we might compromise on the thoroughness of our analysis," cautioned one interviewee (ID 30). Balancing efficiency with rigor is a key challenge for teams relying heavily on process metrics.

Meta-Metrics such as the percentage of business decisions influenced by experimentation, provide a strategic view of the program's impact. "Knowing that experimentation is driving decisions across the company is the ultimate measure of success," remarked one participant (ID 35). These metrics emphasize the alignment between experimentation and organizational objectives, showcasing its broader value. However, these metrics are often difficult to define and measure. "How do you reliably track which decisions were influenced by experiments versus other factors? It's not always clear," acknowledged one respondent (ID 40). This ambiguity can make it challenging to draw actionable insights from Meta-metrics, particularly in complex organizational settings.

5 Discussion and Conclusion

Contributions to Research. This article contributes to several areas of research by providing a systematic categorization of 18 unique metrics for measuring the success of experimentation programs. First, this paper advances the experimentation metrics literature by providing metrics for the success of the experimentation program itself and by categorizing these metrics into six actionable categories: Volume, Outcome-Based, Quality, Engagement and Adoption, Process Efficiency and Strategic Alignment. Existing work, such as Mattos et al.'s metrics framework contains metric categories like the Overall Evaluation Criteria, Guardrail Metrics, Data-Quality Metrics as well as local feature and diagnosis metrics and integrates them in a framework [24]. While these metrics can be defined on a program level, they do not provide guidance to measure the success of the experimentation program itself. Second, this work synthesizes and explicitly addresses gaps identified in the literature [2,16]. Two literature reviews highlighted that while several models for an experimentation process exist there is no guidance to select between these models [2,16]. This paper provides metrics that can measure the success of each of these models by unifying the way organisations track not only the baseline of their current process but also measure the improvements of their experimentation process and thus also helping to identify the adjustment needed for existing models. Third, the article extends the maturity literature by providing metrics for measuring the progress of the experimentation maturity [3,27,29]. While the lack of measurability was already pointed out in initial models, the literature suggests metrics like "Number of A/B tests" or "Number of Training Attendees" for each maturity step in later publications [12]. First, these metrics are not categorised depending on the goal of the experimentation program [12]. Second, there is no guidance provided for what the advantages or challenges are when using these metrics. And third, categories like the engagement and the organisational adoption of the experimentation platform are not mentioned. Our article closes these shortcomings by providing categories not connected to a maturity level, providing guidance on specific advantages and challenges for each of the categories as well as extending potential metrics to also include the organisational adoption and engagement of the experimentation platform.

Practical Contributions. As organizations increasingly adopt experimentation programs, this research offers multiple benefits for experimentation teams and decision-makers. First, the categorization of metrics can guide internal teams in selecting appropriate metrics tailored to their program maturity and objectives. For instance, startups can prioritize volume metrics to measure adoption, while organizations with a higher maturity might focus on quality and outcome-based metrics to refine their processes. Second, the detailed analysis of advantages and disadvantages enables teams to mitigate potential pitfalls, such as overemphasizing speed through process efficiency metrics at the expense of experiment rigor. Additionally, the suggested metrics support the evaluation of third-party experimentation platforms, helping teams assess whether the platform's capabilities align with their organizational priorities. Finally, this research provides a valuable tool for experimentation advocates seeking stakeholder buy-in. By linking metrics like meta-metrics to strategic decision-making, teams can build a compelling case for investing in experimentation programs.

Limitations and Future Research. While this study offers a structured list of experimentation metrics along with benefits and challenges, it is not without limitations. The sample size, though diverse, could be expanded to capture a broader range of industry contexts and organizational sizes. Future research could investigate how metric prioritization varies across sectors, particularly in domains like e-commerce versus software development, where experimentation objectives and challenges may differ significantly. Another limitation lies in the generalizability of certain meta-metrics, such as the percentage of business decisions influenced by experimentation, which may be difficult to measure in less data-driven organizations. Future work could explore methodologies for reliably capturing these metrics, including qualitative approaches such as interviews with decision-makers. Further research could also focus on developing a maturity model integrating the program experimentation metrics. This model could classify organizations based on their metric sophistication, from basic Volume metrics to advanced Meta-Metrics, providing a roadmap for scaling experimentation capabilities. Additionally, mapping the trade-offs and complementarities between metrics could yield insights into designing holistic measurement strategies that balance operational efficiency with strategic alignment.

Conclusion. Previous research has highlighted the importance of robust metrics in experimentation but lacked a comprehensive list for categorizing and evaluating them. This study advances the field by systematically categorizing 18 unique metrics into six actionable categories and analyzing their advantages and disadvantages. By addressing gaps identified by prior studies, this research provides both theoretical and practical tools for improving experimentation programs. The insights offered here will help organizations better measure, manage and optimize their experimentation efforts, paving the way for a more evidence-based approach to decision-making.

References

1. Sudijono, T., Ejdemyr, S., Lal, A., Tingley, M.: Optimizing returns from experimentation programs. arXiv preprint arXiv:2412.05508v1 (2024)
2. Auer, F., Ros, R., Kaltenbrunner, L., Runeson, P., Felderer, M.: Controlled experimentation in continuous experimentation: knowledge and challenges. Inf. Software Technol. **134**, 106551 (2021)
3. Fabijan, A., Dmitriev, P., McFarland, C., Vermeer, L., Olsson, H.H., Bosch, J.: Experimentation growth: evolving trustworthy A/B testing capabilities in online software companies. J. Software Evol. Process **30**(12), e2113 (2018)
4. Yaman, S., et al.: Introducing continuous experimentation in large software-intensive product and service organizations. J. Syst. Softw. **133**(2017), 195–211 (2017)
5. Dmitriev, P., Gupta,S., Kim, D.W., Vaz, G.: A dirty dozen: twelve common metric interpretation pitfalls in online controlled experiments. In: Proceedings of the 23rd ACM SIGKDD International Conference on Knowledge Discovery and Data Mining (Halifax, NS, Canada) (KDD '17), pp. 1427–1436. Association for Computing Machinery, New York, NY, USA (2017)

6. Dmitriev, P., Frasca, B., Gupta, S., Kohavi, R., Vaz, G.: Pitfalls of long-term online controlled experiments. In 2016 IEEE International Conference on Big Data (Big Data), pp. 1367–1376 (2016)
7. Lindgren, E., Münch, J.: Raising the odds of success: the current state of experimentation in product development. Inf. Softw. Technol. **77**, 80–91 (2016)
8. Ha-Thuc, V., Dutta, A., Mao, R., Wood, M., Liu, Y.: A counterfactual framework for seller-side a/b testing on marketplaces. In Proceedings of the 43rd International ACM SIGIR Conference on Research and Development in Information Retrieval, pp. 2288–2296 (2020)
9. Li, L., Kim, J.Y., Zitouni, I.: Toward predicting the outcome of an A/B experiment for search relevance. In Proceedings of the Eighth ACM International Conference on Web Search and Data Mining (WSDM '15), pp. 37–46. Association for Computing Machinery, New York, NY, USA (2015)
10. Tang, D., Agarwal, A. O'Brien, D., Meyer, M.: Overlapping experiment infrastructure: more, better, faster experimentation. In: Proceedings 16th Conference on Knowledge Discovery and Data Mining, pp. 17–26 (2010)
11. Wan, R., Liu, Y., McQueen, J., Hains, D., Song, R.: Experimentation platforms meet reinforcement learning: bayesian sequential decision-making for continuous monitoring. arXiv preprint arXiv:2304.00420 (2023)
12. Fabijan, A., Arai, B., Dmitriev, P., Vermeer, L.: It takes a flywheel to fly: kick-starting and growing the A/B testing momentum at scale. In: 2021 47th Euromicro Conference on Software Engineering and Advanced Applications (SEAA), pp. 109–118 (2021)
13. Olsson, H.H., Bosch, J.: From opinions to data-driven software R&D: a multi-case study on how to close the 'open loop' problem. In: 2014 40th EUROMICRO Conference on Software Engineering and Advanced Applications, pp 9–16. IEEE (2014)
14. Fagerholm, F., Sanchez Guinea, A., Mäenpää, H., Münch, J.: The RIGHT model for continuous experimentation. J. Syst. Softw. **123**, 292–305 (2017)
15. Gupta, S., et al.: Top challenges from the first practical online controlled experiments summit. ACM SIGKDD Explor. Newsl. **21**, 20–35 (2019)
16. Quin, F., Weyns, D., Galster, M., Silva, C.C.: A/B testing: a systematic literature review. arXiv preprint arXiv:2308.04929 (2023)
17. Jeunen, O., Baweja, S., Pokharna, N., Ustimenko, A.: Powerful A/B-testing metrics and where to find them. arXiv preprint arXiv:2407.20665 (2024)
18. Jeunen, O., Ustimenko, A.: Learning metrics that maximise power for accelerated A/B-tests. arXiv preprint arXiv:2402.03915 (2024)
19. Deng, A., Shi, X.: Data-driven metric development for online controlled experiments: seven lessons learned. In: Proceedings of the 22nd ACM SIGKDD International Conference on Knowledge Discovery and Data Mining, pp. 77–86 (2016)
20. Machmouchi, W., Buscher, G.: Principles for the design of online A/B metrics. In: Proceedings of the 39th International ACM SIGIR conference on Research and Development in Information Retrieval (SIGIR '16), pp. 589–590. Association for Computing Machinery, New York, NY, USA (2016)
21. Dmitriev, P., Wu, X.: Measuring metrics. In: Proceedings of the 25th ACM International on Conference on Information and Knowledge Management - CIKM '16, pp. 429–437. ACM Press (2016)
22. Deng, A., Lu, J., Chen, S.: Continuous monitoring of A/B tests without pain: optional stopping in bayesian testing. In: 2016 IEEE International Conference on Data Science and Advanced Analytics (DSAA), pp. 243–252. IEEE (2016)

23. Deng, A.: Objective bayesian two sample hypothesis testing for online controlled experiments. In: Proceedings of the 24th International Conference on World Wide Web - WWW '15 Companion, pp. 923–928. ACM Press (2015)
24. Mattos, D.I., Dmitriev, P., Fabijan, A., Bosch, J., Olsson, H.H.: An activity and metric model for online controlled experiments. In: Product-Focused Software Process Improvement, pp. 182–198. Springer International Publishing (2018)
25. Sauvola, T., et al.: Towards customer-centric software development: a multiple-case study. In: 2015 41st Euromicro Conference on Software Engineering and Advanced Applications, pp. 9–17. IEEE (2015)
26. Gioia, D.A., Corley, K.G., Hamilton A.L.: Seeking qualitative rigor in inductive research. Org. Res. Methods **16**(1), 15–31 (2013)
27. Olsson, H.H., Alahyari, H., Bosch, J.: Climbing the "stairway to heaven": a multiple-case study exploring barriers in the transition from agile development towards continuous deployment of software. In: Proceedings of the 38th Euromicro Conference on Software Engineering and Advanced Applications, September 5–7, Cesme, Izmir, Turkey (2012)
28. Olsson, H.H., Bosch, J., Alahyari, H.: Towards R&D as innovation experiment systems: a framework for moving beyond agile software development. In: IASTED Multiconferences - Proceedings of the IASTED International Conference on Software Engineering, SE, pp. 798–805 (2013)
29. Fabijan, A., Dmitriev, P., Olsson, H.H., Bosch, J.: The evolution of continuous experimentation in software product development: from data to a data-driven organization at scale. In: 2017 IEEE/ACM 39th International Conference on Software Engineering (ICSE), pp. 770–780. IEEE (2017)
30. Bosch, J., Olsson, H.H.: Toward evidence-based organizations: lessons from embedded systems, online games, and the internet of things. IEEE Software **34**(5), 60–66 (2017)
31. Erthal, V.M., de Souza, B.P., dos Santos, P.S., Travassos, G.H.: A literature study to characterize continuous experimentation in software engineering. In: CIbSE 2022 - XXV Ibero-American Conference on Software Engineering (2022)
32. Mattos, D.I., Dakkak, A., Bosch, J., Olsson, H.H.: The HURRIER process for experimentation in business-to-business mission-critical systems. J. Software Evol. Process **35**(5), e2390 (2023)
33. Kohavi, R., Henne, R.M., Sommerfield, D.: Practical guide to controlled experiments on the web: listen to your customers not to the HiPPO. In: Proceedings of the 13th International Conference on Knowledge Discovery and Data Mining, KDD, pp. 959–967 (2007)

Open Access This chapter is licensed under the terms of the Creative Commons Attribution 4.0 International License (http://creativecommons.org/licenses/by/4.0/), which permits use, sharing, adaptation, distribution and reproduction in any medium or format, as long as you give appropriate credit to the original author(s) and the source, provide a link to the Creative Commons license and indicate if changes were made.

The images or other third party material in this chapter are included in the chapter's Creative Commons license, unless indicated otherwise in a credit line to the material. If material is not included in the chapter's Creative Commons license and your intended use is not permitted by statutory regulation or exceeds the permitted use, you will need to obtain permission directly from the copyright holder.

Product and Design

Exploring Documentation Strategies for NFR in Agile Software Development

Igor Moreira[1]($\boxtimes$), Luciane Adolfo[2], Jorge Melegati[3], Joelma Choma[4], Eduardo Guerra[3], and Luciana Zaina[5]

[1] Institute of Technological Research (IPT), São Paulo, Brazil
igor.moreira@ensino.ipt.br
[2] Tribunal de Justiça do Estado do Rio Grande do Sul, Rio Grande do Sul, Brazil
luadolfo@gmail.com
[3] Free University of Bozen-Bolzano, Bolzano, Italy
{jorge.melegati,eduardo.guerra}@unibz.it
[4] Federal University of São Carlos (UFSCar), São Carlos, Brazil
jchoma@ufscar.br
[5] Federal University of São Carlos (UFSCar), Sorocaba, Brazil

Abstract. Companies adopt agile methodologies for various reasons, primarily due to their adaptability to change and evolving business demands. In this context, addressing non-functional requirements (NFRs) may not always be a priority and can present challenges for agile teams. The focus on User Stories present in agile methods and tools often does not offer explicit alternatives for documenting NFRs. In this research, we perform a survey to explore five different strategies for documenting NFRs, to identify which fits better for different types of quality attributes and to understand the strengths and drawbacks of each one. As a result, the participants considered certain strategies as being more or less suitable for specifying different types of quality attributes. For instance, while Story Labeling was rarely recommended for security requirements, using Story Sub-sections or Verification Rules were highly recommended for this kind of quality attribute. Our results also evaluated the strategies considering several factors, such as the level of detail and requirement duplication. As a practical implication, the results of this work can provide guidance to agile development teams in choosing the most suitable alternative for each NFR documentation.

Keywords: Quality attributes · Agile software development · Documentation · Non-functional Requirements

1 Introduction

Companies adopt agile methods for various reasons, primarily due to their adaptability to change and evolving business demands, where the software functionality supports the business. In this context, addressing non-functional requirements

(NFRs) or "quality requirements"[1] may not always be a priority and can present challenges for agile teams [2,8,21]. Despite the challenges involved, professionals agree on the importance of NFRs for the success of the project [1,10,12], as well as their relationship with the project's quality aspects and attributes [13,18]. Particularly in critical systems, such as aircraft or health software systems, the failure to satisfy NFRs can seriously compromise the operations [13].

Documentation plays an essential role in software development, serving as a means to record knowledge and the reasoning behind decisions. In Agile, documentation tends to be minimal and adaptable [22], which can be challenging when handling NFRs [20]. Requirements documentation in agile teams is usually based on User Stories which focus on functional aspects of the software. Because of that, several methods and tools do not provide any guidance on how to document NFRs. Behutiye et al. [5] warn that NFRs are so varied and complex that no single document can always fully capture their significance and meaning.

Some studies have explored this topic [9,17] identifying appropriate practices to handle different kinds of NFRs. One of these studies inspected the requirements and interviewed professionals from three different companies [17], identifying five practices for documenting NFRs. However, since this study was restricted to a small number of companies, it was not possible to generalize the results. Besides that, none of these studies evaluated the consequences and the suitability of these practices to specific quality attributes. In this paper, we tackle this limitation by performing a survey with professionals in which they evaluate the practices for documenting NFRs. In the questionnaire, we focused on the five practices identified by Nasir et al. [17] and asked the participants questions about their adoption, their strengths and weaknesses, and, for each type of quality attribute, which strategy they perceive to be more appropriate.

Our results confirmed that the practices were recognized, used, and considered useful by a significant amount of the participants. Moreover, we also found out that some practices are considered more or less appropriate according to the specific type of quality attribute requirement. Besides that, the participants also pointed out the positive and negative aspects of each practice. As a practical implication, our results provide guidance to agile development teams in choosing the most suitable alternative for each NFR documentation.

2 Non-functional Requirements in Agile Software Development

Requirements Engineering (RE) focuses on defining what needs to be developed to meet business demands, by employing specific processes and techniques. However, the context of agile methods can represent challenges to adherence to RE principles due to the dynamic and adaptive nature of the employed practices. Some studies have focused specifically on NFRs that are considered challenging

---

[1] Some authors consider "non-functional requirements" and "quality requirements" as synonymous [2]. In this paper, we will adopt this position.

in environments using agile methodologies [1,8,21]. For example, some studies proposed new artifacts to complement those already used by agile teams. Farid and Mitropoulos [7] proposed a modeling framework based on two artifacts focused on quality attributes: Agile Loose Cases for NFRs, and Agile Choose Cases for NFRs operationalization. Rahy and Bass [20] suggested two artifacts: the Documentation Work Item, for requirements related to regulatory compliance, and the Safety Critical Work Item, designed to include safety-related features.

Other authors propose solutions for specific quality attributes. Azham et al. [4] focused on the limitations in Scrum regarding security activities and proposed a "Security Backlog" dedicated to this concern. Considering User Experience (UX) requirements, Guerra et al. [19] proposed a set of patterns, which, besides adapting existing artifacts, also propose the UX Concern, designed to handle UX requirements related to multiple Stories. Other studies favored the use of existing documents instead of designing new ones. Behutiye et al. [5] provided guidelines for choosing the most suitable artifact (among Epic, User Story, and Acceptance Criteria) for NFR documentation. Alsaqaf et al. [3] investigated the challenges practitioners face regarding quality requirements and identified 15 challenges, 13 mechanisms behind them, and 9 practices that could mitigate their impact. Similarly, based on 36 interviews conducted in four companies, Karhapää et al. [11] identified 40 challenges classifying them into six categories.

Unlike previous approaches that propose novel specific artifacts [7,20] or deal with quality attributes [4,19], Nasir et al. [17] identified five practices used in real software development environments for documenting NFRs. We based our study on these practices which are described below.

Tasks and Acceptance Criteria. The NFR is defined in tasks associated with a feature defined by a User Story or in an Acceptance Criteria, containing one or more conditions that a feature must satisfy once completed. These two artifacts are already part of the standard User Story structure, so its adoption does not require much adaptation. In the companies that this practice was identified [17], it was used mostly to small quality requirements.

Story Labeling. This practice adds specific keywords or labels into user stories to flag that a specific NFR should be considered. That allows easy identification of the presence of a given NFR and enables documents to be queried and searched for them.

Dedicated Documents. This practice suggests introducing a dedicated document containing requirements associated with a specific NFR type. It can contain requirements that apply to several features of the same software or even to different projects. This document can contain more detailed information, including practices and implementation strategies to be followed. Even being considered more traditional approaches, these practices have been used in agile teams for security and UX/UI Guidelines [17].

Story Sub-sections. In this practice, specific sub-sections related to NFRs are added to the User Stories template. In tools, these sub-sections may be implemented through simple text fields or might ask for more structured information. In this case, for all user stories, there is a dedicated place for information regarding a specific quality attribute. When adopting this practice for more than one quality attribute, some caution is advised to not overload the User Story, harming its agile nature.

Verification Rules. This practice involves using rules defined for verification, as well as a way to define NFR requirements. In this way, the same quality-related constraints included within tools that perform automated checks can also be used for requirements purposes. This practice is analogous to using acceptance tests to document functional requirements, but in this case, the goal is the verification of a quality attribute.

Jarzębowicz and Weichbroth [9] conducted a systematic literature review and obtained similar results. They identified "Documenting NFRs with acceptance tests," "acceptance criteria," and "definitions of done and tasks" in several studies. However, Nasir et al. [17] grouped them as a single practice, **Tasks and Acceptance Criteria**, since they were represented in a similar way in the companies that participated in the study. **Story Sub-sections** were referred to as "structured story cards," and **Dedicated Documents** had a similar structure to what was called "instances of requirements templates dedicated to particular categories of NFRs." None of the identified practices were similar to **Story Labeling** and **Verification Rules**.

3 Research Design

To tackle the identified gap, we defined the following research questions:
RQ1. Are the identified practices recurring and recognized by professionals?
RQ2. Are the identified practices more suitable for documenting requirements of specific quality attributes from the participants' perspective?
RQ3. What are the benefits and drawbacks pointed out by the participants about each practice?

To answer them, we conducted a survey with professionals who participate in software development projects, encompassing participants from academia and industry. The survey study was conducted in three phases: pilot, response gathering, and data analysis. In the first phase, we released the pilot to collect feedback on the questionnaire, engaging 4 professionals with prior experience in NFRs. The evaluation focused on the list of NFR types, the format of the questions, adherence to the topic, and the general understanding of the research. The goal was to gather initial feedback to refine the questionnaire. The pilot participants provided extensive input on the research approach and examples of practices.

In the second phase, we implemented improvements based on the pilot participants' feedback, and we adjusted the overall structure of the questions to better target the practical use and knowledge of NFR documentation practices.

We refined the questions and adopted a list of types of NFRs based on ISO 25010 [23]. The revised questionnaire was then disseminated through email lists and social media and to the researchers' professional networks. As a result, we obtained 50 valid responses from 51 received.

In the third and final phase, we conducted an exploratory data analysis and discussed the findings. We applied a quantitative method to analyze the close-ended questions, addressing RQ1, about the recognition of the practices, and RQ2, with explored the suitability of each practice for specific types of NFRs. For the open-ended questions, we employed a thematic analysis [6] to answer RQ3, which examined the benefits and drawbacks of each practice.

3.1 Questionnaire Design

The questionnaire was divided into two parts. The first part collected participant information, such as gender, age, experience in software development, their self-perceived experience with agile methods, the role they have played, and their self-perceived experience with NFRs. The goal of this part is to understand the profile of the participants and assess the sample's suitability to answer the questionnaire. In the second part, we ask the same set of questions, presented in Table 1, for each practice under study. Before presenting the questions, a brief explanation of the practice is provided, followed by an example of its usage. We highlight that from Q1 to Q4, the questions are close-ended. The options from Q4 were based on ISO 25010 [23], and we added an explanation in each one in case the participant was not familiar with this classification. Questions Q5 and Q6 were open-ended, allowing the participants to freely express their opinions.

Table 1. Questions about each practice for the documentation of NFRs

Q1	I recognize this as a practice for documenting non-functional requirements.
	Options: Strongly agree, Agree, Don't agree or disagree, Disagree, Strongly disagree.
Q2	I have already used or seen this practice being used in projects that I have participated in.
	Options: Strongly agree, Agree, Don't agree or disagree, Disagree, Strongly disagree.
Q3	The usage of this practice can be useful to document non-functional requirements in a project that I have already participated in.
	Options: Strongly agree, Agree, Don't agree or disagree, Disagree, Strongly disagree.
Q4	For what kind of non-functional requirements can this practice be useful (mark as many as you like):
	Options: Functional Suitability, Performance Efficiency, Compatibility, Usability, Reliability, Security, Maintainability, Portability.
Q5	What are the benefits of using this practice? Illustrate with concrete scenarios.
Q6	What are the main drawbacks of using this practice? Illustrate in which cases its usage is NOT indicated.

3.2 Data Analysis

To answer RQ1, we conducted a quantitative analysis, examining the number of responses for each practice to identify trends and distributions in the data. This included tabulation, visualization, and analysis of data related to the use of different practices to handle NFRs. Q1, Q2, and Q3 were used to answer RQ1.

To answer RQ2, we performed three analyses based on Q4. First, we executed a Kruskal-Wallis Test to assess whether there are significant differences between experts and non-experts regarding the selection of NFRs that are most aligned with specific practices. Then, we conducted a frequency analysis to identify the top three NFRs most indicated in each practice from the perspective of experts and non-experts. Finally, we performed a Chi-Square Test to determine whether there is a significant association between participants' responses and the relevance of NFRs to each practice.

Further, we conducted a qualitative analysis of the open-ended responses to questions Q5 and Q6, employing a thematic analysis [6] to extract the insights from teams' experiences and perceptions regarding the benefits and drawbacks of each practice for managing NFRs answering RQ3. To ensure the robustness of the coding process, one researcher performed the initial coding, and a second researcher cross-validated the codes, resolving discrepancies through consensus.

By combining these quantitative and qualitative approaches, we were able to gain a comprehensive understanding of how the identified practices are employed by agile teams in their projects, as well as their benefits and drawbacks from the participant's perspective. This analysis guided our findings, assisting us in providing significant insights into the results of this study.

4 Survey Results

The survey received 50 valid responses during the period it was open. In this section, we present results with the answers given to the closed-ended questions and a general view of the analysis conducted using the open-ended questions.

The dataset containing all the responses, the complete survey structure, complementary graphs, and the tables for the analysis from the perspective of experts and non-experts, as well as the Chi-Square Test and Kruskal-Wallis Test, are included in the replication package [15].

4.1 Participant Profile

The majority of participants have substantial experience in software development, suggesting a relevant sample for this study. Approximately 43% of the survey participants have over 10 years of experience and around 41% have more than one but less than 10 years of experience, and only around 16% have less than a year of experience. Regarding the roles performed by participants in the agile development process (the participants were able to select more than one role), the most common one was developer, with 41 responses, followed by software architects with 16 answers and business analysts with 12 responses. The other roles were: product owner (10 answers), product manager (8), tester (8) and designer (3). This suggests that most participants had greater involvement in the role of implementing NFRs, making them the audience with the greatest impact on how NFRs are specified and presented. Of the participants who responded about their experience with NFRs, 43% stated that they were familiar as users, while 57% worked with their specifications.

Comparison Between Experts and Non-experts. When analyzing the perspective of experts (30 participants) and non-experts (20 participants) in NFRs regarding the alignment of NFRs with a specific practice, for most documentation practices, the KW test [14] did not reveal significant differences between the expert and non-expert groups (see Table 2). However, the KW test indicated a significant difference between experts and non-experts regarding the Story Labeling practice in the NRF of Functional Suitability (p-value 0.012). Since this difference occurred for only one practice for one NFR, we considered that all the answers came from the same population. Therefore, in this paper, we did not make a distinction between answers from the different groups.

Table 2. NFRs adherence to documentation practices from experts (N = 30) and non-experts (N = 20)

	Tasks and Acceptance Criteria	Story Labeling	Dedicated Documents	Story Sub-sections	Verification Rules
Functional S.	0.490	0.012*	0.360	0.067	0.783
Performance E.	0.491	1.000	0.073	0.634	1.000
Compatibility	0.418	0.568	0.814	0.309	0.703
Usability	0.475	0.728	0.490	0.243	1.000
Reliability	0.212	0.469	1.000	0.909	0.817
Security	0.908	0.783	0.908	0.334	0.725
Maintainability	0.806	0.410	0.783	0.904	0.560
Portability	0.469	0.560	0.568	0.434	0.309

* KW test results with statistical significance (p-value < .05).

4.2 NFRs and Practices' Usage

To determine whether the practices are recognized and used and if they are perceived as useful by participants, we tallied the affirmative responses "strongly agree" and "agree" for questions Q1 to Q3 for each practice and displayed the results in Fig. 1. We noticed that all practices had more than 70% of recognition from the survey audience, with Tasks and Acceptance Criteria and Dedicated Documents being the most recognized practices, with 84% and 80%, respectively. The least recognized practice is Verification Rules, with 70%.

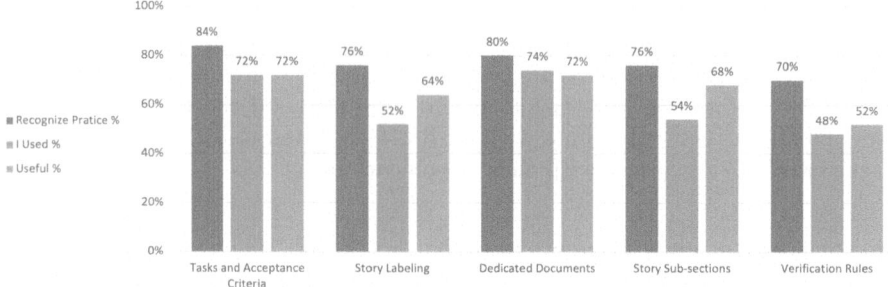

Fig. 1. Recognition and usefulness perception of the practices.

When looking at whether the practices are used by participants, we have a slightly different result. Despite Tasks and Acceptance Criteria being the most recognized practice, Dedicated Document is the most used practice among participants, with 74% of participants stating that they use it, compared to 72% for Tasks and Acceptance Criteria. When looking at the least used practice, we find that Verification Rules is the least used practice among participants, with a result of 48%, showing that less than half of the participants use the practice to handle NFRs.

Regarding whether these practices are useful in the participants' view, the numbers are close to the previous question. With the exception of Dedicated Documents, the other practices had a number of respondents equal or higher who saw the practice as useful compared to the number that actually used it. This fact shows that these practices have the potential for a higher adoption.

Looking at which type of NFR is most suitable for which practice, as shown in Fig. 2, we have some highlights such as Security with 86% of participants saying Verification Rules is a useful practice for dealing with this type of NFR, followed by Usability with 80% for Task and Acceptance Criteria, and Maintainability and Performance with 78% and 76%, respectively, for Dedicated Documents.

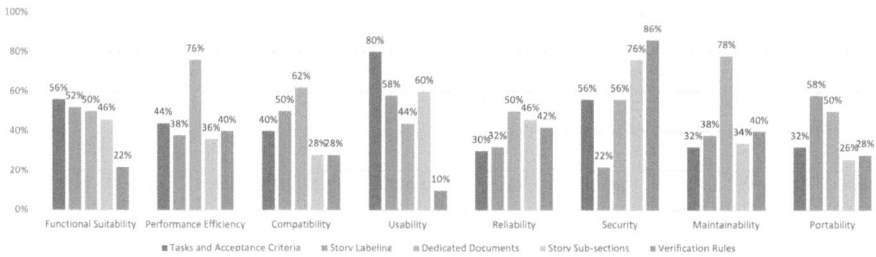

Fig. 2. Adherence of different types of NFRs to different practices.

Tasks and Acceptance Criteria. This was the most recognized practice among our participants, with 84% of the respondents recognizing it as a method for documenting NFRs. When asked if they use this practice to document NFRs or have seen it used in projects they have participated in, 72% responded affirmatively. This makes it the most recognized and one of the most relevant practices for NFR documentation, according to our participants. Regarding which types of NFR are most suitable for documentation using this practice, both in the overall perspective and from the perspectives of experts and non-experts, we observe that Usability is the highest at 80% overall, with 85% for non-experts and 77% for experts. Functional Suitability at 56% overall, with 50% for non-experts and 60% for experts. And Security at 56% overall, with 55% for non-experts and 57% for experts. Reliability is the least useful for this practice, with 30%. Maintainability and portability also received a low number of answers, with only 32% each. Chi-square test results indicate a significant association between responses related to Functional Suitability and Portability ($\tilde{\chi}^2 = 4.38$, p $= 0.036$), as well as between Security and Performance ($\tilde{\chi}^2 = 8.57$, p $= 0.003$).

Story Labeling. For 76% of the participants, Story Labeling is recognized as a practice for documenting NFRs, but only 52% said they use or have used this practice for documenting NFRs. Additionally, 64% believe it is useful for documentation. In terms of which types of NFRs are most suitable for the practice of Story Labeling, Portability appears at 60% overall, with 55% for non-experts and 63% for experts. Usability at 58% overall, with 55% for non-experts and 60% for experts. And Functional Suitability at 52% overall, with 30% for non-experts and 67% for experts, showcasing the greatest discrepancy between the two groups. Security and Reliability, with 22% and 32%, respectively, are considered the least suitable types of NFRs for the practice of Story Labeling. Different from the other practices, Story Labeling did not had a type of NFR that received a high acceptance from the participants. The analysis confirms significant associations in the following types of NFRs: Usability with Functional Suitability ($\tilde{\chi}^2 = 5.05$, p $= 0.025$), Usability with Compatibility ($\tilde{\chi}^2 = 4.02$, p $= 0.045$), and Portability with Compatibility ($\tilde{\chi}^2 = 8.33$, p $= 0.004$).

Dedicated Documents. Dedicated Documents is also a popular practice, recognized by 80% of the participants, making it the most used practice at 74%, and indicated by 72% as a useful practice for documenting NFRs. Regarding which types of NFR are most suitable for documentation using this practice, the findings include: Performance Efficiency at 78% overall, with 65% for non-experts and 87% for experts. Maintainability also at 78% overall, with 80% for non-experts and 77% for experts. Unlike the other practices, all types of NFR are above 44%, which may indicate the versatility of this practice in handling various types of NFR. Significant relationships were observed between Compatibility and Functional Suitability ($\tilde{\chi}^2 = 5.12$, p $= 0.024$), Compatibility and Performance ($\tilde{\chi}^2 = 3.93$, p $= 0.047$), Security and Reliability ($\tilde{\chi}^2 = 8.12$, p $= 0.004$), as well as Maintainability and Security ($\tilde{\chi}^2 = 4.72$, p $= 0.030$).

Story Sub-sections. While Tasks and Acceptance Criteria and Dedicated Documents had similar results, Story Sub-sections and Story Labeling also showed comparable outcomes. With 76% of participants recognizing the practice as a way to document NFRs, 54% affirmed they have used it in a project, and 68% indicated it would be useful for dealing with NFRs. For the type of NFR most suited to the practice, Security was highlighted, at 76% overall, with 85% for non-experts and 73% for experts. Usability followed in second place at 60% overall, with 50% for non-experts and 67% for experts. Functional Suitability at 46% overall, with 30% for non-experts and 57% for experts. On the other hand, Portability and Compatibility were the types of NFRs least indicated for this practice, with 26% and 28%, respectively. The results highlight associations between Usability and Compatibility ($\tilde{\chi}^2 = 5.36$, p = 0.021), Reliability and Performance ($\tilde{\chi}^2 = 11.04$, p = < .001), Security and Reliability ($\tilde{\chi}^2 = 4.39$, p = 0.036), and Functional Suitability with Maintainability ($\tilde{\chi}^2 = 9.63$, p = 0.002).

Verification Rules. Verification Rules was recognized by 70% of the participants, making it the least recognized practice. Only 48% have used this practice in a project, and 52% consider it a useful practice for NFRs. Security was the most recommended type of NFR for use with Verification Rules, at 86% overall, with 85% for non-experts and 77% for experts. Followed by Reliability in second place at 42% overall, with 50% for non-experts and 60% for experts. Performance Efficiency at 40% overall, with 55% for non-experts and 57% for experts. Usability was the least recommended, with only 10% of participants indicating it as a useful practice for documenting NFRs. The findings also confirm a significant association between Security and Reliability requirements ($\tilde{\chi}^2 = 4.94$, p = 0.026).

4.3 Thematic Analysis

For the thematic analysis, we initially selected all the participants' answers from the open-ended questions that were not empty and had relevant content. Based on those criteria, we evaluated the answers, from which we extracted 130 unique quotes that were classified into 18 unique codes that represent the benefits and drawbacks of the analyzed techniques, as shown in Fig. 3. The detailed results for each technique are reported in the discussion in Sect. 5.3.

5 Discussion

In this section, we use the results obtained from the survey answers to respond to our research questions defined in Sect. 3.

5.1 Practices Recognition and Usage (RQ1)

The practices identified in our study and evaluated in our survey are recurring and widely recognized by the participants, as can be observed in the survey

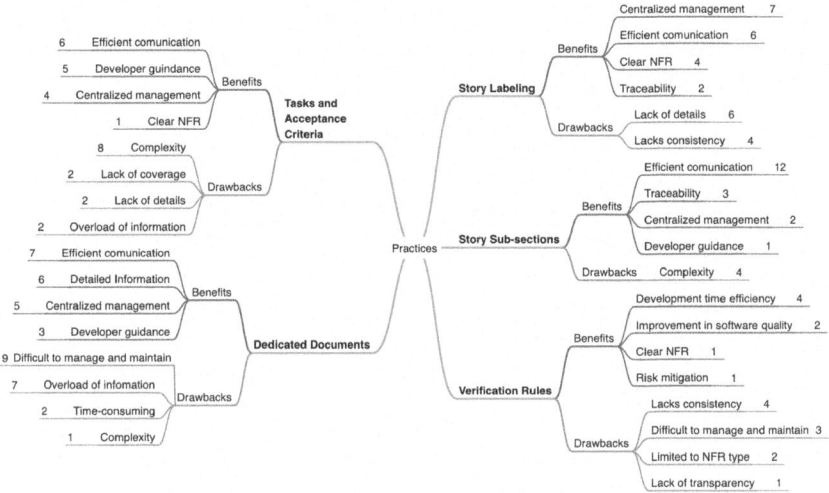

Fig. 3. Benefits and drawbacks by practices.

results. All five practices were recognized by at least 70% of the participants, indicating their significant relevance in the professional context. Among them, "Tasks and Acceptance Criteria" and "Dedicated Documents" were the most recognized practices for documenting NFRs, with 84% and 80% of participants recognizing them, respectively.

These numbers suggest that the practices are common and relevant in the context of NFR documentation in their projects. We also noticed that they are also widely used, with Dedicated Documents reported as the most used practice, with 74% of participants stating they use or have used it in their projects, followed by Tasks and Acceptance Criteria with 72%. These numbers reinforce that these practices are recognized and recurring in the professional market. Even though Verification Rules was the least recognized practice, it was still acknowledged by a large portion of participants, with 70% recognizing it as a practice for documenting NFRs. However, when we look at the number of professionals who stated they use it in their projects, the percentage was 48%, which may indicate that, despite being among the more recognized practices, its use may occur in more specialized scenarios or be less applicable than the other practices, being more used for specific types of NFRs.

5.2 Suitability for Types of NFR (RQ2)

The data collected from the participants' responses indicate that, from their perspective, each practice has a better adherence to certain types of NFRs. We can observe from the results that there is a dispersion of NFR types across the practices, with each practice having a greater adherence to specific types of NFRs. This dispersion can be better observed in Fig. 2. This suggests that the participating professionals handle different types of NFRs with different practices in their agile software development process. This is aligned with the anti-pattern Invariant Management [24], that classifies as a bad practice using the same approach to handle different kinds of NFRs.

When we examine the adherence between NFR types and the practices assessed in this study, we noticed that certain NFR types are highly recommended for specific practices. For instance, the Story Sub-section and Verification Rules were both considered useful for documenting Security NFRs, with 76% and 86% of participants, respectively, recommending these practices. That confirms the findings from the multiple case studies conducted by Nasir et al. [17]. Task and Acceptance Criteria were recommended by 80% of participants as a useful practice for documenting Usability NFRs, being a practice listed for defining UX constraints [19]. Additionally, Dedicated Documents were indicated by a large portion of participants as a useful technique for documenting Maintainability and Performance Efficiency NFRs, with 78% and 76% of participants respectively recommending it, indicating that even within agile methodologies, Dedicated Documents remain a relevant practice.

When we look at the less recommended practices, we find Verification Rules with only 10% of participants indicating it as useful. Despite the availability of tools to automatically perform usability checks [16], the adherence to this practice is low. Additionally, for NFRs of the type of Functional Suitability, only 22% of the participants stated that Verification Rules would be useful for documentation. Lastly, Story Labeling is the least recommended practice for handling Security NFRs, with only 22% of participants signaling it as useful.

Another interesting fact is that for reliability, no practice stood out. None exceeded 50% participants, indicating that there is no preferred way to document this kind of NFR, suggesting a potential future work to identify other practices that may be more suitable and effective for addressing this type of NFR.

This result also indicates certain types of NFRs can be better addressed by using a more appropriate practice, thereby utilizing a variety of practices. From a practical perspective, practitioners can use these results when choosing approaches for documenting a NFR. On the other hand, the use of various practices can make managing NFRs in a unified and centralized way more difficult.

5.3 Practices Benefits and Drawbacks (RQ3)

Tasks and Acceptance Criteria. In this practice, the category `Efficient communication` stood out the most in terms of benefits. Participants mentioned that it provides easier communication with different stakeholders and a clearer understanding. According to one participant, keeping the NFR closer to the User Story *"can provide additional context and information that can help to avoid misunderstandings"*. The second most frequent category is `Developer Guidance`, which highlights benefits such as keeping functional and NFRs closer to developers, clarifying the requirements, and reducing uncertainties about what needs to be done, since *"you can show for the developers the final result expected"*. On the drawbacks side, the category `Complexity` appeared most frequently. While one of the benefits was the ease of making user stories clearer and reducing uncertainties, the major drawback is that *"when defining non-functional requirements as tasks or acceptance criteria, it can introduce unnecessary complexity"*. This fact was also associated in some cases with Overload of Information, since *"overloading User Stories with too many non-functional requirements can make them unwieldy and challenging to manage"*.

Story Labeling. In this practice, we observed a significant emphasis on two points Centralized Management and Efficient communication. One of the advantages mentioned is that it is *"easy to filter cards with the same label"*, making the management more centralized. On the side of efficiency, practitioners point to a good compromise between the time needed to implement it and how fast this information can be absorbed since it *"can be understood in one sight without much time needed for reading"*. On the downside, we have Lack of details as the major drawback, pointing out that it may not provide sufficient details or fully capture the complexity, as well as not having an explicit goal for that NFR. According to a participant, *"labels alone may not provide enough detail or specificity to fully capture complex non-functional requirements"*. The fact that it might Lack consistency was also a concern since *"practice may turn bad if the team comes up with labeling that is confusing or not self-explanatory"*.

Dedicated Documents. In this practice, we identified Efficient communication as the greatest benefit of using it, as stated by some participants: *"these documents will outline the exact constraints, rules, and best practices to follow"* and it is *"specifying exactly how a certain functionality will behave"*. As a second benefit, the Detailed information was cited since the *"details regarding the requirements and reasoning behind them can be properly described"*. We also identified a significant amount of statements highlighting Centralized management and Developer guidance. As drawbacks, Difficult to manage and maintain and Overload of information were the most mentioned. One participant observed that *"in agile development environments that prioritize flexibility and collaboration, extensive documentation, including dedicated NFR documents, can become a hindrance"*. And a load of updating the documentation was also a concern since *"this kind of documentation gets outdated if not managed properly"*. Regarding the overload, it might *"generate excessive documentation"* and that *"extensive documentation may be impractical and counterproductive"*.

Story Sub-sections. In this practice, the most prominent category was Efficient Communication. According to participants, it provides *"alignment with compliance standards, documentation, and traceability"*. From the point of view of who specifies the stories, *"having dedicated sub-sections for NFRs ensures that each story's specific constraints and dependencies are clear and not ambiguous"*. Traceability, Centralized management, and Developer guidance were also mentioned. As for drawbacks, Complexity was the only identified category. According to one participant, *"these sub-sections can make user stories more complex since they will be present in all stories"*. Another comment mentions the complexity of this practice when used for several NFRs, since *"depending on the amount of NFRs and fields to fill in, the user story could be very extensive"*.

Verification Rules. In this practice, the most mentioned category was Development time efficiency. According to the participants *"this practice eliminates the huge amount of time that developers usually spend checking their own code"* because it *"saves time in NFR testing since they are automatically checked"*. As a drawback, the high volume of false positives that can be potentially generated by automated tools was mentioned in relation to Lacks consistency. Because of that, *"in scenarios where the tool generates a high volume of false positives, teams may find it less useful"*. The fact that the application is limited to NFR type also might prevent the usage of this technique in some cases since *"the number of things you can automate is very limited and hard to state"*.

6 Conclusion

In this study, we evaluated with professionals the agile practices for documenting NFRs identified by Nasir et al. [17]. We conducted a survey to collect insights regarding how these practices are recognized and used. Our findings reveal that the practices identified are both recurring and widely recognized among professionals. Practices such as Tasks and Acceptance Criteria and Dedicated Documents emerged as the most recognized and utilized, indicating their relevance in agile processes. Despite Verification Rules being the least recognized and used, it still showed significant recognition to be applied in more specific contexts.

Our results also fill the gap in the literature regarding the applicability of these NFR documentation techniques. Based on the survey, we identified that some techniques are more suitable for the documentation of certain types of NFRs. Moreover, we identified the benefits and drawbacks of each of them regarding different properties, such as the level of detail, communication, and management easiness. As a practical implication, development teams can rely on our results to decide the most suitable approaches to document a NFR.

Future studies can investigate the properties of other practices that were out of the scope of this study. For types of NFRs that did not receive a high amount of answers on these documentation practices, future efforts might be focused on adapting the existing approaches or developing new ones tailored to their characteristics. Finally, case studies can also be conducted in agile development teams, in which the adoption of these practices is performed in a systematic way, guided by the characteristics identified in this study.

Disclosure of Interests. The authors have no competing interests to declare that are relevant to the content of this article.

References

1. Aljallabi, B.M., Mansour, A.: Enhancement approach for non-functional requirements analysis in agile environment. In: 2015 International Conference on Computing, Control, Networking, Electronics and Embedded Systems Engineering (ICCNEEE), pp. 428–433. IEEE (2015)
2. Alsaqaf, W., Daneva, M., Wieringa, R.: Quality requirements in large-scale distributed agile projects – A systematic literature review. In: Grünbacher, P., Perini, A. (eds.) REFSQ 2017. LNCS, vol. 10153, pp. 219–234. Springer, Cham (2017). https://doi.org/10.1007/978-3-319-54045-0_17
3. Alsaqaf, W., Daneva, M., Wieringa, R.: Quality requirements challenges in the context of large-scale distributed agile: an empirical study. Inf. Softw. Technol. **110**, 39–55 (2019)
4. Azham, Z., Ghani, I., Ithnin, N.: Security backlog in scrum security practices. In: 2011 Malaysian Conference in Software Engineering, pp. 414–417 (2011)
5. Behutiye, W., Karhapää, P., Costal, D., Oivo, M., Franch, X.: Non-functional requirements documentation in agile software development: challenges and solution proposal. In: Felderer, M., Méndez Fernández, D., Turhan, B., Kalinowski, M., Sarro, F., Winkler, D. (eds.) PROFES 2017. LNCS, vol. 10611, pp. 515–522. Springer, Cham (2017). https://doi.org/10.1007/978-3-319-69926-4_41
6. Braun, V., Clarke, V.: Using thematic analysis in psychology. Qual. Res. Psychol. **3**(2), 77–101 (2006)
7. Farid, W.M., Mitropoulos, F.J.: Novel lightweight engineering artifacts for modeling non-functional requirements in agile processes. In: 2012 Proceedings of IEEE Southeastcon, pp. 1–7 (2012)
8. Inayat, I., Salim, S.S., Marczak, S., Daneva, M., Shamshirband, S.: A systematic literature review on agile requirements engineering practices and challenges. Comput. Hum. Behav. **51**, 915–929 (2015)
9. Jarzebowicz, A., Weichbroth, P.: A qualitative study on non-functional requirements in agile software development. IEEE Access **9**, 40458–40475 (2021)
10. Kamata, M.I., Tamai, T.: How does requirements quality relate to project success or failure? In: 15th IEEE International Requirements Engineering Conference (RE 2007), pp. 69–78. IEEE (2007)
11. Karhapää, P., et al.: Strategies to manage quality requirements in agile software development: a multiple case study. Empir. Softw. Eng. **26**(2), 1–59 (2021). https://doi.org/10.1007/s10664-020-09903-x
12. Kopczyńska, S., Ochodek, M., Nawrocki, J.: On importance of non-functional requirements in agile software projects—A survey. In: Jarzabek, S., Poniszewska-Marańda, A., Madeyski, L. (eds.) Integrating Research and Practice in Software Engineering. SCI, vol. 851, pp. 145–158. Springer, Cham (2020). https://doi.org/10.1007/978-3-030-26574-8_11
13. Kotonya, G., Sommerville, I.: Requirements Engineering: Processes and Techniques. Wiley Publishing (2002)
14. Kruskal, W.H., Wallis, W.A.: Use of ranks in one-criterion variance analysis. J. Am. Stat. Assoc. **47**(260), 583–621 (1952)
15. Moreira, I.: Replication package for: exploring documentation strategies for NFR in agile software development (2025). https://doi.org/10.5281/zenodo.14742725
16. Namoun, A., Alrehaili, A., Tufail, A.: A review of automated website usability evaluation tools: research issues and challenges. In: Soares, M.M., Rosenzweig, E., Marcus, A. (eds.) HCII 2021. LNCS, vol. 12779, pp. 292–311. Springer, Cham (2021). https://doi.org/10.1007/978-3-030-78221-4_20

17. Nasir, S., Guerra, E., Zaina, L., Melegati, J.: An exploratory study about non-functional requirements documentation practices in agile teams. In: Proceedings of the 38th ACM/SIGAPP Symposium on Applied Computing, pp. 1009–1017. SAC 2023, Association for Computing Machinery, New York, NY, USA (2023)
18. Paech, B., Kerkow, D.: Non-functional requirements engineering-quality is essential. In: 10th International Workshop on Requirments Engineering Foundation for Software Quality (2004)
19. Pereira, A., Cleto Filho, A., Guerra, E., Zaina, L.: Towards a pattern language to embed UX information in agile software requirements. In: 26th European Conference on Pattern Languages of Programs. EuroPLoP 2021, Association for Computing Machinery (2021)
20. Rahy, S., Bass, J.M.: Managing non-functional requirements in agile software development. IET Software **16**(1), 60 72 (2022)
21. Ramesh, B., Cao, L., Baskerville, R.: Agile requirements engineering practices and challenges: an empirical study. Inf. Syst. J. **20**(5), 449–480 (2010)
22. Selic, B.: Agile documentation, anyone? IEEE Softw. **26**(6), 11–12 (2009)
23. International Organization for Standardization: ISO/IEC 25010: 2011: systems and Software Engineering-Systems and Software Quality Requirements and Evaluation (SQuaRE)-System and Software Quality Models. ISO/IEC (2011)
24. Viviani, L., Guerra, E., Melegati, J., Daniel, J.: Anti-patterns in managing uncertain non-functional requirements. In: Proceedings of the 28th European Conference on Pattern Languages of Programs, pp. 1–10 (2023)

Open Access This chapter is licensed under the terms of the Creative Commons Attribution 4.0 International License (http://creativecommons.org/licenses/by/4.0/), which permits use, sharing, adaptation, distribution and reproduction in any medium or format, as long as you give appropriate credit to the original author(s) and the source, provide a link to the Creative Commons license and indicate if changes were made.

The images or other third party material in this chapter are included in the chapter's Creative Commons license, unless indicated otherwise in a credit line to the material. If material is not included in the chapter's Creative Commons license and your intended use is not permitted by statutory regulation or exceeds the permitted use, you will need to obtain permission directly from the copyright holder.

Adapt and Overcome - How Agile Practitioners Adapt to Issues that Impede the Delivery of Value: An Interview Study

Jan-Niklas Meckenstock[1](✉) [iD] and Victoria Wallmichrath[2] [iD]

[1] Chair for Industrial Information Systems, University of Bamberg, Bamberg, Germany
jan-niklas.meckenstock@uni-bamberg.de
[2] Babtec Informationssysteme GmbH, Wuppertal, Germany

Abstract. Continuously delivering valuable software is a core principle of agile software development (ASD). In practice, value delivery is often impeded by several key issues, including low customer involvement, volatile requirements, technical debt, delivery pressure, excessive rework, or meeting overhead, which affect the product or the process. Despite their negative influence, the different consequences for the delivered value remain to be better understood. In addition, a collection of measures to help practitioners adapt to these issues is missing, as previous work only offers limited guidance on how to mitigate them. To address this situation, we conducted 19 semi-structured expert interviews to identify the consequences of key issues for value delivery and empirically derive measures to adapt to these issues. We find 34 value-reducing consequences, which primarily affect product quality and capabilities, delivery timeliness, and process efficiency. We also develop a collection of 48 measures to address the issues, including procedural changes, process artifacts and roles, technical means, and different ways to approach customers. With our work, we provide practitioners with actionable measures to adapt to issues encountered in daily practice and avoid their value-reducing consequences, thereby facilitating continuous value delivery. For research, we extend knowledge on the dark side of ASD by illustrating how key issues affect the delivered value, which was less regarded in related studies. In addition, we encourage future investigations into how micro-tailoring fosters sustained value delivery, along with examinations of resilience engineering in the context of ASD to improve the performance of software development processes.

Keywords: Agile software development · Agile business value · Issues impeding value delivery · Countermeasures to sustain value delivery · Interview study

1 Introduction

Agile software development (ASD) methodologies such as Scrum, Extreme Programming (XP), or Kanban have transformed the software development (SD) industry, receiving considerable attention from various research communities [3, 12]. At its core, ASD was conceived to "*satisfy the customer through early and continuous delivery of valuable software*" [4], as proclaimed in the Agile Manifesto. Research has revealed significant benefits that form the value of ASD [25], particularly with regard to the provided software products. Among other benefits, these include higher product quality with fewer defects [2, 16], reduced time to market [26, 29], or better meeting of requirements [2, 26]. Together, these benefits contribute to the steadily increasing adoption of ASD methodologies, as frequently reported in the annual State of Agile Reports [11].

In practice, "*continuous delivery of valuable software is not an easy task,*" [18] as various issues [24, 28] or barriers [1] can impede value delivery. In this regard, a literature study by Meckenstock [24] systematizes issues that occur frequently in ASD. *Lacking customer involvement, technical debt, volatile requirements, delivery pressure, required rework,* and *meeting overhead* appear especially problematic [24], inter alia, due to their potential effects on the timeliness of deliverables [17], product quality [13], or the correctness of requirements [19]. In analogy, a study by Alahyari et al. [1] on value in ASD finds several barriers that can impede value delivery. As a commonality, however, the studies do not thematize the consequences for value delivery if these issues or barriers are not overcome. Similarly, Petersen and Wohlin [28] investigated benefits and issues in ASD, but did not assess the specific consequences of the identified issues for value delivery. Besides lacking insights into the consequences for the delivery of value, prior work also did not provide measures to adapt to these issues. Identifying the consequences of key issues in ASD and adapting to them appears important, though, to ensure the continuous delivery of value and improve the application of ASD.

To address the lack of insights into the consequences of six key issues for value delivery and provide a collection of measures that can help practitioners uncover better ways to deliver valuable software products, we conducted an interview study with 19 ASD experts. Our study investigates the following research questions (RQ):

- *RQ1: What are the consequences of key issues in ASD methodologies for the sustained delivery of valuable software products?*
- *RQ2: Which measures do practitioners apply to adapt to critical issues and avoid their negative consequences that affect a sustained value delivery?*

The paper is structured as follows: in Sect. 2, we describe the theoretical background of the study and related work. Section 3 contains the methodology behind our work. Section 4 presents the results of the study and illustrates the consequences of the six issues and measures to adapt to them. Section 5 discusses the key findings, suggests paths for future research, and addresses limitations. Section 6 concludes the paper.

2 Theoretical Background and Related Work

Delivering value to the customer is deeply rooted in the principles of the Agile Manifesto [4], making it a core objective of ASD methodologies. The Scrum guide emphasizes this value delivery by continuously providing increments towards a product goal [34], i.e., a software product, with ASD methodologies generally "*contributing to perceived customer value*" [9]. The term *value* is often perceived differently, but implies a "*benefit, whether tangible or intangible, economic or social, monetary or utilitarian, [...] aesthetic or ethical*" [5] that can be derived from such a software product. While IS research, for instance, views value from a more economic-financial stance [33], research on the value of ASD adopts a wider perspective, emphasizing that *"value is not only dollars"* [29]. In this vein, [25] find that the value of delivered products materializes in the following ways: better meeting of customer demands through frequent feedback, higher software quality, reduced time to market, better responsiveness to changing requirements, and increased productivity, among other non-product-related benefits, i.e., developer satisfaction [29] or improved communication [2]. In analogy, [1] suggest that ASD value is mostly perceived to manifest in product functionality, maintainability, quality, and time to availability, with financial aspects being less frequently mentioned. While ASD can also imply other beneficial effects [1, 25, 26, 29], our study focuses on product-delivery-related benefits, given the promise of ASD to continuously provide valuable software [4, 34]. In line with prior research, we consider the core value proposition of ASD to imply an *early, frequent, and sustained delivery of a high-quality software product that can be evaluated with the customer in short iterations, leading to a better meeting of requirements through higher responsiveness to change.*

In practical settings, several issues impede the delivery of valuable products and affect ASD's core value proposition. Six issues seem especially critical [24], as they affect the product, reinforce other issues, or imply negative effects on the process. These include *lacking customer involvement, technical debt, volatile requirements, delivery pressure, required rework,* and *meeting overhead*. Similarly, potential barriers that impede value delivery found by Alahyari et al. [1] align with the issues discussed in Meckenstock [24], i.e., vague requirements, late scope changes, lack of access to customers, or tight deadlines [1]. Below, we describe these critical concerns for value delivery:

Lacking customer involvement is problematic, as ASD teams rely on the customer to clarify and prioritize requirements and seek feedback on recent increments [19] to align the product with the requirements. *Volatile requirements* lead to inadequate estimates [30] that often cause delays [17]. In addition, *delivery pressure* results in shortcuts in development that degrade product quality and create technical debt [23]. *Technical debt* implies deficiencies in the code resulting from time pressure [23], which hampers product quality and maintainability in the long run [13]. *Required rework* of increments due to missed requirements and technical debt [24] may also be problematic, as it increases project costs [37]. Finally, despite their importance in steering the development process, *meeting overhead* disrupts the workflow and reduces developer productivity [39].

These six issues all imply certain negative effects, but how they specifically affect the delivery of valuable software is less clear. While [24] illustrates which issues occur most frequently and how they are related, the specific consequences for the delivered value are less regarded. Similarly, [1] only list barriers toward achieving value, yet the consequences, if these barriers are not overcome, remain unaddressed. Together, previous studies only describe which issues generally occur and which barriers exist in ASD, with the specific consequences for value delivery being less understood.

In addition, previous work does not provide a comprehensive collection of measures to adapt to these issues. Adaptation is a key principle of ASD, though, as suggested in the key managing rule of XP to "fix XP when it breaks" [38]. Therefore, inspecting and adapting the process to fix aspects that are not working well is embedded in virtually all ASD methodologies, i.e., XP or Scrum [3, 38]. Still, [1] only describe practices that should generally be in place for value creation, while measures to overcome the identified barriers are missing. This also holds true for [24], which generally does not thematize how to adapt to issues to ensure value delivery. With regard to adaptation, research on ASD method tailoring [8, 36], i.e., "*customizing the agile method to meet the context and circumstances of use*" [36] also primarily focuses on tailoring motives and criteria [8], the effects of tailoring on success [36], and the main approaches of contingency-based method selection or method engineering [8]. How to customize ASD with measures or micro-adaptations [16] to sustain value delivery is less investigated, though. While some suggestions are scattered in the literature, i.e., how to address low customer involvement [19] or technical debt [23], a comprehensive set of measures to help ASD teams adapt to key issues thus remains to be defined.

To address these shortcomings, this study sheds light on the consequences of the six key issues derived from [24] for the core proposition of ASD to deliver valuable software products. In so doing, we aim to extend findings on the value [1, 25] and the dark sides of ASD [24] by clarifying the specific impact of the examined issues on the delivered value. Our study also intends to provide an empirically-derived collection of measures that practitioners can apply to adapt to these issues, as a consolidated set of practical measures is lacking. Thereby, we also contribute insights into how ASD practitioners adapt to critical issues, which was missing in [1, 24]. Together, this study should equip ASD practitioners with actionable measures to help them find better ways to deliver valuable software products when facing these issues in daily practice.

3 Methodology and Study Design

Study Design. To answer our RQs, we conducted semi-structured expert interviews [6], relying on the guidelines by Myers and Newman [27] to enable a rigorous data collection. Doing so appears suitable, as we investigate a variety of practical problems [35] that ASD practitioners face in daily development practice. An interview protocol with three sections guided the interviews to ensure that all experts were asked a consistent set of questions. The interview protocol is featured in the online appendix[1]. After the first three interviews, we refined the protocol to address observed gaps in the questions and achieve better alignment with the research objectives. In each interview, we first presented the goal of the study and asked the experts about their experience with ASD, the methodologies they apply, and their perception of the value of ASD. In the second part, we asked about the negative consequences of each investigated issue derived from [24] for the delivery of valuable software. In this section, we also inquired about how the experts specifically adapted to these issues to continuously deliver valuable software. In the wrap-up section, we asked which issue the experts deemed to be the most problematic. We also inquired if they wanted to add an issue or a consequence that was not mentioned before, however, most experts considered the six investigated issues as the main sources of negative consequences for a sustained value delivery.

Data Collection. The interview study was conducted between September and December 2024. We performed 19 interviews with experts from 14 organizations to gain a

---

[1] The online appendix can be found at: https://doi.org/10.6084/m9.figshare.28190441.

Table 1. Overview of participating ASD experts

ID	Role	Country	Industry	Agile Experience	No. of Employees	Applied Agile Methodologies
E1	Agile Coach	USA	Banking	13 years	50.000	SAFe, Scrum
E2	Developer	Switzerland	Groceries and Retail	4 years	2.200	SAFe, Scrum
E3	Agile Coach	Australia	Insurance	9 years	90.000	Scrum
E4	Scrum Master	Germany	ICT Services	4 years	1.000	Scrum
E5	Business Analyst	Germany	IT Consulting	4 years	300.000	Scrum
E6	Developer	Portugal	IT Consulting	3 years	370.000	Scrum
E7	Scrum Master	Germany	ICT Services	7 years	1.000	Scrum
E8	Product Owner	Germany	ICT Services	6 years	1.000	Scrum
E9	Developer	Germany	Banking	5 years	1.100	Scrum
E10	Head of Software	Germany	ICT Services	15 years	250	Scrum
E11	Product Owner	Germany	HR Services	5 years	50	Scrum
E12	Developer	Switzerland	ICT Services	6 years	180.000	Scrum, Kanban
E13	Head of Technology	Germany	Marketing	11 years	200	Scrum, Kanban
E14	Agile Coach	Germany	ICT Services	12 years	450	Scrum, Kanban
E15	Agile Coach	Germany	Healthcare	13 years	300.000	Scrum, Kanban, Lean
E16	Scrum Master	Germany	ICT Services	8 years	1.000	Scrum
E17	Developer	Germany	ICT Services	8 years	250	Scrum
E18	Head of Software	Spain	ICT Services	17 years	20	Scrum
E19	Head of Software	Germany	ICT Services	15 years	250	Scrum

broad perspective on the topic with a *"variety of voices"* [27]. Following the definition of *expert* in [6], we considered an *expert* in ASD as someone who *"has technical, process, and interpretive knowledge [in the field of agile development], by virtue of the fact that the expert acts [as a developer, coach, Scrum Master or Product Owner, i.e., any role associated with the application of ASD]"*, (cf. [6], p. 54). Table 1 contains an overview of all experts [E1-E19]. This selection ensured that diverse perspectives on issues, their consequences, and applicable adaptation measures could be obtained. The experts were recruited using a combination of purposive and convenience sampling [20] and approached via LinkedIn or referred to the authors after an interview. All interviews were conducted in Microsoft Teams and recorded after the experts had given their consent, with the first author serving as the interviewer in all cases. On average, the interviews lasted 43 min, ranging from 32 to 58 min. Most interviews were conducted in German, while five were in English. The recordings were subsequently transcribed, with all German interviews being translated into English for the analysis step. The first author transcribed and translated the interviews, which the second author later validated, while potential disagreements were resolved in joint discussions.

Data Analysis. The collected data was analyzed in a three-step cycle with inductive and deductive characteristics. We followed the recommendations by Saldaña [32] and Kuckartz [21] to identify relationships between the six issues and their consequences for value delivery as well as measures to adapt to these issues. The qualitative analysis was performed in MAXQDA, with the two researchers separately coding the data to avoid bias and ensure reliability, while disagreements were again resolved in joint discussions. In the first step, we identified negative consequences for the delivered value based on 1108 statements from the interviews. The consequences were assigned to the specific issue of the six investigated in this study that caused them. In the second step, we distilled measures the experts applied to adapt to these issues. In the third step, we revisited the initial results and refined them for the results presentation. Overall, we found 34 value-reducing consequences to result from the six issues. We also merged related consequences into 9 consequence types to allow further abstraction, see Table 2. Furthermore, we derived 48 measures that the experts used to adapt to the six issues, with related measures grouped into 7 measure types, see Table 3. The online appendix features a more detailed account of the analysis and provides the code book behind our work. We also sent out a follow-up report to five interested experts to reduce misinterpretations, receiving three responses that clarified statements we deemed as difficult to understand. One expert supplied an additional list of points to further expand on statements that lacked information, thereby enriching the existing data. The preliminary results were also presented to three experts to allow for further validation of the study.

4 Findings

In this section, we first illustrate the value-reducing consequences of the six examined issues. All consequences are listed in Table 2. Subsequently, the measures the experts applied to adapt to the key issues are described. Table 3 contains all identified measures.

4.1 Negative Consequences of Key Issues for Value Delivery

Delivery Pressure had a particularly negative effect on software quality, as developers *"cut corners and focus on the wrong thing, which is deliver on time rather than deliver a good outcome"* [E3]. Under pressure, also technical deficiencies in the code accumulated, since having to provide a continuous *"feature firework"* [E8] often resulted in the negligence of testing and other quality measures [E6,E7,E8,E11]. Besides poor quality, *"pressure creates anxiety"* [E1] and endangers psychological safety [E7,E10,E12,E16], which caused developers to experience stress and health issues [E2,E7,E8,E16]. As a related consequence, the delivered scope shrunk, given the team's capacity was reduced due to pressure-related cases of illness, causing them not to deliver to the full extent [E8,E16]. In addition, when pressurized, some teams focused on providing fewer features to avoid sacrificing quality, again at the expense of the scope [E5,E8,E12]. Most developers saw delivery pressure as the most problematic issue, i.e., [E2,E6,E12,E17].

Lacking Customer Involvement had negative consequences for the specification of requirements, the delivered functionality, and the timeliness of deliveries. Delivered products were often misaligned with requirements, as teams built features that are *"not in line with what was actually desired"* [E2]. Low customer engagement also impeded teams from receiving feedback [E2,E8,E17,E19] to assess the delivered increments. Besides deviations from actual requirements, obsolete functionality *"that nobody uses and then ends up in the bin"* [E16] resulted, further suggesting a waste of resources [E6,E9,E13,E16]. Several experts also cited incomplete requirements as a source of this issue, i.e., [E2,E4,E6,E9,E16], causing teams to operate in *"the fog of uncertainty"* [E5,E6] due to a lack of customer feedback. Finally, low customer involvement slowed development, causing delays when *"decisions are pending that would define subsequent steps"* [E17]. Especially Product Owners and Scrum Masters [E3,E4,E7,E8,E16] deemed low customer involvement as the most critical issue, since *"Product Owners cannot challenge their requirements and have to pull something out of thin air"* [E4].

Meeting Overhead and Interruptions affected the developers' concentration and focus, especially during coding work, as *"getting back into what you had been working on before is often difficult and takes time"* [E12]. Other experts [E8,E9,E16,E18] also reported frustration when spending much of their day in meetings, as it took away time for the development of functionality and implied an interruption of the workflow [E2, E4,E6,E12,E17]. Overall, many experts perceived meetings as a loss of time [E3,E8,E9, E12,E15,E17], but particularly those with large numbers of participants, lacking goals and minimal speaking time for some of the members. For the most critical consequence, developers reported reduced productivity, as *"not only the duration of the meeting itself but also the time before and afterward impedes us from making actual progress"* [E17].

Required Rework was identified by [24] to be an issue causing further problems, for instance, cost increases. However, most experts saw rework as a value-enhancing aspect rather than being problematic. [E3] described rework *"as the only way to get value"*, but only if it is *"a meaningful optimization or extension of extant work"* [E10]. [E19] added that *"rework improves the product, but the extra time required may come at a cost"*, in line with [E2,E14]. The experts generally highlighted that it is essential to differentiate the kind of rework that occurs, i.e., whether amendments to existing features deliver a value add or merely imply extra work that *"rather represents gold-plating"* [E10]. As will be described in Sect. 4.2, using a good / bad / ugly approach when assessing rework was suggested by the experts [E7,E10,E17] to ensure that only value-adding rework is

Table 2. Observed consequences of examined issues for value delivery

Key Issue	Consequence Type	Consequence	Expert IDs
Delivery Pressure	Additional Efforts	Additional Work Required	E2, E12, E14, E16
	Emotional Issues	Stress and Health Issues	E1, E2, E5, E6, E7, E8, E9, E11, E12, E14, E16, E17, E18
	Product Quality	Reduced Code Quality	E1, E2, E3, E4, E6, E7, E8, E11, E12, E13, E14, E15, E17, E19
	Product Capability	Reduced Delivery Scope	E5, E8, E12, E14, E16
Lacking Customer Involvement	Emotional Issues	Demotivation of Developers	E4, E6, E9, E17
	Product Capability	Obsolete Functionality	E6, E9, E13, E16
		Product-Requirement-Misalignment	E2, E3, E4, E5, E8, E9, E11, E16, E17, E19
	Requirement Issues	Unspecific / Incomplete Requirements	E2, E3, E4, E5, E6, E8, E9, E12, E15, E16, E17
	Time-to-Market	Delay of new Features	E2, E4, E6, E9, E15, E17
	Waste Issues	Waste of Resources	E6, E9, E13, E16
Meeting Overhead and Interruptions	Emotional Issues	Developer Frustration	E8, E9, E12, E16, E18
	Process Efficiency	Loss of Focus	E4, E6, E8, E9, E11, E12, E13, E17, E19
		Reduced Productivity	E2, E6, E8, E12, E19
		Workflow Interruption	E2, E4, E6, E12, E17
	Waste Issues	Loss of Time	E1, E3, E7, E8, E9, E12, E15, E17
Required Rework	Additional Efforts	Additional Time Required	E2, E9, E14
Technical Debt	Additional Efforts	Additional Cost	E1, E2, E6, E9, E12, E17, E19
		Additional Rework	E1, E4, E6, E10, E12, E14, E17

(*continued*)

Table 2. (*continued*)

Key Issue	Consequence Type	Consequence	Expert IDs
	Customer Satisfaction	Deteriorating Customer Relationship	E2, E14, E16
	Process Efficiency	Reduced Velocity	E7, E9, E16, E17, E18
	Product Quality	Difficult Code Understanding	E2, E8, E12, E16, E17
		Difficult Maintainability	E9, E12, E16, E17
		Reduced Software Quality	E2, E6, E12, E14, E15, E16, E19
		Security Issues	E5, E9, E10, E15, E16
	Time-to-Market	Delay of new Features	E4, E6, E7, E9, E14, E16, E17
	Waste Issues	Loss of Time	E2, E4, E7, E8, E11, E14, E19
Volatile and Unclear Requirements	Additional Efforts	Additional Cost	E2, E4, E5, E7
	Emotional Issues	Frustration of Developers	E6, E8, E14, E15, E16, E17
	Product Capability	Incoherent Functionality	E7, E12, E16, E17, E19
		Reduced Delivery Scope	E2, E11, E16
	Product Quality	Technical Error	E2, E4, E11, E12, E16, E17
	Requirement Issues	Feature Creep	E5, E10, E16
	Time-to-Market	Delay of new Features	E6, E9, E10, E11, E16, E19
	Waste Issues	Wasted Time and Effort on Obsolete Functionality	E7, E8, E9, E14

performed, which follows [15]'s good-bad-ugly-taxonomy for iterative rework. Hence, rework is essential for value but requires adequate consideration.

Technical Debt was especially problematic for quality-related aspects. The experts reported that software quality declined, i.e., [E2,E6,E12,E15,E19], with cross-cutting concerns such as security issues, scalability, and maintainability emerging as critical side-effects [E5,E9,E12,E16]. Technical debt also slowed the development, as *"maintenance tasks to allow new features to be implemented at some point become rampant"* [E4].

Consequently, delays occurred [E4,E6,E9,E14,E17], as teams lost time fixing the accumulated debt. Besides time loss, dealing with technical debt [E1,E6,E9,E12,E17] also caused significant cost increases, as *"fixing debt is often not accounted for in the budget"* [E17]. Technical debt may therefore also contribute to a deteriorating customer relationship [E2,E14,E16]. Consequently, technical debt was considered a major concern by developers as well as Product Owners and managers [E2,E4,E6,E12,E17,E18, E19], particularly due to its *"medium to long-term implications"* [E19] if not addressed.

Volatile and Unclear Requirements caused incoherent products with *"low functional consistency"* [E19], forming a *"patchwork carpet of features"* [E7]. With changing requirements, the experts also reported that technical errors were induced [E2,E4, E11,E12,E16,E17], as previous work needs to be adapted to support the altered requirements. To add, the uncertainty accompanying requirement volatility *"causes mistakes to happen and creates a mess in the implementation"* [E4]. In this vein, frustration also emerges [E6,E8,E15,E16,E17], as due to volatility, *"developers start something, but are again interrupted and need to focus on something new"* [E16]. This volatility also causes a waste of resources on *"developed features that are not bulletproof"* [E9], leading to delays due to time spent on changing requirements [E6,E9,E10,E11,E16,E19].

4.2 Measures to Adapt to Issues and Sustain Value Delivery

Delivery Pressure was usually managed with three types of measures. First, experts reported that conservative estimates and smaller, manageable stories focusing on *"key aspects required for a go-live for each iteration"* [E11] helped to reduce pressure. Here, reducing the story size to a *"minimal degree of value, almost like an MVP within each story, helped us minimize the feature pressure"*, reported [E16]. Second, the experts strongly involved the customer in the planning sessions and sought their agreement for conservative estimates, as it *"helped the customer understand how things get delivered and provided transparency"* [E4]. In addition, involving the customer in demos to present the value of delivered features, *"but keeping dates away from developers and instead focus on delivering quality work"* [E3] further alleviated the pressure. Moreover, *"providing transparency will put customers at ease"* [E1]. The expert added that with transparency, *"customers forgot about dates because they saw that the team was actually working on delivering the promised value"*. Third, the experts emphasized a strong Scrum Master as a *"firewall"* [E9,E16] that *"protects the team"* [E3]. Especially visualizing the short- and long-term consequences of delivery pressure for value delivery *"caused a rethink on the customer side and reduced constant feature pressure"* [E16].

Lacking Customer Involvement was handled with a range of measures, such as the installation of technical consultants. These consultants, as opposed to a regular on-site customer as part of the team, sit on the customer side, *"enabling a direct connection to the customer"* [E12]. Technical consultants acted as *"fire extinguishers"* [E13] and could quickly provide necessary information, given their role to manage the customer side of development and the *"stronger relationship basis and better know-how of the customer side of the project"* [E13]. This measure was appreciated by several experts, i.e., [E5,E12,E13]. Other experts adapted to low customer involvement with proactive visits [E4,E8,E9,E16] or repeated inquiries to the customer [E2,E7,E17]. Here, asynchronous communication tools, i.e., Microsoft Teams channels and chats, proved beneficial to "*reaching relevant contacts on the customer side*" [E2]. In addition, with a "*pac-man approach*" [E8], i.e., by "*continuously feeding the customer with something tasty*" [E3], customer involvement happened naturally, as it "*iteratively convinced them of the value that the team delivered*" [E5]. As with the issue of delivery pressure, also convincing the customer to be constantly involved by visualizing the consequences of lacking engagement is beneficial, as it helps to "*sensitize them for the importance of their role*" [E16]. As a last resort, escalations to higher levels may be an option to secure involvement, yet this step "*is rather unpleasant and implies further pressure*" [E5].

Meeting Overhead and Interruptions were managed using procedural changes, i.e., by eliminating unnecessary meetings and only focusing on the meetings that ASD prescribes. Especially jour fixes (i.e., regularly recurring, fixed meetings to discuss the current status of projects) and touchpoints that [E8] called a "*typical consulting issue*" were eliminated. For necessary meetings, experts eliminated wasteful aspects, i.e., members bringing laptops into [E3,E16] or performing work during these meetings [E4,14]. To add, Scrum Masters reduced the participating members to only those that "*can contribute substantially and not only have 30 s of participation*" [E7], so others can instead focus on coding work. [E8] defined representatives within the team, "*similar to scaled approaches where the use of representatives works well*". [E11,E14, E16] supported meetings with meeting-minute-keeping tools to ensure non-participating members could also keep themselves in the loop if desired. [E8,E15] further implemented a so-called 16th minute for daily meetings. This 16th minute implies adding a small time slot after the actual 15 min daily scrum to discuss certain issues that do not require everyone to participate, thereby saving time for other members to focus on development tasks and ensuring that the daily meeting does not significantly exceed the defined time frame. As another measure, several experts [E4,E7,E15] enforced a strict routinization of meetings to "*carve out slots for productivity*" [E5], along with a standardized agenda and a clear goal. This instilled "*a routine, which leads to efficiency in the meetings*" [E7]. Lastly, [E4,E8,E11,E16] implemented a 3-week sprint with a core focus week. Instead of spending "*two of ten working days every two weeks for sprint transition day*" [E8], a week of focus on development in between had a "*great psychological but also productivity-enhancing effect*" [E16], as it reduced meeting overhead.

Required Rework was not considered a critical issue per se, as depicted in Sect. 4.1. Still, certain measures emerged that helped to manage occurring rework. Most experts followed a good / bad / ugly rework approach, similar to the rework taxonomy by [15] to classify types of iterative rework. In this vein, good rework implies aspects that add value through beneficial adjustments toward improving the software, while bad rework entails additional efforts required due to preventable, recurring mistakes [15]. Ugly rework, meanwhile, refers to excessive amendments that cause the SD process to run out of control or that imply gold plating [15], i.e., overengineered solutions. Consequently, the experts classified rework into "*valuable improvements in the direction of the agreed vision, or rework that rather implies knocking over previous implementations, thus bad rework*" [E16]. For ugly rework, [E10] described that "*gold-plating is also undesirable, as it does not add value, takes time, and causes you to never actually finish the functionality*". To accommodate expected, beneficial rework, experts defined a rework buffer for each iteration [E3,E4,E14,E16,E19]. ASD is designed to accommodate rework, so "*this buffer is essential during release planning since amendments will always occur somehow*" [E4]. Lastly, several experts emphasized the need for a modular and flexible architecture, thus "*setting up the product in an easily adaptable manner*" [E14] to allow demands for valuable rework to be more manageable.

Technical Debt was primarily managed through new process artifacts or technical measures. For process artifacts, experts defined a refactoring buffer that "*made up 20–30% of our capacity to look into technical aspects*" [E11]. In addition, experts created a backlog item that labels technical debt, thereby "*giving teams the psychological safety to continuously include necessary debt fixing in their planning*" [E10]. Concerning technical measures, code reviews proved particularly helpful when three developers (six-eyes-principle) inspected the code, as it prevented "*happy path testing and mutual nodding, while helping to find inconsistencies in the code*" [E11]. [E6,E18,E19] supported this identification of debt with additional tools such as CodeScene. To add, with continuous (unit) testing, potential debt can also be identified, while the system is generally "*built more modularly and more flexibly defined*" [E14]. This falls in line with several experts who emphasized modular or microservice architectures to reduce the accumulation of technical debt [E4,E5,E14]. To fix technical debt, developers applied a Boy Scout rule for clean coding, i.e., "*always leaving the software better than you found it*" [E9]. While developers adhered to this approach during regular sprints, sometimes performing a technical sprint is necessary [E8,E13,E16–18]. While such a sprint did not deliver new features per se, "*the performance gains, reduced fault likelihood, and better maintainability are convincing arguments to perform such a sprint*" [E16]. Still, in a few cases, a complete rewrite was required [E8,E9,E17]. While this is a drastic step, it eliminated "*the pain of prior implementations and allowed to get rid of inherited liabilities*" [E8], but should "*only be the ultima ratio to address technical debt*" [E9].

Volatile and Unclear Requirements could be handled with collaborative vision and expectations definitions between the team and the customer, paired with the derivation of requirements and a roadmap that aligns with the vision and expectations [E1-E3,E7,E10,E16]. Should volatility occur, assessing whether this deviation in the requirements aligns with the overall vision is essential, thereby "*challenging if this new or altered requirement is what the customer truly wants or needs*" [E5]. Here, both the Product Owner and the technical consultant can act as firewalls to assess the volatile requirements, thus "*cushioning some of the volatility*" [E13] and "*steering it in the right direction*" [E10]. These roles can also help to clarify vague and ambiguous requirements [E1,E12,E13,E16]. The experts also emphasized continuous prioritization of requirements to ascertain which "*needs are truly of high importance, and if a shift in the requirements falls in this category*" [E14]. Lastly, several experts incorporated a scope change buffer to "*accommodate things that emerge from this volatility, which we sometimes called 'surprise of the quarter'* " [E16]. This buffer allowed to capture some volatility without compromising the sprint goal [E4,E5,E11,E16]. Still, if the buffer cannot absorb the volatility, "*postponing it to the next sprint is also an option*" [E10].

Table 3. Applied measures to adapt to examined issues and sustain value delivery

Key Issue	Measure Type	Measure	Expert IDs
Delivery Pressure	Customer Approach	Demo Sessions to Show Value	E1, E3, E4, E8, E16
		Involve Customers in Planning Stage	E1, E2, E4, E13
	Procedural Changes	Inter-Sprint-Workload Balancing	E8, E10
		Workload Balancing within Team	E2, E17
	Req. Eng. Practices	Conservative Estimates	E5, E6, E8, E11, E12, E19
		Cut Small Stories	E3, E5, E16, E17
		Prioritize Key Requirements	E4, E11, E19
	Role Installation	Scrum Master as a Firewall	E3, E5, E4, E8, E10, E16
Lacking Customer Involvement	Customer Approach	Escalation to Higher Levels	E5, E10, E17
		Pac-Man Approach	E2, E3, E5, E8, E9, E19
		Proactive Customer Visits	E4, E8, E9, E16
		Repeated Inquiry	E2, E7, E17
		Visualize Consequences	E8, E9, E16, E17
	Req. Eng. Practices	Joint User Story Mapping	E1, E8, E19
	Role Installation	Implement an On-Site Customer	E8, E12, E16
		Implement a Technical Consultant	E1, E5, E12, E13, E16
	Tool Support	Asynchronous Communication Tools	E2, E6, E16, E19
Meeting Overhead and Interruptions	Procedural Changes	16th Minute added to Daily Meeting	E8, E15
		3-Week Sprint with Core Focus Week	E4, E8, E11, E16
		Eliminate Unnecessary Meetings	E3, E5, E7, E11, E15, E16
		Eliminate Wasteful Meeting Elements	E1, E3, E4, E7, E14, E15

(*continued*)

Table 3. (*continued*)

Key Issue	Measure Type	Measure	Expert IDs
		Minimize Number of Participants	E5, E7, E8, E9, E17
		Routinization of Meetings	E4, E5, E7, E15
		Set up Fixed Agenda with Goal	E1, E3, E7, E9
	Role Installation	Install a Meeting Chair as Facilitator	E1, E3, E7, E14
	Tool Support	Asynchronous Communication Tools	E11, E14, E16
Required Rework	Process Artifacts	Define Rework Buffer	E3, E4, E14, E16, E19
		Good / Bad / Ugly Rework Approach	E2, E7, E8, E10, E13, E16, E17
	Role Installation	Involvement of Design Experts	E5, E8, E9, E14
	Technical Measures	Modular and Micro-Service Architecture	E4, E9, E14, E16, E17
Technical Debt	Process Artifacts	Dedicated Refactoring Buffer	E4, E8, E9, E10, E11, E12, E13, E16, E18, E19
		Technical Debt Backlog Item	E9, E10, E16, E17, E18
	Role Installation	Involve Architecture Experts	E4, E9
	Technical Measures	Boy Scout Rule for Clean Coding	E8, E9, E10, E14
		Code Guidelines	E2, E6, E9, E12, E16
		Code Reviews	E5, E10, E11, E19
		Continuous Testing / Unit Testing	E1, E10, E12, E14, E17
		Modular Architecture	E4, E5, E14
		Rebuild from Scratch	E8, E9, E17
		Technical Sprint	E8, E13, E16, E17, E18
	Tool Support	AI Code Analysis Tools and CodeScene	E5, E6, E11, E18

(*continued*)

Table 3. (*continued*)

Key Issue	Measure Type	Measure	Expert IDs
Volatile and Unclear Requirements	Process Artifacts	Scope Change Buffer	E1, E4, E5, E10, E11, E16, E19
	Req. Eng. Practices	Check Vision-Requirement-Alignment	E5, E7, E11, E12, E16
		Continuous Prioritization	E4, E11, E14, E18, E19
		Joint Requirements / Roadmap Definition	E1, E2, E3, E6, E9, E10, E14, E17
		Joint Vision and Expectation Definition	E1, E3, E5, E7, E12, E16
	Role Installation	Product Owner as a Firewall	E1, E4, E10, E14
		Technical Consultant as a Firewall	E1, E12, E13, E16, E17

5 Discussion

5.1 Key Findings and Future Research Opportunities

In this study, we examined the value-reducing consequences of six key issues in ASD and how practitioners adapt to them to sustain value delivery, which was less regarded in prior works [1, 24, 28]. Our study addresses this gap by examining the consequences of these issues if not mitigated, as illustrated in *RQ1*. In addition, a set of actionable measures to adapt to key issues was lacking. Here, our study contributes a collection of 48 measures that ASD teams can employ to enable continuous value delivery, see *RQ2*.

Concerning *RQ1*, reduced product quality and capabilities, security concerns, delays, inefficient development, and wasted effort were reported as the main consequences that affect the delivery of value in ASD. While all issues seemed problematic in some way, *lacking customer involvement*, *delivery pressure*, *technical debt*, *meeting overhead*, and *volatile requirements* appeared particularly influential. This aligns with issues identified in [1, 10, 19, 23, 24], while we extend these prior findings by detailing their specific value-reducing consequences. Consequences such as security issues induced by technical debt and delivery pressure, product-requirement-misalignments due to low customer involvement, and volatile requirements causing incoherent features suggest that adapting to these issues is essential to uphold the promise of ASD for continuous delivery of valuable software. Our work also indicates that the abovementioned issues are the key concerns that affect ASD's value proposition, except *rework*, as explained next.

As such, our work shows the need for a differentiated perception of the importance of rework for value creation in ASD research. While rework was seen as a consequence of various issues in [24] with negative implications such as increased costs [19, 30, 37], almost all experts saw rework as a "*value-enhancement with additional time needed as the cost involved, which is, however, necessary for a better product*" [E19] and "*the only way to get value*" [E3]. This seems logical, as rework is embedded in the key XP practice of refactoring [38], making it an integral aspect of ASD. Still, some types of rework are less desirable, as apparent with the good / bad / ugly classification for rework suggested by the experts, which aligns with the rework taxonomy proposed by [15]. Overall, our study highlights rework as a key ingredient of ASD to achieve value in practice, which was somewhat misrepresented in [24], while it also emphasizes the importance of evaluating the nature of the rework that should be performed. Hence, our findings can help to resolve differing perspectives on rework between research and practice by underlining its importance for the continuous delivery of value with ASD.

Concerning *RQ2*, we present a collection of 48 measures that the experts employed to adapt to key issues encountered in ASD, which features technical measures, different ways to approach customers, or adaptations of the development process, together with new artifacts and roles. This set can assist practitioners in dealing with difficult situations that could negatively affect the delivery of value and offer strategies to improve the ASD process, thereby helping to address key issues and avoid their negative consequences from the outset. In this vein, we extend prior knowledge with insights into how to adapt to typical issues that affect value delivery, which was not addressed by [1, 24]. Additionally, while measures to adapt to certain issues were previously scattered across the literature [10, 19, 23], this study provides an empirically derived, consolidated collection. Based on this set, future research can evaluate how these measures may enhance ASD frameworks and validate their effectiveness in case studies. Research could also assess how combinations of measures stimulate each other to improve value delivery, or determine the impact of these adaptations on development success, similar to [36].

To add, our work suggests reassessing how tailoring is done when adapting to critical issues. The experts tailored ASD with method engineering [7], i.e., "*micro-level tailoring of development practices at a finer level of granularity*" [16], such as adding a 16th minute to daily meetings or following the Boy Scout rule for clean coding to reduce technical debt. Tailoring, however, is often considered from a macro perspective, i.e., if a practice is adopted or omitted [3, 36], and how these granular adaptations affect the development success [36]. In contrast, this study emphasizes the need to examine how small, nuanced adaptations improve value creation and project success. Early research on ASD customization also shows the importance of "*micro-level tailoring*" [16] of ASD practices, which may thus be further examined in research on method tailoring.

The measures can also help practitioners to better address anti-patterns that affect ASD [14], i.e., lacking client feedback due to "*long or non-existent feedback loops*" or disruptions during development, which stem from the customer side [14]. With Eloranta et al. [14] making several recommendations for various anti-patterns, our work can enrich their suggestions with different approaches to help mitigate issues in the SD process and ensure value delivery, even when facing certain problematic anti-patterns.

Lastly, resilience engineering (RE) [22] to improve the performance of ASD when facing issues provides a novel perspective for research. Applying RE in the context of ASD seems promising, as it serves to identify strategies "*to help resolve problems so that software development can progress*" [22], which aligns with the measures identified in our study to sustain value delivery. Recent work by Lopez et al. [22] shows RE as a useful approach to detect issues and find ways of adaptation or compensation to enable resilient performance in software engineering, which also seems applicable in ASD. In line with [22], we encourage further investigations using the RE technique to develop strategies to improve ASD use. Our findings can inform these future inquiries.

In sum, our study offers actionable measures to address common issues in ASD practice, emphasizes the importance of rework to create value, and encourages scholars to investigate the role of micro-tailoring to maximize value creation and project success, which can also be enhanced with studies using the RE technique in the context of ASD.

5.2 Limitations

We discuss potential threats to validity along the dimensions by Runeson and Höst [31]. For *construct validity*, the experts may have different interpretations of the investigated issues. This can result in responses that do not accurately reflect the phenomena under study. To avoid these problems, misunderstandings related to the issues were clarified during the interviews. Further unclarities identified during the analysis were resolved with a report sent to five participants, as described in Sect. 3. We also ensured consistent questions with an interview protocol, which was refined after three interviews to prevent unclarities. To add, as an inherent limitation of our research approach, we cannot confirm if the suggested measures had the intended effects, despite specifically inquiring about measures that have proven beneficial. Given the consistency in the suggested measures, however, the collection offers valuable adaptations to common issues. Concerning *external validity* threats, the interview sample mostly consists of experts from the DACH-region, while ICT services and IT consulting bear a similarly large proportion. Thus, a regional and industry bias may influence generalizability. To reduce these concerns, we interviewed experts from other regions and industries, finding corresponding statements on issues and measures, i.e., the Pac-Man approach or the classification of good-bad-ugly rework. To add, after ~ 10 interviews, we observed answers consistent with previous interviews, indicating a certain level of saturation. We also acknowledge an inherent limitation of our research approach, as it cannot capture the details of the context in which practitioners encountered issues or employed measures to address them. Depending on the context, some measures may thus be more or less effective, while certain issues can be more problematic compared to other settings. Also, *internal validity* concerns may arise, which relate to the value-diminishing consequences. Different issues may have similar consequences, which can make it difficult to distinguish the origin of a certain value-reducing consequence. We addressed this concern by cross-checking whether other issues had similar consequences, which are therefore explicitly stated in multiple issue categories in the tables in the results section. We also ensured that a large selection of issues was examined to limit *internal validity* concerns. Lastly, for *reliability* concerns related to data collection, analysis, and reporting, we adhered to the guidelines by [6, 21, 27]. During the development of the interview protocol, the transcription, and the analysis, both authors were involved to avoid bias. Especially the analysis was performed separately, though, to ensure an unbiased interpretation. By reaching out to interviewees to avoid misinterpretations, as illustrated in Sect. 3, we further enhanced the *reliability* of our work. Despite potential limitations, our work can provide meaningful insights to support a sustained value delivery in ASD.

6 Concluding Remarks

The core proposition of ASD to continuously deliver valuable software products [4, 34] is often hampered by several issues [1, 24]. In this study, we interviewed 19 ASD experts to examine how six issues impede value delivery and to uncover how practitioners adapt to them. 34 consequences were identified, which include reduced product quality, incoherent products, delivery delays, and wasted efforts, among other consequences. To mitigate these issues, we derived a collection of 48 measures that can help ASD practitioners to sustain value delivery. Our work underlines the key role of rework for value creation, while also encouraging future studies on the benefits of micro-tailoring and the RE technique to improve the application of ASD. In sum, this study contributes helpful approaches to ensure ASD's key value proposition is upheld in daily practice.

References

1. Alahyari, H., Berntsson Svensson, R., Gorschek, T.: A study of value in agile software development organizations. J. Syst. Soft. **125**, 271–288 (2017)
2. Alami, A., Krancher, O.: How scrum adds value to achieving software quality? Empir. Softw. Eng. **27** (2022)
3. Baham, C., Hirschheim, R.: Issues, challenges, and a proposed theoretical core of agile software development research. Inf. Syst. J. **32**, 103–129 (2022)
4. Beck, K., et al: Manifesto for agile software development. (2001). https://agilemanifesto.org. Accessed 22 Jan 2025
5. Biffl, S., Aurum, A., Boehm, B., Erdogmus, H., Grünbacher, P.: Value-Based Software Engineering. Springer, Berlin, Heidelberg (2006)
6. Bogner, A., Littig, B., Menz, W.: Interviewing Experts. Palgrave Macmillan London (2009)
7. Brinkkemper, S.: Method engineering: engineering of information systems development methods and tools. Inf. Soft. Technol. **38**, 275–280 (1996)
8. Campanelli, A.S., Parreiras, F.S.: Agile methods tailoring – a systematic literature review. J. Syst. Soft. **110**, 85–100 (2015)
9. Conboy, K.: Agility from first principles: reconstructing the concept of agility in information systems development. Inf. Syst. Res. **20**, 329–354 (2009)
10. Dasanayake, S., Aaramaa, S., Markkula, J., Oivo, M.: Impact of requirements volatility on software architecture: how do software teams keep up with ever-changing requirements? J. Softw. Evol. Process **31**, 1–19 (2019)
11. Digital.ai: 17th Annual State of Agile Report. (2024). https://digital.ai/resource-center/analyst-reports/state-of-agile-report/. Accessed 22 Jan 2025
12. Dingsøyr, T., Nerur, S., Balijepally, V., Moe, N.B.: A decade of agile methodologies: towards explaining agile software development. J. Syst. Soft. **85**, 1213–1221 (2012)
13. Elbanna, A.R.: Identifying the risks associated with agile software development: an empirical investigation. In: Proceedings of the 8th Mediterranean Conference on Information Systems (2014)
14. Eloranta, V.-P., Koskimies, K., Mikkonen, T.: Exploring ScrumBut—an empirical study of scrum anti-patterns. Inf. Soft. Technol. **74**, 194–203 (2016)
15. Fairley, R.E., Willshire, M.J.: Iterative rework: the good, the bad, and the ugly. Computer **38**, 34–41 (2005)
16. Fitzgerald, B., Hartnett, G., Conboy, K.: Customising agile methods to software practices at Intel Shannon. Eur. J. Inf. Syst. **15**, 200–213 (2006)

17. Hannay, J.E., Benestad, H.C.: Perceived productivity threats in large agile development projects. In: Proceedings of the 2010 ACM-IEEE International Symposium on Empirical Software Engineering and Measurement, pp. 1–10. ACM (2010). https://doi.org/10.1145/1852786.1852806
18. Highsmith, J.: Agile Software Development Ecosystems. Addison-Wesley, Boston (2002)
19. Hoda, R., Noble, J., Marshall, S.: The impact of inadequate customer collaboration on self-organizing agile teams. Inf. Soft. Technol. **53**, 521–534 (2011)
20. Kitchenham, B., Pfleeger, S.L.: Principles of survey research. ACM SIGSOFT Soft. Eng. Notes **27**, 17–20 (2002)
21. Kuckartz, U.: Qualitative Inhaltsanalyse: Methoden, Praxis, Computerunterstützung. Beltz Juventa, Weinheim, Basel (2018)
22. Lopez, T., et al.: Accounting for socio-technical resilience in software engineering. In: 2023 IEEE/ACM 16th International Conference on Cooperative and Human Aspects of Software Engineering (CHASE), pp. 31–36 (2023). https://doi.org/10.1109/CHASE58964.2023.00012
23. Martini, A., Bosch, J., Chaudron, M.: Investigating architectural technical debt accumulation and refactoring over time: a multiple-case study. Inf. Soft. Technol. **67**, 237–253 (2015)
24. Meckenstock, J.-N.: Shedding light on the dark side – a systematic literature review of the issues in agile software development methodology use. J. Syst. Soft. **211** (2024)
25. Meckenstock, J.-N., Hirschlein, N., Schlauderer, S., Overhage, S.: The business value of agile software development: results from a systematic literature review. In: ECIS 2022 Proceedings (2022)
26. Meckenstock, J.-N., Schlauderer, S., Overhage, S.: How do individual social agile practices influence the development success? an exploratory study. In: Wirtschaftsinformatik 2022 Proceedings (2022)
27. Myers, M.D., Newman, M.: The qualitative interview in IS research: examining the craft. Inf. Organ. **17**, 2–26 (2007)
28. Petersen, K., Wohlin, C.: A comparison of issues and advantages in agile and incremental development between state of the art and an industrial case. J. Syst. Soft. **82**, 1479–1490 (2009)
29. Racheva, Z., Daneva, M., Sikkel, K., Buglione, L.: Business value is not only dollars – results from case study research on agile software projects. In: PROFES 2010, pp. 131–145. Springer (2010). https://doi.org/10.1007/978-3-642-13792-1_12
30. Ramesh, B., Cao, L., Baskerville, R.: Agile requirements engineering practices and challenges: an empirical study. Inf. Syst. J. **20**, 449–480 (2010)
31. Runeson, P., Höst, M.: Guidelines for conducting and reporting case study research in software engineering. Empir. Softw. Eng. **14**, 131–164 (2008)
32. Saldaña, J.: The Coding Manual for Qualitative Researchers. SAGE Publications, Thousand Oaks (2021)
33. Schryen, G.: Revisiting IS business value research: what we already know, what we still need to know, and how we can get there. Eur. J. Inf. Syst. **22**, 139–169 (2013)
34. Schwaber, K., Sutherland, J.: The scrum guide. Scrum Alliance. (2020). https://scrumguides.org/scrum-guide.html. Accessed 22 Jan 2025
35. Seaman, C.B.: Qualitative methods in empirical studies of software engineering. IEEE Trans. Software Eng. **25**, 557–572 (1999)
36. Tripp, J., Armstrong, D.J.: Agile methodologies: organizational adoption motives, tailoring, and performance. J. Comput. Inf. Syst. **58**, 170–179 (2016)
37. van Waardenburg, G., van Vliet, H.: When agile meets the enterprise. Inf. Soft. Technol. **55**, 2154–2171 (2013)

38. Wells, D.: Extreme programming: a gentle introduction (2001). http://www.extremeprogramming.org. Accessed 6 Mar 2025
39. Wiesche, M.: Interruptions in agile software development teams. Proj. Manag. J. **52**, 210–222 (2021)

Open Access This chapter is licensed under the terms of the Creative Commons Attribution 4.0 International License (http://creativecommons.org/licenses/by/4.0/), which permits use, sharing, adaptation, distribution and reproduction in any medium or format, as long as you give appropriate credit to the original author(s) and the source, provide a link to the Creative Commons license and indicate if changes were made.

The images or other third party material in this chapter are included in the chapter's Creative Commons license, unless indicated otherwise in a credit line to the material. If material is not included in the chapter's Creative Commons license and your intended use is not permitted by statutory regulation or exceeds the permitted use, you will need to obtain permission directly from the copyright holder.

Author Index

A
Adolfo, Luciane 229
Augner, Tabea 52

B
Bretschneider, Ulrich 52
Broomandi, Fateme 37

C
Choma, Joelma 229

D
Daniel, João 129
Deshpande, Advait 19
Drews, Paul 210

E
Eilers, Karen 52

F
Farshchian, Babak A. 100

G
Gregory, Peggy 19
Guerra, Eduardo Martins 145, 176
Guerra, Eduardo 129, 229

H
Hyrynsalmi, Sami 3
Hyrynsalmi, Sonja M. 37

I
Ihantola, Petri 69
Irgens, Marius 186

L
Lee, Sean Jonathon 195

M
Mäkitalo, Niko 69
Marchand, Rob 160
Martini, Antonio 186
Matthes, Florian 81, 116
Meckenstock, Jan-Niklas 245
Melegati, Jorge 145, 229
Mikkonen, Tommi 69
Moalagh, Morteza 100
Moreira, Igor 229
Mota, Gabriel 129

N
Neri, Giulia 160

O
Obode, Ehikioya 19
Özkan, Necmettin 52

P
Paasivaara, Maria 37
Pancher, Juliano Cesar 145
Peters, Christoph 52

S
Salman, Iflaah 37
Senapathi, Mali 195

Siemon, Dominik 3
Silveira, Fábio Fagundes 176
Somerville, Derek 19
Stotz, Nils 210
Suomi, Tomi 69
Svesengen, Vegard 100

T
Teixeira, Tiago Samuel Rodrigues 176
Tobisch, Franziska 81, 116

W
Walkinshaw, Neil 160
Wallmichrath, Victoria 245
Wang, Xiaofeng 3, 129

Y
Yang, Nan 3

Z
Zaina, Luciana 229
Zhang, Zheying 3

The manufacturer's authorised representative in the EU is Springer Nature Customer Service Centre GmbH, Europaplatz 3, 69115 Heidelberg, Germany. If you have any concerns regarding our products, please contact ProductSafety@springernature.com

Printed and bound by CPI Group (UK) Ltd, Croydon, CR0 4YY

26/03/2026

02078961-0001